TO

THE

ARCTIC

The Wiley Science Editions

TO
THE
ARCTIC

An Introduction to the Far Northern World

STEVEN B. YOUNG

The Center for Northern Studies

WILEY POPULAR SCIENCE

John Wiley & Sons, Inc.

NEW YORK • CHICHESTER • BRISBANE • TORONTO • SINGAPORE

Photography by Steven B. Young
Art by Nancy Behnken, Cynthia Steed, and Ann Young

This text is printed on acid-free paper.

Library of Congress Cataloging-in-Publication Data

Young, Steven B.
  To the Arctic: an introduction to the far northern world /
  Steven B. Young.
    p.   cm.—(Wiley Popular Science)
  Includes index.
  ISBN 0-471-078891 (paper) --- ISBN 0-471-62082-3
  1. Natural history—Arctic regions. 2. Arctic
  regions—Description and travel. I. Title. II. Series.
  QH84.1.Y68 1988
  508.311'3—dc19   88-17423

Printed in the United States of America
10 9 8 7 6 5 4 3 2 1

For fifteen years of Northern Studies students

Preface

I returned to my book—Bewick's *History of British Birds:* . . . there were certain introductory pages that, child as I was, I could not pass quite as a blank. They were those which treat of the haunts of sea-fowl; of "the solitary rocks and promontories" by them only inhabited; of the coast of Norway, studded with isles from its southern extremity, the Lindeness, or Naze, to the North Cape—

> Where the Northern Ocean, in vast whirls,
> Boils round the naked, melancholy isles
> Of farthest Thule; and the Atlantic surge
> Pours in among the stormy Hebrides.

Nor could I pass unnoticed the suggestion of the bleak shores of Lapland, Siberia, Spitzbergen, Nova Zembla, Iceland, Greenland, with "the vast sweep of the Arctic Zone, and those forlorn regions of dreary space—that reservoir of frost and snow, where firm fields of ice, the accumulation of centuries of winters, glazed in Alpine heights above heights, surround the pole, and concentre the multiplied rigours of extreme cold". Of these death-white realms I formed an idea of my own: shadowy, like all the half-comprehended notions that float dim through children's brains, but strangely impressive. The words in these introductory pages connected themselves with the succeeding vignettes, and gave significance to the rock standing up alone in a sea of billow and spray; to the broken boat stranded on a desolate coast; to the cold and ghastly moon glancing through bars of cloud at a wreck just sinking.

—CHARLOTTE BRONTE, *Jane Eyre*

For centuries, the polar regions have occupied a unique place in Western people's perception of the world in which they live. Remote, forbidding, and presumably of little or no practical value to civilization, the polar regions were largely ignored during the early portion of the Age of Discovery, while the outlines and general features of the continents became subjects for speculation and exploration. The presence of a major land mass in the high latitudes of the Southern Hemisphere was not even established as a fact until nearly the middle of the nineteenth century, and maps of both the arctic and antarctic regions continued to show immense blanks in many areas for several decades into the twentieth century.

Meanwhile, a recognition extended back through the centuries that certain unique products and features of the polar world were valued by Western civilization. These values were often related to the rarity and the exotic origin of goods from the polar regions, and the romance, mystery, and danger involved in bringing them back to the known world. Narwhals' tusks were the stuff of legends; they apparently gave rise to stories of the unicorn, with its supernatural attributes and the magical properties of its spiraling horn. The great white falcons of Greenland were worth a king's ransom, and northern furs found their way into the trade routes of the civilized world as had exotic spices and perfumes. Not much later in history came more prosaic contributions from the North: codfish and oil and baleen taken from the bodies of the great whales gained increasing importance in European and, later, American markets. Commercial exploitation of the North, particularly the northern seas, became a factor to be reckoned with in world commerce and politics.

At the same time, the romance of the polar regions, rather than being dispelled by the beginnings of exploration and commerce, was deepened and enhanced. Exotic peoples whose ways of life were thought to represent archaic stages in human progress toward "civilization" were met with in northern areas. The expeditions that penetrated the northern fastnesses were led by explorers who became cultural heroes in Western countries. The legend of the Northwest Passage as an alternate route to the Indies refused to die until long after it had lost its possible commercial significance. Intrepid explorers, and men whose judgment and abilities would later come into question and cause endless controversy, disappeared into the northern ice. They were often followed by others whose main objective was to discover the fate of their predecessors.

The romance and significance of the North were reflected in Western culture in a way that is perhaps too deep to formulate in any articulate fashion. The civilizations of western Europe contain in their very foundations cultural stones that can be traced to the sculpted fiords and glaciers of Scandinavia and the bleak lava plains of Iceland; they form the bases for the legal systems, legends, and literature of Atlantic Europe. And always there have been legends and stories going back to the beginnings of European Christianity, with the hermit saints of Ireland and the Hebrides, or deeper still, into the classical past, to Pliny the Elder, to the Greeks themselves, involving strange hyperborean regions and people or near people.

It seems to be the fate of the human endeavor, which we loosely term science, to demythologize the areas of human concern that come under its umbrella: to explain, often by reductionism and overanalysis, aspects of human perception and imagination that earlier were encompassed in a legendary, nonrational framework. We are now in a position to do this with respect to much about the polar regions. In fact, it is one purpose of this book to do precisely this. Many of the most remarkable features of the Arctic and Subarctic are indeed amenable to rational, scientific explanation. The state of our knowledge is such that we can paint a precise, factual, and comparatively detailed picture of the polar lands and seas; of the players, human and otherwise, who are on stage; and of the subtleties of the interactions involving the physical and biological processes unique to, or characteristic of, the Arctic regions. In fact, our detailed knowledge of this environment is far more extensive than can be contained even in a fairly voluminous work such as this and is greater than can be encompassed by a single author, no matter how deep his commitment to the subject or how cooperative and supportive his colleagues are.

All advances in knowledge push the frontiers of knowledge farther and farther out from the original source. Hence, the boundaries of what is "beyond" our knowledge are continually expanded by the very process by which things become known and understood. Because factual knowledge is our focus here, it is outside the scope of this book to concentrate on the unknowns of the Arctic, particularly since these unknown areas are uncodified and trackless; speculating about them slides into the realm of philosophical and spiritual concerns at least as readily as it leads to an increase in factual knowledge. However, the call of the polar regions is no less now than it was in the days of St. Brendan, Leif Ericson, or of Scott, Shackleton, or Peary; it has been neither dispelled nor contaminated by the scientific approach of the recent past. The call is a familiar mood or presence to those of us who follow in their footsteps, even if we do so in helicopters rather than open boats or dogsleds.

The following chapters explain many of the phenomena that were mysteries in the truest sense to people of earlier generations who were concerned with the polar regions. But a mile-wide river of moving ice flowing from the interior of a frozen continent and harboring the ghost images of events that occurred millennia ago can never be "only" a mass of material subject to certain physical laws or a potential storehouse of information for understanding the earth's processes. The polar regions have always meant more to us than this; they will never lose their aura of the unknown and the ineffable for those who choose to see it.

SUGGESTIONS ON HOW TO USE THIS BOOK

This book is designed to function as a field guide and general introduction to the common physical and biological features that the scientist, naturalist, or interested traveler will find in the arctic regions. Included here are at least brief descriptions of most of the more conspicuous vertebrates, higher plants, and geomorphic features that stand out in the arctic environment. At the same time, there is no way that this book can replace the array of excellent field guides, floras, and more narrowly focused scholarly works that deal with the far north. A much-abbreviated list of books is incorporated at the end of each chapter; any serious students of the Arctic will wish to acquire the ones that are particularly related to their field of interest. For example, tundra birds are treated here in some detail, but information on their identification can be more profitably sought in the several excellent works that provide keys to identification, pictures, often distribution maps, and even information on songs, feeding habits, and breeding biology. What is supplied here, instead, is the supplementary information that may help the naturalist understand the role of the individual bird species or group in the overall environment of the Arctic.

Similarly, the number of illustrations has been kept to a minimum. There's no sense in trying to picture each mammal, bird, fish, or flowering plant that might be encountered in the North. Instead, illustrations have been chosen to display representative specimens of important groups or examples that epitomize some particular feature. Additionally, the choice of illustrations here emphasizes little-known or seldom-illustrated phenomena. In many cases, this lack of knowledge is a result of the fact that the feature or process in question is not particularly photogenic. Even the most spectacular pingo is little more than a lump on the landscape, particularly as compared to a large alp. But its history is at least as fascinating as that of an alp, and it justifies the inclusion of a number of illustrations that are neither awe inspiring nor self-explanatory.

This book concentrates on patterns and processes, rather than individual species or phenomena, and presents in some detail subjects usually available only in more advanced or technical works, which are either hard for the general reader to obtain or too heavy and expensive to cart around in a bush plane: hence the emphasis on areas such as periglacial processes and peatland ecology. It is true that we cannot really understand any natural environment without some sort of a picture of the events and processes that led up to the present state. This is especially true in the North, where the rich tundra environment we see may have been under a mile or so of ice only a few thousand years ago. A major Soviet periodical is called *Problems of the Pleistocene and Arctic;* the title demonstrates the Russians' clear perception that geography and environmental history are inseparable—a perception that is to be applauded. Chapters 7 and 13 here reflect this connection, treating the Ice Ages and the overall history of the Arctic specifically.

In spite of this book's lip service to comprehensiveness, it may horrify people in fields such as entomology, invertebrate biology, and limnology-oceanography. The average reader's concern with mosquitoes or internal parasites is generally limited to avoiding them; people whose interest in these topics is serious and compelling will wish to make forays into the more specialized literature.

Acknowledgments

Twenty-five years of wandering around the polar regions of both hemispheres have left me deeply in debt to hundreds of people, not only for hospitality and support but also for the germs of all sorts of ideas. Most of these ideas are too deeply intertwined by now for their sources to be identified, so a blanket thank you will have to suffice, along with an apology for the innumerable things that have been left out by oversight, for lack of space, or for my lack of understanding of their importance. Some people do need to be singled out, though. These include Geoffrey Bibbey, who does not know me, but whose book *The Testimony of the Spade* not only sparked my awareness that *time* is a crucial dimension for understanding anything but also gave me a standard of what scientific writing for the intelligent public can be at its best. Dave Hopkins helped me extend the concept of time into the far north, and I've spent many a pleasant hour trying to visualize a herd of woolly mammoths on the now drowned plains of the Bering land bridge. I didn't go to enough far places with Jan Young, but, whatever the future brings, this book is hers as well as mine.

The artwork in this book is the work of several people whose talent should be obvious, but whose careful cooperation and patience may not be. Cynthia Steed made the fine drawings of plants in Chapters 8 and 9, as well as some of the diagrams; Ann Young contributed drawings of many of the animals and birds, as well as some diagrams. Nancy Behnken drew many of the chapter headings. The cruder efforts at diagrams are my own. Tom Young and The Camera Store, of Steve, Vermont, processed the photographs.

STEVEN YOUNG

Contents

Chapter 1

Bears, Boreas, and Celestial Mechanics:
How We Define and Subdivide the Polar Regions

THE Arctic is not an easily definable geographic entity such as Madagascar, Lake Michigan, or even Antarctica. It is a sort of an irregular, free-form hat on the globe, with the North Pole roughly at its center. From there it extends southward with earflaps, frills, and sequins dipping into the temperate regions. Included in the Arctic are parts of three continents, an entire ocean, the largest island in the world, and a broad array of seas, straits, islands, rivers, and mountain ranges (see Figure 1–1).

The word *arctic* is derived from *arctos,* Greek for *bear.* In the northern sky, two constellations circle endlessly around the one

Figure 1–1. Polar projection outline map of the northern part of the Northern Hemisphere, showing approximate boundaries of the arctic and subarctic regions. The solid line approximately follows the traditional boundary between the Arctic and Subarctic; it is close to both the latitudinal or coastal timberline and to the location of the 10°C July isotherm. The forested area of the Subarctic is shown by the tree symbols, but much of the area is actually treeless and tundralike, particularly immediately south of timberline. The stippled area in the North Atlantic Basin and the vicinity of Bering Strait is the marine Subarctic, characterized by a mixing of waters and organisms from the Arctic Ocean and temperate oceans. The unstippled area in the Arctic Basin is considered to be the true marine Arctic. The waters of Hudson Bay, although reaching to temperate latitudes, are derived mainly from the Arctic Basin.

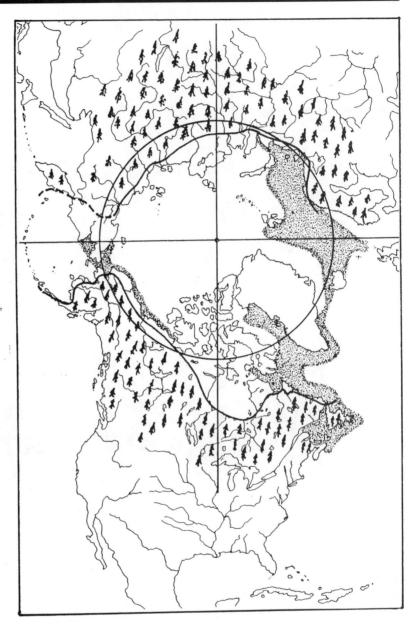

fixed point in the heavens: Polaris, the North Star. The constellations are called *Ursa Major* and *Ursa Minor,* the *Great Bear* and *Little Bear;* they contain the familiar Big and Little Dippers. As one travels northward, the Bears rise ever higher in the sky, flickering briefly through the white nights of the northern summer or gazing frostily down over the long polar winter night.

There is no more compelling case for the transmission of myth and legend down from high antiquity than the association of the celestial Bears with the north. Later, we will follow our own remote ancestors northward with the retreat of the Ice Age glaciers some 15,000 years ago. Bears loomed large in the lives of these people. People hunted bears, competed with them for food and shelter, made shrines of their bones and hides in the deep recesses of their caves. It seems more likely than not that they saw bears among the stars, and that they felt their northward journeys bringing them more and more under the domination of *Arcturus,* the Bear Star.

Another legendary figure who still appears in our northern lexicon is *Boreas,* the North Wind of Greek mythology. When we speak of boreal forests or hyperborean lands, frost seems to lie in the word itself.

Our modern concepts of the Arctic still depend for their definitions on cold winds, spinning earth, and the relationship of the earth to the stars, most particularly our own star, the sun.

THE NORTH POLE AND OTHER POLES

"Oh!" said Pooh again. "What is the North Pole?" he asked.

"It's just a thing you discover," said Christopher Robin carelessly, not being quite sure himself.

—A. A. Milne, *Winnie the Pooh*

The spinning earth is impaled on an imaginary axis, and the unseen points where the axis protrudes through the surface of the earth are the North Pole and the South Pole. The earth is a very stable top, and the poles are solidly fixed in place, giving us two of the few fixed geographical points we'll be dealing with. We call the north and the south rotational poles the true, or geographic, poles; they mark latitudes 90° north and south. These are the poles the explorers Peary, Amundsen, Scott, and Shackleton sought, but they are not the poles that a compass points to, or that the northern lights cluster around during the polar night. To someone who goes there, the North Pole is No Place, just an imaginary point on the shifting pack ice of the Arctic Ocean. The South Pole, a bit more stable, lies on a two-mile-thick ice sheet in the heart of the Antarctic continent.

The magnetic poles are the places where the poles of the earth's magnetic field intersect the surface of the earth. They are the spots to which the compass needle points. In fact, at the north magnetic pole the north end of the needle should point directly earthward. The locations of the magnetic poles are only roughly connected with the rotational poles. The north magnetic pole is currently located in the Canadian high Arctic on Bathurst Island, at about 76° north; the south magnetic pole lies in the Southern Ocean at about 65° south in the vicinity of Dumont D'Urville, a French Antarctic research station.

Traditional navigation requires taking magnetic compass readings and then converting directions to *true north*. Even at low latitudes the differences in the location between true north and magnetic north are so great as to require major compensations to be made. These correction factors are printed on maps and charts as degrees, minutes, and directions, and are known as the magnetic declination. Magnetic declination becomes so extreme in areas such as the Canadian Arctic that a magnetic compass is often nearly useless; the needle wanders around confusedly or points southward! On maps and charts, magnetic declination is stated as of a specific date; this is because the magnetic poles "wander"—change location—rapidly; their location can alter by hundreds of miles over a few decades.

Not only do the magnetic poles wander, they even occasionally reverse, changing magnetic north to south. Reversals seem to occur at irregular intervals, often hundreds of thousands of years apart. We don't know what effect these reversals have on living things. It has been suggested that they may expose the earth's surface to massive amounts of high energy radiation; this could disrupt life and perhaps result in widespread extinctions of plants and animals. Evidence is scanty, though. In any case, reversals of the magnetic poles do leave evidence in rocks, and these reversals can often be dated by geochronometric techniques. They can then sometimes be traced on a worldwide scale and provide a basis for dating other significant events, such as Ice Ages.

The magnetic poles are associated with the distribution of charged particles in the earth's exosphere. These particles originate mainly in the sun, and they tend to be aligned along magnetic lines of force that are related to the earth's magnetic field. Under some conditions, the interaction between the charged particles and the upper levels of the earth's atmosphere is visible as light. This interaction produces the aurora borealis, or northern lights, so widely associated with northern legends and perceptions. Similar lights in the Southern Hemisphere are called the aurora australis. Auroral displays are most common in the vicinity of the magnetic poles, but they frequently extend to middle latitudes. They can often be seen in temperate North America, particularly in the spring and fall, and when sunspot activity is at a peak.

THE POLAR CIRCLES

In addition to the latitudinal lines that circle the globe with the geographical poles at their center, geographers often draw four parallels that are related not to the spherical geometry of the earth but rather to the orientation of the earth to the sun. These lines are the Tropics of Cancer and Capricorn, located at approximately 23°27' north and south latitude, respectively, and the Arctic and Antarctic Circles, located at 66° 33' north and south latitude. The location and significance of these circles depends on a peculiarity of the relationship of the earth's axis of rotation with respect to the plane of its orbit as shown in Figure 1–2. The axis is tilted to the plane at an angle of about 23°27'. Although the poles do not move, the earth and its axis actually wobbles; and the angle of the tilt, called the ecliptic, oscillates predictably over the millennia. A complete cycle, during which the angle varies from about 21.8° to 24.4° and back, takes about 40,000 years. This oddity needn't concern us now, but it does seem to be associated with the waxing and waning of Ice Ages, as is further discussed in Chapter 7.

The tilt of the earth in relation to the plane of its orbit causes the seasons, and the angle of the ecliptic provides the basis for the location of the Arctic and Antarctic Circles. The warm season of each year occurs when the hemisphere in which summer is occurring is tilted toward the sun; winter occurs when the tilt is away from the sun. Thus, the seasons in the Northern and South-

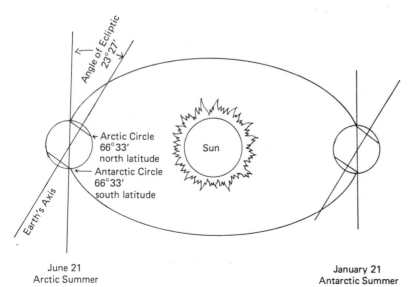

June 21
Arctic Summer

January 21
Antarctic Summer

Figure 1–2. The relationship of the axis of the earth's rotation to the plane of its orbit around the sun. The axis is currently tilted 23°27' from the perpendicular to the plane of the orbit. This tilt causes the seasons and defines the tropics (23°27' north and south) and Polar Circles (66°33' north and south).

ern Hemispheres are opposite from one another. Figure 1–2 also demonstrates why day length varies increasingly from season to season as latitude increases. Seasonal changes in day length cause the seasonal variations in solar energy available in polar regions; extremes in seasonality combined with generally low levels of available energy are the two most important physical characteristics of the polar environment. These are, in effect, the armature on which the rest of this book is built. The Arctic, as everyone knows, is the place of deep cold, the midnight sun, and the long polar night.

The Polar Circles are defined by the angle of the ecliptic. In theory, they are defined by the rotation of the exact location at which the rays of the sun are tangent to a point on the earth's surface at midnight on the longest day of the year, and at noon on the shortest day. Hence, any location within the Polar Circles is in the Land of the Midnight Sun. Figure 1–2 also shows that the midnight sun would appear to remain higher in the sky with increasing latitude. The number of days during the summer when the midnight sun is visible also increases with latitude, as does the length of the dark, sunless period in the winter. Ultimately, at the rotational poles themselves, there is no difference between night and day; the sun appears to circle above the earth's surface at a constant altitude during a given day, and this altitude changes only with the seasons.

Actually, the exact location of the Polar Circles can't be observed directly from the earth's surface. This is due to the presence of the atmosphere, which causes refraction of the sun's rays and causes the sun to appear somewhat higher in the sky than it actually is, as shown in Figure 1–3. As a result, the midnight sun is visible some distance (nearly 100 miles at sea level) outside the Polar Circles. This has led to the misnaming of the village of Circle, on the Yukon River in Alaska; the midnight sun appears over the river on the longest day of the year, but the village actually lies well south of the Arctic Circle.

Because of this atmospheric refraction, the total time that the sun is visible over the horizon during the year is actually greater at high latitudes than in more temperate locations. Also, since the sun "drops" below the horizon at a shallow angle in the polar regions, dawn and dusk persist for long periods before and after the sun is visible. One result is that winter days in polar regions are much longer than summer nights. On a summer visit to Leningrad or Anchorage you will experience the famous white nights; you can read a newspaper outdoors without artificial light at midnight. But at Christmas there are several hours of sunshine

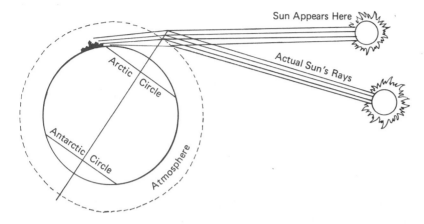

Figure 1–3. Effect of refraction of light rays in the earth's atmosphere on the apparent position of the sun above the horizon. The sun appears about 2½ times its own diameter above its actual position, so that the midnight sun is visible some distance south of the Arctic Circle on the longest day of the year.

in the middle of the day, as well as several additional hours of dawn and dusk.

COLD AND SEASONALITY

We always associate the polar regions with cold. In fact, the term *cold regions* is often used as a virtual synonym for polar regions. Scientifically, it is more accurate to think in terms of lack of energy, specifically, heat energy. Equally important is the distribution of available heat energy over the course of the year—seasonality. This comparative lack of energy from the sun and the uneven distribution over the course of the year of such energy as is available are crucial factors. They determine many of the other physical and biological characteristics of the polar regions. There are also, of course, wide variations within the polar regions in terms of the amount of energy available and how this energy is distributed through the seasons. These variations are predictable, and are useful for subdividing the polar regions into smaller zones and sectors on the basis of similarities of climate and other physical and biological features.

The amount of radiation coming from the sun is essentially invariable over historical time—centuries—although it seems to fluctuate over longer periods. The amount of energy transmitted in a beam of a certain given cross-sectional area is known as the solar constant. However, the amount of solar energy that actually arrives on an area of a particular size on the earth's surface is variable and depends on several factors. The most important of these is a result of the angle at which the sun's rays strike the earth's surface. Also important are the amount of radiation that is dispersed in the atmosphere through absorption and scattering as well as the energy lost to space from reflection from the earth's surface and from clouds and other atmospheric phenomena. In the polar regions, the angle of the sun's rays to the earth is always comparatively oblique. The available energy of a beam of energy from the sun is spread over a broader area, directly related to the obliqueness of the angle of incidence, as shown in Figure 1–4. Also, the more oblique the angle of incidence, the greater the distance the beam of solar energy must travel through the atmosphere, with some loss of energy through scattering. The result is that earth's surface at high latitudes receives much less solar energy in an equivalent area than in temperate and tropical regions. Overall, this would be true even if there were no seasonality, or no angle of the ecliptic.

The polar regions would be even colder than they are if temperature were directly proportional to the amount of incoming radiation reaching the ground. Atmospheric circulation and, to a lesser degree, oceanic circulation redistribute solar energy over the earth's surface. Some of the energy arriving in temperate and tropical regions is transmitted to high latitudes in the form of warmed air and water. This transfer of energy is the major driving force of the earth's atmospheric circulation, and it is the determining factor in our climate and weather. Circulation resulting in energy transfer to the polar regions is affected by geography. So, as we have seen, polar conditions are not uniformly distributed in the higher latitudes. The coast of Labrador at the same latitude as Glasgow, in Scotland, is Arctic, according to most definitions, while the more northerly Trondheim, in Norway, doesn't even make it into the Subarctic. In these cases oceanic circulation is principally responsible for the anomaly. The North Atlantic Drift warms the coast of western Europe, while Labrador is bathed in the ice-laden waters of the Labrador Current, flowing from the Greenland coast. So, definitions of the polar regions need to take into account factors besides latitude and the location of the Polar Circles if they are to reflect the physical and biological conditions we think of as typifying the polar regions.

ENERGY AVAILABILITY AND PHYSICAL AND BIOLOGICAL FEATURES

Physical and biological processes in polar regions are crucially related to the freezing point of water and whether water exists in a liquid or solid state. Almost equally important are the phe-

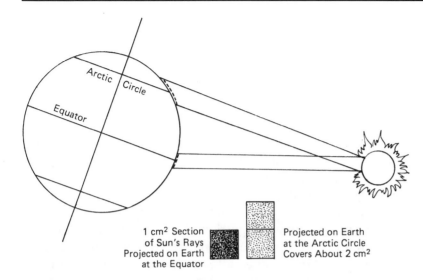

Arctic Circle

Equator

1 cm² Section
of Sun's Rays
Projected on Earth
at the Equator

Projected on Earth
at the Arctic Circle
Covers About 2 cm²

Figure 1–4. Concentration of solar energy in relation to the angle of incidence of the sun's rays on the earth's surface. Even during summer, solar energy per unit of area at high latitudes is less concentrated than near the equator. This helps create a net annual deficit of energy in the polar regions, one that is partially made up by atmospheric and oceanic circulation.

nomena associated with water's phase change between liquid and solid states.

In temperate and tropical regions, the amount of energy available normally allows water to exist as a liquid; ice is rare and temporary. In the polar regions, water in the form of ice is common, recurrent, or even essentially permanent. Ice profoundly affects physical and biological processes on all scales, from the molecular to the continental. At below-freezing temperatures, precipitation occurs as snow or ice, and it may remain in this state as glacial ice. This results in geological and geomorphic processes in the polar regions that are profoundly different from those in warmer regions.

The presence of snow and ice on the land has tremendous implications for the local heat budget. The surface of snow and ice is highly reflective; a snow-covered landscape is said to have a high *albedo*. This causes increased reflection of solar energy back into space from snowy terrain. It exacerbates the already low level of available energy in polar regions, and this powerfully affects global and local patterns of atmospheric circulation.

The transformation of water to ice and ice to water is a much more complicated process than one would suppose. Freeze-thaw cycles occur often in cold regions, and they have a major effect on the land and its living things. Crystallizing ice can split rock and explode living cells. Thawing ice can turn the cozy snow nest of a lemming into a dank, uninhabitable mudhole or cause the earth to slump and collapse.

Essentially all biological activity is dependent on the presence of liquid water. The cells of many organisms can *exist* for a more or less extended period of time at temperatures below freezing, but *living* requires water in the cells. For plants and many lower animals, energy to keep water liquid comes directly from the sun, so they are immediately dependent for this energy on the local, daily climate. Higher animals control the temperature of their own internal environment, but they do this by utilizing solar energy fixed and stored by plants.

It is a widely held perception that the polar regions are mainly lifeless areas of ice and snow, but the vast majority of the polar lands and seas support life in tremendous quantity and variety. The living systems that occur in any given portion of the polar regions provide much of the local character; they are also the basis for differentiating that portion from other polar regions. So the nature of various polar environments is critically affected by the intensity and extent of conditions that allow temperatures to stay above the freezing point of water. As we will see, it is not the duration and intensity of cold that provides the basis for defining the polar regions. Much more important is the nature of the short time each year when there is enough energy available to allow biological systems to function. Since energy availability is so marginal for these systems, minor variations in available energy can have profound effects on the nature of the organisms and ecosystems that can flourish in polar regions.

Stated in another way, most polar organisms, particularly in terrestrial environments, exist close to an absolute threshold of temperature and energy availability, below which life cannot survive in an active state. Relatively small variations above this threshold can then profoundly affect the composition of the array of forms of life that are actually able to exist. Thus, there is a clear correlation between the kinds of organisms present and the amount of available energy. A practical example is the presence or absence of trees in far northern regions. As we will see later, this is closely related to the amount of summer warmth, and the resulting *timberline* is a traditional boundary between the Arctic and the Subarctic. More generally, this means that subdivisions of terrestrial polar regions made on the basis of climatic phenomena are closely related to those made on the basis of biological phenomena. The general definitions of the Arctic and Subarctic are likely to be compatible for climatologists, biologists, and even social scientists. Inuit (Eskimos) live in the treeless Arctic, Indians in the forested Subarctic.

A very different situation prevails in marine ecosystems and in some freshwater ecosystems. Here, temperatures are generally at or above freezing (that is, above the freezing point of seawater) in all portions of the water mass except the surface layers. Furthermore, temperatures don't vary much seasonally; as long as there is floating ice, the water can't warm significantly above freezing. Temperature can be an important factor in the distribution of arctic marine organisms, but it is neither as crucial or as direct at sea as it is on land. Instead, the distribution of marine organisms in polar regions depends on a variety of interrelated factors, including temperature, ice cover, and the availability of nutrients and oxygen and energy in the form of light. Since no single physical feature is correlated well with the nature of the polar marine ecosystem, it is not easily or clearly subdivided by comparison to land areas. An additional difficulty in classifying or subdividing these ecosystems is that bodies of water are in motion and may carry a set of conditions and organisms far from where we would expect them. For example, the coast of Maine is infamous (among swimmers, at least) for its cold waters. This is the result of the Labrador Current, flowing southward from Baffin Bay and bringing a near-arctic sea to a temperate coast that is nearer the equator than the pole.

In summary, then, we can say that the nature of the polar environment is a function of the orientation of the higher latitudes of the earth to the sun, that this orientation results in low amounts of available energy in polar regions, and that such solar energy as is available is distributed in an uneven, seasonal fashion. The distribution of energy exercises a major control on the nature of atmospheric, land, and marine conditions, particularly with respect to the state in which water exists. There are also feedback mechanisms by which these factors affect energy distribution and climate in return. Finally, these combined factors exert a controlling influence on the presence and nature of biological systems in the polar regions.

Biological features provide much of the basis for delineation of subregions within the polar regions. Because polar region biology is so directly shaped by polar conditions, subdivisions based on biological factors also clearly reflect the physical and astronomical characteristics of the polar regions. So we now have a conceptual framework on which to define and perhaps subdivide the polar regions.

The arctic and antarctic regions are surprisingly interchangeable in the public mind. Never in all history has an Eskimo hunter stepped out of an igloo to come face to face with a penguin, magazine cartoons notwithstanding! While the main focus of this book is the Arctic, in order to provide some perspective, we will take a brief look at all of the polar regions before settling down to the far north for the rest of the book. Of course, many of the generalizations we can make about the Arctic hold true in the far south as well. While the idea that ice is ice is a gross over-simplification, the ice in Antarctica behaves in most ways pretty much like the ice in Greenland.

Except in a few areas such as quantum physics, scientists tend to be uncomfortable with ambiguity. This is probably the reason that most articles and books dealing with the polar regions start out with a map showing clearcut boundaries: north of this line is the Arctic, south of it the Subarctic. Such a map appears in Figure 1–1. The basis of drawing these boundaries is not nearly as clear as the maps might imply.

Deep within the continents the treeless barrens that are often equated with the Arctic begin to give way to scattered patches of cold woodland. To the south of these vanguards of trees lies a mosaic of treeless peatlands, meandering forested watercourses, and barren, windswept ridgetops, often lying in a belt hundreds of miles wide. Somewhere within this seemingly uninviting and almost unpopulated expanse lies the boundary between what is traditionally called the Arctic and the Subarctic.

Near the seacoast, conditions are radically different. Cold currents penetrate deep into temperate latitudes, dragging a coastal strip of the Arctic with them into Maine, as we saw. Even farther to the south, mountaintops penetrate into an arctic layer of the atmosphere, creating "islands" that are more or less related to the true Arctic, depending on many factors of history and geography. We call these *alpine* areas.

If we go back only a few millennia, the wink of an eye in terms of geological time, the extent and location of the polar regions was dramatically different. In 15,000 B.C., the climate and overall environment of the location of the present New York City would have been roughly equivalent to that of parts of Greenland today. Over geological time, the polar regions have repeatedly undergone these radical migrations. Although they seem to occur at a glacial pace in relation to individual human lifespans, changes of this sort are clearly happening to this day. So we need to be aware that the edges of the polar regions are not only fuzzy and frayed in space, but mutable over time.

Although we will be concentrating on the Arctic, we will be using a much broader concept of the Arctic than do most geographers. Much of the information we will be looking at applies as well to interior Labrador as it does to Baffin Island, to Fairbanks as to Nome, and we need not let the presence of an occasional spruce tree, or even a fair-sized patch of forest, drive us back into the treeless tundra of the Arctic as traditionally defined.

Given all these caveats and limitations, then, let's look now at some of the classic ideas of what constitutes the polar regions. Some of the more important geographical features are shown in Figure 1–1.

DEFINING THE POLAR REGIONS

The Arctic

The Arctic is the region in the Northern Hemisphere that extends from the North Pole southward in an irregular fashion to between about 70° and 55° north latitude. The Arctic terrestrial environment is characterized by an absence of tree growth. The absence of coniferous trees, which are often the most conspicuous feature of the vegetation in the areas immediately south of the Arctic, is particularly striking. Treeless vegetation in the far north has in recent decades generally come to be classified as *tundra,* and ecologists often equate the *tundra biome* with the terrestrial Arctic. (*Biome* is a broadly inclusive ecological term. Examples of biomes equivalent to the tundra biome are tropical rain forest or temperate grassland.)

Most of the terrestrial Arctic is free of snow and ice during some portion of the summer, and it supports a complex and varied ecosystem. The great exception to this is the ice cap that covers most of the island of Greenland. This, the only extensive polar ice sheet in the Northern Hemisphere, is a true biological desert, which supports virtually no life.

The southern limit of the Arctic is defined by two related phenomena, one biological, the other climatic. As we have seen, the Arctic's lack of tree growth biologically distinguishes it from other regions. Forest is generally replaced by tundra vegetation over a relatively narrow zone that is commonly called the timberline. The timberline can be formally defined as the poleward or seaward limit of arborescent coniferous forest growth. While this definition implies that there is a clear-cut line between forest and tundra, in fact the "line" is more commonly a zone some 50 to 100 miles or more wide in which forest and tundra interweave in a complex way. The situation is further complicated in areas of high relief and rugged terrain, since forests drop out as mountain altitude increases. Transitional areas such as the timberline are commonly called *ecotones.* The forest-tundra ecotone, in fact, is the example often used to illustrate this phenomenon. The timberline is discussed in detail in Chapter 8.

Although the timberline delineates the Arctic from the Subarctic, many anomalous situations appear if we rely entirely on the timberline to define the two areas. The most serious difficulties in classification arise in coastal areas that are treeless but have a climate that hardly falls within any generally accepted concept of the Arctic. The aspect of the islands off the northern and western coast of Scotland is tundralike in many respects, yet snow and subfreezing temperatures are rare and sporadic. A similar situation occurs in the Aleutian Islands of western Alaska. On the other hand, some forested inland areas classified subarctic in Siberia and Canada have extremes of winter cold far exceeding those of the exposed ice pack at the North Pole.

As was suggested earlier, the absence of tree growth in some far-northern situations is believed to be related to low temperatures and lack of heat energy during the growing season. This idea gained support during the early 1900s, when climatic data from polar regions began to become available. It was soon discovered that a correlation existed between the isotherm for 10°C (50°F) for the warmest month of the year (normally July in the polar regions) and the location of the timberline. (An isotherm is a line connecting locations of equal temperature, in this case, the equal mean temperatures of 50°F for July.) Once this correlation was established, given the isolation of the Arctic and the distance between weather stations, it is likely that researchers have relied on extrapolation—or fudging—in establishing the location of the isotherm between weather stations by basing it on the timberline. In fact, it is safe to say that the presence or absence of trees has probably been a major factor in estimating the location of the isotherm. In any case, this concept led to the widely accepted definition of the Arctic as the area in which the mean temperature for all months of the year was less than 10°C. In order to exclude marginal situations such as the Outer Hebrides, the proviso was added that the mean temperature for at least one month of the year must be below freezing.

It was already mentioned that the maritime Arctic is much more difficult to define satisfactorily. The map in Figure 1–1 shows generally accepted boundaries, which are based on factors such as water chemistry, ocean currents and the origin of water bodies. You will see immediately that there is little relationship between the distribution of "arctic" conditions in terrestrial and marine situations. Some arctic coasts are bounded by waters that are considered temperate, for example. In general, marine scientists define arctic waters comparatively narrowly, and include mainly water masses that are included in the Polar Basin and that are affected only minimally by mixture with other water masses. A rough-and-ready definition of the marine Arctic is simply the area that is more or less permanently covered by pack ice. This ice pack is discussed in Chapter 3.

High Arctic and Low Arctic

Although the terms *high Arctic* and *low Arctic* often crop up in older technical literature and in popular treatments of the polar regions, these terms have no clear-cut technical meaning. They do reflect a recognition of the great variation in conditions between arctic areas immediately adjacent to the timberline and those lying far to the north, as in northern Greenland and the Canadian Arctic archipelago. (In Chapter 9 some zones within the Arctic are discussed; the zone definitions are more useful than the terms low Arctic and high Arctic.)

The term *high Arctic* generally refers to the various islands lying within the Arctic Basin, such as the Svalbard archipelago, and to the northern portions of Greenland and the Canadian Arctic islands. The area is characterized by a desertlike environment, with a thin, discontinuous cover of low vegetation. Much of the high Arctic is heavily glaciated and surrounded by ice-covered seas during all or most of the year.

The term *low Arctic* refers to a much richer tundra environment, with closed, often meadowlike, vegetation, and often including shrubby growth, even dwarf woodland. Areas such as northern Quebec and Labrador, most of northern and western Alaska, and, according to some definitions, northernmost Scandinavia, lie within the area traditionally considered to be the low Arctic.

The Subarctic

The Subarctic, as traditionally defined, includes immense areas of primarily forested country in the interior portions of the two major land masses in the Northern Hemisphere, North America and Eurasia. Measured by the total land area involved, the terrestrial Subarctic is by far the largest part of the area we consider within the northern polar regions, as it includes the majority of Canada and Siberia as well as most of Scandinavia and Alaska. Iceland, although mostly treeless, is usually thought of as subarctic, and some people suggest that the southwestern corner of

Greenland, where sheep can be raised and even some grain crops grown, should be called subarctic.

The Subarctic is immense both in the area it involves and its potential significance to modern civilizations; geographically, more of it is closer to heavily settled areas than is the true Arctic. Even so, the Subarctic has in many respects remained *terra incognita* compared to the Arctic. The vast distances involved, its inaccessibility from the sea, and the extreme climatic conditions, particularly in winter, of the Subarctic made it comparatively difficult to access until recent times. This is even true in the areas where the Subarctic extends southward to latitudes generally thought of as lying in the temperate zone. Included here are even parts of the United States' lower 48 states, such as northern Minnesota, northern Michigan, northern New England, as well as parts of Atlantic Canada.

Over most of its extent, the Subarctic is a vast and almost continuous coniferous forest. Hence, it is known to ecologists as the *boreal forest biome;* it is also sometimes called the *taiga* (tié·gah), from a Russian word for a dwarfed, open coniferous forest. This forest is discussed in Chapter 8.

The northern border of the Subarctic is the southern edge of the Arctic, which has already been defined in terms of climate and vegetation in the preceding section. The definition of the southern boundary of the Subarctic is also based on vegetational and climatic factors, although these aren't clear cut as in the Arctic. Typically, in the southern border of the subarctic boreal forest, tree species are replaced by other trees of more temperate and local distribution such as oak, beech, hemlock, and hickory, or sometimes by steppe, grassland, and semiarid woodlands. As in the case of the timberline, the boundary is more of a zone than an exact line, and its definition is further complicated in areas of high relief, where boreal forest vegetation may occur as a zone related to elevation, but may merge imperceptibly with "true" boreal forest lying to the north. We see islands or peninsulas of boreal forest in the southern Appalachians, the Alps, and even as far south as the tropics in Mexico.

The presence of boreal forest vegetation is related to climatic factors, as is the case with timberline and tundra. A generally accepted climatic definition of the Subarctic establishes that it includes the area in which at least one month, but no more than four months, of the year have a mean temperature of 10°C or above. Again, the added proviso that at least one month must have a mean temperature below freezing eliminates such coastal situations as the rain forests of the North American Pacific

Northwest from consideration within the Subarctic. One rather odd boundary that defines the southern edge of the Subarctic could be called the *vine line*. Vines and creepers—honeysuckle, grape, poison ivy, and such—stop at the southern edge of the taiga.

The marine Subarctic is of comparatively limited extent, irregular in distribution, and difficult to define. Oceanographers generally think of the marine Subarctic as the area in which polar waters are mixed with water from the temperate oceans; thus, the limits of the marine Subarctic are related to ocean currents, and particularly areas in which the ocean waters are affected by outflow from the Polar Basin. This means that the Bering Sea coasts of Alaska, which lie within the terrestrial Arctic, are bordered by seas that have little connection with the Arctic Basin and are considered to be temperate in their affinities, rather than either Arctic or Subarctic. On the other hand, the coastal waters of Atlantic Canada and northern New England are affected by the Labrador Current, which originates in the Arctic and brings subarctic conditions as far south as Cape Cod. While these concepts do not accord well with a land dweller's view of what constitutes polar conditions, they are clearly reflected in a variety of aspects of the marine environment, including water temperature, chemistry, fauna, and flora. The most serious difficulties with these definitions arise in the eastern North Atlantic Ocean, where the North Atlantic Drift, a continuation of the Gulf Stream, affects marine conditions as far north as 80° in the vicinity of the Svalbard archipelago. Here, the juxtaposition of high arctic land conditions and an ocean that in some ways is temperate to subarctic is incongruous.

As in the case of the marine Arctic, the presence or absence of pack ice provides a reasonably accurate and useful definition for the marine Subarctic. In general, ocean waters that are covered by pack ice during a portion of the year, but which are outside the limit of the permanent polar ice pack, can be considered subarctic waters.

The Circumpolar North

The northern polar regions form a nearly continuous ring of land, surrounding a mediterranean sea, the Arctic Ocean. The only major break in this continuous terrestrial environment is in the North Atlantic; even here the gap is fairly narrow and partly bridged by islands: Iceland, the Faeroes, Shetlands, Orkneys, and Svalbard. The circumpolar distribution of land masses in the far north has provided migration pathways for many of the important plants and animals of northern polar ecosystems. An important biological feature of the Arctic and Subarctic is the circumpolar distribution pattern of many of the organisms that live there. This means that arctic areas tend to be biologically similar whatever sector of the circumpolar regions they may be located in. So, biological information acquired in one portion of the Arctic is usually applicable elsewhere in the circumpolar north. We've become more aware of this situation in recent decades as biologists have recognized the identity of species of many Eurasian and North American animals. For example, the caribou of the New World and the reindeer of Eurasia are now considered to be a single species, *Rangifer tarandus;* similarly, American moose and Eurasian elk are now all included in the single species, *Alces alces.*

Similarities within the circumpolar regions have additionally been influenced by their common history during recent geological time. At the same time, polar conditions provide similar evolutionary selection pressures for polar organisms wherever they occur in the circumpolar north. We'll look at these factors in more detail when we consider the Ice Ages in Chapters 7 and 13.

The circumpolar similarity of physical and biological conditions is more obvious the farther north one goes. The flora and fauna of high arctic regions are often nearly identical, no matter their location around the Polar Basin. As one moves south, on the other hand, the southern Subarctic derives some of its most typical features from adjacent temperate regions, so the circumpolar similarity is reduced.

Circumpolar distribution patterns lead to a circumpolar approach by northern scientists. International cooperation in northern exploration and research is the rule, with a few sad exceptions. The Cold War is a temperate region phenomenon, ignored by polar scientists the world over.

Alpine Regions

We've stressed the effect of climate, particularly temperature, on defining and controlling the distribution of polar environments and their biological constituents. It has also long been known that the higher elevations of temperate mountains are similar to true polar situations in terms of physical and biotic features. Polar and alpine research efforts, therefore, often go hand in hand.

Temperatures in the troposphere (the lower atmosphere) usually decrease progressively and predictably as one goes high-

er. Temperatures drop about 0.6°C per 100-meter rise in elevation, or about 3°F per 1,000 feet; this figure is known as the
Standard Lapse Rate. Near-arctic conditions, then, occur in
mountainous regions, with the lower alpine limit occurring at
progressively higher elevations toward the Equator as shown in
Figure 1–5. At low latitudes, alpine areas are usually small and
isolated from the Arctic by intervening temperate (and tropical)
lowlands. Seasonality in alpine areas is, of course, dependent on
latitude. Although there are glaciers on Mt. Kilimanjaro and in the
high Andes, there is no midnight sun, and really no winter or
summer. Alpine situations at high latitudes are more or less
indistinguishable from nearby arctic regions, but the similarity
decreases in temperate and tropical areas. The alpine tundra of
the mountains of New Guinea or the *paramo* of Peru bears only a
superficial similarity to the Arctic, while only an expert could
distinguish alpine areas in the Canadian Rockies from the true
Arctic.

The factors involved in these relationships are complex; they
include the location of the alpine area and its history of long-term
climatic change, tectonic activity, and even continental drift.
These lead to concerns like the kind of selection pressures
brought to bear on the organisms inhabiting the particular alpine

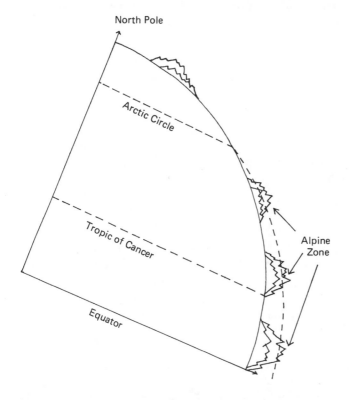

Figure 1–5. The relationship between arctic and alpine zones. Within the Arctic, both mountains and
lowlands lie beyond the timberline.
Southward, the timberline intersects
hills and mountains at a progressively higher elevation, so that
alpine regions become smaller and
more widely separated.

environment. Therefore, the relationship of any given alpine region to the circumpolar north is unique. It has been theorized that the alpine environment is older than the arctic tundra, and that the high mountains were the sources for many polar organisms: alpine regions served as staging areas from which the expanding tundra was populated as the world climate deteriorated during the latter part of the Cenozoic period or Age of Mammals.

We can see biological and climatic zonation, or division into zones, associated with elevation within the polar regions, too. Arctic conditions occur on mountain tops within the boreal forest regions, and mountains in the Arctic have biological and climatic conditions typical of even higher latitudes. The summits of the Brooks Range, near the Arctic Circle in Alaska, are much like the lowlands of northernmost Greenland or Ellesmere Island, in the Canadian high Arctic.

The Antarctic

The terrestrial Antarctic includes the antarctic continent itself plus a few associated islands near the coast, such as the Balleny Islands, Ross Island, Peter I Island, and the South Shetlands. If we think of the Arctic as a frozen sea surrounded by more or less open land, we can directly contrast it to the Antarctic, which is a frozen continent surrounded by seas. Most of these seas are only frozen solidly for part of the year, however. Unconfined by land and subject to some of the fiercest storms on earth, pieces of the ice pack are constantly dispersed northward.

Over 90 percent of the antarctic continent is covered with permanent ice and has been ice covered for at least several million years. The ice averages nearly 3,000 meters (almost two miles) thick; its maximum depth is over 4,000 meters. Because of the thickness of the ice, Antarctica is the highest of the continents, as well as the coldest.

In parts of coastal Antarctica, the ice sheets from the interior spread out over the sea, forming ice shelves. These thick layers of floating ice are distinct from pack ice, which is frozen sea water. The outer edges of the ice shelves regularly split off, forming huge, flat-topped icebergs that look like floating sugar tablets. These *tabular bergs* are typical of antarctic seas.

There is some open, ice-free land in Antarctica. It occurs principally in mountainous regions where peaks (called *nunataks*) rise above the surrounding glaciers. These are most common near the coast, where the ice is thinner. There are also a series of *dry valleys,* or ice-free glacial canyons, of the scale of the

Grand Canyon of Arizona. The largest are inland from the Victoria Land coast. Even in the ice-free areas, nothing is biologically comparable to the tundra biome of the Arctic. In a few places mosses, lichens, and even two species of flowering plants (a grass and a tiny member of the carnation family) occur. Insects, spiders, and a few other invertebrates are associated with these simple communities. However, there are no terrestrial vertebrates, and the vast, ice-covered major portion of the terrestrial Antarctic is biologically dead.

On the other hand, the coastal regions of Antarctica support a rich array of life, including higher vertebrates such as penguins, seals, skuas, and albatrosses. Without exception, all depend on the surrounding seas for their livelihood; they are land animals only in that they come ashore to rest, escape predation, and breed.

The marine Antarctic consists mainly of the cold seas in the immediate vicinity of the continent; there are no clear biological boundaries. We might think of the marine Antarctic as being the area of sea adjoining the continent and covered by pack ice during a significant portion of the year. These seas would extend up to several hundred kilometers out from the continent, depending on location. Politically, antarctic waters extend out to the sixtieth parallel, and the seas south of this line are subject to agreements in the Antarctic Treaty.

Unique to the marine Antarctic is the unfrozen sea underlying the millions of square kilometers of floating ice shelves. Although a drill hole or two has penetrated the ice, we know nothing about the underlying seas: they are as alien as Mars.

The Subantarctic

With a few exceptions, the Subantarctic is an exclusively marine environment. It is the southern portion of the Southern Ocean, a circumpolar belt of open sea where the South Atlantic, South Pacific, and Indian Oceans merge at the higher latitudes of the Southern Hemisphere. A good northern boundary for the subantarctic seas is a phenomenon called the Antarctic Convergence. At the convergence the cold waters of the southern seas are overlain at the surface by much warmer subtropical waters. One can easily see this from shipboard: the subantarctic waters are cold, gray-green, and fog bound, in contrast to the blue water to the north. The change in temperature is as much as 3° to 6°C over a distance of a few kilometers or even less. There are clear-cut differences in the organisms inhabiting the two bodies of water, and fog banks and other unsettled weather conditions are often associated with the convergence. Much of the antarctic and subantarctic water originates as upwellings from deep currents from the more temperate ocean basins. When it arrives at the surface, this water is exceedingly rich in nutrients. The action of sunlight then allows the rapid growth of marine algae, and this in turn supports an immense biomass of other life, ranging from tiny invertebrates to whales.

The terrestrial Subantarctic consists of a few small, generally extremely isolated islands scattered in the Southern Ocean. Although it could be argued that only those islands south of the Antarctic Convergence are truly subantarctic, some more northern islands are usually included. For example, Tristan da Cunha, in the South Atlantic, Campbell Island and Auckland Island both south of New Zealand, are generally thought of as subantarctic. On the other hand Bouvet Island, at about 55° south in the Atlantic, is best described as truly antarctic, as are the South Sandwich and South Orkney Islands of the Scotia Arc. Also, the southernmost portion of South America, sometimes called the Magellanic or Fuegian region, is often termed subantarctic. This area is forested, and is the only part of the Subantarctic that bears any similarity to the forested portions of the Subarctic, although these similarities are superficial.

The larger subantarctic islands support glaciers, and were more heavily glaciated within the past ten to fifteen thousand years. Most islands have a thin, sparse vegetation cover, somewhat similar in appearance to arctic tundra. But the similarity is only superficial; taxonomically, arctic and antarctic plants are mostly unrelated. Many of the antarctic plants come from the southern Andes and New Zealand. A few are world travelers found in the north as well: grasses, ferns, and, of course, dandelions!

The antarctic and subantarctic regions are among the most isolated and little-known places on earth. Except for southern South America, they were never inhabited by any native people. Most of them were not discovered until the late eighteenth or nineteenth century; in fact, the first sighting of the antarctic continent was probably made about 1820. In spite of their isolation, the islands have been as much damaged by human activities as more temperate and accessible areas. Their herds of fur seals were generally destroyed within a few years of their discovery, and elephant seals and even penguins followed within a few more years. Processing plants for whales were set up on the islands, and rabbits, cats, and rats were often introduced. Many of the subantarctic islands have become biological ruins compared to what they had been for all history until the past 150 years.

SUGGESTED FURTHER READING

A few of the more general books dealing with the Arctic are listed below, including several older works that will help a reader trace the ways in which our understanding of the polar environment has evolved. Many of the other books listed at the end of later chapters also include general introductory material that may be useful. Additionally, several periodicals deal with a wide variety of arctic or polar concerns. The most important of these are *Arctic,* published quarterly by the Arctic Institute of North America (AINA); *Arctic and Alpine Research,* published quarterly by the Institute of Arctic and Alpine Research (INSTAAR), Boulder, CO; *Polar Geography and Geology,* published quarterly by V. H. Winton and Sons, and dealing largely with Soviet activities in the polar regions; and *Polar Record,* published three times a year by the Scott Polar Research Institute, Cambridge, England. Scott Polar Research Institute also publishes *Recent Polar and Glaciological Literature,* an annotated compendium of current literature, three times a year.

Armstrong, T. E., and G. Rowley. *The Circumpolar North; a Political and Economic Geography of the Arctic and Sub-Arctic Regions.* London: Methuen, 1978.

Baird, P. D. *The Polar World.* London: Longman, 1964.

Breummer, F. *Arctic World.* San Francisco: Sierra Club Books, 1985.

Central Intelligence Agency. *Polar Regions Atlas.* Washington, DC, 1978.

Ives, J. D., and R. G. Barry. *Arctic and Alpine Environments.* London: Methuen, 1974.

Lopez, Barry. *Arctic Dreams.* New York: Charles Scribner's Sons, 1986.

Kimble, G. H. T., and D. Good, eds. *Geography of the Northlands.* Special Publication no. 32. Washington, DC: American Geographical Society, 1955. (One of the classic older publications on the North.)

Müller, Fritz. *The Living Arctic*. Toronto: Methuen, 1977 (English ed. 1981).

Nordenskiold, O., and L. Mecking. *The Geography of the Polar Regions*. Special Publication no. 8. Washington, DC: American Geographical Society, 1928. (This classic is long out of print but is of more than historical interest.)

Sage, Bryan. *The Arctic and its Wildlife*. New York: Facts on File Publications, 1986.

Thorèn, R. *Picture Atlas of the Arctic*. Amsterdam: Elsevier, 1969.

Chapter 2

Polar Weather and Climate

THE study of weather and climate is a purely physical science. The human element rarely goes beyond people's names given to typhoons and hurricanes. When we deal with polar climates, though, it is important to remember that we humans are tropical animals, at least in our origins. We have an intuitive awareness that, away from the tropics, all that stands between us and a miserable death from hypothermia is our technology—our clothing and manufactured shelter. And most of us have a great deal more experience with heat deprivation than we do with hunger. A fear of the polar chill probably lurks at several levels of our unconscious. It shows up as *windigo* legends—tales of fearsome creatures with hearts and guts of crystal ice—who were once men. When the pitiful frozen body of some nineteenth century explorer is exhumed from the permafrost, chinalike eyeballs still staring, not many of us can avoid a cold shiver.

We learn from physics that cold is a nonentity, a void, only the absence of energy. But this knowledge is counterintuitive. If we bring a chunk of metal, say a bulldozer part, out of the polar cold into a warm room, it seems to radiate cold onto our exposed faces and hands. If we look across the jagged ice and hissing snow of the Arctic Ocean in the half light of a polar noon, we may well feel like candles about to gutter out, consumed by cold.

It's important to remember that an organism that has been physically adapting to the polar climate through a million generations or so has a different outlook. A moose appears content munching willow twigs at 60 degrees below zero. A fur seal will die of heatstroke if it is forced to scuttle any distance over cold, wet tundra. Shoot a caribou in zero weather, fail to dress it, and the meat will begin to spoil from its own body heat, so effective is the fur as insulation. Even a chickadee, a few grams of fluff with naked legs, will begin breeding behavior when there are 50 or 60 Fahrenheit degrees of frost in the air.

These and other organisms are remarkably well adapted to polar climate, polar cold, and polar seasonality. But many adaptations to the polar environment are no better than standoffs: compromises or jury-rigs of some kind. We humans may have left the tropics only an ice age or two ago, but all warm-blooded animals are tropical in some archaic sense. Just as land animals carry the ancient sea around with them in the form of their body fluids, homiotherms—animals whose internal temperature does not vary in reaction to outside temperatures—carry around an internal climate probably dating from the Age of Dinosaurs. Warm-blooded animals may be almost unbelievably good at maintaining a temperature differential between their inner core and the surrounding environment, but it is a differential that *must* be maintained. The differential may be close to that between the freezing point and boiling point of water, and yet be separated only by a few centimeters of fur, hide, and flesh.

The Achilles' heel of homiotherms in the polar regions isn't cold per se. It is the energy required to maintain the temperature differential with the external environment. To remain alive in the polar winter, a homiotherm needs a concentrated energy source. The frozen, windswept winter tundra is not usually a good place to find it.

Other problems abound. If you are a seal in the polar sea, you have little more heat control problem in winter than in summer. But how do you breathe air when there is a meter-thick layer of pack ice sealing the surface of the sea? If you are an evergreen tree, you need to accommodate water loss from your leaves when your roots are frozen and can take on no water—a problem called physiological drought. Or the problems may be mechanical: windborne snow crystals that scour off needles and bark.

Staying alive in cold climates, then, is a complicated problem for all forms of life. For homiotherms, the most basic concern is getting enough energy to maintain body temperature and keeping this energy from dispersing. Plants and cold-blooded animals must avoid damage to cells that are below freezing and must complete life cycles during the comparatively short time when temperatures are high enough to allow biological activity. Of course, accommodating to temperature change, as well as temperature extremes, is critical for these organisms.

We've seen that the major features of polar climates are cold—lack of heat energy—and variability, or seasonality. In Chapter 1 we saw that, other things being equal, the closer to the Pole the less energy there is, and the more energy that is present is seasonally distributed. Theoretically, we should be able to draw a series of concentric belts around the Pole and characterize the climates we would find in each. Such a drawing would have little relevance to the real world, however. The study of climate is really a study of relationships, and the relationships studied are much more complex than the straightforward ones of latitude and temperature, ecliptic and seasonality. The physics of water is the critical factor in understanding the climate and weather in the cold regions. The most obvious physical characteristic of water in the polar regions is simply that it regularly changes back and forth between the solid and the liquid state; this change is fundamentally important to nearly all aspects of the polar environment. But water does many things besides changing from liquid to solid; the complexity of these changes affects polar weather and polar organisms.

THE PHYSICS OF WATER

To understand the complex changes in water that affect polar weather, we need to review briefly the physics of water, particularly properties called *specific heat, latent heat of fusion,* and *latent heat of vaporization.*

A calorie, in physics, is the amount of energy needed to raise the temperature of a gram of liquid water one degree centigrade. (Nutritional calories—*large calories*—are 1,000 times greater.) Water is the standard substance against which others are compared; at one degree temperature difference for the addition or subtraction of one calorie per gram, water is said to have a specific heat of 1.0. Other substances also have a characteristic specific heat, which is expressed as a relationship between that substance and water. For example, the specific heat of aluminum is approximately 0.21, so that the amount of energy that would raise the temperature of a given weight of water one degree would raise the temperature of the same weight of aluminum nearly five degrees. Most solid materials, such as rock and soil, have a specific heat even lower than that of aluminum. Let the sun shine on dry rock, sand, or gravel, and it will warm up rapidly. But the heat departs quickly after sunset, as any desert traveler can tell you. So, the surface temperature of terrestrial environments varies widely, as the quantity of radiant energy reaching it changes with the seasons or over the course of a day. On the other hand, bodies of water change temperature only slowly as heat energy is gained or lost. This tendency to change temperature more slowly is exacerbated by the fact that radiant energy is absorbed in water to some depth, rather than only on the surface, since water is transparent to most common wavelengths of radiant energy. In addition, the liquid state of water allows mixing and a more uniform distribution of temperatures throughout a body of water than would occur in rock and soil.

Bodies of water, then, are reservoirs of heat as the air cools in the fall; as temperatures climb in the spring, they keep surrounding air cooler. In either case, bodies of water flatten extremes of temperature in their proximity, both daily and seasonally, in what we might call a damping effect.

Specific heat is only the beginning of the story. Two other properties of water, and of other substances that change from a solid to a liquid to a gaseous state, are the latent heats of *fusion* and *vaporization. Heat of fusion* refers to the amount of energy absorbed or released in a change between a liquid and a solid state at the same temperature. In the case of water, 80 calories per gram must be released before liquid water at 0°C solidifies into ice. Conversely, ice must absorb 80 calories per gram, nearly as much energy as would raise liquid water at the same temperature to boiling, before it can become liquid water. This is why you should never eat snow when you are suffering from hypothermia—lowered body temperature—no matter how thirsty you are. You would be putting a near-perfect heat sink right into the core of your body where it would do the most damage.

The high latent heat of fusion of water (ice) means that an ice-covered body of water (or an ice- and snow-covered landscape) must absorb large quantities of energy and melt all of the ice before the surrounding water or underlying wet soil can begin to warm up to temperatures above freezing. Practically, this means that many polar seas never reach temperatures significantly above freezing even during the summer. Any sea breeze blowing from these waters will always be chilled to near the freezing point.

A change in state from liquid to gas involves even more energy gain or loss. The heat of vaporization of water is 585 calories per gram. Unlike freeze-thaw (fusion), *vaporization* (and condensation) can take place at any temperature. For example, ice and snow can change directly to water vapor in a process known as *sublimation*. This is the same process by which frozen laundry on a line can dry: in either case, it involves the absorption of at least 665 calories per gram of ice transformed to water vapor (80 plus 585). Similarly, the deposition of dew or frost releases great quantities of energy, inhibiting further cooling of the air.

If dry air passes over open water or a wet surface, it tends to evaporate water from that surface, so that large amounts of heat are lost in the process. Thus, an air mass that passes over open water is generally cooled by contact with the cold surface, and also by losing the energy required to evaporate water from the surface.

This brings us to another important feature of air that has been in contact with water: It is generally close to being saturated—that is, its relative humidity is high. Since the ability of the air to contain water vapor is related to temperature and increases as temperature increases, the cooling of maritime air precipitates the water. It may remain suspended in the form of cloud or fog, or it may drop to the ground as precipitation. In either case, it is an important feature of the climate.

MARITIME AND CONTINENTAL CLIMATES

We see, then, that the relationship between land and water could be practically as important as latitude in determining temperature, seasonality, and other features of the climate. In terms of temperature, inland climates are the most strongly seasonal; they are called *continental climates*. Coastal locations have climates with subdued seasonality, called *maritime climates*.

This can be illustrated in a diagram. Figure 2–1 shows the difference in annual temperature regime on a month-to-month basis between a highly maritime and a highly continental climate. We can easily see that a continental climate shows great temperature swings from season to season. The same is true, to a lesser degree, from day to night. A maritime climate, on the other hand, displays much less variation over both shorter and longer periods of time. Cool summers and mild winters are characteristic of maritime climates, while hot summers and cold winters are characteristic of continental climates of comparable latitudes. Variations in such factors as precipitation, cloud cover, and fog are also associated with these climate types, and these variations can be important, particularly at the local level.

Figure 2–1 also shows the time lag between the longest day of the year, when the most energy reaches the earth's surface, and the warmest period. A comparable lag also occurs in winter. The lag is considerably longer in maritime than in continental situations, again because of the damping effect of water. The summer solstice, the longest day of the year, is usually June 21. In most parts of the Arctic, July is the warmest month of the year. In a few highly maritime areas like northern Norway, August is the warmest, and winter bottoms out in February rather than January.

Obviously, there is a continuum from the most extreme maritime to the most extreme continental climate, and many factors affect the degree of continentality. Among these are distance from a body of water, size of the water body, direction of prevailing winds, and the presence of barriers to wind flow, such as mountains. Wind flow and weather patterns are changeable, and a coastal region may be in the grip of maritime influence one day, but subject to a continental air mass shortly afterward.

Locally, an important feature of polar maritime climates is their relationship to the formation of sea ice. Once a layer of pack ice has formed, heat exchange between the air and the underlying water is strongly inhibited, and air temperatures can drop far below what they would be over open water. This means that many coastal regions at high latitude have cool, damp, typically maritime summers but become much more continental in winter, with long stretches of clear, intensely cold weather. The mean annual temperature of a location under such conditions may be several degrees colder than what would be predicted without this effect.

A final comment on maritime climates is that they are often *exotic,* in the sense that the water affecting the climate may have traveled great distances as ocean currents. The classic case of this, of course, is the Gulf Stream. It turns Iceland and Norway into temperate countries, with warm summers, blue ocean water, and ice-free ports. Only a few hundred miles away, and at similar latitudes, the eastern Greenland coast is bathed in the frigid East Greenland Current. Pack ice covers the sea for most of the year,

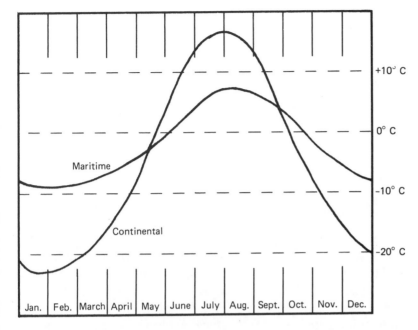

Figure 2–1. Annual temperature regimes of two northern localities. One is a highly maritime situation, such as occurs in the Aleutian Islands or Iceland. The other, a more intensely seasonal one, is typical of a subarctic location in Siberia, northwestern Canada, or interior Alaska. Although the maritime location is warmer on a year-round basis, it has a cooler summer and is located within a treeless arctic area, while the continental site lies within the forested region. Note that the temperature peaks occur well after the longest day of the year, and later at the maritime station than at the continental one.

and the narrow, bleak, tundra-covered coast backs up against the largest glacier in the Northern Hemisphere.

CATEGORIES OF POLAR CLIMATES

We are now ready to put together a classification scheme for polar climates. Climates of cold regions of the Northern Hemisphere are usually divided into three groups, based on summer temperature regimes. These are:

1. *Ice cap climates* (called simply *polar climates* by climatologists): mean temperature of all months below freezing
2. *Tundra (arctic) climates:* mean temperature of all months below 10°C, with at least one month below freezing
3. *Taiga (subarctic) climates:* mean temperature of no more than four months above 10°C, and one or more below freezing

Each of these types can vary from being intensely maritime to intensely continental; so we can think of six polar climatic types, all of which occur in the far north. Southern Hemisphere polar climates are not exactly comparable, since nowhere in the far south is there anything equivalent to the highly seasonal, highly continental climate of some arctic and subarctic regions. Typical examples of the types are diagrammed in Figure 2–2.

Figure 2–2. Diagrams of typical ice cap, tundra, and boreal forest temperature regimes. In each case, the summer temperatures define the nature of the environment. Winters in these stations are similar, but could vary widely without significantly affecting the overall situation.

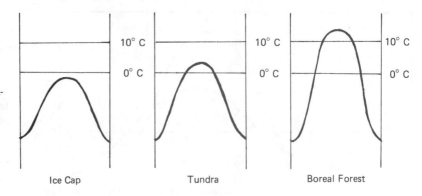

Ice Cap   Tundra   Boreal Forest

Ice Cap Climates

Glaciers can form only under conditions where the quantity of precipitation falling as snow is relatively high and the summer is cool enough so that this snow doesn't all melt. (Chapter 4 discusses glaciers in detail.) This means that the initial formation of glaciers must take place at high latitudes or high elevations or some combination of both. Once a glacier has become established, however, as it becomes larger and thicker, it provides a sort of feedback mechanism for its continued growth: It sets in motion a cycle that promotes its growth. Temperatures drop as the surface of the ice sheet rises in elevation as more ice accumulates; at the same time, the year-round snow-covered or ice-covered surface causes a change in albedo, or light reflection. Almost every area covered by an extensive ice sheet has a characteristic climate, with no month of the year having a mean temperature above freezing. Conversely, there are no examples of extensive ice-free terrain in areas where the temperature for the warmest month of the year is below freezing. The closest approach to an ice-free, below-freezing terrain is in the Dry Valleys of Antarctica, where some gaps in the polar ice cover several hundred square miles. An ice cap climate, then, is a specific type of polar climate characterized by mean temperatures remaining below freezing during all months of the year. If the ice cap is large, as in the case of Greenland or Antarctica, the inland climate will also be extremely cold, far below freezing, during all or most of the year.

The coldest known place on earth is the Soviet Vostok Station, high in the interior of the Antarctic Plateau. The mean annual temperature is –55.6°C, a record of –88° has been recorded, and temperatures seldom rise above –15° in midsummer. By comparison, Centrale, in the middle of the Greenland ice cap, has a mean annual temperature of –28.1°C. But temperatures still rise to freezing only briefly and fleetingly during the summer, although the latitude is about the same as northern Norway. In fact, ice cap climates extend southward in Greenland nearly to Cape Farvel, at roughly the same latitude as Aberdeen, Scotland.

Precipitation in ice cap climates varies widely. Because of the feedback relationship between the presence of perennial ice and snow and the climate, an ice cap climate normally occurs only when there is enough precipitation to maintain the snow or ice cover. Where minor exceptions occur, as in the Dry Valley area of Antarctica, a combination of low annual precipitation and a sub-glacial topography that guides the moving ice sheet away from the area results in ice-free areas with an ice cap climate. A similar situation probably occurs locally in parts of Peary Land, North Greenland, and in northernmost Canada. On most inland por-tions of major ice sheets, however, the climate is highly con-tinental, and precipitation is low. Only where glaciers approach the coast do they come under a maritime climate with heavy precipitation.

Arctic (Tundra) Climates

As discussed in Chapter 1, the timberline is often accepted as the southern limit of the Arctic and is closely congruent with the 10°C isotherm for the warmest month of the year. If the tem-perature for the warmest month of the year were below 0°C, an ice cap climate would prevail and the land would probably be glaciated. Therefore, a tundra climate is one in which at least one month of the year has a mean temperature above freezing but below 10°C.

Because tundra climates by definition depend on low summer temperatures, they are often associated with maritime situations. Even at latitudes north of the Arctic Circle, tundra climates do not occur at low elevation at a distance of more than 200 to 300 miles from large bodies of water. However, the presence of pack ice during much of the year may provide a strong continental in-fluence in high latitudes. For example, parts of Ellesmere Island and northernmost Greenland (Peary Land) have comparatively warm, dry summers and intensely cold winters; these areas are surrounded or bordered by nearly permanent polar pack ice.

Most tundra climates are moderately maritime during the sum-mer, moderately continental during the winter, and have by standards of temperate regions low to very low precipitation. Precipitation may range from a low of about 5 centimeters (2 inches) per year in northernmost Canada and Greenland to 50 to

75 centimeters (20 to 30 inches) in coastal regions such as the shores of the Bering Sea. Low precipitation is particularly significant, in that it means that snow cover is generally thin, even though it may last for many months. Since there is very little tall vegetation to impede the wind, the tundra snow cover is generally redistributed by drifting. Deep snow patches may occur in hollows, but much of the land is nearly snow free throughout the winter. This is important for grazing animals such as caribou, and it also causes patches of snow-free terrain to appear within a few days of the first spring thaw, providing habitat for ground-nesting birds and other organisms. Also, as is discussed in Chapter 4, this low snowfall goes a long way toward explaining why much of the Arctic is not covered by glaciers and even escaped glaciation during the Ice Ages. (See Chapters 7 and 13 for a full discussion of the Ice Ages.)

An atypical climate, generally considered as a variation of a tundra climate, occurs where the land is near to or surrounded by cold oceans that are nevertheless too warm, or too open and subject to currents, to develop an extensive or long-lasting ice cover. These conditions occur in the Aleutian Islands and in parts of Içeland. The vegetation of areas such as these is tundralike in that it is generally treeless. Mean summer temperatures are usually within a degree or two of 10°C, and mean winter temperatures are generally slightly below freezing. However, the growing season is much longer than in a typical arctic environment, and the vegetation is generally enriched by a wide variety of temperate species. Furthermore, agriculture is possible, with cool-weather crops such as cabbages and potatoes often thriving. Even cattle ranching can be successful, to the point that cattle interests and brown bears on Kodiak Island, Alaska, have been on a collision course. In these borderline tundra situations, a temperature change of a degree or two, enough to raise summers above 10° and winters above freezing, would move the area into the temperate zone. Thus, areas such as the Faeroe Islands, the Shetland Islands, and the west coast of Norway are seldom considered as being in the polar regions, although their climate and vegetation is only marginally different from that of the Aleutians.

Although the difference in summer temperature between a tundra climate bordering an ice-cap climate and one near timberline appears to be small, there are great variations in the vegetation between areas at these two extremes, and these variations are strongly correlated with differences in temperature and related parameters such as length of growing season, frost-free days, and soil conditions. How these variations in the tundra climate affect the distribution of arctic plants and animals is examined in Chapters 8 and 9.

Subarctic Climates

Most typical areas in which subarctic climates prevail lie deep in the interior of major land masses and are highly continental. Exceptions to this are in areas along the east coasts of North America and Asia, where prevailing westerly winds from the interior tend to mitigate the influence of the nearby oceans. In areas such as Newfoundland, Labrador, and the Siberian coast of the Sea of Okhotsk, the climate and vegetation are typically subarctic, although winters are generally somewhat moderated and precipitation is increased.

On an annual basis, subarctic climates are not necessarily warmer than those of tundra areas. In parts of interior Siberia, mean July temperatures are on the order of 15°C, while mean January temperatures may be as low as –40° to –50°. Thus, mean annual temperatures in such a subarctic climate may be as low as –15°, colder than virtually all of the tundra areas of the world. The effects of the high summer temperatures are augmented by the predominately clear skies, low cloud cover and precipitation, low snow cover and hence early spring, and low albedo of the dark forest.

Precipitation in subarctic regions is extremely variable, but generally low by temperate region standards. Measured at typical inland stations, mean annual precipitation is 150 to 300 millimeters (6 to 12 inches). So snow cover is usually fairly light and summer drought is common, although the soil may remain wet if it is underlain by permafrost. In some coastal regions, such as in Atlantic Canada, precipitation is much higher, as much as 1,000 millimeters (40 inches) or more. This results in a deep, late-lying snow cover, which in turn causes a late spring and shortened growing season.

Alpine Climates

In alpine areas in temperate regions, the local climate is in many ways comparable to that of the true Arctic. In fact, ice cap climates occur at the highest elevations in major mountain ranges such as the Himalayas. As would be predicted by the Standard Lapse Rate, the actual temperature regime of an alpine area is closely correlated with elevation. In general, alpine climates have much heavier precipitation than is typical of the Arctic, since major mountain ranges tend to intercept moisture-bearing clouds. This means that snowfall is usually high, glaciation may occur and be a major factor even where an ice cap climate does not prevail, and deep snow drifts lasting far into the summer are common.

As the tropical regions are approached, alpine situations become increasingly less comparable to the Arctic. Seasonality decreases until, in the case of the *paramo* of the high Andes, the climate at certain elevations is comparable to a tundra summer climate throughout the year. While it is never warm, there is no true winter, and such snow cover as does occur is unpredictable. Day length is virtually the same throughout the year, air pressure is much lower than on the arctic lowland tundra, and short wavelength radiation is much more intense in these regions, which lie above much of the atmosphere. The result of all of these factors is that organisms are subject to a radically different array of selection pressures than would occur in the Arctic. In addition, alpine regions in the tropics are generally separated geographically from the polar regions, and their flora and fauna are mostly derived by specialization of the biota of the surrounding lower lands. In terms of both climate and biology, the alpine regions of the world are increasingly divergent from the Arctic with decreasing latitude.

Antarctic Climates

Most of Antarctica has an ice cap climate. We have seen that the few ice-free areas on the main part of the continent are bare by virtue of the low precipitation associated with the extreme continentality of the interior, combined with orographic, or mountain-related, features that exclude the spread of ice into certain areas.

In a few local areas on the Antarctic peninsula and on the associated island groups, mean temperatures may rise to a few degrees above freezing for as long as two or three months during summer. Although these areas are surrounded by pack ice, the climate is generally somewhat maritime. Winter temperatures are comparatively mild, and there is heavy snowfall. The only ice-free areas are exposed cliffs, headlands, and islets. These have a climate comparable to some areas in, for example, west Greenland, but they are too small and too isolated to be biologically comparable to any tundra areas of the Northern Hemisphere.

The islands of the Scotia Arc, except for South Georgia, also are considered to be antarctic and have a climate similar to that of the Antarctic peninsula, although somewhat more maritime. Tiny and isolated Bouvet Island, in the South Atlantic, also has an antarctic climate.

Subantarctic Climates

Subantarctic climates are unique, although somewhat similar to some anomalous Arctic areas such as the Aleutian Islands. A typical subantarctic island displays minimal seasonality, with summer (January) temperatures only a few degrees above winter. On the Kerguelen Islands, for example, the mean January (summer) temperature is about 7.5°C, while the mean for July is about 3.5°. This is the result of an extreme type of maritime situation (sometimes called a hyperoceanic climate). Because of the minimal difference between summer and winter temperatures, it is also called a microthermal climate. Although occurring at relatively high latitudes, subantarctic island climates are most comparable to those of some tropical highlands, because of the reduced seasonality.

While humidity is generally high and cloud cover heavy in subantarctic regions, the precipitation of the subantarctic islands is not particularly high, at least near sea level. Snow cover tends to be light, variable, and temporary, and much of the precipitation falls as a cold drizzle. In the mountains, however, snow is heavy, and mountainous subantarctic islands are well glaciated, as in the case of Kerguelen, Heard, and South Georgia.

WEATHER THROUGH THE ARCTIC YEAR

Climatic information is fine so far as it goes, but it takes a good deal of interpretation to imagine what it is like to *be* there. A quick overview of the weather and the march of the seasons in a typical arctic area can make it easier. Such weather can be found in the vicinity of the Bering Strait in Alaska or Siberia, in southern Baffin Island, East Greenland, or the Kola Peninsula of arctic Russia. This overview will survey a climate somewhat north of the Arctic Circle, and will start in March, when the sun has returned for half of each day.

Temperatures are still well below zero Fahrenheit (−18°C) each night and don't rise to freezing during the day. In the bright noonday sun, though, the snow may actually melt a bit. Offshore, the pack ice is solidly frozen, covered with a white blanket of snow. Most days are calm and sunny; little new snow falls. By late

April there is some real thawing. Exposed ridges are bare, and ponds and puddles appear during the day and only skim over with ice during the brief night. The pack ice still appears solid from shore, but hunters would be aware of more open leads; perhaps bowhead and belukha whales would be seen for the first time. By mid-June, thaw is progressing rapidly. There are still deep snow patches where drifting occurred, but most level land in the lowlands is bare; grasses and sedges are beginning to show green or white tufts, and a few early flowers appear. Ponds and lakes are rapidly becoming ice free. Birds are back, many of them already nesting, and the first mosquitos and black flies are about during the heat of the day. Nights, although the sun is shining brightly, are still brisk; ice may still skim a thaw puddle for a few hours as the sun ricochets along the northern horizon. Pack ice is still much in evidence but it is broken into discrete pans and pressure ridges. When the wind blows offshore, the ice may retreat toward the horizon for a day or two. The open sea is full of feeding birds, although most of the returning waterfowl have already disappeared quietly into the tundra.

The weather has become much more unsettled as the land thaws. Bright, clear days are interspersed with overcast days, and an occasional light drizzle falls, often driven by a cold wind. A fresh swath of snow still appears every now and then on the surrounding hills.

Mid-July is the height of summer, and everything is happening at once. Arctic summer days can be amazingly gentle, like those of April or May in the temperate regions. With the sun shining day and night, mild winds, temperatures well above freezing, the constant trickle of water from the melting snow, and the presence of birds and flowers in vast numbers, winter seems to have disappeared almost instantly. Particularly in continental areas, arctic summer days can be hot, humid, and uncomfortably insect ridden. Although storms are more prevalent than during winter, they are still few and nonviolent by temperate standards. Thunderstorms are rare or nonexistent, and rains are mostly gentle, foggy drizzles.

The most prominent feature of an arctic summer is its shortness; May gives way to October overnight, and the birds are flocking up to migrate when it seems that the eggs have hardly been laid. Mid-August sees the sun dipping below the horizon for a couple of hours. The tundra sedges take on a tawny color, the air is full of fluffy willow seeds, and fall color, as spectacular as a New England October on a minute scale, begins to show on barrens and mountain slopes. A line of frost begins to creep down the hillsides, and one day there is ice around the edges of the thaw ponds.

The sea, on the other hand, is now ice free as far as one can see. The first fall storms build great, long swells and sometimes wild breakers on the exposed coast. Birds are in the air and at sea: auks flocking in deep water, the last molting waterfowl hanging forlornly around the coastal lagoons, and the birds of prey hawking their way south.

The October sunlight is thin and wan; days at a time go by with the temperature hovering a bit below freezing. Thin, blowing snow fills the air, dead grass and leafless twigs rattle and hiss in the wind, and the ponds are frozen enough to walk on. Wild storms still occur out to sea, but the first calm days of winter will be along soon, and *young ice* will make a flexible, greasy covering for the cooling ocean.

Late November brings the return of sea ice in earnest, although it is still mostly unsafe for travel. The land is now frozen solid, temperatures are falling far below zero, and much of the year's supply of snow has already fallen to drift across the tundra, fill the hollows, and scour the ridgetops.

January brings the intense cold—frosty stars, auroras, and the boom and crash of the thickening pack ice offshore. In the clear cold, temperatures sometimes approach 40 below, the point at which the centigrade and Fahrenheit thermometers meet. One day, however, the sun bounces along the ridgetops to the south for an hour or so!

Weather in the Arctic is about as variable as it is anywhere else. In general, though, it is seldom extreme by the standards of the temperate regions. A typical winter day at a location well within the Arctic would have cloudless skies or a low overcast, little or no wind, and temperatures somewhat below zero Fahrenheit, perhaps $-10°$ to $-30°C$. It would correspond to a normal January day in any of the northern tier of U.S. states or the Canadian prairie provinces during a cold snap. What is significant is that these conditions last for anywhere from four to eight or nine months, depending on how deep into the Arctic the location. During the arctic winter, storms are rare. Most of the snowfall has occurred during the fall, and further storms are mainly windstorms which may pick up and redistribute the snow in a fashion similar to a desert sandstorm. (See Chapter 3 for more on snow movements.) During windstorms temperatures generally rise, perhaps to the vicinity of zero degrees Fahrenheit. Winter weather of greater violence is typical of the more marginal portions of the Arctic in the North Atlantic Basin and Bering Sea. Intense storms regularly form in the vicinity of Iceland, Baffin Bay, and the Aleutian Islands. In areas subject to these storm systems, temperatures only rarely fall far below zero Fahrenheit, and this happens mainly when air from deeper in the Arctic breaks out toward the south. But typical winter weather is wild, stormy, and full of heavy snowfall, feeding the glaciers of Greenland, Iceland, and the Alaska Range. Although winters last for a shorter time than in other parts of the Arctic, and show greater variation in temperature, they are much more fierce and inimical to human activities, particularly those that take place on the sea.

MICROCLIMATES: WEATHER ON THE SCALE OF LIFE

For living things, the regional climate has only the roughest connection with the day-to-day needs of life. A spruce tree doesn't respond to the 10°C July isotherm. Its concerns are whether it will be warm enough, for long enough, to put on a new annual set of needles, to mature a crop of cones, or for the seeds of a new generation to germinate. Or the crucial question may be the likelihood that a late frost may occur and destroy a year's seed crop. These concerns involve local phenomena: the temperatures maintained on the south-facing side of a twig, for example. At the same time, they also involve combinations and sequences of events, often in a complex and as yet poorly understood way. For example, in a developing new shoot, a week with a mean temperature of 10°C and a minimum of 1° would be radically different from a week with a similar mean but a minimum of −1°. And this, of course, is a grossly oversimplified example. Suppose that the maintenance of a spruce woodland at timberline would be possible if one year in 40 resulted in viable seeds, but that the trees would die out, over the centuries, if only an average of one year in 80 was a seed year. While it is obvious that the phenomenon would be largely a climate-dependent one, getting a handle on it would be extremely difficult.

In terms of the numbers of questions still to be answered, it would be hard to find a potentially more fertile field than the relationship between microclimates and living things, particularly in the Arctic. Given the complexities hinted at here, though, it should be clear that this is an enormously complex field and that advances require time, money, and sophisticated experimental techniques. The relatively few details known of the interrelationships between microclimate and life will be skipped here to go on to some more conspicuous microclimatic concerns.

Temperature Inversions and Extreme Cold

Every northern gardener knows better than to plant in a frost pocket—a hollow or valley floor where plants get nipped by frost during clear, still nights in June or late August. The microclimatic situation here is called a temperature inversion, and it is a very common feature of arctic and boreal environments.

Temperature inversions occur most commonly in areas where cold air drains toward the floor of a broad, shallow valley. In some subarctic areas, temperature inversions may create differentials of as much as 20°C over only 100 meters or so of elevation. Most extreme winter cold temperature recordings in the far north are from sites where inversions occur. Northern towns and cities are often built on hillsides, above the still coldness pooling in the valley floor. The campus of the University of Alaska, Fairbanks, is built on a bluff above the Tanana River valley, and a long flight of wooden stairs leads down to the valley floor. Walking down the stairs on a cold winter day is as bone chilling as entering deep space. Still air is absolutely necessary for this kind of temperature inversion to form and persist, and the dead calm of an inland subarctic winter creates perfect conditions. Even an intense and deep temperature inversion can be broken up in a matter of minutes by the onset of wind. This is one of the factors responsible for the sudden rises in temperature often observed in mountainous northern areas during winter, and commonly known in North America as *chinooks*.

Precipitation and Moisture

Most polar climates are characterized by extremely low precipitation, although there are important exceptions. Many tundra areas characteristically receive no more than 10 to 25 centimeters of precipitation annually, including both rain and snow. Nevertheless, many tundra areas are more or less covered with standing water, at least on level areas and hollows, whenever they are not frozen solid. There are a number of reasons for this situation. For example:

1. Low evaporation associated with low temperatures
2. Low plant transpiration associated with that low evaporation, plus short growing seasons
3. Drainage impeded by permafrost (See Chapter 6 for more on this.)

In general, differences in moisture and precipitation account for variations within the various types of polar climates, rather than defining the climatic types themselves. Therefore, precipitation regimes are discussed individually under the various climatic groups.

Windchill

If we leave a chunk of rock or a piece of equipment outside in cold weather, it will rapidly reach the same temperature as the surrounding air, and will then stay at this temperature whatever the wind is doing. The human body, however, is constantly producing heat and trying to maintain its temperature far above that of the surrounding air. One component of maintaining body temperature is keeping a cushion of heated air in contact with the skin surface. This, of course, is the principle of clothing or other forms of insulation. Any air movement disrupts this cushion, replacing warmed air with cold. Heat loss is therefore increased by air movement or wind; this heat loss increases with windspeed, but the change in heat loss is most important at relatively low windspeeds. Specialists in cold weather biology and survival have established a table of *windchill factor,* which is of some use in predicting the effects of windspeed on the human body, particularly with respect to the onset of frostbite on exposed skin surfaces. Windchill is now commonly reported in the daily weather forecasts in colder areas, with the quoted figures indicating appallingly low temperatures during the average winter storm in, say, Chicago. These windchill temperatures are somewhat subjective, but they do serve a useful purpose in that they emphasize the extreme danger that a person may be in during even a temperate winter. They also indicate that the danger from cold temperatures in the Arctic is often surprisingly slight, due to the calm air.

The windchill factor is of much less value in understanding and predicting the relationship between weather and hypothermia, since hypothermia often occurs when temperatures are moderate, but accompanied by high winds and rain or wet snow.

SOLAR WEATHER AND THE AURORA

A feature powerfully associated with the Arctic is the aurora borealis, or northern lights. (A similar phenomenon of the Southern Hemisphere is known as the aurora australis.) The auroras are not strictly weather, since they occur far above all but the most minimal remnants of the atmosphere, and their occurrence is related to charged particles arriving from the sun.

Auroras occur most commonly and most intensely in a belt around the magnetic poles, and they tend to be most spectacular at times when sunspot activity and solar flares are at peaks. They are important in their effect on telecommunications, and they have therefore been studied in great detail in recent decades. An aurora occurs as bands of light, often white or greenish, less commonly red or pink. These bands may have the appearance of curtains descending from near the apex of the sky, and they quiver and flicker. They are often bright enough to cast wavering shadows on the snow-covered landscape and provide enough light to aid in travel and landmark recognition. Since the north magnetic pole is in Canada, auroral displays are particularly prevalent in the Western Hemisphere, where they are quite common in temperate latitudes. They often reach their peak visibility in fall and spring.

SUGGESTED FURTHER READING

Most of the general readings suggested for the last chapter include sections on weather and climate, and most elementary climatology and meteorology texts provide some information on polar climates. Additional references stressing climatic change are listed after Chapter 7.

Barry, R., and R. Chorley. *Atmosphere, Weather, and Climate.* London: Methuen, 1982.
Lockwood, J. G. *Causes of Climate.* London: Edward Arnold, 1979.
Orvig, S. *Climates of the Polar Regions.* World Survey of Climatology, vol. 14. Amsterdam: Elsevier, 1970.
Weller, G., and S. Bowling. *Climate of the Arctic.* Fairbanks: Geophysical Institute, University of Alaska, 1975.

Chapter 3

Ice and Snow

ICE dominates the polar environment. This claim may seem implausible, now that we have debunked much of the popular idea that the Arctic is a land of eternal ice and snow. But while travelers on the endless muskeg of Canada are wiping sweat and mosquitos from their eyes, cursing the heat, and dreaming of iced beer, evidence of the presence of ice is around them on every side and in every detail of what they see. Underfoot is soil, along with the lenses and layers of crystalline ice that keep the top layers of the soil saturated and soggy, providing breeding places for the myriads of insects. Frogs, snakes, and turtles are conspicuous by their absence; they can't burrow through the deep frost to sleep away the winter. Ice has shaped everything here. It has sculpted the landforms through ancient glaciers. It has shattered the rocks, heaved the soil, and dammed the rivers. It has the final say on whether any organism will live or die. Perhaps most important, it provides a challenge to every living thing to adapt, to change, to improvise, and to survive. Nothing in the polar regions escapes the ice.

Paradoxically, ice in one form or another provides shelter, warmth, and safety for myriads of polar organisms. Few polar plants and animals would survive a single temperate winter, where they might be deprived of their safe blanket of snow by a January thaw or stimulated into dangerous early growth by the false spring of a bright March day.

ICE AS A SUBSTANCE

The study of ice and the phenomena related to cold temperatures is now known as *cryology.* It is related to *glaciology,* a term that now tends to be used mainly in relation to a specific type of ice, the glacier. Another related term, *geocryology,* refers to periglacial (permafrost related) phenomena. (See Chapter 6 for more on permafrost.)

To physicists and chemists, no substance is more enigmatic than water, and many of the most mysterious properties of water become evident as it solidifies into ice. Ice is actually considered by geologists to be a mineral. It fits the accepted definition in that it is a naturally occurring, crystalline, inorganic substance with a definite composition. However, it has a number of properties that make it a unique mineral, at least under the conditions that prevail on the earth. Many of these properties have to do with ice's ability to be deposited or dispersed at temperatures at which all other familiar minerals are obdurately solid.

Much of our knowledge of the nature of ice is a by-product of metallurgical research associated with the aerospace industry and engineering. With the advent of supersonic aircraft and of missiles and space travel, it became important to understand the properties of metals at temperatures near their melting point. Naturally occurring ice is always at high temperature with respect to its melting point, and it exhibits a number of properties in common with space-age metals.

Water is the basis of all life as we know it. No living cell can carry out its life processes without liquid water to facilitate them. But when water is cooled to the point that it crystallizes and becomes a solid, it is deadly to cells. As any gardener knows, unprotected plant cells exposed to frost are destroyed almost instantly. Certain cells have the ability to resist the formation of ice within themselves or to minimize the disruptive effects of freezing, but they do so by suspending most of their life activities and going into an inactive state. This condition can be sustained for long periods of time, but the various activities that we know as life do not start up again until the temperatures within the cells rise above freezing and liquid water is available again. The ways in which organisms have come to deal with ice and cold are fascinating and complex.

Just as ice is antithetical to life at the cellular level, it is also a destroyer on a larger scale. The advance of glaciers obliterates all living things. While life is found in the driest deserts and the ocean depths, and even colonizes the craters of active volcanos, there is no life whatsoever on the inland ice of Greenland or Antarctica. The spread of an ice sheet is more deadly to anything in its path than a nuclear holocaust.

While glacial ice is inexorable, the seasonal ice and snow of the cold regions has provided a challenge to living organisms. Any plant or animal that attempts to survive in the cold regions must adapt to conditions that are at least temporarily inimical to life. The variety and ingenuity of these adaptations are remarkable; they could easily be the subject of an entire book themselves.

Ice also affects the physical environment in complex and subtle ways. The results of the advance of glaciers are generally obvious. While many polar regions are not glaciated and never have been, the fabric of their environment, soils, erosional processes, and landforms is ultimately dependent on the endless, largely invisible action of ice.

Ice from the Air: Snow and Its Relatives

Most of the ice in the terrestrial portion of the polar environment is in the form of snow or had its origin as snow. Broadly speaking, snow is simply precipitation of water in a solid state. In fact, rain that falls in warmer regions is often in the form of snow until a few moments before it reaches the earth's surface.

Everyone is familiar with the typical six-sided snowflakes that constitute snowfall. While the first literary reference to them is in a Chinese manuscript less than 2,000 years old, snowflakes must have been observed with wonder for millennia before then. Classic studies of snowflakes were made in the nineteenth century, not long after the development of photography. While it is often said that no two snowflakes are alike, it soon proved possible to distinguish a number of types (see Figure 3–1). Most are clearly based on the six-sided crystalline structure of ice, but they vary in their shape and structure according to the atmospheric conditions under which they form. They range from the graceful, feathery structures, which we think of as typical, to thin plates, hard pellets, and aggregates of flakes that have been altered in the atmosphere through various processes.

Figure 3–1. A variety of snow crystals. Although snow crystals vary greatly, they all share the characteristic hexagonal crystalline structure.

Snow that has fallen through a warmer air layer, then dropped into the colder air of a temperature inversion, can be refrozen into compact bits of ice known as sleet; if the refreezing is partial, it is freezing rain. Under some circumstances of atmospheric turbulence, sleet is carried in updrafts and aggregates into larger particles of ice called hail. Since hail is usually associated with thunderstorms, it is more common in temperate regions than in the far north. Sometimes snow crystals are aggregated together without refreezing and thawing, so that they form hard, round, white pellets, known as graupel.

At very low temperatures tiny ice crystals may precipitate out of a cloudless sky; these are called ice prisms or sometimes diamond dust. They fall slowly through the clear air, often glittering brilliantly in the sun or moonlight. In some cold, dry, inland areas these ice crystals form a significant proportion of the snowfall, building up an accumulation with the consistency of fine sawdust.

Ice from the air may also be deposited on surfaces directly, as hoarfrost. This appears as very fine, white particles on surfaces and may build up as delicate needlelike or featherlike structures. If the ice is deposited out of clouds or fog, rather than clear air, it is somewhat different in appearance. It builds up as a white, spongy crust known as rime ice, which is the result of tiny droplets of water freezing to the surface. In some cloudy regions, particularly on mountain slopes, rime ice may build up deep layers on exposed surfaces and persist over most of the winter. In these circumstances it is a significant form of precipitation and may also protect the exposed surfaces of plants.

The larger droplets of freezing rain form a layer of clear ice on whatever surface they land. This glaze ice can build up and cause serious problems, breaking down trees, making roads impassable, icing structures, or worst of all, icing aircraft in flight. Similar types of icing may occur from salt spray on ships at sea or on coastal structures.

SNOW DEPOSITION: THE FORMATION OF THE SNOWPACK

Snow may be deposited as a gentle sifting down of feathery crystals in still air, in a blizzard, or in any condition or combination of conditions in between. A blizzard, sometimes also known by the Russian word *buran,* is a storm characterized by heavy snowfall, high winds, and low temperatures. By this definition, blizzards are rare in the far north, since snowfall is generally relatively light and winds are often calm for long periods, particularly in interior areas.

As it is deposited on the ground in still air, wild snow has an extremely low density. Although the ice in the crystals has a specific gravity of about 0.9 (that is, it is nine-tenths as dense and heavy as water), the density of the lightest, fluffiest, new-fallen snow may be only one-hundredth to three-hundredths that of water. Thus, the topmost layer of new-fallen snow is composed almost entirely of air that surrounds the crystals. This situation begins to change almost instantly. Within a matter of hours, new-fallen snow has generally compacted to several times the density it had in the few moments after falling. A rule of thumb used by meteorologists is that 10 centimeters of fresh snow is the equivalent of 1 centimeter of rain, so that the snow would have a density one-tenth that of water, or a specific gravity of 0.1. This is only the roughest generalization, since the actual density will depend on such factors as the wetness of the snow, the temperature, and how much the snow has been blown by wind. Snow, then, is subject to processes that immediately begin to alter its characteristics after it has been deposited on the ground. In the more temperate regions, where the snow usually melts within a few days of its arrival, these processes usually do not proceed very far before the snow cover is destroyed by warm weather. In the cold regions, however, where the snow may lie on the ground for months at temperatures generally below freezing, the processes that continue to occur result in the creation of a different and in many ways a more complex substance than that which fell out of the sky. The long-lasting blanket of snow covering polar lands during much of the year is commonly known as the snowpack.

Dry snow landing in an open, windswept environment such as the arctic tundra is usually redistributed by wind. Although the actual amount of snow falling in tundra regions is generally low compared to temperate environments, the drifting of snow often creates local areas of deep snow in the lee of ridges, along river banks, and in hollows in the terrain. The snow in these drifts has already undergone one kind of transformation, due to the abrasion and breakage of the fragile crystals as they are swept over the land. The broken crystals are much more tightly packed, and more cohesive than new snow. They often form a hard crust known as wind slab, which is different from the icy crust formed by melting of the surface of an undisturbed snow pack. The snow in wind slab has again increased in density several times, so that it has become a heavy, rather strong substance, which may be half as dense as water. Snow deposits of this consistency can be "quarried" with a snow knife, and the blocks used to construct a traditional igloo or other snow structure. The surface of snow heavily compacted and drifted by wind often has a wavelike or dunelike appearance; the ridges are known as *sastrugi*.

Snow deposition is particularly interesting in situations of rough terrain above or beyond the timberline. Irregularities in the landscape create complex eddies in the wind. The strongly cohesive windblown snow crystals are often deposited in fantastic forms that seem to have little relationship to the force of gravity. One of the commonest and most important of these is called a snow cornice. In forming this, wind blowing across a feature such as a sharp ridge will rapidly lose large amounts of snow in an eddy on the lee side of the ridge. This snow will be plastered against the back of the ridge, creating a structure with a vertical or overhanging face and a sharp edge (see Figure 3–2). Snow cornices can extend out for many meters, becoming increasingly unstable as they enlarge or as weather changes. They may give way unexpectedly, quite possibly triggering an avalanche. A similar situation occurs in crevasses on glaciers. (For more on this, see Chapter 4.) In a glacier, a snow cornice may extend out from one edge of a crevasse until it ultimately covers the entire opening with a snowbridge. These features are the greatest single hazard in traveling on a glacier.

Since the distribution of snow in treeless, windswept areas is so uneven, on the local scale there is tremendous variation in the nature of the snow deposits and their effect on the environment. The top of a ridge or hummock may be virtually snow free throughout winter, while a hollow a few meters away may be filled with snow for most of the year or even throughout the entire year. These effects are often not obvious to the casual visitor in the summer, but are critical to the distribution and survival of tundra organisms. The arctic environment isn't comprehensible unless it is seen or at least imagined throughout the long months of the polar winter.

In the interior of the continents, particularly in the arctic woodlands and boreal forest, fallen snow has a remarkably different fate. Here, snowfall tends to be somewhat greater, wind is less prevalent, and trees and brush may virtually eliminate the effects of wind at ground level. Although the tree branches themselves may intercept a good portion of the snowfall, snow generally builds up to a more or less uniform cover. This snow cover can vary tremendously in thickness and duration from place to place, but the majority of it falls fairly early in the winter.

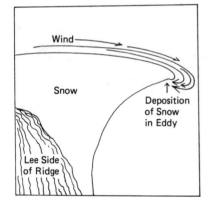

Figure 3–2. How a snow cornice grows. Snow crystals caught in an eddy below the sharp edge of the ridge are plastered against the underside, allowing the edge to grow outward. Growing snow cornices are extremely unstable and can collapse under little pressure or even spontaneously, and collapsing, can cause avalanches.

Typically, a snow deposit of half a meter to a meter is established by December, persists into April or May without changing radically in depth, and then disperses rapidly in the warm spring weather.

Whether in tundra or woodland, arctic snow typically has a lifespan of many months if it lands on open ground, frozen lakes, or pack ice, or years or centuries if it lands on a glacier or ice cap. Annual snow of extended duration is known as the snowpack, and it undergoes numerous transformations before it disperses in spring breakup. Snow landing on older snow and on ice deposits such as glaciers has a different fate, which is discussed in Chapter 4.

Metamorphism

Once the snow has become more or less permanently settled, whether in drifts or in an even snowpack, additional processes come into play. These processes are known collectively as *metamorphism*. Metamorphic processes alter the nature and relationship of the crystals in the snowpack, changing the crystals differently according to their level in the snowpack and in response to different weather conditions.

A crucial property of snow, related to metamorphism, is its exceptional insulating value. Snow, particularly when it is dry and loosely packed, can be thought of as a natural equivalent of Styrofoam insulation. As long as snow remains at or below freezing, its insulating value is matched by few other naturally occurring substances. This is the reason for the effectiveness of the snow igloo.

The insulating value of snow is of little importance in temperate regions, where the snowpack is short lived and often saturated with melt water, and where the temperature differential between the ground surface underlying the snow and the air above is comparatively small. However, it becomes extremely significant in deep, long-lasting snowpacks where air temperatures remain low for long periods of time. Such conditions prevail in the following situation, which is more or less typical of a cold continental area in the vicinity of the timberline, such as much of Alaska or northern Canada.

Within a very few meters of the soil surface, soil temperatures remain essentially unchanged throughout the year. The soil temperature at these depths closely approximates the mean annual air temperature at the site. Unless the soil of the site is underlain by permafrost (see Chapter 6 for more on permafrost), it remains at a temperature above freezing throughout the winter within a meter or so of the surface, even if the surface is bare of snow. If the air temperature remains far below freezing for long periods of time, the soil thus provides a heat source.

Once a snowpack has been created, the heat from the underlying soil is mostly trapped in the upper layers of the soil and in the lower layers of the snowpack. Farmers and gardeners in northern areas notice that snow falls on deeply frozen ground in the fall, but find that there is no frost in the ground as soon as the snow has melted in the spring. This is due to the insulating blanket of snow, which allows thaw to progress in the shallow soil layers, even though the air immediately above the snow may have been bitterly cold for months during the winter.

The result of this situation is that a sharp temperature gradient is established within the snowpack. This gradient is particularly strong when the air temperatures are extremely low. The temperature differential between the snow-soil interface and the air at the snow surface may be as much as 40°C. (See Figure 3–3.)

Since the snow in the pack is at a density of perhaps 0.2 to 0.3, it is thoroughly suffused with air. Furthermore, because the crystals are small and have complex surfaces, the contact between the air and the crystal surfaces covers much surface area. Molecules of water are directly transferred from the surface of the crystals to the entrapped air, in a process known as *sublimation*. Within a snowpack, the entrapped air rapidly becomes saturated with water vapor.

The amount of water in the form of vapor that can be held in air is directly related to the temperature of the air: the warmer the air, the more water molecules per unit of volume at 100 percent humidity. If the air is warmed, it will take up more molecules from the adjacent snow crystals. If it is cooled, it will deposit water molecules on an adjacent surface, such as that of a snow crystal.

Since warm air rises, and since the crystals in the snowpack are loosely enough packed to allow air circulation, saturated air from the low part of the pack moves upward. It is then cooled, and it deposits some of the water molecules on the surrounding snow crystals. At the same time, cooler air is dropping toward the bottom of the snowpack, where it becomes warmed and picks up more water molecules. In short, an air circulation pattern is established within the snowpack, and this results in a steady transfer of water molecules from the crystals in the warmer lower

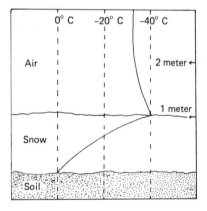

Figure 3–3. Graphic representation of the temperatures within and immediately above a snowpack during a spell of extreme cold. Under these conditions, metamorphic processes within the snowpack accelerate.

layers to those in the upper layers. This results in a change in density at different levels of the snowpack. The lower layers come to consist of delicate, weak, loosely packed crystals, while the upper layer becomes denser and is cemented into a hard crust, somewhat similar to wind slab. The lowermost layer may be reduced in density to about 0.2 grams per cubic centimeter, less than half that of the top layer. The appearance of the crystals in the lower layer is distinctive; they become long, fine, and needlelike. This substance has come to be known as depth hoar; it is also sometimes called *pukak*. Because of its low density and delicate structure, this material is structurally weak and cannot support much load. The continued formation of depth hoar allows the snowpack to settle and become denser through the repeated collapse of the lowermost layer. Northern farmers are familiar with this phenomenon: the steadily settling upper layer of hard snow wreaks havoc on wire fences and the lower branches of trees and shrubs. The weak layer at the snow-soil interface is easily traversed by small mammals, and this *subnivean space* is of tremendous importance to their survival in polar regions.

Depth hoar is also of great importance in mountainous areas, since it is a major factor in the initiation of avalanches. The formation of depth hoar is an ongoing process that is only partially related to additional snowfall. Thus, new snow is not necessary to trigger an avalanche. It is only required that the depth hoar reach a level of structural weakness such that the overlying layers can break loose, where they can also trigger the fall of nearby, slightly more stable portions of snowpack.

The process of the migration of water molecules within the snowpack and the formation of layers of differing density described above is often called *constructive metamorphism*. A different process, known as *destructive metamorphism,* usually goes on concurrently.

Destructive metamorphism is not well understood though it seems to involve a number of processes. The complex crystals of new-fallen snow are known to tend to break down spontaneously, as well as by abrasion and other mechanical action. Snowflakes lose their sharp, feathery points. The tiny shards thus formed seem to disappear; their mass seems to accrue to the larger remaining crystals, probably partly by redeposition of sublimated water vapor and partly through the melting together of crystals at points of contact. The speed with which the processes of destructive metamorphism take place, and probably their relative importance, depends on such factors as temperature, stresses imposed by overlying snow, the original nature of the crystals, and probably many others. In any case, destructive metamorphism tends to make snow denser and more compact and to strengthen the bonds between particles. It appears to be particularly effective in the case of rapid deposition of heavy snow.

Constructive and destructive metamorphism take place when the temperature in the snowpack remains below freezing. Additional changes take place when temperatures rise and actual melt begins. The various phenomena involved, known collectively as *melt metamorphism,* are particularly important in situations where there are repeated freeze-thaw cycles as in spring weather, or in alpine regions at low latitudes. In these cases, larger and larger compact crystals tend to form. This is the *corn snow* familiar to spring skiers and maple syrup makers. It can be strongly cemented together by frozen meltwater when temperatures drop, then rapidly become loose and weak with the onset of warm conditions again.

There are many variations on this theme. For example, an abnormally warm stretch of weather may result in melt at the snow surface. The top few centimeters may become suffused with meltwater, which may then refreeze, creating a dense crust. Freezing rain may fall through a temperature inversion, creating a surface of glaze ice. These hard surfaces may then be buried by additional snowfall; in time they would be at least partially converted back into normal snowpack material.

It should be clear that the regime of a snowpack is a complex one involving a large number of subtle physical processes, and is dependent on such factors as time and temperature. Many of these processes are only weakly displayed if the snow cover is thin and of short duration. Given the situation typical of polar conditions, with a long duration of the snowpack and considerable depth in at least local areas, a highly variable complex of substances results.

Most of the discussion up to now assumes that the snowpack will ultimately melt away before the end of the summer and the onset of a new snow season. In many arctic and alpine situations, the snow may fall on a layer of old snow remaining from the previous year. If this process continues over a period of years, additional changes take place deep within the snowbed and result in a transformation of the snow to glacial ice. We'll pick up that story in Chapter 4.

Avalanches

Avalanches are a phenomenon mainly of mountainous alpine regions, since they usually occur where there is a heavy snowfall, a deep snowpack, and steep slopes. These conditions occur commonly enough within the Arctic, as we define it, to be of some interest here. This may become increasingly true as arctic development proceeds, given avalanches' somewhat detrimental effect on humans and their activities and structures.

Avalanches are simply masses of snow that slide downhill. To anyone who has watched one in progress or seen the results of a major avalanche, this is a rather bland description. Avalanches can move literally millions of tons of snow at speeds sometimes exceeding 300 kilometers per hour. At such velocities, masses of snow can become airborne and ride for long distances across valleys on a cushion of compressed air. Some of the worst disasters attributed to avalanches have occurred far up the valley on the *opposite* side from the original avalanche. Nor does the snow necessarily stop there; it may slosh back and forth several times, reducing anything on the valley floor to splinters.

Avalanches may be triggered by the falling of a snow cornice; or they may occur apparently spontaneously as the layer of snow in contact with the underlying rock or soil is weakened by metamorphism and the creation of depth hoar. Earthquakes are an exceedingly effective trigger. The faces of some mountains in southern Alaska were drastically altered as a result of the Good Friday earthquake of 1964. Of course, avalanches may trigger other avalanches, as may human activities on unstable slopes.

Attempts at avalanche control include the triggering of small avalanches by artificial means, such as howitzer fire or explosives, and various techniques intended to stabilize the snowpack on avalanche-prone slopes. The most effective damage control technique, of course, is to identify avalanche-prone locations and avoid them. However, since ski developments are necessarily at the bases of steep, snowy mountains, a certain amount of compromise is in order.

Relatively little is known about the effects of avalanches on the arctic environment, but they are probably of some importance. For example, they could well be a major source of accumulation of snow on the surface of a glacier (see Chapter 4), or could account for the presence of large snowbed communities at the foot of mountains (see Chapter 9). Certainly an avalanche track provides an environment in which the number of organisms able to survive the conditions is necessarily sharply limited.

ICE FROM FREEZE UP: LAKES, RIVERS, AND THE SEA

Ice seals the surface of the polar environment, whether land or water, for a good part of the year. The role of the ice covering bodies of water is fully as crucial as that of the snow discussed in the last section, and the processes this ice undergoes are comparably complex.

A fundamental characteristic of water is that, as it changes from a liquid to a solid state, it expands and decreases in density by about 8.5 percent. We will see the effects of this phenomenon over and over again in this book. One of the most important effects is simply that it causes ice to float. The floating ice on lakes and seas then provides a barrier to further energy transfer from the warmer liquid water to the air above. This barrier affects every phase of the polar environment, from the climate to the metabolism of microscopic algae.

Chapter 2 discussed some other features of the relationship between liquid water and ice, such as the latent heat of vaporization, in relation to climate. That information is relevant to the discussion of types of ice.

River and Lake Ice

By definition, all of the polar regions experience temperatures averaging below freezing during some portion of the year. So rivers, lakes, and ponds in polar regions freeze each year. Although the ice cover may be thin and ephemeral in some marginal polar regions, it generally lasts for several months each year, and profoundly affects many aspects of the polar environment. Of course, many of the cooler temperate areas also have cold winters and a consequent buildup of lake and river ice, which have their own effects on enterprises ranging from fishing to navigation to power generation.

Freshwater ice is generally more or less solid ice, which doesn't go through the transformations that snow undergoes. It is initially formed by the cooling of the surface layer of open water through the transfer of heat to air that is below the freezing temperature. The initial stages of this freezing are quite complex and variable; spectacular crystals may form on the solidifying surface. The ice that forms in this way is clear and hard and is known as black ice. The same process occurs on rivers. However, if there is a strong current, areas of the river are often kept open, even at cold temperatures. If the open water is supercooled, it may contain quantities of tiny, finely dispersed ice crystals known as frazil ice. These may aggregate into a loose slush of crystals, sometimes called brash ice. (The term *brash ice* more commonly refers to finely broken, loose floating ice at the edge of a glacier or around disintegrating icebergs.) Frazil ice may rapidly coagulate around any solid structure or under the river ice, forming what is known as anchor ice. This coagulation can cause a rapid and uneven buildup of ice at certain locations. It can also cause problems in situations such as spillways and water intakes.

Black ice is usually snow covered before it becomes very thick. The snow loading on the ice surface depresses the ice, allowing water from the lake to percolate up through cracks and flaws, saturating lower layers of the snow. With continued cold conditions, this layer of mixed water and snow crystals freezes solidly. However, the crystalline structure of the snow remains, and the ice is less dense than the lake ice and has a granular consistency. This snow ice thickens as more snow is deposited, often forming discrete layers. It also insulates the underlying lake ice, so that little further thickening of this layer takes place. In fact, under some conditions, it appears that the original lake ice may thin out, or even melt entirely away, leaving a layer of pure snow ice.

Since snow ice is much weaker than lake ice, the nature as well as the thickness of ice is important in determining whether it is safe for traffic. In addition, snow ice disperses differently from lake ice. When pure lake ice melts, it becomes progressively thinner, but its strength in relation to its thickness remains about the same. Only in the very late stages of disintegration does lake ice rather rapidly change into discrete crystals. These are vertically oriented columnar crystals known as candle ice. Candle ice has essentially no cohesive strength and, since it can form irregularly and unpredictably on the surface of a pond or river, it is very dangerous. Snow ice breaks up because of loss of cohesion between the old snow crystals, so that it may quickly change from thick, solid ice to a layer of slush with virtually no strength. Whether covered with snow ice, black ice, or a combination of both, northern lakes often break up literally overnight, particularly if there is any current. River ice is generally broken up by rising water associated with snow melt, so rotten ice is less likely to occur there.

An effect common in frozen rivers occurs at breakup, when

large masses of ice may accumulate. These masses can form immense ice dams that back up water far upstream in areas of low relief. The effects can be especially serious in areas where the mouths of large rivers lie in a colder climate than the upriver areas where snow melt is taking place. Huge areas in the deltas of such rivers as the Yukon, Mackenzie, Lena, and Ob are inundated every spring by ice-choked flood waters. There is some evidence that the Yukon river may undergo drastic changes in its course as a result of ice damming.

Even without ice damming, the effect of river ice during breakup can be awe inspiring. Blocks of ice a couple of meters thick and as big as a house are carried along by the current of the flooding rivers, bulldozing everything in their way and scouring the shores, bars, and islands down to bare ground. This yearly scouring limits the type of vegetation that can become established on river shores. On the other hand, the disturbance can encourage colonization by weeds, similar to a poorly cultivated garden. Even after the flood waters have retreated, huge blocks of ice may remain stranded for months far inland from the summer shores. These may crush vegetation, cover it with ice-rafted mud and silt, or, conversely, supply it with water from melt during the dry summer. There is no English word for the overall situation described here, but the Siberians apply the term *becevnik;* it must affect thousands of square kilometers in the lower reaches of the great Siberian rivers.

Another river ice phenomenon is known as overflow ice, also sometimes called *aufeis* or *naled* (see Figure 3–4). This ice forms in the beds of relatively small fast-moving streams that flow throughout the winter. It can involve the buildup of anchor ice, the freezing of seepage from springs, and the saturation of snow that has fallen on river ice. *Aufeis* deposits quite commonly reach a thickness of two or three meters; they may extend for several kilometers along rivers and last through most of the summer. They may occasionally be used as insect-free summer resting areas by caribou. They also have a peculiar significance for bush pilots and explorers since maps often show them as lakes, as a result of misinterpretation of aerial photographs, but they are not the equivalent of lakes for landing with float-equipped aircraft.

Sea Ice

Sea ice is a much more complex and dynamic substance than lake and river ice. The presence of sea ice is central to polar ecosystems. It affects the seas and the adaptations of the organ-

Figure 3-4. An extensive field of *aufeis* in interior Alaska. The ice may be several meters thick and last for most of the summer.

isms that live in them, but it also has a profound effect on terrestrial and coastal ecosystems. It is a major controlling influence on the climate of ice-bound coastal regions. It is also of great importance in determining the type of human activities that take place in coastal arctic situations. The technology developed by sea ice hunters to deal with and exploit the frozen ocean is complex and formidable. A good portion of the vocabulary of most Inuit (Eskimo) dialects is related to sea ice conditions, travel, and hunting technology. Most of the early expeditions by Westerners into the polar regions were seaborne, and the polar ice pack was a formidable, and often fatal, challenge and adversary.

Sea ice, or pack ice, originates in the same fashion as lake ice, in that it begins as ice crystals forming on the cooled surface of the sea. In the early stages of freezing, salt water takes on a greasy appearance, as myriads of individual ice crystals form and float in the top few millimeters of the sea. This is known as slob ice, or grease ice. Soon the crystals coagulate into flexible plates or sheets, sometimes called *nilas*. If there is any wind or wave action, the edges of these plates collide and thicken, creating pancake ice. The pancakes, in turn, thicken and freeze together to form an ice cover.

Sea ice commonly takes one of two forms. Near shore and in closed bays, the ice remains more or less smooth and flat and is easily traversable. This shore ice (fast ice or ice foot) may extend for many kilometers out to sea in some locations. In the open sea, the forces of wind, current, and wave action keep large masses of ice in constant motion. These large ice masses are called floes. Often, the floes separate, leaving stretches of open water called leads. In cold weather the leads will soon freeze over again, causing thin areas in the pack ice. The newly formed ice in leads is commonly known as young ice.

A recurring lead tends to form at the intersection between fast ice and the moving pack. This is often known as the flaw lead or shore lead. Experienced sea ice travelers are able to divine the presence of leads and closed pack because the pattern of dark leads and light floes is reflected on the undersides of the low-lying clouds, which commonly blanket the polar seas, particularly in spring and summer. This is sometimes called water sky or iceblink.

In certain locations currents or upwellings cause leads to be more or less permanent. These ice-free areas may be a few meters across or may cover hundreds of square kilometers, as in the case of the North Water in northern Baffin Bay. They are often now known as *polynas* or *polynyas,* a term earlier applied to areas of thin ice. Polynyas are a lively area of study, since they may be of tremendous importance to overwintering marine mammals and birds, and since they are rare, local, and could very easily be damaged by oil spills, navigation, or any other human activities in the area.

While some portions of the open pack ice separate to form leads, in other areas adjacent floes collide. Floes may underride or override each other or simply break against each other. The result in any case is normally a high ridge of jumbled ice, called a pressure ridge. These ridges may reach a height of ten meters or more above the surrounding pack. Since ice is nearly as dense as water, the major portion of the pressure ridge will extend downward toward the sea bottom. Some shallow polar sea floors are plowed by downward extending pressure ridges at depths of probably as much as 30 meters. According to one respected glossary of ice terminology, a downward project-ing ice hummock is known as a bummock; it was presumably named by submariners, who might well take a personal interest in this phenomenon. The potential effect of bummocks on undersea cables and pipelines on the shallow sea floor is easily imagined.

Open leads and pressure ridges make travel on the open pack of the polar seas difficult. When the pack disperses in summer, the remnants of pressure ridges may ride the winds and currents and pile up against shores, inhibiting navigation. Massive remnants of pressure ridges are sometimes called floe bergs. They are not icebergs in the usual sense, since icebergs are derived from glacier ice.

In the Polar Basin, much of the pack ice remains frozen from season to season. This multiyear pack differs from annual ice in a number of features, perhaps the most interesting of which is the fact that the salt contained in the original pack ice leaches out, normally within a year after the ice's formation, so that multiyear pack can be melted as a source of fresh water.

The problems of traversing ice by ship are the reverse of foot or vehicle travel. Leads can open and tempt a ship deep into the pack, then close with appalling suddenness and power. In the nineteenth century, fleets of whaling ships were lost in the area near Point Barrow, Alaska, as they were nipped and then beset by the pack ice. Many of the early polar expeditions came to grief under similar circumstances, as did the ill-fated Franklin and DeLong expeditions. Later explorers built special polar ships with intricate systems of heavy cross braces and round bottoms that would allow them to be forced upward by the colliding floes. Perhaps the most famous of these is Nansen's *Fram,* which was designed to become beset and to drift across the entire Arctic Ocean.

Even today polar sea ice remains a severe impediment to navigation. The Soviet Union has built immensely powerful nuclear-powered icebreakers and uses them to keep open the Northern Sea Route along the Siberian coast. Even with the most modern equipment, there are periodic scares as the pack closes unexpectedly and winter threatens to close in on convoyed ships.

The most awesome pack ice phenomenon is called *ivu* by Eskimos. Large, fast-moving floes pile up against the shore and, driven by the ice behind, can override broad stretches of beach, sandspit, and island. Archaeologists at one well-known site near Point Barrow have uncovered a house and its inhabitants who were overwhelmed by *ivu,* leaving a sort of arctic Pompeii with the frozen bodies remaining for hundreds of years. Since the preferred means of drilling for oil in shallow arctic seas involves the creation of artificial gravel islands, the significance of *ivu* can't be overlooked. Yet it is a relatively rare phenomenon and, because of its unpredictability, difficult to study.

Glacier Ice and Icebergs

Glacier ice results from the buildup and compression of snow falling on the surface of a glacier. The process is discussed in detail in the next section. Glacial ice is relevant in this section because the larger and more polar glaciers transport quantities of ice to the sea, where it is *calved* off into icebergs, which may be enmeshed in the pack ice or are sometimes free-floating in otherwise ice-free areas of sea.

In the Northern Hemisphere the vast majority of icebergs are derived from the Greenland ice sheet. Along much of the coast of Greenland, distributary glaciers continually spew huge, irregular chunks of ice into fiords and the open sea. These icebergs are then carried by ocean currents, mainly the Labrador Current, to the vicinity of western Newfoundland, the Grand Banks, and the shipping lanes of the western North Atlantic. Because of the difference in temperature between the iceberg and the surrounding sea, large icebergs are commonly accompanied by fog banks, enhancing the danger to shipping. Most of the mass of the iceberg is below the surface of the sea (eight-ninths submerged, according to a commonly quoted figure). Tongues of subsurface ice may extend far beyond the visible edges of the berg. These rams are a great danger to ships. Bergs are also often highly unstable and may capsize violently. As icebergs disintegrate, they break into smaller chunks of ice called bergy bits. Even smaller pieces, which are awash in the waves, are called growlers.

In the antarctic regions many of the continental glaciers reach the coast in the form of immense ice shelves that extend sometimes hundreds of kilometers out over the surface of the sea. As the ice shelves spread out from land, enormous pieces are detached and begin to float away. These tabular bergs sometimes are 100 kilometers or more long. Smaller ones have a characteristic flat top, like a floating sugar cube. Because the bergs extend much deeper into the water than the surrounding pack ice, they are often moved by different currents; it is common to see a large berg plowing through the ice pack like an immense, slow-moving icebreaker, piling up pressure ridges in front and leaving an open lead behind.

In the Northern Hemisphere the only ice shelves are along the north shore of Ellesmere Island. These apparently calve large bergs only occasionally; these are the well-known ice islands of the Arctic Ocean. The ice islands may have patches of gravel, soil, and even vegetation on their surfaces. They are probably the source of rumors of unknown lands lying within the Polar Basin, such as the famous and elusive Crocker Land, which was reportedly sighted several times in a part of the Arctic Ocean where no land exists.

Ground Ice

In areas where the mean annual temperature is below freezing but the terrain is unglaciated, large amounts of ice may build up in the soil and deep sediments. The ice is normally under the surface of the soil, so that it is not directly observable in the undisturbed environment. In some places such as the vicinity of Barrow, Alaska, and in some parts of northern Siberia, some 50 to 90 percent of the total volume of the upper layers of sediments (the top 10 meters or so) may consist of ground ice. This may exist as wedges, lenses, or massive blocks of clear ice. It is often relatively close to equilibrium with the prevailing physical environment and vegetation, and a slight alteration of conditions may lead to instability and meltout. Hence, ground ice often presents major engineering difficulties in polar regions. (See Chapter 6.)

SUGGESTED FURTHER READING

Most of the basic readings suggested at the end of Chapter 1 contain information on ice and snow. Chapters 4, 5, 6, and 7 also contain material on ice and snow within the context of the topics of those chapters. Among the few reference and textbooks devoted specifically to ice and snow, the following are useful.

Bentley, W. A., and W. J. Humphreys. *Snow Crystals.* NY: Dover, 1962. (This is a classic photographic record of the variety of shapes of snow crystals.)

Gray, D. M., and D. H. Mole, eds. *Handbook of Snow: Principles, Processes, Management, and Use.* Toronto: Pergamon, 1981.

LaChapelle, E. *Field Guide to Snow Crystals.* Seattle: University of Washington Press, 1969.

Marchand, P. *Life in the Cold.* Hanover, NH: University Press of New England, 1987.

Seligman, G. *Snow Structure and Ski Fields.* Cambridge, England: International Glaciological Society, 1980.

Chapter 4

Glaciers and Glaciology

WHILE *glaciology* is, strictly speaking, the study of ice in all of its various forms, the term usually refers to the study of one type of naturally occurring ice deposit—glaciers. Glaciology, then, is the study of the physical characteristics of ice that combine to give glaciers their unique attributes. The scale on which glaciological research is performed ranges from the molecular level to studies of ice movement and properties in areas of continental proportions.

Although people have been living near glaciers and have been affected by them throughout much of the latter history of the human species, the science of glaciology is little more than a century old. The early study of glaciers began in areas in which present-day glaciers impinged on the lives and livelihoods of people. The first systematic studies of glaciers were made in the Alps and in Scandinavia. More recently, glaciological studies have concentrated on the much larger and more inaccessible areas of glacial ice in the far polar regions such as Greenland and Antarctica. The difference in scale between the vast polar ice sheets and the friendly local glaciers of Swiss mountain villages is several orders of magnitude; the physical properties of the ice that constitutes all glaciers are similar, though, as are the responses of glaciers to a variety of climatic and geographic factors. So, the broad outlines of the study of glaciers are relevant to all present-day glaciers, as well as to the much more extensive glaciers that occurred in the past.

Glaciers are of fundamental significance in understanding the polar environment. They currently cover a significant portion of the arctic regions, are widespread in alpine areas, and dominate the Antarctic. Their presence has a great impact on the heat budget of the earth and on the global climate, and is often crucially important in controlling climate more locally. The volume of glacial ice is critically connected to the volume of water in the oceans and the location of sea level and shorelines. Glaciers are also perhaps the prime agent of erosion, deposition, and geomorphic processes in general in many polar and alpine regions. Finally, the existence of glaciers was much more widespread in the recent geological past than it is today. Their area and volume was some four times that of the present as recently as 18,000 years ago. Thus, the past history of the polar regions must be understood in the context of the creation and dissolution of immense continental ice sheets. Chapters 7 and 13 look at the history of the Ice Ages in more detail.

THE CREATION OF GLACIAL ICE

A glacier is simply a naturally occurring deposit of ice that has attained such a mass and thickness that some of the ice is subject to alteration and movement under the impetus of its own weight and pressure. For this to occur, the ice deposit must normally be on the order of 50 meters thick.

With minor exceptions, all of the ice that makes up a glacier originates as snow deposited on the surface of the glacier. Although a glacier must originate as the result of deepening deposits of snow on the land surface, the birth of a glacier has seldom been witnessed in historical times, since most glaciers have been stable or shrinking for the past 15,000 years or so, with a few interesting exceptions.

The early stages in the development of a glacier and in the feeding of an established glacier with new ice involve the transformation of snow to glacier ice. Chapter 3 described some of the processes by which newly fallen snow is transformed into a variety of substances that display differing physical characteristics. Most of these newer materials are characterized by greater density than the approximately 0.1 gram per cubic centimeter of new-fallen snow. Firn, the material that makes up deep, perennial snow patches, has been compacted to a density (0.4 to 0.8) half or more of that of liquid water. A density of 0.55 is sometimes considered to mark the transition from old snow to firn. At this point, there can be no further increase in density by means of a simple rearrangement of the granules, so other phenomena must come into play. As the firn is further compacted by the weight of additional layers of snow above it, it undergoes a final transformation into glacier ice. The steps in this transformation are somewhat dependent on whether the firn remains dry and at a temperature below freezing or is soaked by percolation of meltwater formed by snow melt on the surface of the glacier or firn patch. The end result is pretty much the same.

In deep firn, molecules are transported to the zone of contact between particles by sublimation, so that bonds between the particles are increased and the material takes on the characteristics of a three-dimensional latticework. This process is known as sintering; as it continues, the density increases to the point that the volume of air-filled interstices is greatly reduced. From this point on, further transformation is brought about mainly by recrystallization. The size and shape of the crystals change by molecular diffusion and by deformation of the crystals in such a manner as to reduce stresses. When the density of the firn has reached approximately 0.82 to 0.84 gram per cubic centimeter, the trapped air included in the material is no longer contained in a series of connecting spaces. Much of it has escaped to the surface; the remainder is contained in closed pockets. At this point, the firn has become glacier ice. Any further increase in density will occur because of the further compression of the trapped air. The bubbles of trapped, compressed air are responsible for the fact that deep glacial ice, as obtained from, for example, a large iceberg, will fizz if put in a drink. This is standard fare on the cruise ships that increasingly ply Greenlandic waters. There was even a fad (fortunately short-lived) of importing glacier ice farther south for this effect.

The speed of the processes described above varies depending on the temperature; similarly, the speed varies according to the depth at which the processes are likely to occur. Furthermore, they are considerably altered in the presence of meltwater. Meltwater provides lubrication for the grains, allowing increased packing from pressure. In addition, surface tension of the water tends to pull the grains together. Finally, meltwater may fill in the interstices that, in dry firn, would contain air. Hence, the presence of meltwater hastens the process by which the firn increases in density and allows it to occur at a shallower depth in the glacier. As a result, in a warm glacier, such as occurs in more temperate regions, the transformation of snow to glacier ice may take place in the top ten meters or so of the glacier and may take only a few years. In a cold glacier, such as the antarctic ice cap, the transformation process may still be occurring at a depth of perhaps as much as 100 meters, and it may take 100 or more years.

Although it displays an array of unusual properties, glacial ice is technically a mineral. It is a naturally formed chemical compound with a definite composition and a crystalline molecular structure. Furthermore, glaciers can accurately be described as consisting of a type of metamorphic rock that near the surface grades to a sedimentary rock. The characteristics that make glacial ice unique among rocks and minerals are related to the fact that glacial ice occurs naturally on earth at temperatures near its melting point. It is also unique in that its deposition is the result of a change of state, from liquid or gas to a solid. Finally, it is one of the few minerals, and the only common one, that is ultimately eliminated from the environment under natural conditions, also by a change of state. Thus, glacial ice is constantly being created and dispersed in the natural environment. Furthermore, the sites of its deposition are distant from the sites of its dispersal. All of these properties combine to provide what are perhaps the most significant aspects of glaciers. They are constantly in motion; they are constantly being replenished and dispersed; and their size and volume is in a state of equilibrium with climatic factors and changes with changing climate.

GLACIAL BUDGETS

Glaciers have often been compared to conveyor belts, on which material is constantly added at the top and carried to the bottom, or glacial terminus, where it is dispersed. The energy that drives this conveyor belt is solar energy. It is transmitted to the glacier by the deposition of snow, which is ultimately derived from the oceans through evaporation and raised to the mountaintops, to be brought back to the oceans by gravity.

If we use this conveyor belt analogy, it is obvious that the existence and health of a glacier is dependent on the continued accumulation of snow, and that this accumulation is counterbalanced by the dispersal of the snow, now transformed into glacier ice. If more snow accumulates than is dispersed, the glacier will grow. If more ice is dispersed than is accumulated, the glacier will shrink. If dispersal, which is technically called *ablation,* and accumulation are in balance, the size of the glacier will remain the same. Note, however, that a glacier that is of stable size, neither advancing nor retreating, is nevertheless in a dynamic equilibrium (see Figure 4–1). The ice is in constant motion, moving from areas of accumulation in inland or upland regions to areas of ablation in the lowlands or at the seacoast. From this concept, it follows that a change in climate that alters the balance between accumulation and ablation will not cause the glacier to grow or shrink indefinitely. Instead, it will seek to establish a new equilibrium, with accumulation and ablation back in balance. A glacier, then, always either has what might be thought of as a "balanced budget" or is actively in the process of seeking a new balanced budget in response to changing conditions of accumulation and ablation.

All accumulation on a glacier is similar, in that it all involves the deposition of snow on the glacier's surface. This usually occurs as snowfall, but it might also occur through avalanching. In a few cases, the terminus of one glacier discharges ice chunks over the edge of a cliff, and the ice then reconstitutes itself into a new glacier. While some of the new snow may be ablated before it has undergone the transformation through firn to glacial ice, it is nonetheless significant in the glacial budget, since it provides insulation and protection to the ice lying beneath it. The energy expended melting this seasonal snow accumulation is energy that cannot be utilized to ablate the underlying ice.

Ablation can take place in several ways. In lower latitude gla-

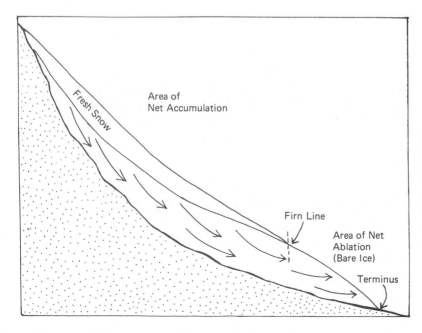

Figure 4–1. Idealized model of a typical alpine glacier. This diagram depicts a steady-state glacier, in which the location of the terminus remains stable; the glacier is thus in equilibrium. Nonetheless, ice is constantly being deposited on the surface of the glacier by snowfall and, mainly in the lower portions, is constantly being removed by melt and other forms of ablation. Ice is thus constantly in motion downslope toward the terminus.

ciers, ablation most commonly occurs through direct melting of ice on the lower portions of the glacier. However, it can also occur through sublimation. Some glaciers in dry, cold portions of northern Greenland and the Canadian high Arctic islands undergo much of their ablation through this process. Another form of ablation, also characteristic of high latitude glaciers, is the formation of icebergs. This process is known as calving. In certain parts of Antarctica, net accumulation continuously takes place over the entire surface of the glacier. Net debits to the antarctic glacial budget take place through the calving of icebergs, some of which may be of immense size. The calving of an iceberg is one of the most awe-inspiring of natural phenomena. Even the terminus of a relatively small sea-level glacier (such as can be seen at Glacier Bay, Alaska, for example) generates an impressive amount of noise and commotion, usually resulting in no more than the regular sloughing off of brash ice and bergy bits. The calving of a real berg can toss a ship around; at one site near Glacier Bay, the calving of an iceberg created a "tidal wave" that destroyed forests hundreds of meters above sea level. In the Northern Hemisphere, the most impressive calving occurs mainly along the coast of Greenland, and the resulting icebergs have been seen as far south as Bermuda waters. The final dispersal of the Greenland ice may thus occur far out at sea, at a great distance from the ice front. Smaller sea-level glaciers, such as occur in places like Alaska, usually produce only small icebergs that disappear rapidly if they reach the open sea. Even these small bergs may be a hazard for shipping if they are confined to bays and fiords.

In most glaciers, ablation and accumulation take place simultaneously throughout the year. During winter, snow may be accumulating over the entire surface of the glacier, but some of this snow is immediately dispersed through sublimation or some other process without ever being incorporated in the glacier. In warm periods, ablation may temporarily occur over the entire surface. This condition cannot, however, continue for long. Furthermore, it cannot occur to the extent that the entire accumulation of snow from the preceding winter is ablated above the area of the terminus. Should this happen, the glacier would be in serious trouble, since it would have no "net income" for the year in any portion of its "operations." As would be true in corporate economics, this state of affairs would rapidly lead to bankruptcy—here, the disappearance of the glacier.

The necessary presence of snow that has not yet been transformed into ice on at least some portion of a glacier provides a visible separation between two distinct portions of a glacier. The upper parts will appear to be smooth and white, as they are covered with firn or fresh snow (see Figure 4–1). At a point down the glacier, a line will mark the transition from fresh snow to glacial ice on the surface. Any part of the glacier that displays bare ice at the surface is losing more material by ablation than it is accumulating over the course of a year. Such a bare area is thus said to lie within the area of *net ablation.* As the warm season progresses, an increasingly large area on the lower portion of the glacier is stripped down to bare ice. The line between the bare ice surface and the smooth, snow-mantled surface is progressively displaced up the glacier throughout the period of melt. When this line reaches its highest point, and the greatest area of bare ice is exposed, the line accurately delineates the overall area of net ablation and net accumulation. This uppermost location of the delineation between the two zones is known as the *firn line.* In a stable glacier, it tends to be located at approximately the same level on the glacier year after year. The yearly variation depends on whether a given year was a heavy snow year or a year with a warm summer.

TYPES OF GLACIERS

Glaciers are generally classified as one of three types. These are: *alpine glaciers, piedmont glaciers,* and *ice sheets* or *continental glaciers.* The types are not always distinct from one another, and there are subtypes within the categories. Glaciers also commonly occur in *glacial systems,* which may contain examples of all the types. And, as glaciers expand and contract over time, they may change from one type to another.

Alpine glaciers occur in areas of high relief (see Figure 4–2). The smallest ones are sometimes known as *cliff glaciers, cirque glaciers,* or *glacierets.* At minimum, a glacier must be deep enough for the formation and flow of glacial ice. Thus, if a glacier is confined to a small, deep depression, it can cover a small area, perhaps less than one square kilometer. Deep snow patches that have not attained sufficient depth to be glaciers are also common in alpine regions. They are known as firn patches or nivation patches.

The distinguishing feature of alpine glaciation is that it does not totally inundate the terrain. Alpine glaciers are generally confined to valleys and separated into individual rivers of ice by intervening unglaciated ridges and peaks. Hence, a typical alpine

Figure 4–2. Alpine glaciation in the
St. Elias Range, near the boundary of
northernmost British Columbia, the
Yukon Territory, and Alaska. This
area contains the largest alpine glacial system in the world, and it is
clear that a relatively small amount
of additional spreading and thickening of the ice would result in true
continental glaciation. Note the
wave ogives on the surface of the
large glacier near the bottom of the
picture.

glacier is also known as a valley glacier. Valley glaciers are similar
to rivers in that they increase in size and volume downstream
through the coalescence of tributaries. A large valley glacier may
thus be the downstream aspect of a glacial system involving the
inflow of many smaller tributary glaciers.

Valley glaciers occur in mountainous regions throughout the
earth. In tropical and warm temperate regions, they are small and
confined to high elevations. Alpine glaciers reach progressively
lower elevations as one travels poleward, particularly in areas of

heavy snowfall, as along the west coasts of continents. The glaciers may extend to sea level at latitudes 50° to 60°, forming what are known as tidewater glaciers such as occur in southeastern Alaska and southern Chile.

Piedmont glaciers (see Figure 4–3) form when the lower reaches of alpine glaciers spread out over lowlands at the foot of mountainous regions. They are generally the result of the coalescence of several alpine glaciers. Piedmont glaciers are comparatively rare and are generally confined to the higher

Figure 4–3. Piedmont glacier. The Bering glacier, near Yakutat, Alaska, is formed by the merging of hundreds of alpine glaciers near the foot of the St. Elias Range. The history of the glacier, and the fact that the photograph shows the area of net ablation, is revealed by the large number of medial moraines.

latitudes. Classic examples occur in southern Alaska. There, the Malaspina glacier covers an area as large as Rhode Island state.

Alpine glaciers may thicken and coalesce in their upper reaches, overriding the surrounding terrain with sheets of ice (see Figure 4–2). Smaller examples of this situation are common in the Northern Hemisphere, north of about latitude 60°. The Vatnasjokull in Iceland, the Harding and Juneau icefields in Alaska, and the Baker icefield in Patagonia are good examples. At higher latitudes glaciers of this type become larger and more prevalent. Large portions of Svalbard, Novaya Zemlya, and Ellesmere Island are deeply buried in glacial ice. The most extreme examples are in Greenland and Antarctica. There, glaciers reach continental proportions and cover millions of square kilometers. The ice sheets reach depths of over 3,000 meters. Their weight is so great that they depress the underlying crust of the earth. If the Greenland ice cap were to melt suddenly, the central portion of the island would temporarily be a shallow sea.

In areas where the terrain underlying continental ice sheets is mountainous, the tallest mountains may protrude through the encompassing ice. These isolated peaks are known as *nunataks*. This is an Inuit, or Eskimo, word, one of the few that have come into general use among polar scientists. The word means eating land—the mountains seem to be being engulfed. Nunataks occur deep within the inland ice of Greenland. They are also found within a few hundred kilometers of the South Pole in Antarctica.

Continental glaciers are often separated from the sea or lowlands by ranges of coastal mountains, as is the case along most of the coast of Greenland, for example. The ice passes through mountain valleys as glaciers that are similar to other valley glaciers, but that generally move faster and are often much larger than typical alpine valley glaciers. Known as distributary glaciers, they often dump phenomenal quantities of ice into coastal waters by calving.

FEATURES OF A GLACIER

The surface of a glacier often appears to be a featureless expanse of snow. Nonetheless, we have already seen that there is a visible distinction between the area of net accumulation and the area of net ablation during the melt season. Other zones and features can also be distinguished visually on a glacier. Surface features generally reflect processes occurring deep within the ice. They may provide clues to the nature and activity of the glacier, and to the nature of the underlying substrate. Some glacial features are common to the entire glacier, while others may be localized in particular zones. Many are also masked by the overlying layer of firn and snow characteristic of much of the glacier's surface during most or all of the year.

The uppermost reaches of valley glaciers are often on steep slopes. The surface of the glacier may be surmounted by deep deposits of firn lying at a steep angle. This firn may occasionally slump under its own weight, breaking loose from the slope along a line, so that a deep fissure is formed in the firn deposit (for a diagrammatic version of this process, see Figure 4–4). These features are familiar to alpine climbers; they are known as *bergschrund*.

Somewhat similar cracks also occur on the surface of the glacier itself. These form as a result of stresses associated with glacial flow, particularly in response to irregularities in the underlying topography. The cracks, known as crevasses (see Figures 4–4 and 4–5) are a common feature of most glaciers. They are generally narrow, have steep, nearly vertical sides, and may extend 25 to 50 meters deep into the glacier. Their depth is limited by the internal movement and flow of the glacier; it theoretically varies in relation to certain physical characteristics of the ice of the particular glacier.

Crevasses are of particular interest to mountain climbers and travelers on glaciers, since they are exceedingly dangerous. The

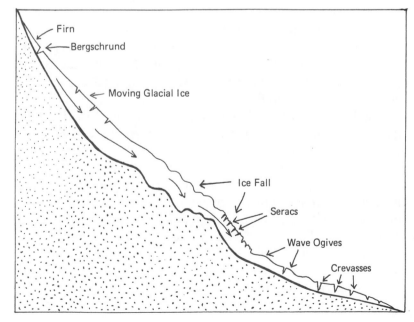

Figure 4–4. Diagrammatic view of a glacier, showing a number of common features and their relationship to each other.

Figure 4–5. Crevasses near the edge of a large icefield on Anvers Island, Antarctica. The ice front is some 50 to 70 meters high. The huge crevasses are partially bridged by snow, and the deadly danger to a traveler on such a surface is evident.

danger is increased on the portions of a glacier that are covered with snow and firn, since the opening of the crevass may be masked by the loose snow, forming weak and unstable snow bridges.

Icefalls are a glacier's equivalent of river rapids and are generally associated with an underlying cliff or steep slope. They take the form of jumbled and unstable areas of immense blocks of ice. Some glaciers, as in the Dry Valleys of Antarctica, are separated into two parts by a zone of unglaciated terrain. In these unusual situations, the upper glacier feeds the lower one by dropping a steady flow of ice blocks that slide and roll down the steep rocky slope onto the surface of the lower glacier. More typical ice falls do not create a complete break between portions of a glacier but are similar in principle.

Regularly spaced wavelike ridges commonly found on the glacier's surface are known as ogives. (See Figure 4–2). They often develop down-glacier from icefalls where they are known as wave ogives. The nature of their formation is not fully understood; it appears that they are related to a periodic surge of ice over the ice fall, which is presumably seasonal. One explanation suggests that because a glacier dropping over an icefall is spread out and its surface area increases, so that a comparatively great deal of ablation would take place in summer, thinning the ice. This could be reflected in a depressed area on the glacier surface downstream from the fall. The crescent shape of the ogives then would result from the fact that the ice moves faster in the middle of the glacier than on the edges.

As alpine glaciers move through a valley, they scour and undercut the valley walls. This results in the deposition of rock and rubble from the valley sides on the surface of the glacier, so that the sides of the glacier commonly incorporate a good deal of rock and debris. If two valley glaciers coalesce, these strips of "dirty" ice merge. The result is an elongated dark-colored stripe that is clearly visible on the surface of the combined glacier, at least in areas where it is not covered by fresh snow. This feature is known as a medial moraine. Large valley glaciers and piedmont glaciers may contain dozens or hundreds of these moraines, each running parallel to the others and following the sinuous curves of the flowing glacier (see Figure 4–6). They provide information on the number and comparative volume and flow of the tributary glaciers that lie far upstream.

The lowermost portion of a glacier is known as the terminus,

Figure 4–6. Medial moraines. It is evident in this view that these formations are merged lateral moraines. The exposed bare ice and the rock and rubble of the moraine confirm that this photograph was taken within the area of net ablation.

or snout. It is typically lobate in form and rises steeply up to the surface of the main body of the glacier. The composition of the terminus may be complex and difficult to characterize. It may be located in or on the shores of a large meltwater lake, and it may consist of jumbled masses of ice. Since the glacier is commonly carrying a large load of rock and rubble, the terminus may be mantled in this material to a considerable depth as the ice melts out. This may result in the presence of large areas of ice-cored moraine, which may make it difficult to determine the exact location of the terminus (see Figure 4–7).

The terminus may also be found at a sea coast, or the glacier may even be "grounded" in shallow water and extend a considerable distance beyond the shoreline. In this case, much of the ablation occurring may take place through the calving of icebergs rather than through melt. A terminus of this type is often precipitous, as much as 100 meters or more high, and characterized by active and continuous ice fall. As has been discussed, the events that take place at the terminus of a large tidewater glacier can occur on an awesome scale. Even large ships can be swamped by the waves associated with the calving of an iceberg, and the rumble and roar of constantly falling ice is a most impressive sound.

An ice cap differs from a valley glacier in that its terminus is the entire margin of the glacier, at least if the margins of the glacier are located on flat terrain. In many cases, of course, ice sheets

Figure 4–7. Ice-cored moraines near the terminus of the Kastner glacier in the Alaska Range near Paxson, Alaska. Although the terrain appears to be mainly rock and gravel, most of it is actually ice. A large, fast-moving, and extremely dangerous river is emerging through the rubble. This stagnant ice will ultimately melt away, causing the ground to slump, and karst-and-kettle topography to develop.

discharge through mountain systems. In the mountains, there may occur a succession of large individual valley glaciers, each fed by the ice cap, but each with its own separate terminus. These distributary glaciers occur along much of the mountainous coast of Greenland.

The margins of some large continental ice sheets extend far out over the surface of the sea, forming floating ice shelves such as the Ross Ice Shelf in Antarctica. Ice shelves are often afloat. They continue to grow until some event or combination of events separates large portions of them from the main body of the glacier, whereupon they float away as enormous flat-topped icebergs. At any given time, several such ice islands are usually floating about in the Arctic Ocean, sometimes giving rise to rumors of undiscovered land such as the legendary Crocker Land. These islands are actually tabular bergs, calved from the north coast of Ellesmere Island.

Until about 10,000 years ago, continental ice sheets extended deep into temperate latitudes in North America and Eurasia. Their margins extended for thousands of miles across the face of the continents. We can only speculate on the nature of these ice margins, since no one in record-keeping times ever saw a continental ice sheet on land in low latitudes. What are probably the closest modern equivalents are the margins of some of the glaciers in Iceland. The presence of these huge ice sheets in the geologically recent past has had a profound effect on the northern environment, as well as that of many temperate regions. The ancient glaciers and some of their effects will be discussed later in this chapter and in Chapter 5.

GLACIAL FLOW

The definitive feature of a glacier is its constant movement. During most of the history of glaciology, it was assumed that an appropriate analogy for glacier movement was a viscous liquid, such as cold molasses. Only in the past few decades has it been recognized that glacial ice should, and does, act like any normal polycrystalline solid at a temperature near its melting point. Perhaps the tardiness of this recognition is a result of scientists' paucity of opportunities for observing other substances occurring in vast volumes at high temperatures—that is, temperatures near the substance's melting point. This relatively recent reconception of the movement and characteristics of glacial ice provided great impetus for the study of glaciers, since it was then also recognized that the information gained was relevant to physical and engineering problems of space age metals and ceramics.

Much of the information relevant to an understanding of glacial flow is highly technical and is built upon complex physical and mathematical concepts. Those who study glacial flow theorize about it using mathematical models, which are then compared with observations from the glaciers themselves. One reason that use of these models is valuable is that glaciers are often inaccessible. Studying glaciers in the flesh is an expensive and time-consuming proposition. Since many of the processes of glacial movement take place only deep within the glacier, they are more or less inaccessible to direct observation by researchers. No one has ever been at the bottom of even a relatively shallow glacier. Attempts to probe deeply into a glacier are difficult and frustrating, since the plastic flow of the glacial ice tends to fill in bore holes and entrap even sophisticated drilling equipment. Millions of dollars were recently spent in a frustrating, although ultimately successful, attempt to bore through the Ross Ice Shelf in Antarctica and reach the underlying sea.

The following examination of some of the processes of glacial movement can only scratch the surface of a complicated and often controversial subject. Theoretically, glaciers move through two discrete processes: *basal slippage* and *ice deformation*. Each of these is a complex process.

Basal slippage is simply, as the term implies, the sliding of the ice mass along the surface of the underlying substrate. It is theoretically possible only in the case of a warm glacier, where temperatures are high enough to allow melting to occur at the base of the ice as a result of the pressure of the overlying material. If the glacier is frozen to the base, slippage cannot occur, since the strength of the bond created would considerably exceed the strength of the ice itself. There is some evidence, obtained by tunnelling under the terminus of cold glaciers, that this theory is correct.

Assuming that temperatures are such that basal slippage can occur at all, a number of factors would determine its relative importance in overall movement. Among them is the amount of liquid water present, which would act as a lubricant. The nature of the underlying bedrock and its irregularities are also important.

Ice deformation is a result of slippage of planes within the ice crystals in response to stress. In essence, it is possible to bend an ice crystal, given the right combination of circumstances. In a glacier in which there is no basal slippage, all movement theoretically occurs through this process. However, the speed and extent of this movement is complexly related to alterations to the engineering properties of ice in response to temperature, pressure, and stress. Since most of these alterations occur at a microscopic or even molecular level, direct observation is difficult or impossible. We'll simply say that ice crystals do deform under various conditions, that these conditions are well enough understood to provide some theoretical and predictive basis for understanding glacier movement, and that ice deformation is a major component of most, if not all, glacial movement.

Many of the theoretical models that have been proposed to describe glacial movement could be tested experimentally if simple, "perfect" glaciers existed. For example, if an ice sheet were to spread out over perfectly flat terrain, a careful measurement of its slope and contours would provide a great deal of information regarding the processes through which it reached its current state. In real glaciers innumerable variables cloud any simple understanding of their nature. For example, accumulation is likely to be uneven over the surface. It may be affected by weather patterns, and may, of course, vary from year to year. Temperatures within the glacier can also be expected to vary, and the nature of the underlying terrain will obviously affect movement.

Leaving aside theoretical considerations, glacier movement can, of course, simply be measured. This is commonly done by placing markers on accurately surveyed lines on a glacier and making repeated measurements over a period of time. But if ice deformation is a component of the movement, surface movement will tell only part of the story. Measurements at depth, in bore holes, have also been made in response to this concern. It appears that surface observations can provide a reasonably accurate measurement of total flow in a glacier.

As might be expected, the rate of flow of glaciers varies greatly. A typical valley glacier may have a velocity over most of its length of from 10 to 200 meters per year. Movement will be slower near the terminus, where ablation is occurring, and faster in situations such as ice falls, where the cross-sectional area is reduced and flow must increase accordingly. The great valley glaciers that drain major ice caps flow much more rapidly. Some antarctic glaciers of this type have been observed to flow at a speed of over 1,000 meters per year, and one of the major iceberg-producing glaciers on the Greenland coast flows at some 10 kilometers per year.

In small valley glaciers, there is also a good deal of variation in flow on a shorter-term basis. This may be related to seasonal variations in melt, and even such factors as heavy rainfall. An extreme example of this situation is known as a surge or, popularly, a galloping glacier. In this case, the terminus of a glacier may advance several kilometers in the course of a year or two. It then normally begins to retreat to near its original position. One of the best known galloping glaciers is the Black Rapids glacier in central Alaska, which periodically threatens to engulf the Richardson Highway, and which caused some concern over the location of the Trans-Alaska oil pipeline.

The reasons for glacial surges are not well known. It has been suggested that avalanches might deposit abnormal amounts of snow on the area of accumulation. A plausible explanation in some cases is that a glacier might warm enough that it would change from a cold glacier to a warm one, with a consequent sudden facilitation of basal slippage. Glacial surges could, at least theoretically, have a profound effect on climatic change. If a major ice sheet, such as the one that covers West Antarctica, should suddenly surge, it would increase its surface area markedly and alter the overall albedo of the earth. It has been suggested that this could trigger a new ice age.

EXTENT AND VOLUME OF GLACIERS

The land area of Antarctica covered by glacial ice is on the order of 12 million square kilometers, a considerably larger area than the United States or all of Europe. It has been calculated that the average depth of ice is nearly 2,000 meters, with a maximum of over 4,000 meters. Hence, the total volume of the antarctic ice cap is over 20 million cubic kilometers, enough to cover the entire earth, including both land and sea, to a depth of as much as 25 meters. In spite of the immense quantities of ice on Antarctica, there are a few areas on the continent that are unglaciated.

It has been estimated that the antarctic ice cap contains about 90 percent of the glacial ice on the earth. Most of the rest is contained in the Greenland ice cap. Other glaciers, no matter how large and impressive they are individually, are negligible in terms of the total amount of the earth's glacial ice.

However, even these tiny local glaciers are immense by human standards. The Malaspina glacier covers over 1,000 square kilometers and its depth has been measured at over 1,000 meters in some places. Even alpine valley glaciers may be several kilometers in width, over 100 kilometers in total length, and reach a depth of up to 1,000 meters. Finally, the total extent and volume of glacial ice at present is only about one quarter what it has been as recently as 18,000 years ago. The evidence of previous glaciation is ubiquitous in many temperate regions, and glaciers have been a major force in creating the temperate landscapes we live in, as well as the landscapes of most of the Arctic and Subarctic.

SUGGESTED FURTHER READING

Much of the glaciological literature is highly technical and seldom finds its way into publications for the general public. The *Journal of Glaciology,* published by the International Glaciological Society at Cambridge, in England, is the leading periodical in the field. Most of the works listed after Chapters 5 and 7 contain sections on straight glaciology as well as on glacial geomorphology and history. The following are useful works dealing specifically with glaciology.

Andrews, J. T. *Glacial Systems: An Approach to Glaciers and Their Environment.* Belmont, MA: Duxbury Press, 1975.

Paterson, W. S. B. *The Physics of Glaciers.* Oxford: Pergamon Press, 1969.

Chapter 5

Polar Landscapes:
Glacial Geology and Geomorphology

MOST elementary earth science textbooks have, early on, a diagram and explanation of the hydrologic cycle. Such a diagram shows water from the oceans evaporated, deposited as rainfall, and ultimately finding its way back to the sea, taking with it sizable chunks of the landscape. Differences in the nature of stream erosion between humid and arid environments are generally mentioned, and a paragraph may be included on the fact that erosion can also take place through the action of wind or ice, albeit mainly in bleak and hardly habitable regions.

Much of the water involved in erosion and deposition in the polar regions spends a good deal of its tenure there in a solid state, as discussed in Chapter 4. Since much of the polar ice is in the dynamic form of glaciers, its involvement in the creation of the polar landscape takes place through the processes of glacial erosion and deposition.

Erosional processes differ greatly depending on whether the water involved is in a solid or a liquid state; the landscapes created by glacial ice are easily distinguishable from those formed by the action of liquid water. Long after a glacier has disappeared from an area, the evidence of its previous existence is indelibly engraved on the rocks, gravel deposits, and on the overall face of the land. Since glacial ice covered much of the boreal and north temperate regions as recently as 15,000 to 18,000 years ago (see Chapter 7 for more on the Ice Ages), many northern landscapes can be properly understood only in relation to their history of inundation by glacial ice.

As agents of geomorphic change, glaciers are similar to water and wind in that they involve erosional and depositional cycles. However, erosion and deposition by glacier take place very differently than erosion and deposition by the other agents. In addition, glaciation often results in related secondary water- and wind-dependent geomorphic processes whose nature is defined by the presence of the nearby glacier.

GLACIAL EROSION

Roughly equivalent volumes of water derived from precipitation flow over the landscape to the sea, whether this water is in the form of glacial ice or streams of water. However, a unit volume of ice traverses the landscape at only a miniscule fraction of the speed of even slow-moving water. In order for a comparable amount of water to return to the ocean, the volume of ice that is in active movement at any given time on a glaciated landscape must be many orders of magnitude greater than would be the case if it were in the form of liquid water. This, in turn, means that a much greater proportion of the surface of the land will be subject to glacial erosion at a given time than would be eroded by liquid water, if we ignore the usually relatively minor effects of sheet erosion associated with the sources of small rivulets.

Figure 5–1 illustrates the contrasting situation in two valleys that carry identical amounts of water, in one case in the form of a valley glacier, in the other as a stream of liquid water. Liquid water moves only in direct response to the force of gravity, and thus can move only downslope. Also, the erosional ability of a stream of water is directly related to the amount of material it is carrying in the form of suspended particles. The size and erosional energy of these suspended particles are directly dependent on the speed at which the water is moving, and thus on the slope of the land. Since glacial ice is a solid, its movement is affected by the volume of ice upstream. Ice can be forced to move up a

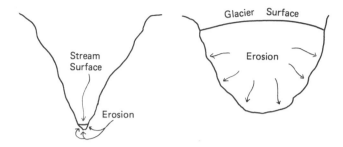

Figure 5–1. Idealized cross section of two valleys carrying identical volumes of water over time. Water traverses the valley on the left in a liquid state, while glacial ice, moving at only a fraction of a millionth the speed of the liquid, fills the valley on the right. The erosive action of the glacier effects the entire valley floor and sides, creating a characteristic U-shaped trough.

slope, pushed from behind. Erosion can take place in the course of this upslope movement. Furthermore, glacial ice itself can cause erosion, whether or not it includes a significant amount of such suspended material as rock. Finally, the effectiveness of glacial erosion is not closely dependent on the speed at which the glacier is moving. This also means that glacial erosion can actively take place at the bottom of a deep, ice-filled depression. If a similar depression were filled with liquid water, as in a lake, only deposition could occur.

Erosion of the substrate by the passage of glacial ice takes place by means of two discrete processes, known as abrasion and plucking, or quarrying. Abrasion, as the word implies, is simply the wearing away of material in sandpaper fashion. It is particularly effective in cases in which a large amount of hard material, such as rock fragments and gravel, is included in the lower strata of the overriding glacier. Since its effectiveness is also related to the direction of ice flow in relation to the substrate, a steep slope facing the direction of ice movement is likely to be subjected to intense abrasion (see Figure 5–2). Abrasion generally proceeds in small increments, so that relatively fine material is produced and incorporated into the load of detritus carried by the glacier.

Plucking is the removal of large blocks of rock. It is particularly effective on slopes that are in the lee (downstream) of the direction of glacial movement. In general, plucking is a more effective means than abrasion for the removal of bedrock material. This is particularly true in the case of a comparatively clean glacier, which has incorporated relatively little rock. Continental glaciers are able to incorporate new material into the ice mass only along their bottoms, while in alpine glaciers much material falls on the glacier from the valley sides. Hence, plucking is a particularly important phenomenon in the erosion caused by large ice sheets. If a hilly landscape is overridden by ice, the upslope sides of the hills are usually ground into smooth, gentle inclines, while the downslopes are rugged and steep because of

Figure 5–2. Ice-scoured bedrock near Glacier Bay, Alaska. The direction of ice flow can be clearly deduced from the direction of the striations, or scratches, caused by rock and sand dragging over the surface.

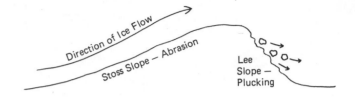

Figure 5–3. The two major erosive actions of a glacier, abrasion and plucking (or quarrying). Abrasion sandpapers the upstream (or stoss) slope, leaving a scoured, scratched, and polished surface. Plucking, more effective in removing material, pulls large blocks from the downstream (or lee) slope. The resulting asymmetrical bedrock formation is commonly called a *roche moutonnee.*

the plucking of large blocks. This terrain is known as stoss and lee topography. The individual asymmetrical hills are called *roche moutonnees;* their shape clearly indicates the direction of ice travel (see Figure 5–3).

Alpine Scenery and Glacial Erosion

Without exception, the spectacular scenery seen in alpine regions is the result of glaciation, either past, present, or in combination. As varied as alpine scenery may appear to be, it is the result of a very few basic processes in which relatively small glaciers interact with the elevated terrain. Figure 5–4 shows a typical example of alpine scenery, including a variety of features that are the result of an earlier episode of glaciation.

The basic feature associated with alpine glaciation and geomorphology is known as a cirque. A cirque is a bowl- or

Figure 5–4. Typical alpine scenery in the central Brooks Range, Alaska. Most of the glaciers have retreated, leaving a deep glacial valley and side valleys, cirques, arêtes, and related features.

amphitheater-shaped depression in the side of a slope (see Figure 5–5). It is usually formed by the erosional forces of the uppermost portion of a glacier, although there is some evidence that a deep snowbed that is not deep enough to exhibit the internal movement characteristic of a glacier may also be able to form a cirque under some circumstances.

In its initial stages, a cirque is a naturally occurring hollow or ravine on the side of a hill. During the winter a snowbed forms in this hollow from drifting, and the deep snow buildup often causes snow patches to remain in incipient cirques through the summer. These early stages of cirques can commonly be observed in polar and alpine regions; they are clearly evident in summer because of the snow patches they contain, and they are generally known as nivation hollows, or corries. Old, empty cirques, remnants of previous glacial episodes, are often found in the same vicinity.

The transformation of a nivation hollow into a cirque generally

Figure 5–5. Two small cirques with active glaciers. The slumping of the glacial ice results in the formation of a bergschrund and the over-steepening of the headwall of the cirque.

takes place when the buildup of annual deposits of snow is such that internal movement begins under the weight of the accumulated snow and ice, forming a glacier. Movement of the ice begins to gouge the cirque floor and to undercut the sides and back wall of the hollow. Steep deposits of firn and ice often form at the back wall, or headwall, of the cirque. These become effective plucking agents as they break free and carry material down onto the surface of the glacier. Sometimes large areas of ice pull away from the headwall but leave the upper reaches of the firn deposit intact, so that a gap is formed. This situation is known to climbers as *bergschrund.*

Since cirque erosion is taking place around the periphery of the original depression, the classic bowl-shaped cirque, with a U-shaped cross section, is formed. Should the glacier then melt away because of a change in the climate, the empty cirque will remain as an indication of previous glaciation. Whether or not a cirque can form is a function of the snow line on a mountain; the snow line is the line above which, because of climatic conditions, snow is able to persist in hollows throughout the summer. If a series of now-empty cirques were all formed during the same episode of lowered snow line, their floors will generally be at nearly identical levels, indicating the snow line at the time of their formation. Groups of old cirques, then, can provide valuable information with respect to past climates.

If climatic conditions are such that the initial cirque glacier continues to expand and extend downslope from the original cirque, the U-shaped cross section will continue to be produced downslope, forming a valley with oversteepened sides and a more or less flat floor. These U-shaped valleys are a classic feature of glaciated terrain. Valleys of this type commonly have streams in their bottoms after the glacier has left, but stream erosion has usually not had time since deglaciation to recreate the V-shaped valley configuration characteristically produced by stream erosion.

As long as a cirque is occupied by a glacier, erosion continues to take place at the headwall, so that the cirque bites progressively deeper into the hillside. Since cirque glaciers generally occur on both sides of the ridge or spine of a mountain, the tendency is for there to be back-to-back cirques whose headwalls progress toward each other until they meet. The point of coalescence is characterized by a knife-edged ridge known as an arête (see Figure 5–6). Should the coalescence continue to the point that the ridge is overridden by the confluence of the two glaciers, the ridge is generally smoothed and rounded, forming a more

gentle feature known as a col. (Much of the terminology used in the study of glacial geomorphology is derived from words in common usage in languages used in glaciated areas. So the words are often picturesque and evocative, in contrast to the technical jargon of many other scientific fields.)

It is common for headward erosion to occur simultaneously in three or more cirques around the periphery of a mountain. As this erosion proceeds, all of the headwalls may converge on a central point, leaving a faceted spire of rock called a horn. These are among the most spectacular features of alpine glaciation; such famous peaks as the Matterhorn were formed in this fashion.

The high elevation features of alpine scenery, then, are largely the result of cirque erosion taking place on the sides of features that have never been subject to complete inundation by ice. They are characterized by slopes oversteepened by the action of alpine glaciers, mainly at the headwalls of cirques, but also along the

Figure 5–6. The intersection of several cirques, causing a typical array of knife-edged ridges (or arêtes).

borders of valley glaciers. If the mountaintops project far above the limits of past or present glaciation, they may owe their contours to subaerial, rather than glacial erosion. For this reason, some alpine areas are characterized by precipitous terrain at lower elevations surmounted by gentle, rolling summits. Since glaciation was much more extensive in the recent past than now, this situation is relatively uncommon. It is well illustrated in portions of northern and western Alaska (see Figure 5–7).

A related phenomenon occurs in areas that were subject first to continental glaciation followed by partial deglaciation and the production of alpine features as the waning glaciers were confined to cirques and valleys. Careful interpretation of this type of terrain can provide valuable information on the glacial history of an area. Excellent examples of the results of local glaciation following the retreat of continental ice sheets can be seen on the island of Newfoundland (see Figure 5–8).

Alpine Valley Features

In most alpine situations, the terrain has developed by the action of an extensive network of valley glaciers. As we saw, these glaciers are the continuation of cirque glaciers, and alpine valleys with a U-shaped cross section are, in a sense, elongated cirques.

The effectiveness of erosion by valley glaciers is related to such factors as the depth of the ice, the speed at which the ice is

Figure 5–7. View of a cirque from above in the upper Charley River drainage, central Alaska. The photograph shows the contrast between the deep bite of the now-vanished cirque glacier and the surrounding more gentle terrain.

Figure 5–8. Results of residual alpine glaciation after a continental glacier has retreated. These deep, fiordlike valleys in western Newfoundland were oversteepened after the general leveling and smoothing of the land caused by continental glaciation.

moving, the nature of the substrate, and the load of abrasive material contained within the glacier. Erosion is most effective in a deep, narrow valley through which a glacier moves rapidly. As a result, downcutting, or gouging, by the glacier is often most effective well upstream from the terminus. This means that deep hollows may be gouged out on the floor of a glacial valley. After glaciation, the hollows generally fill with water, forming deep ponds and lakes known as tarn lakes. Tarn lakes are common in the floors of cirques (see Figure 5–9).

A related situation occurs in tidewater glaciers. There the weight and depth of the ice may erode the valley floor to a depth well below sea level, so that the valley is filled with an arm of the sea after deglaciation has occurred. This formation is known as a *fiord* or *fjord;* it is of common occurrence wherever alpine glaciation has taken place on coastal mountain systems, as in Norway, Greenland, southern Alaska, Patagonia, and New Zealand.

The drowned valleys of fiords are often extremely deep in their inner reaches; depths of over 500 meters are not unusual. However, in the vicinity of the terminus of the vanished glacier erosional forces were generally reduced because of thinning of the ice due to lack of confinement in a valley, and because of melt and the flotation of the ice by sea water. Consequently, the mouths of fiords are generally comparatively shallow. This situation has had practical consequences for wartime shipping, for example. The fiord may provide a large, deep, and protected

Figure 5–9. A tarn lake in the Brooks Range, Alaska. A cirque glacier dug deeply here, creating a basin that became a tarn after the glacier retreated.

harbor whose entrance is shallow and difficult to navigate for submarines or surface vessels unfamiliar with the area.

Fiordlike lakes may occur in areas where valley glaciers have extended down from the mountains into the edges of a flat plain. The large lakes along the eastern margin of the Andes in southern Argentina are examples of this phenomenon.

Valley glaciers, as discussed in Chapter 4, tend to converge in a *dendritic* (treelike) pattern. Given the nature of glacial erosion, there is no impetus for the smaller or less active of two merging glaciers to erode its floor to the depth of the floor of the larger or faster-moving glacier. When the glaciers have retreated upstream from the point of confluence, the resulting feature is a juncture of two valleys in which the floor of one intersects far up the steep side of the other. This feature is known as a hanging valley. Since glacial valleys are commonly occupied by streams, the mouth of a hanging valley generally discharges a waterfall, one of the characteristic features of alpine scenery (see Figure 5–10).

Erosional Features of Continental Glaciers

By definition, continental glaciation overrides the entire surface of the terrain, although isolated nunataks may occur. As a result of complete inundation by ice, continental glaciation produces erosional features markedly different from those produced by alpine glaciation. In general, landscapes that have been subjected to continental glaciation are characterized by smoothed and subdued terrain, although secondary alpine glaciation may superimpose alpine features on areas previously subjected to continental glaciation.

As is true of alpine glaciers, continental glaciers alter the landscape by abrasion and plucking; although the processes are similar, the features formed are generally distinctive. Although the erosional force of continental glaciers is immense, the nature of the features formed under the glacier depends to a large extent on the structure and composition of the underlying substrate. The direction of ice flow is affected by the presence of subglacial hills and valleys, and the effectiveness of erosion is related to the resistance of the bedrock. Hence, glaciated terrain, although rounded and subdued on a large scale, is often rough and uneven locally, even when it has been subjected to long episodes of continental glaciation. Perhaps the most characteristic feature of hilly terrain that has been glaciated is the *roche moutonnee* (sheep rock), mentioned at the beginning of this chapter.

Most land surfaces that have been subjected to subglacial erosion show evidence of abrasion, whether or not plucking has also taken place. The presence of earlier glaciers can often be ascertained by smooth, polished surfaces of the bedrock, produced by abrasion (see Figure 5–2). The polished surfaces often display a pattern of parallel grooves and ridges. These indicate the direction of ice flow and can serve as valuable indications of the local movement of the ice sheet. Glaciers also apparently sometimes chatter over the bedrock surface, like a dull carpenter's plane over wood. This process leaves evidence in the form of shallow fractures and gouges, which are often crescent-shaped.

Perhaps the most characteristic feature of glaciated landscapes is the obliteration of drainage patterns associated with stream flow. Again, unlike stream erosion, the erosional processes associated with glaciers are not dependent on downslope motion. As a result, recently deglaciated landscapes have not developed drainage patterns such as those normally associated with

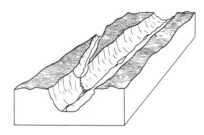

Figure 5–10. Cross section of a hanging valley. Here the main glacier was a much more effective erosive force than the smaller side valley glacier. When the glaciers retreated, the side valley was left hanging, with a waterfall.

streams and rivers. Glaciated landscapes are characterized by numerous lakes and ponds, wildly meandering streams with highly variable flow patterns, and waterfalls and rapids. The boundary of previous continental glaciation in eastern North America can easily be determined by these drainage patterns, and, particularly, by the abundance of lakes and ponds. This can easily be seen by comparing a map of a previously glaciated area such as New York state with one of a nearby unglaciated area, such as Virginia.

Depositional (Glacio-fluvial) Features

Glaciers are in contact with various kinds of bedrock at their base and, in the case of alpine glaciers, along their sides. This means that they constantly incorporate material that has been dislodged from the substrate by abrasion and plucking. They also pick up great quantities of rock and debris by undercutting valley walls, so that rockslides constantly fall onto the surface of the glacier.

At the terminus of the glacier, the ice disappears through melt, calving, or sublimation. The incorporated rock, gravel, sand, and silt that has been carried along by the conveyor-belt action of the glacier is then deposited in the vicinity of the terminus. If the terminus later advances, this material may be reincorporated into the glacier and redeposited at the new terminus. Similarly, if the glacier is retreating, it will leave behind it a succession of depositional features as its terminus retreats upstream. These features generally are conspicuous on previously glaciated terrain. Although variable in their appearance and composition, they are known collectively as moraines. The material that together composes the features is known as moraine, till, or drift. Morainal material is often classified in two major types, unstratified or stratified till. The difference between the two is in the mode of deposition, whether directly by ice or by water action associated with ice melt. Features consisting of till are known as *ice contact features,* in contradistinction to water-laid deposits that are associated with glaciers but that occur at some distance from the site of glacial deposition.

Since a glacier itself is composed of ice, mechanisms for sorting of included materials on the basis of the size of the particles, as occurs with particles suspended in water, are absent (with some minor exceptions). The deposits left directly by a melting glacier are thus unsorted; fine and coarse material is simply dumped, with little or no stratification. The presence of large deposits of unstratified glacial till provided the first evidence in support of the contention that drift deposits in Europe were the result of glacial action, rather than evidence of the biblical great flood. (The idea of a great flood did not die instantaneously, however; ingenious scenarios by which unstratified deposits could be created by a flood were current in some circles for years. Most of these posited rafting of sediments from glacier ice by icebergs that had presumably drifted over the surface of the land when it was inundated by the waters of the great flood.)

Since the ablation and retreat of a glacier involves the presence of a good deal of meltwater within and in the immediate vicinity of the terminus, some forms of moraine are at least partially the result of water deposition; the presence of sorting and stratification provides evidence of water. The various kinds of moraines, both stratified and unstratified, are often complexly merged with each other.

The most widespread type of morainal material is known as ground moraine. It is unsorted material that has accumulated at the zone of contact between the glacier and its substrate; it may also have been deposited on the surface of the ground in thin, irregular sheets as the glacier retreated more or less steadily or rapidly.

Ground moraine of the first type is called lodgement till; that deposited during glacial retreat is ablation till. Since ablation till is often deposited on the surface of already existing lodgement till, a more or less clear delineation between the two types is often evident in a cross section through the material; this is one of the few ways in which stratification of materials directly laid by ice can occur.

The surface topography of an area that has been traversed by a glacier at some time in the past is generally a mosaic of bare polished rock and ground moraine; these features provide incontrovertible evidence of glaciation. (See Figure 5–11).

Ground moraine can vary in its composition. Most generally, it consists of a matrix of fine, claylike material that is blue or gray in color, with rounded boulders of various sizes making up a greater or lesser portion of the volume of the material. The unsorted nature of the deposit, which is commonly known as boulder clay, reflects its glacial origin. The included boulders also bear evidence of their transport by glaciers, although they superficially resemble stream-washed stones. Glacial boulders generally have been ground into faceted shapes as they slid along

Figure 5–11. A deposit of glacial till, or unstratified drift or moraine. The material is a mixture of fine and coarse material dropped directly by a melting glacier and not affected by liquid water, which would have tended to sort the material according to size.

the interface between the ice and the substrate; further evidence for this process is the presence of scratches and grooves on their surfaces.

A conspicuous feature of glaciated terrain is the presence of large, isolated boulders on the surface of the ground or protruding from it. These are known as glacial erratics (see Figure 5–12). Erratics have often been transported some distance. If the location of their origin can be pinned down, they provide evidence of the local direction of movement of the glacier. Erratics are often perched in precarious positions, and they are commonly associated with legends of past human or supernatural agencies. Glacial erratics often persist in place after ground moraine and till have been dispersed by subaerial erosion, and after the evidence of glaciation on exposed bedrock has been destroyed by weathering and frost action. Under some circumstances, the presence of erratics may provide the only compelling evidence for past glaciation. It is hard to argue with the evidence of a ten-ton chunk of exotic rock on a mountain peak.

Most of the material transported by a glacier is deposited in the vicinity of its terminus. If the position of the terminus remains stable for a long time, deep deposits of till are formed along the entire ice front (see Figure 5–13). These deposits generally take the form of mounds and ridges outlining the location of the terminus. Deposits of the type that delineate the farthest extension of the glacial margin are called terminal moraines. In large continental glaciers, these terminal moraines may be immense, forming ridges as high as 100 meters and extending for hundreds of kilometers along the glacial margin. Terminal moraines of this type are particularly conspicuous on flat terrain, as in the American Midwest. They have also been important in forming coastal features, and they are a major constituent of Cape Cod and Long Island, as well as some submerged features on the continental shelf.

When a glacier retreats, it generally does so in a somewhat sporadic and uneven fashion, so that a new equilibrium is often established some distance above the terminal moraine. These periods of stasis result in the formation of additional morainal deposits that are identical to terminal moraine in structure and mode of formation. These are known as recessional moraines. A series of them may be found along a valley floor or on flat terrain, each indicating a period of re-equilibration and achievement of temporary stability of the overall retreating glacier. They may also be partially obliterated by minor episodes of readvance, through the bulldozing action of the glacier.

Figure 5–12. A typical glacial erratic, left by a rapidly retreating continental glacier in Labrador. In Europe, a formation as spectacular as this would undoubtably have given rise to legends of little people or giants.

In a valley glacier, most of the included rock and gravel is deposited along the sides of the glacier, because of the undercutting and slippage of the valley walls. During retreat, this material is dumped *in situ* by the melting ice, forming long ridges of rubble that run parallel to the direction of ice movement, unlike terminal and recessional moraines. The ridges are known as lateral moraines (see Figure 5–14). The highest point on the valley wall reached by the glacier is often clearly evident immediately above lateral moraines; it is called a trim line. Medial moraines, like lateral moraines, are also deposited as rubble ridges by retreating glaciers but are located in from the margins of the glacier.

The terminus of a glacier is often an extensive, chaotic-appearing area extending over several square kilometers even in the case of a relatively small valley glacier. Ablation of the ice mainly proceeds from the surface downward, so that any included rubble is left on the surface of the glacier. As melt proceeds, a thick layer of morainal material may be left on the

Figure 5–13. Glaciated landscape on the Kenai peninsula, Alaska. The retreating glacier has left a large recessional moraine that forms the dam for a proglacial lake. A river has partially breached the dam and is carrying sediment-laden water to the sea, where it remains clearly visible.

Figure 5–14. Lateral moraine along the side of a valley glacier.

surface. It often is difficult to determine whether any ice remains underneath. The layer of rubble provides effective insulation from the sun and warm air, so that continued melt of any underlying ice is inhibited. Common results are formations called ice-cored moraines, which may remain downstream from the current active terminus of the glacier. In some cases, they may even develop a vegetation cover and show little evidence of the continued melting of the underlying ice. Over time, the gradual melting out of the stagnant, or dead, ice may result in uneven slumping of the ground surface, resulting in rough terrain called karst-and-kettle topography. This is often an area of impeded drainage, with many small lakes and ponds that may lack inlet and outlet streams and are often quite deep. These ponds are particularly susceptible to becoming choked with floating vegetation over a long period; they are the origin of many of the smaller bogs characteristic of cool temperate regions that were glaciated in the past (see Figure 5–15).

Morainal features may form underneath a glacier, caused by processes not fully understood. They take place deep within the glacier, but their results are evident only after the glacier has retreated. The best known of these features are called drumlins. These are generally low, rounded hills, often occurring in groups in areas that have been subject to continental glaciation. Classic drumlins are teardrop shaped, with the tail oriented downstream

Figure 5–15. Karst-and-kettle topography on the north shore of the Alaskan peninsula. The irregular topography is caused by slumping associated with the melting out of ice-cored moraine. The absence of a clear drainage pattern is typical of this formation; the level of water in the kettle ponds fluctuates according to the water table.

to the direction of ice travel; they show up well in aerial photographs. Drumlins apparently form in several ways. In some cases, they may form in the lee of a protrusion of bedrock that has apparently caused a cavity to form in the glacier; this is subsequently filled with ground moraine. These are crag-and-tail features. The origin of other drumlins is less clear; they may be formed by some irregularities or internal stresses in the ice sheet such that cavities or crevasses are formed and filled with morainal material. They may also be the result of thin ice overriding material in a recessional moraine during a readvance. Drumlins merge into a number of less distinct features that are streamlined in shape, oriented to the direction of ice flow, and unstratified.

STRATIFIED ICE-CONTACT FEATURES

Since melt occurs over the whole surface of the ablation zone of the glacier, not just near the terminus, the resulting meltwater must disperse in some way. Some water may flow on top of the ice or along its sides, but most percolates downward through crevasses and joins subglacial streams or streams contained within the body of the glacier itself. These streams also pick up quantities of morainal material from the glacier and transport it as typical streams and rivers would. Streams within a glacier change drastically both in their location and in the speed and volume of flow as the regime and position of the glacier itself changes. A subglacial stream may flow with great volume for a period of time, then abruptly disappear or change its bed, leaving behind the accumulated material deposited in its old bed. Later, as the glacier continues to retreat, these stratified deposits are themselves dropped on the surface of the emerging terrain.

The most characteristic and easily identified of these features are eskers. They are normal streambeds in many respects, but they have been deposited on the terrain as raised ridges in what amounts to a mirror image of a typical river bed. In large continental glaciers, eskers extending for tens of kilometers and reaching elevations of 10 to 100 meters are common. Eskers are particularly conspicuous in the barren grounds of northwestern Canada, where they look like immense yellowish-brown serpents superimposed on the ice-scoured bedrock. They can be an important habitat for animals that excavate dens, such as wolves and ground squirrels. In more populated areas, they may be important sources of sand and gravel.

Kames are features related to eskers that generally form by the deposition of stratified material in hollows and cavities in the glacier, particularly during the rapid disintegration of the terminus area of a retreating glacier. These deposits are ultimately dropped on the surface of the underlying terrain, where their stratigraphy is often disrupted by slumping. Since the surface of the lower reaches of a valley glacier is usually somewhat convex, kamelike deposits are often found along the valley sides. As the glacier retreats and thins, some of these deposits slump away, but some may remain perched on the valley sides. They form flat-topped, steep-sided benches and platforms known as kame terraces. These can be important agricultural land where farming is difficult because of the rough, undulating terrain associated with other glacial deposits.

Ice-Rafted Sediments

Glaciers that calve icebergs discharge most of their incorporated morainal material out to sea in the icebergs. The material is ultimately deposited on the sea floor as the icebergs melt. The distribution of these sediments can be discovered in the course of deep sea drilling studies; the sediments provide information on the distribution of icebergs in past times.

Depositional Features Associated with Glacial Meltwater

An actively ablating glacier whose terminus is on land supplies much meltwater to the surrounding environment, whether the glacier is in retreat, advance, or steady state. The features associated with this meltwater are not strictly glacial, ice-contact features but do have many characteristics that are a giveaway of their glacial origin.

When the front of a glacier has retreated from a terminal or recessional moraine, it often leaves a hollow between the terminus and the moraine. This depression generally fills with water, forming a proglacial lake (see Figure 5–13), which often contains small icebergs. The waters of a proglacial lake are generally rich in suspended materials. This usually causes the lake to have a milky appearance; at a distance the water looks blue-green. Most publicly accessible glaciers have a "Turquoise Lake" associated with them.

Normal lake depositional processes, involving the sorting of material according to size, take place in a proglacial lake, with the result that stratified deposits are superimposed on, and sometimes mixed with, the underlying till. Proglacial lakes are usually short-lived because of the unstable position of the glacial terminus. In addition, the moraines forming the downslope shore of the lake are unconsolidated and easily breached by outflow streams that may carry high volumes of water during periods of active ablation. A recessional moraine sequence will therefore generally contain evidence of the presence of a series of more or less ephemeral proglacial lakes.

Streams running away from a glacier's terminus or from a proglacial lake are generally choked with sediment. They continually drop the sediment load and build up the streambed and valley floor. The resulting flat, gently sloping deposits are called valley trains (see Figure 5–16). The meltwater streams constantly change their channels as they become choked with sediment and overflow their banks so that channels are constantly coalescing and separating in a shifting network of watercourses. This feature is known as a braided stream or braided channel system.

The topography of valley trains may be somewhat hummocky near the glacier terminus, particularly if the glacier is retreating rapidly, because of the melting out of ice-cored moraines and the development of karst-and-kettle topography. If the glacier is more stable, these features will be subdued by erosion and deposition.

Because of the unstable nature of braided drainage patterns,

Figure 5–16. Valley train near Lake Clark, Alaska. The flat, gently sloping deposit has been carried down by meltwater from a large glacier a short distance upstream. The plain continues to build up from the sediment-rich waters, which also give the lake a milky appearance.

and also because of the widely fluctuating volumes of water carried by the streams, valley trains and other outwash plains are generally lightly vegetated as long as the terminus is near. Glacial streams on outwash plains can be terribly dangerous to cross. Their volume, depth, and speed change hour by hour according to the melt of the glacier. Alpine climbing parties have been trapped or killed by glacial torrents that had been only rivulets a few hours before. As is discussed in Chapter 6, this may have been the fate of the famous frozen mammoths of Siberia.

Loess

The surface of outwash deposits, such as valley trains, includes much fine silt and rock flour. This is often blown from the surface by wind, but it is constantly replenished by sediments carried in meltwater. Great quantities of fine material are carried away from the outwash area and deposited in the form of layers of dust, and even dune fields, often far away from the outwash plain. This phenomenon is often intensified by the strong, dry winds (katabatic winds) that rise on the upper areas of the ice cap and blow down-valley. The windblown material deposited is known as loess (the German word is pronounced approximately *lurse*). Loess particles are generally angular and tend to be cohesive, so that loess deposits have a blocky structure and a high angle of repose. Stream erosion of deep loess deposits thus results in the formation of deep, steep-sided ravines (see Figure 5–17).

Some of the most productive agricultural land in the temperate regions is located in areas of deep loess deposits, which were derived from the broad outwash plains of earlier continental glaciations. These are particularly evident in Poland, Hungary, the Ukraine, and large areas of the American Midwest. Modern-day loess deposition is generally local; excellent examples of the process occur in portions of Alaska, particularly along the southern borders of the Tanana River Valley near Fairbanks.

DISTRIBUTION OF GLACIAL GEOMORPHIC FEATURES

The nature of the terrain uncovered by a glacial retreat depends on factors that control which of the various features and groups of features discussed above predominate. These factors include the nature of the topography and bedrock before the onset of glaciation, the type, extent, and duration of the glaciers, the speed of glacial retreat, the location of the area with respect to cen-

Figure 5–17. Loess deposit along the Yukon River, downstream from Tanana, Alaska. In this region of central Alaska, windblown silt built up deposits as much as 100 meters deep during the last Ice Age. Loess particles are strongly cohesive, so that steep bluffs are formed when the deposits are dissected by river erosion.

ters of glaciation, and the geomorphic history subsequent to deglaciation.

Land that is of comparatively low relief and that was near the margins of long-lasting continental ice sheets is likely to be characterized by a preponderance of depositional features including ground moraine, broad ridges of terminal moraine and associated recessional moraine, eskers, drumlins. The land is likely to be overlain by a thick blanket of loess, and to contain numerous large lakes. This type of terrain is characteristic of much of the American Midwest and the plains of eastern Europe.

Similar terrain that lies nearer to the original centers of glaciation (usually farther north) was generally deglaciated much more rapidly, so that depositional features are much less in evidence. The landscape may be dominated by scoured and polished bedrock with quantities of glacial erratics scattered about on the surface. The abundant lakes tend to be bowls and grooves carved into the bedrock, and large canyons called meltwater channels abound where immense quantities of captive meltwater broke their bounds suddenly and created catastrophic but temporary floods. Landscapes of this type are common in much of eastern Canada and Scandinavia. They are particularly well displayed in northern areas where forest growth and soil formation have not progressed to the point of masking the underlying glacial features. (See Figure 5–18.)

In areas of greater original relief, but where the thickness of the ice was such as to totally override the landscape, features such as roche moutonnees and crag-and-tail features abound. The topography is controlled by the nature of its surface prior to glaciation, by the relative resistance of the often complex bedrock, and by the interaction between the relief of the terrain and the movement of the overriding glaciers. Uplands and valleys can exert a strong influence on the local ice flow and thus clearly affect the local erosional characteristics of the glacier. Lakes in these hilly areas are often long and deep, similar to fiords. Examples include the Finger Lakes of western New York state and some of the lochs of Scotland.

In areas of truly mountainous terrain, continental glaciers have often left the summits of the highest peaks unglaciated, or, more likely, subjected to the action of subsidiary local alpine glaciers. The higher peaks were thus nunataks, and their features are typical of alpine glacial activity.

This phenomenon becomes particularly relevant in high

Figure 5–18. Terrain exposed by a rapidly retreating continental glacier along the southern coast of Labrador. Because a typical continental ice sheet is clean and retreats rapidly, most of the features here are erosional rather than depositional. The feature on the right is a typical *roche moutonnee.*

mountain systems located near a seacoast, particularly if deep water lies immediately offshore. As discussed in Chapter 4, the various characteristics of glacial ice limit ice sheets with respect to the gradient from their margins toward their center. If inland ice is flowing to the sea through valleys in coastal mountain ranges and is discharging into deep water, increased accumulation will result in increased speed and discharge, but not in an overall thickening of the ice sheet. Hence, the uplands will remain unglaciated, while intense erosion takes place on the valley floors and sides. This situation results in particularly spectacular scenery, with high alpine peaks, precipitous crags, and deep valleys and fiords. This process has provided the basis for the renowned scenery of Norway, New Zealand, and southern Alaska, while many of the coastal regions of Greenland and Antarctica are currently undergoing the same process.

Where glaciers approach the coast in less precipitous terrain, they may remain grounded far outward from the present seacoast, overriding and polishing to bedrock any islands, and producing a partially drowned glaciated landscape. The smooth outcrops of more resistant bedrock protrude as scattered islands, known as skerries (see Figure 5–19), which are common in the Baltic Sea and along the coast of Norway and eastern Canada.

Figure 5–19. Skerries along the south coast of the island of New-foundland. Skerries are a characteristic feature of glaciated coastlines, where the rising water has drowned the ice-scoured terrain, creating an intricate shoreline and innumerable islands, channels, ledges, and coves.

Past alpine glaciers were similar to those that are currently widespread, and the features they left behind are essentially identical to those that are presently being formed in most of the higher mountain regions of temperate and some tropical latitudes. A careful study of features generally associated with alpine glaciation in hilly regions that are not presently glaciated can provide considerable insight into the processes of glaciation and deglaciation of these regions in times past. In some cases, the continental ice sheets retreated rapidly and completely, leaving only exposed, ice-free terrain with no residual glaciation. In other areas, alpine glaciers persisted for some hundreds or thousands of years, and the features of alpine glaciation superimposed on the generally glaciated terrain are clearly evident.

Proglacial lakes were often large and abundant in hilly terrain as the glaciers retreated. In many cases, these lakes were impounded by dams of ice, as in the case of a major valley glacier persisting when some of its tributary glaciers had already retreated. Large lakes, often at high elevations, can be formed in this fashion, but they are exceedingly unstable because of the tenuous nature of the ice dams. Thus, otherwise inexplicable temporary shorelines and lake deposits, and a variety of other features, are common in some hilly areas. They are particularly evident in northern New England.

SUGGESTED FURTHER READING

Many sources of information on glacial geomorphology also deal more broadly with the Quaternary Period and are listed after Chapter 7.

Davies, J. L. *Landforms of Cold Climates.* Cambridge, MA: MIT Press, 1969.

Embleton, C., and C. A. M. King. *Glacial and Periglacial Geomorphology.* London: Edward Arnold, 1975.

Flint, R. F. *Glacial and Quaternary Geology.* New York: John Wiley, 1971.

Sugden, D. E., and B. S. John. *Glaciers and Landscape.* New York: John Wiley, 1976.

Chapter 6

The Periglacial Environment

WE discussed the nature of ice in some detail in Chapter 3 and looked at conspicuous icy phenomena there and in the chapters on glaciers. As important as all of these features and processes are, their total effect on the polar environment is at least matched by more subtle processes that occur within the soils, surface deposits, and even the bedrock of the cold lands. Because these processes and the features associated with them are often buried in otherwise normal-appearing ground, they were largely undiscovered, or at least unappreciated, until the mid-twentieth century march into the polar regions.

The beginnings of understanding in Westerners of the action of deep, prolonged cold on the soil may well have been the result of the need to deal with someone's dead body, following the European tradition of burying corpses. This would have been a common problem in the early days of arctic exploration and colonization, or with the Greenland colonists of the tenth and eleventh centuries. During the warm arctic summers, there is good reason to get a fallen comrade under ground as expeditiously as possible, but normal gravedigging is doomed to failure in most arctic areas. The ground from about the depth of an average coffin is permanently frozen and has the consistency of concrete. Ice and its effects are inescapable in the far north, even if no ice is visible for miles in any direction. Somewhere within a few inches of the traveler's footsteps is ice, a continuous, frozen infrasurface hidden just below the visible top layer of the ground.

In counterpoint to the burial problem, any organic matter, once incorporated in frozen ground, is preserved intact as long as the ground is frozen. The famous frozen mammoths of Siberia did not fall into glaciers as is sometimes suggested in the popular press; they were frozen in permafrost. We'll see how they may have gotten there later in this chapter. Recent eerie and macabre studies have been carried out on the remains of early Greenland colonists, unlucky explorers, and Eskimo victims of *ivu*. As a result, we know a remarkable amount about various physical pathologies of earlier polar people, and probably at least one murder by poisoning has been discovered, if not solved.

Perennially frozen ground, or permafrost, underlies most of Siberia, and efforts to extend agriculture east of the Urals brought about the first serious confrontations between Western technology and adamantly frozen soil. Soviet scientists continue to be among the world leaders in the field of study dealing with what are now generally known as periglacial phenomena. This is something of an unfortunate term, since it seems to imply a connection with glaciers. It actually refers to the climate found in the vicinity or on the periphery of glaciated regions. Periglacial climates are characterized by intense cold, but with enough thaw, or with low enough precipitation, as to exclude the formation of extensive glaciers. Periglacial phenomena comprise those aspects of the soil, sediments, and substrate that are associated with prolonged or intense frost action, or both; and with temperatures below freezing. By this definition, it is easy to see that periglacial phenomena commonly occur in areas that are not now, and may never have been, associated with glacial activity. Some scientists refer to frost soil phenomena to avoid confusion, and many Western scientists have now adopted the term *geocryology* for the study of frost soil phenomena.

Some periglacial phenomena occur where intense cold in winter and deep seasonal freezing are followed by complete thaw in the following warm season. But most typical features of the periglacial zone are associated with mean annual temperatures below freezing, resulting in the soil or substrate being permanently, or at least perennially, at a temperature below freezing.

PERMAFROST

The word *permafrost* is also misleading, since it technically refers to ground that is frozen during two or more successive cold seasons and the intervening summers, rather than necessarily being permanently frozen. Also, the term *permafrost* doesn't necessarily mean that the material referred to is frozen in the sense of containing water in the form of ice. Desiccated sands or bedrock can also be called permafrost. On the other hand, glacial ice and liquid water at temperatures below 0°C, as occur in some areas where water has a high content of salts, are not normally considered to be permafrost. Though these provisos can be important, the majority of permafrost conditions and most of the features characteristic of permafrost are found in soils and other unconsolidated sediments.

Permafrost is distributed throughout the colder portions of the earth's surface and can normally be found wherever local mean annual temperatures are at least slightly below freezing. Permafrost may or may not underlie glaciers; by definition, a warm glacier (see Chapter 4), with a film of liquid water at its base, would not allow formation of permafrost underneath its bed. The effects of permafrost usually are best seen on terrain that is currently unglaciated and that has not been subject to glaciation in the recent past.

Because its presence is dependent on low annual temperature regimes, permafrost is a phenomenon of higher latitudes and altitudes. However, because permafrost depends on low annual temperature, rather than on temperature during the growing season, the distribution of permafrost has little or no relationship to the distribution of biologically defined subdivisions of the polar regions such as the tundra and boreal forest. Not all tundra areas are underlain by permafrost, and deep and continuous permafrost is found hundreds of kilometers inside the timberline in areas of intensely continental climate. Surprisingly, as much as 25 percent of the land area of China is believed to be underlain by permafrost. Such permafrost would be found mainly in the high mountains and plateaus of Tibet and Inner Mongolia.

Permafrosted regions are often separated into two zones, the *zone of continuous permafrost* and the *zone of discontinuous permafrost*. The southern portions of the latter zone, where permafrost may exist only in isolated locations under special conditions, is sometimes further separated as the *zone of sporadic permafrost*. The general distribution of permafrost zones in the Northern Hemisphere is shown in Figure 6–1.

Permafrost also occurs in alpine regions in low latitudes. Since this occurrence is generally on alpine summits of bare rock, talus, and fell field, most features generally associated with lowland permafrost are usually absent in alpine situations.

Extensive areas of permafrost under the sea floor on the continental shelf of many northern areas have recently been discovered. Some scientists believe that its presence dates from a period when the continental shelves were exposed by eustatic changes in sea level, rather than being an effect of current below-freezing temperatures of the sea. In any case, a number of features typical of terrestrial lowland permafrost environments also occur on shallow sea floors. This is of more than passing interest for petroleum production and shipping. Small, steep-sided permafrost hills called pingos (discussed below) are known to protrude from the otherwise level sea floor, and these could be disastrous for heavy oil tankers.

Permafrost extends to depths of 1,500 meters or more in parts of Siberia and probably goes nearly as deep in some areas of northern Canada and Alaska. Most of the information on this subject is gathered in the process of oil exploration, so its distribution is spotty. It is clear, though, that the overall depth of permafrost penetration is variable and related to present and past conditions. Other factors being equal, permafrost depth should depend on the coldness of the climate and the duration of the cold climate regime. The lowermost level to which permafrost extends is theoretically a function of an equilibrium point at which the geothermal heat gradient of the earth's interior intersects with the cooling gradient, related to low atmospheric temperatures and the heat budget at the soil surface. Hence, the depth to which permafrost can penetrate is ultimately limited. It probably takes a cold temperature regime lasting for many thousands of years to force permafrost to penetrate to the depths recorded in Siberia and Alaska. Deep permafrost is therefore generally thought to be fossil or relict permafrost, reflecting extreme low temperature regimes reaching far back in time. The

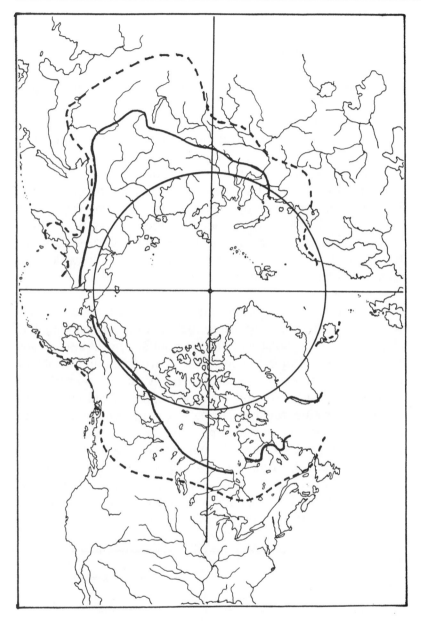

Figure 6–1. Distribution of permafrost throughout the circumpolar North. The solid line marks the approximate boundary of continuous permafrost and the broken line the limit of discontinuous permafrost at low elevations. Sporadic permafrost in mountainous regions such as Tibet is not indicated. Data on the depth of permafrost is sketchy, but the deepest freeze is in parts of Siberia and northern Canada, where frozen ground is encountered over 1,000 meters down.

presence of deep permafrost also reflects glacial history, since the presence of a continental ice sheet 1,000 or more meters thick should have an inhibiting effect on frost penetration, even if it were a cold glacier. Some support for this view comes from the Canadian high Arctic, most of which was heavily glaciated; here permafrost depths are generally shallower than in unglaciated areas in Alaska and Siberia that now have comparable temperature regimes.

Since permafrost only includes the portion of the soil or substrate frozen throughout the warm season, permafrost is normally surmounted by a layer of seasonally thawed ground, the active layer. The depth to which thaw penetrates is directly related to summer temperatures. Other factors being equal, warm summers cause a deep active layer, whatever the annual temperature and total depth of permafrost. The depth of the active layer has some effect on the biota of an area. The distribution of deep-rooted plants and burrowing animals depends on a deep active layer, both locally and regionally.

Permafrost, then, is the layer of perennially frozen material bounded on top by the deepest penetration of the active layer and on the bottom by the depth of permafrost penetration. Where the active layer and the underlying unfrozen layer intersect, permafrost is not present, and the area in which this situation occurs locally is the zone of discontinuous permafrost (see Figure 6–2).

Many factors besides atmospheric temperature affect depth of freeze and depth of thaw. These include direction and angle of slope exposure, insulation of the soil surface by various means, variations in moisture content of the active layer, and insolation (the rate of delivery of direct solar energy) at the soil surface as affected by cloud cover and vegetation cover. Variations in these factors determine whether permafrost is present locally in the zone of discontinuous permafrost and determine the depth of the active layer in the zone of continuous permafrost. Figure 6–2 shows a schematic representation of the distribution of permafrost on an ideal transect, or sample area, from north to south.

Most kinds of permafrost are impervious to the percolation of water. This means that there can be no subsoil drainage of free

Figure 6–2. An idealized cross section showing changes in depth and continuity of permafrost and of the active layer from north to south. To the left is continuous permafrost, ranging progressively deeper and with a shallower active layer toward the north.

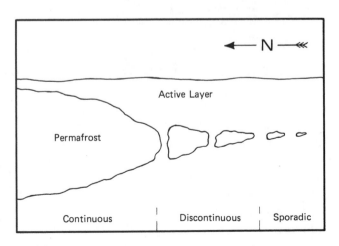

water from thawed topsoil underlain by or surrounded by permafrost. The active layer often consists of saturated material of a soupy consistency, called *talik* (tah-leek'). Talik may flow and slump under the force of gravity. This causes phenomena typical of permafrosted landscapes, which will be examined later in this chapter. It is possible for deep masses of talik to form within areas of deep continuous permafrost, for example, in thawing that may occur under a lake or river. These talik masses have important implications for other phenomena such as pingos, which will be examined later in this chapter.

FROST PHENOMENA

We've mentioned that the change of water between a liquid and a solid state is a complex process with special implications for polar environments and organisms. Most processes and results of freeze-thaw cycles depend on the fact that water expands as it freezes and can exert great pressure on whatever may contain it, be it a beer bottle or a chunk of rock on the head wall of a cirque.

Frost action depends on freezing and thawing, rather than the duration of low temperatures, so frost effects are not limited to the permafrost zone. They occur wherever temperatures at the soil surface dip below freezing, although the effects are small and ephemeral where frost is rare. Frost action's effectiveness is largely related to the number of transitions between ice and liquid water; the results of frost action are most conspicuous where the freeze-thaw cycle occurs often, rather than in areas of extreme cold. Frost action is dependent on the presence of water, so frost features are usually weakly developed in arid lands. On the other hand, a continental climate, with its great seasonal and daily variations in temperature, is an ideal site for freeze-thaw cycles.

Frost Wedging

Frost wedging is one of the most characteristic features associated with the freeze-thaw cycle. It is simply the splitting apart of material, generally rock, by the action of freezing water. We have seen how important this can be in breaking off material from headwalls of cirques and along the oversteepened sides of glacial valleys; it is the process responsible for much of the morainal material incorporated in alpine glaciers.

Frost wedging is equally effective on gentle slopes and level

Figure 6–3. Block field, or *felsen-meer,* near the summit of Gros Morne, Newfoundland. The large, angular blocks of quartzite have been split off from the underlying bedrock by frost wedging.

areas of exposed bedrock, such as are often left behind after glaciers have retreated. Over time, exposed bedrock is often mantled by a deep layer of frost-shattered rubble associated with frost wedging on the surface. The rubble may destroy or mask evidence of earlier glacial activity. It confuses efforts to determine the exact extent of previous glaciation. Fields and slopes of frost-shattered rubble are called *felsenmeer* (see Figure 6–3). On a steep slope, rubble will generally collect in an apron at the bottom, forming a scree or talus slope.

The effectiveness of frost wedging depends on such factors as the number and intensity of freeze-thaw cycles, the presence of water, and the nature of the substrate. Hard rocks, such as are often found in dikes and sills, may be exposed by continued frost wedging and the mass wasting of the surrounding softer matrix. Precipitous crags, called tors (see Figure 6–4), formed in this fashion are common on slopes and ridge tops in areas that now have, or once had, a periglacial climate; they can also result from other, nonfrost processes.

Frost Heaving

The effects of frost action do not cease when the surface layer of exposed bedrock has been reduced to rubble. Rock fragments and boulders embedded in a matrix of finer material show the effects of frost action in an array of related phenomena called collectively frost heaving. Frost heaving tends to affect different-sized particles differently and so results in the sorting of material

Figure 6–4. Tors in the Tanana upland, central Alaska. These masses of resistant bedrock have been exposed by the solifluction of surface debris down the gentle slope.

on the basis of size. For example, boulders embedded in un-stratified glacial till are often segregated and raised to the surface of the deposit, as is well known to farmers of previously glaciated terrain such as New England. This process is equally effective with respect to artificial structures such as foundation walls, and has also often been observed in human burials too shallow to lower the remains below the seasonal frost line. In spite of its ubiquity in cold climates, the actual mechanisms of frost heaving are not well understood. Rather than consider a variety of alternative explanations, we will simply say here that frost heaving is a major cause of the sorting of previously undifferentiated material (such as the surface of glacial till) into size classes. This sorting is an important cause of many types of patterned ground found in the polar regions.

PATTERNED GROUND

Figure 6–5. Ice-wedge polygons on the arctic coastal plain near Barrow, Alaska. The low centers, the raised bordering ridges, and the ditch between the ridges over the underlying ice wedge are clearly visible in this photograph, taken from an airplane at an elevation of about 500 meters.

Most polar terrain that isn't exposed bedrock, covered with glacial ice, or mantled by dense vegetation cover shows patterning on the surface. The patterns are called polygons, circles, nets, stripes, and steps. Their form is related to slope, so that polygons and circles, which occur on level, flat areas, become increasingly elongated as slope angle increases. On steep slopes they become linear features such as stripes. Patterned ground is both classified on the basis of shape and separated into two major categories on the basis of whether its constituent materials are sorted or unsorted.

Unsorted Polygons

Unsorted polygons are perhaps the commonest kind of patterned ground. They occur over vast expanses of low, flat areas, mostly within the zone of continuous permafrost (see Figure 6–5). The processes that cause their formation are apparently weak or inactive at mean annual temperatures above –6° to –8°C. Where these polygons are found in slightly warmer conditions, they are assumed to be inactive relics of past colder climates.

The process by which unsorted polygons form is well understood. It initially depends on another cold climate phenomenon known as frost cracking, which is distinct from frost wedging, although it also involves the formation of wedge-shaped

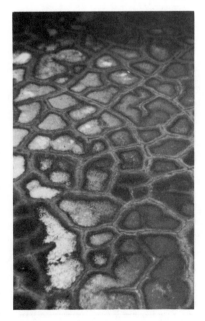

deposits of ice in the soil. These features are commonly called ice-wedge polygons.

If frozen terrain is subjected to temperatures far below freezing for a long time, the surface begins to contract, and stresses build up in the frozen soil. The surface may then crack in much the same way as does drying mud at the bottom of a mud puddle, but on a much larger scale.

Frost cracks can occur in nonpermafrosted areas but cannot penetrate below the depth of freezing. In permafrost conditions, they can extend only to the depth that the cold penetrates during the winter, since, if there are no significant changes in temperature, there can be no expansion and contraction. The amount of contraction, and thus the width of the crack, depends on how much the material is chilled. Since the temperature differential is greatest near the surface of the ground, the crack will be widest at the top and will narrow down to a point, appearing wedge shaped in cross section (see Figure 6–6).

The snow at the soil surface begins to melt on the first warm day, but since the deep soil stays cold, cracks remain open. The frost cracks then fill with water from snow melt in early summer. The water freezes immediately, creating a narrow, wedge-shaped vein of ice filling the crack. Later in the summer, as the deeper permafrost warms up toward the freezing point, it expands. However, since the crack is now filled with ice, the expansion can only take place in an upward direction. The surface of the soil along the borders of the crack is thus raised slightly, forming a ridge along each side of the top of the ice-filled crack (see Figure 6–6).

Because clear, solid ice has a lower tensile strength than frozen soil, during the next winter frost, cracks reoccur in the ice wedges. In the next spring thaw, the process of inflow of meltwater and freezing repeats, adding an increment of ice to the ice wedge. As the sequence of frost cracking, inflow of water, freezing, and expansion is repeated year after year, large bodies of ice form in the upper layers of the sediments. At the same time, the ridges at the border of the ice wedges continue to grow. Since there is no sorting process included in the formation of ice-wedge polygons, they are a type of unsorted polygon.

Ice-wedge polygons range in size from a few meters in diameter to as much as 100 meters. They usually have low centers bordered by the ridges, and the centers are often filled with water during the summer, forming shallow ponds. The minor changes in topography associated with the ridges and centers of

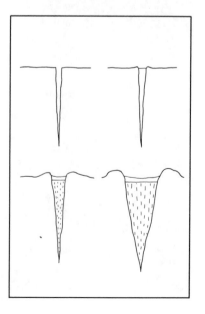

Figure 6–6. Formation of an ice-wedge polygon. At top left is the initial frost crack, extending several meters deep into the frozen ground. At top right, the crack has filled with meltwater, which has frozen immediately, expanding and causing the beginnings of ridges at the sides of the crack. At lower left, the growing ice wedge has gone through several seasons: The ridges are expanding and a layer of moss and debris covers the surface of the wedge. At lower right, the wedge has grown and persisted for many years and is typical of those associated with the patterned ground shown in Figure 6–5.

ice-wedge polygons are enough to cause noticeable differences in vegetation between the centers and the ridges, and this may accentuate the distinctive appearance of the polygons (see Figure 6–5). A low-center polygon may undergo further development by formation of additional secondary ice wedges in the center or by the increase in size of the ice wedges such that most of the interior is raised above the surrounding terrain. It is also common for the upper surfaces of the ice wedges to melt out, generally because changes in the local drainage pattern allow the meltwater to be carried away. The material at the edge of the polygon may then slump into the trough created by the melting wedge. The result is a polygon with a raised center, called a high-center polygon (see Figure 6–7).

Ice-wedge polygons are of great importance in the polar environment. They cover extensive areas, provide microrelief in areas that are otherwise essentially featureless (see Figure 6–8), and are associated with processes that form great volumes of ground ice in the soil. As we might expect, other processes result in the melting out of this ground ice, so that an equilibrium is established. The ice-destructive processes collectively are called thermokarst; they are discussed later in this chapter.

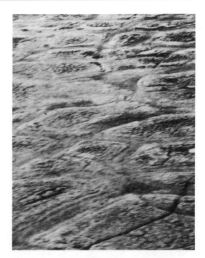

Figure 6–7. High-center polygons. These are mainly the result of alteration, through the partial melting out of the surrounding ice wedges, of normal low-center ice-wedge polygons, with consequent slumping of material into the resulting ditches.

Figure 6–8. The arctic coastal plain of Alaska, a region of deeply permafrosted sediments. Here the interaction of ice-wedge polygons, thaw lakes, river channels, and related features results in a complex landscape dominated by shallow water and shifting ground.

Figure 6–9. Stone nets, or sorted polygons, in western Alaska. Each polygon is a little less than a meter in diameter. The finer material has been segregated toward the center, allowing colonization by moss and other vegetation, and accentuating the differences in size of the particles.

Figure 6–10. Another group of sorted polygons, in the uplands of insular Newfoundland. The larger (greater than two-meter) structures are on a slight slope and tend to be elongated. If the slope were steeper, they would appear as stripes.

Sorted Polygons, Nets, and Stripes

Sorted features that are polygonal or netlike probably result from a combination of patterning processes, probably mainly frost cracking, and sorting processes that result from frost heaving. Sorted polygonal features are common in uplands where the soil includes much coarse gravel and rock. These features tend to become elongated or linear as the angle of the slope increases (see Figures 6–9 and 6–10).

Any of the patterned ground features mentioned creates variability and microtopography in the terrain. These may control such factors as drainage, soil particle size, depth and duration of snow cover, and exposure. This, in turn, affects the nature of the vegetation on a local scale, so that longstanding patterned ground features are often visually enhanced by related patterns in vegetation.

ICE-CORED MOUNDS

Large, steep-sided mounds called pingos are prominent in many arctic areas, particularly where there is otherwise low relief (see Figures 6–11 and 6–12). Smaller mounds, called palsas, are found widely in peatlands south of the zone of continuous permafrost. Although pingos and palsas differ in size, distribution, and mode of formation, they are both associated with permafrost, and both contain masses of ice in their interior. The distinction between the two forms may not always be as clear-cut as was once believed.

Pingos are generally separated into two types, depending on how they form. Here, too, the distinction may not always be justified. The process of the formation of a pingo is as remarkable as its appearance, whether it is a closed system, or Mackenzie Valley-type pingo, or an open system, or East Greenland-type pingo.

The initial stages of the formation of a closed system pingo depend on the presence of a deep and reasonably voluminous body of unfrozen talik, surrounded on the sides and bottom by permafrost. How might this come to be?

When a body of water such as a lake or large river is located in a permafrost environment, the water acts as a heat source that allows thawing under its bed. If the water is too deep to freeze to the bottom, there is no seasonal refreezing because of the insulating effect of the water above. Over many years the thaw goes deep, creating a bulb of talik.

Figure 6–11. A pingo, apparently in the early stages of development, in the arctic lowland of Alaska. The channel by which the earlier thaw lake drained away to a nearby river is clearly visible above the rising mound. The presence of ice-wedge polygons on the pingo surface indicates that additional periglacial processes are taking place simultaneously with pingo formation.

Lakes and riverbeds in permafrost areas tend to be unstable; they may drain or change course in a number of ways, of which thermokarst is generally the most important. If a lake underlain by a deep talik bed drains, the talik begins to refreeze. Freezing proceeds inward from the sides, upward from the permafrost below the talik, and from the top of the newly exposed lake floor.

Figure 6–12. A mature pingo in the Mission lowland, lower Noatak River drainage, arctic Alaska. This pingo is obviously quite old; it supports the only trees in the area, probably because of a combination of drainage and a south-facing slope.

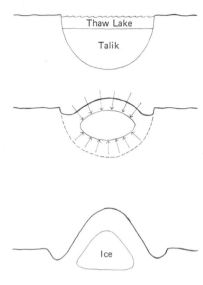

Figure 6–13. How a closed-system pingo forms. In the initial stage (top), a thaw lake develops a deep bulb of unfrozen talik below it. If the lake drains, freezing of the talik proceeds from top, bottom, and sides (center). Water in the talik is segregated as the talik freezes and is forced toward the center of the growing pingo. When all the talik and extruded water are frozen, the pingo ceases to grow (bottom). An open-system pingo depends on an artesian water source and so is more commonly found in areas of discontinuous permafrost.

As freezing proceeds and the water in the saturated talik expands, liquid water is forced out of the freezing sediments. This water wells up under the crust of vegetation and newly frozen soil of the lake bed. It then freezes, causing a raised mound with a core of pure ice to form. The process continues until the entire talik bulb is frozen and all of its liquid water extruded; this water in turn is frozen in the interior of the mound. At this point, the mound has become a mature pingo, with a core of solid ice (see Figure 6–13).

Open system pingos, also known as East Greenland-type pingos, depend on an artesian water source rather than water forced out of talik by cryostatic pressure. Hence, they are likely to occur in areas where permafrost is not continuous or deep. They are otherwise similar to closed system pingos.

The surface of a pingo is composed of old lake bottom sediments. This crust may be several meters thick. It is normally held in place by vegetation, sometimes including trees. If the surface material is disturbed, the ice core melts. The pingo may then collapse in ruins or develop a crater that makes it resemble a volcano.

Pingos range in size from a few meters high to as high as 50 to 75 meters. Large ones may be 500 or more meters in diameter.

Figure 6–14. A palsa near Shef-ferville, Quebec. Although this may be the most intensively studied palsa in the world (note the instrumentation), the process and life history of palsas are still incompletely understood. They are most common in the more temperate portions of the periglacial zone, where the one shown is located.

Although they are most often circular in outline, oval or elongated pingos are also common.

Relatively little information is available on the speed of growth of pingos or on their life expectancy. It has been speculated that most existing pingos were formed during specific periods, but little definitive evidence supports this suggestion. In any case, changes in pingos usually aren't obvious from year to year.

Palsas (see Figure 6–14) are smaller than most pingos and are more inclined to be irregular in outline. They can occur as extended ridges, rather than discrete mounds. Palsas occur in peatlands; their interiors usually consist mainly of peat. The peaty mounds contain ice lenses, generally of small volume. Although the processes by which palsas form are still obscure, differential frost heaving, perhaps associated with variations in snow cover, is likely to be involved.

A feature related to palsas and often associated with them is called string bog or strangmoor. String bogs are wet peatlands with networks of peaty ridges. They enclose small ponds called *flarks,* creating a terraced, or rice paddy, effect (see Figure 6–15). String bogs are widespread in the Subarctic and in warmer parts of the Arctic. They are also seen in some cool, moist, temperate regions free of permafrost. The mechanisms by which string bogs form are, like those that form palsas, poorly understood.

Figure 6–15. An area of string bog, or strangmoor, in western Newfoundland. The small rice-paddy-like ponds are called flarks. The processes by which strangmoors form, like those that form palsas in similar areas, are not fully understood.

GELIFLUCTION AND RELATED FEATURES AND PROCESSES

Loose surface material on a slope tends to move downslope by gravity. This process can be accelerated by factors related to freeze-thaw cycles and the presence of permafrost. The creeping, downslope movement of soil is known as solifluction; solifluction associated with periglacial processes is called gelifluction.

While underlying permafrost provides a barrier to drainage water from above, seasonally frozen soil provides additional water to the soil of the active layer as thaw progresses. The frozen surface below the talik then provides a smooth, lubricated surface over which the thawed, saturated, surficial material may slide in what is called solifluction. The freeze-thaw cycle of the active layer also intensifies solifluction. When the active layer freezes, it increases in volume and hence thickness as a result of the expansion of freezing water. This expansion raises the surface of the soil in a direction perpendicular to the angle of the slope (see Figure 6–16). On thawing, the ground settles, but the direction of its downward movement is directed by gravity—it settles straight downward—so that it is redeposited slightly downslope from its original location.

Gelifluction often forms lobes of downward creeping material that drip down the sides of the slope, giving the appearance of

Figure 6–16. The ratchet effect in soil movement downslope related to frost action. Each winter freezing episode forces the surface of the soil to rise perpendicular to the slope of the hill (left), but each summer thaw allows slumping straight downward.

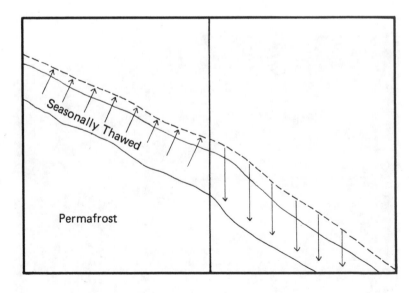

candle wax or poorly applied varnish (see Figure 6–17). Gelifluction interacts with some of the ground patterning phenomena, helping to create stone stripes and steps. Since gelifluction may result in the transport and removal of large quantities of material, including coarse, frost-shattered rubble, it is instrumental in creating tors.

Gelifluction lobes move slowly and last for many years. Vegetation patterns often respond to the stable solifluction lobes and

Figure 6–17. Solifluction lobes on the Seward peninsula, Alaska. The appearance of these slowly slumping lobes is accentuated by a denser growth of vegetation in the protected area along the lower surface of the lobe.

accentuate their outlines. But the lobes can also move rapidly enough to overturn and bury existing vegetation. A cross section of a solifluction lobe may display convoluted soil patterns and inclusions, including frozen and preserved plant material. This situation has implications for investigations that rely on stratigraphy for interpretation. Material found at an archaeological site, for example, might easily be misinterpreted if its stratigraphy has been disrupted by solifluction.

Periglacial processes can affect the movement and orientation of surface material in other ways. Freeze-thaw cycles and frost wedging, for example, can initiate rock slides and rock falls. Talus or scree slopes (see Chapter 5) are a common result. These are simply apronlike deposits of boulders and rubble that have broken away from a steep slope. While talus slopes are not confined to polar regions, they are particularly common at high latitudes and high elevations where intense frost action is common. Their presence is a result not only of periglacial processes, but also of the history of glaciation in many mountainous and polar regions, which has left oversteepened slopes and valley sides.

A common feature of talus slopes in cold regions is a protalus rampart (see Figure 6–18). This garlandlike deposit of boulders and coarse material forms a ridge near the base of the talus slope. It forms in association with a deep, long-lasting snowbed at the base of the slope. Material sliding down the talus lands on the smooth, hard-packed surface of the snow patch and slides to the base. This also occurs at the lip of a cirque containing a deep snowbed or small glacier; the protalus rampart in this case may look like a small recessional moraine. It may also help dam a tarn lake if the snowpatch later melts away.

Rock glaciers, a formation related to talus, consist of the same sort of material as talus slopes. Their surface, however, has a lobate, wavy appearance, indicating that the mass of material is, or was at one time, in motion. Rock glaciers include fine material and ice in their interior portions, apparently the cause of their movement. Rock glaciers may retain their characteristic appearance after the ice has melted out, which explains their occurrence in temperate regions. They therefore may also provide evidence of the occurrence of periglacial conditions at earlier times. As might be expected, rock glaciers can intergrade with ice-cored moraines associated with retreating true glaciers and with protalus ramparts.

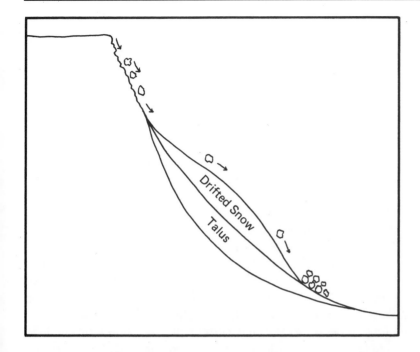

Figure 6–18. How a protalus rampart forms. Ice wedging detaches rock and rubble from the steep slope; the material slides down the smooth surface of the snow and stops at the foot of the drift. After the snow patch melts, visualizing the process that resulted in such a garland of rock and rubble is difficult.

THERMOKARST

Earlier we looked at processes that result in the buildup of ice in the soil and sediments of permafrosted regions. Among the more important of these processes are the formation of ice wedges, the growth of pingos, and the leaving behind of ice-cored moraines as glaciers retreat. The volume of ice contained in the soil and sediments of some polar areas is truly remarkable. It has been estimated that some 50 to 90 percent of the volume of the top 10 meters or so of the terrain in the vicinity of Barrow, Alaska, is solid ice. A permanent underground observation tunnel some 10 meters long was constructed entirely within a single block of massive ground ice near Barrow.

Other processes counteract the continued buildup of ground ice. The amount of ice in the ground can be thought of as the result of an equilibrial system. This means that there is an innate instability in the system at any given time, and the continued buildup of ground ice will tend to set in motion the processes that reverse the buildup. Furthermore, the balance between the constructive and destructive processes can be delicate, and minor perturbations in the environment can trigger massive alterations in the amount of ground ice.

The processes that result in the melting out of ground ice are called thermokarst processes. Karst topography is formed when subsidence of the terrain surface takes place differently in different areas because of the loss of underlying material, as in a limestone topography of caves and sinkholes. Thermokarst is thus a special type of karst situation in which the loss of material is due to melt.

Thermokarst processes are most prevalent in the upper layers of ice-rich sediments where underlying permafrost layers inhibit the draining away of the free water that is formed as a result of ice melt. Consequently, thermokarst processes generally result in the formation of shallow lakes and ponds. These tend to increase in size as melt-out continues.

Thermokarst lakes, also known as thaw lakes, dominate large areas of ice-rich landscapes. Portions of the Arctic Lowland of Alaska, for example, are well over half water covered. An interesting feature of many thermokarst lakes is the parallel orientation of their long axes. Although the development of this situation is not fully understood, the long axes of lakes on the Arctic Lowland are generally perpendicular to the direction of the prevailing winds. Factors other than the wind, however, such as the nature of the underlying substrate, may also be involved.

Thaw lakes tend to increase in size more or less indefinitely through continued ice melt and slumping of the margins. In areas where the terrain contains a certain amount of relief, the expanding margins of thaw lakes usually reach lower-lying ground, which soon results in the drainage of the water from the lake. Hence, drained lake beds, or playas, are common features of thermokarst topography. The unconsolidated sediments of drained lake beds are subject to wind erosion and transport, and dunes commonly develop as a result (see Figure 6–19).

As we saw, drained thaw lake beds also create a situation where pingo formation can take place. In low-lying areas of minimal relief, thermokarst lakes may coalesce to form immense compound lakes. Further breakdown of the shores may result in the merging of the lake with adjacent shallow seas and river mouths, forming deep bays and estuaries such as are common along the northern coast of Alaska and western Canada (see Figure 6–8).

A related phenomenon of gentle slopes is the formation of beaded drainages (see Figure 6–20). These are small rills or valleys that contain series of small, often regularly spaced pools, connected by small streams or rivulets. They result from the

Figure 6–19. Playa, or drained thaw lake, in arctic Alaska.

partial melting out of ground ice where small streams flow over the surfaces of ice wedges. Compound beaded drainages, where a gentle slopes is covered by a network of tiny ponds and intersecting streamlets, are sometimes visible.

The transformation of low-center polygons to high-center polygons is also a form of thermokarst activity involving the partial melting out of ice wedges. This transformation is particularly evident along shorelines and river bluffs. It often results in

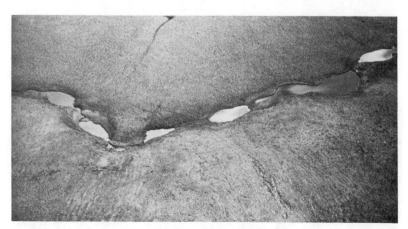

Figure 6–20. Beaded drainage system. The small ponds form as a rivulet crosses a hidden ice wedge and causes some melt out and slumping.

remarkably regular, evenly-spaced, conical hilly formations or triangular, faceted structures along bluffs (see Figure 6–21). Although these are widespread in the north, the only name for them is *baydjarakh,* a Russian word not in common use in North America.

In addition to its significance in creating the specific thermokarst features we have discussed, thermokarst is important in more specialized dynamic processes in ice-rich terrain. Some of these processes appear to be cyclical. They may result in a predictable progression from forested areas to open bog flats and marshes, followed by the reestablishment of forest. This situation can be seen in action in the "drunken forests" common in permafrosted areas in the Subarctic, where trees are actively uprooted by permafrost action. Once the area has been deforested, solar energy can reach the soil surface. Rethawing of the permafrost then occurs, ultimately allowing reestablishment of tree cover.

Thermokarst action may also result in the formation of depressions that do not fill with water and become lakes. These are particularly common in some parts of Siberia, where they are called *alases* (ay'-lus-us). They are seldom identified in North America, but they may be more common than has generally been supposed.

Even where the amount of solid ice in the soil is minimal, thermokarst action can be important. The physical properties of soil change dramatically when soil changes from a frozen to a thawed state. These changes are particularly significant if the newly thawed material is underlain by permafrost, so that drainage is impeded. In this case, thawing produces talik, which has essentially no mechanical strength and is subject to flow and

Figure 6–21. Bluff along the lower Colville River, arctic Alaska. These regular features are apparently formed by the melting out of ice wedges. From the river level they appear to be conical, regularly spaced hillocks. These are apparently similar or identical to features known as *baydjarakhs* in the Soviet Union.

slumping. Talik can be produced through human activities as well, and can have strong effects on engineering projects.

ARTIFICIAL THERMOKARST

Since the balance between constructive and destructive processes in permafrost environments is often delicate, relatively small perturbations in the environment can often set in motion self-sustaining processes that can in turn lead to major changes in the environment that are difficult or impossible to control by any artificial means.

Most artificially induced changes in a permafrosted environment come about through the disturbance of the topmost layer of the soil and the vegetation cover. These changes alter the albedo of the land surface, usually by exposing dark-colored material such as peat, which absorbs solar energy and promotes deep thaw. The destruction of surface cover also changes the insulating properties of the soil, encouraging deeper thaw.

These changes are often caused by construction in permafrosted regions. However, even relatively light traffic by vehicles can be sufficient to initiate thermokarst action (see Figure 6–22). This can rapidly result in roads and tracks becoming permanently impassable, and thus makes the constant alteration of travel routes a necessity.

Figure 6–22. Artificial thermokarst near the village of Barrow, Alaska. A vehicle track crossed a large mass of ground ice. Destroying the vegetation, the vehicle track initiated thaw and slumping, rapidly making the road permanently impassable.

Techniques available to minimize these difficulties include the use of vehicles with high flotation, such as broad tracks or large tires, which create minimal alteration, particularly if travel routes are altered before much damage takes place. Travel during winter is also an option. Heavily utilized winter roads are often constructed by pumping quantities of water over the tundra surface from nearby thermokarst lakes. If ice roads of this type are carefully planned and used, they can carry heavy traffic with little disturbance of the permafrost.

Artificially induced permafrost melt becomes a more serious problem in the case of permanent construction, such as all-season roads, pipelines, and buildings. The engineering techniques developed to deal with these problems generally involve isolating heat sources from the underlying permafrost, artificially increasing the insulating value of the topmost layer, and sometimes artificially maintaining the temperature of the underlying permafrost below freezing by various types of heat-exchange structures. A significant portion of the Trans-Alaska Pipeline was constructed above ground and suspended on pylons, using structures that transfer heat from the frozen ground away into the atmosphere (see Figure 6–23). Without these specialized (and expensive) techniques, the pipeline would almost certainly have become permanently inoperable within a few months of its completion.

Settling due to permafrost melt can often be seen in older construction in many of the towns and villages of permafrosted areas. Cabins and houses often settle into the ground, with settling particularly pronounced in portions that are heated. Land that has been cleared for agriculture also often exhibits thermokarst subsidence, so that swales and ponds form in what had originally been flat, apparently well-drained fields.

FOSSIL PERIGLACIAL PHENOMENA

Many of the features and processes discussed in this section may leave evidence of their existence behind long after the conditions that formed them have ceased to prevail. Ice wedges may be replaced by sand and sediment; in an arid climate, frost cracks may fill with sand and loess, forming sand wedges. The ghost image of patterned ground can commonly be seen in agricultural lands that have not been subject to a periglacial climate for some 10,000 years. These images are particularly evident in parts of England, Poland, and Hungary; they are clearly visible from the air, and the remains of the ice wedges can be seen in excavations.

Fossil periglacial phenomena can be of great interest in efforts to reconstruct and understand past climatic regimes and climatic change associated with the transition from full glacial times some 18,000 years ago to the present interglacial period. With this in mind, we can return to the question of the frozen mammoth carcasses. How, in the natural environment, does one quick-freeze an animal the size of an elephant?

The first part of the answer is that one doesn't. It makes good news copy to suggest that the mammoths are so fresh that a passable steak can be cut from them. In fact, anyone who has had much to do with the organic remains frozen in permafrost can cite powerful olfactory evidence that a good deal of time and biological activity took place subsequent to the death of the organisms and before they were frozen. The fact that dogs were attracted to the thawing remains is hardly proof of their fresh condition, as anyone who has kept a dog in the country should know. What we can say is that after whatever killed the mam-

Figure 6–23. Closeup of the trans-Alaska pipeline as it crosses south-central Alaska. The tall structures on the supporting pylons are heat exchangers that help to keep the underlying permafrost healthy, that is, solidly frozen.

moths did its work, the dead flesh was chilled reasonably rapidly and was deposited in the ground before it could be eaten by scavengers. Once chilled and protected, it could have frozen over a period of months or even years. Several scenarios account for how this could have occurred. The most plausible involve drowning, but this would not exclude other possibilities. There are a lot of organic remains in the permafrost, and they need not have all gotten there in the same way.

It is easy to envision a herd or family group of mammoths, or other animals, grazing on grass and riparian willow on the gravel bars of immense rivers and outwash plains, fed by glacier melt during the last Ice Age. While we can expect that the animals would have had a nearly instinctive sense as to how to deal with this rich but dangerous environment, there must have been times when animals were caught in torrents of rising water as the summer sun beat down on thousands of square kilometers of retreating glaciers. Although we hear of the complete remains of mammoths, most of the frozen organic material from large mammals is horribly mangled and dismembered. This fits with the idea that animals drowned and tumbled, along with rock and boulders, down a glacier-swollen river. Ultimately, the remains might have been deposited as flotsam in a quiet backwater or mixed with a newly formed bar of gravel as the braided streams of the outwash plain overflowed their banks. We can easily imagine a newly formed gravel bar, standing well above retreating flood waters, saturated with frigid glacier water, and containing the chilled, broken carcasses of unfortunate mammoths. Soon the frost table would begin to rise in the new deposit, as it insulated the underlying permafrost from the summer sun. The frozen meat could lie there indefinitely, until it was disturbed by a gold-mining operation or a new change in the river's bed.

SUGGESTED FURTHER READING

Brown, R. J. E. *Permafrost in Canada: Its Influence on Northern Development*. Toronto: University of Toronto Press, 1970.

French, H. M. *The Periglacial Environment*. London: Longman, 1976.

Washburn, A. L. *Periglacial Processes and Environments*. London: E. Arnold, 1973.

Washburn, A. L. *Geocryology: A Survey of Periglacial Processes and Environments*. New York: John Wiley & Sons, 1980.

Chapter 7

Ice Ages

EARLIER, we stressed that it is not possible to understand the arctic environment without a deep awareness of the events of the polar winter, when all good scientists are far away from the tundra in their heated laboratories. From the last chapters, it should be equally obvious that the nature of the northern environment is also a product of its history, and that probably the most significant feature of its history is what has been called the "winters of the world"—the Ice Ages.

We will direct our attention to a day in the year 16,000 B.C. or, as we often express it, 18,000 B.P. (before present). While this is the distant past to us, it is a very late date in the overall history of the earth, which stretches back some 4,600,000,000 years. By 18,000 B.P. something over 99 percent of *human* history had already passed. Our ancestors had long ago developed language, art, a spiritual life, and a firm chin. They had fire, houses, sewn clothing, and probably pets. But the world they looked out onto was dramatically different from that of the present, and much of that difference had to do with *ice*. If our ancestors were living at the site of present-day Paris, Philadelphia, or Seattle, they were living in the Arctic as we have been defining it. When they hunted, they probably hunted caribou; if they picked berries or dug roots, the berries or roots were most likely of species we will be talking about in our discussion of the tundra vegetation (see Chapters 8 and 9). A few days walk would bring them to the edge of the ice, which might even have crept a bit closer since their grandparents' day.

The distribution of ice over the Northern Hemisphere in 18,000 B.P. is shown in Figure 7–1. A number of differences from our familiar world stand out immediately. For example, there simply was no Ontario, no Norway in 18,000 B.P. Everything that lives in these areas has migrated in during the few thousand years since the ice sheets left. On the other hand, much of Alaska and Siberia was as ice free then as it is now. Mammoths wandered over grasslands and steppes in these northern areas during the height of the Ice Age, and they were hunted extensively and effectively by our ancestors. We saw in Chapter 5 how the landscape of many northern areas is still profoundly affected by the vanished glaciers. It would be surprising if the radical differences

Figure 7–1. Distribution of continental glaciers at about 18,000 B.P. (Before Present), the height of the last Ice Age. Although ice covered most of Canada and Scandinavia to an average depth of 2,000 meters or more, note that much of Asia and Alaska were unglaciated. Lowered sea levels exposed much of the continental shelf so that the total extent of unglaciated northern lands was not much less than at present. The major ice sheets were: the Greenland (the only one remaining), the Laurentide (over eastern-central North America), the Cordilleran (over western North America), and the Scandinavian. The presence of an extensive ice-shelf complex over the Barents and Kara seas, and the presence of glacial ice in local areas such as the Gulf of St. Lawrence and the northwestern Canadian high Arctic are still debated.

in the glacial history of northern environments were not reflected in some way in the present biological environment as well; although the differences may be subtle, they are increasingly recognized as basic to our understanding of the arctic environment.

It isn't only the distribution of ice that has changed over the millennia. We can well imagine that a wall of ice stretching across what is now the breadbasket of America would have some effects well beyond the glacial terminus. We would expect to find tundra or spruce forest in the Ohio Valley, rather than oak woods or cornfields, caribou and muskox instead of whitetail deer, and frigid winters lasting from October to May. Similar differences in climate and vegetation would have prevailed in other parts of the world.

Not only the nature of the continents, but even their shape was affected by the Ice Ages. As the ice expanded the seas shrank; the English Channel became dry land, dense spruce forest lived on the banks "offshore" ice-covered New England.

Perhaps most important of all, the ice was never stable over time (nor is it now). The world of 18,000 B.P. was drastically different from that of 14,000 or 22,000 B.P.: 18,000 years ago was the extreme of a glacial expansion. But 30,000 years ago was a time much like the present in many parts of the earth. And before then, over the previous half million or so years, the ice had waxed and waned repeatedly in what are now temperate latitudes.

THE QUATERNARY PERIOD

The Quaternary period is the most recent portion of geologic time. It is, with the Tertiary, one of the two periods in the Cenozoic era, also sometimes called the Age of Mammals. The Cenozoic era is believed to have lasted some 60 to 70 million years, about 1.5 percent of the 4.6 billion years since the formation of the earth. The Quaternary itself is generally considered to encompass only the last two million years or less, so it includes only a minute fraction of the earth's total history.

In spite of its short duration, the Quaternary period is unique in a number of respects. Its climate has, overall, been colder and drier than at any other time during the earth's recent past. Actually, this period of comparatively cool temperatures is the culmination of a long-term trend that has prevailed throughout the latter portion of the Cenozoic, for the past 20 to 30 million years. In the Quaternary, however, the climate has been such that the more northerly and southerly portions of the earth have repeatedly been glaciated. Such glaciation has occurred only rarely in the earth's entire history; the last time was some 250 million years ago, early in the Age of Reptiles.

The Quaternary period has traditionally been divided into two epochs, the Pleistocene and the Holocene. The Pleistocene is the time of repeated episodes of glaciation or the Ice Age, while the Holocene is postglacial time. The Holocene reaches back only some 10,000 years, with the Pleistocene including all the earlier portion of the Quaternary. Recent scientists have downplayed the significance of the division of the Quaternary into the two epochs. They base this on the recognition that postglacial times are not significantly different from the several warm periods within the Pleistocene known as interglacials. In fact, global climates seem to be cooling. The postglacial climatic optimum or hypsithermal was over some three to four thousand years ago. The past few centuries are sometimes known as the little ice age, when mountain glaciers in some places reached their farthest advance in the Holocene. While it generally appears that the cooling trend has been at least temporarily reversed, evidence suggests that another episode of glaciation is probable, and perhaps imminent.

On the other hand, the Holocene has been characterized by one absolutely unique feature: the rise of human civilization. In fact, a certain amount of evidence suggests that the human activities of modern industrial society may well have the effect on the global climate of forestalling or delaying the predicted next onset of ice-age conditions. So, perhaps the Holocene is for real!

THE STUDY OF ICE AGES

With all the glacial erratics, till plains, empty cirques, and so forth that are so prominently visible in Europe and North America, it is surprising that even the scientific community of a little over a hundred years ago was sceptical about ice ages. This attitude can be understood as a product of seeing the Bible as the true, literal source of historical information from the distant past. If the bones of some giant, extinct animal were found, the beast was thought to have died in the Noachian Flood, a few thousand years before the birth of Christ. If an exotic boulder were found on the summit of a hill, the Flood in some way was thought to have been responsible for bringing it there. Even after the idea of the Ice Ages was beginning to be well accepted, a curious hybrid concept posited that glacial drift had been transported by icebergs ("ice-rafted sediments") in the Flood and dropped onto the surface of the drowned land.

By the middle of the nineteenth century, the geological principle of uniformitarianism was gaining general acceptance in place of the earlier theory of catastrophism. *Uniformitarianism* considers the present to be the key to the past, whereas *catastrophism,* as the name implies, accepts that events such as the Flood were crucial to the present nature of the world. In uniformitarianist theory, the features found in ancient deposits are considered results of processes of erosion and deposition that have more or less exact counterparts still operating at present. If something left piles of unstratified rubble in Yorkshire or Connecticut, it seemed reasonable to look for the modern counterpart of the process somewhere in the world. As it turned out, the Swiss Alps and the mountains of Norway were the places to find processes that could produce the observed effects, and the idea of the Ice Age rapidly took hold. It was soon possible to chart the distribution of glacial features over the surface of the earth, and the outlines of the extent of past glaciations (as we saw in Figure 7–1) took shape within the next few decades.

Quite a few surprises emerged as well. It rapidly became obvious that there were substantial differences between one terminal moraine and another. Some appeared quite fresh, others so old that the enclosed boulders were oxidized and fragmented. Alpine glaciologists recognized four separate episodes of glaciation. They named these for local rivers: *Gunz, Mindel, Riss,* and *Würm,* in sequence from oldest to youngest. Similar investigations were made in other areas. North America also appeared to have a four-chapter glacial history. With admirable conservatism, the glaciologists agreed that it was premature to correlate North American ice ages with those of Europe, so they gave them different names: *Nebraskan, Kansan, Illinoian,* and *Wisconsinan.* In North America also began the tradition of naming interglacials as well; we have *Yarmouth, Aftonian,* and *Sangamon.* The unwillingness of glacial geologists to cross-correlate glacial episodes continues to this day, with the result that a complete list of terminology for local glacial events would fill many pages.

This concept of cycles of glaciation further complicated a concern that was already being addressed: What is (are) the cause(s) of ice ages? An explanation for both the overall cooling trend of climate and the perturbations within it was needed. A small library of books and papers has addressed these questions.

The view summarized here is that of a majority but certainly not a consensus of Quaternary scientists. The majority has become a more solid one since the 1960s, as scientists have accepted theories of plate tectonics and continental drift.

The continents have reached their present location only within the past few million years. Antarctica was once attached to India and supported a jungle of tree ferns and other plants of warmer regions. Reptiles, amphibians, and even primitive mammals crept around on the forest floor. As the continent of Antarctic broke away and moved southward, it began to pick up ice on its higher mountains. As the glaciers expanded into the lowlands, they began to change the energy balance of the earth by significantly increasing its albedo. Now the center of Antarctica is the South Pole, almost totally ice covered, and subject to almost unimaginable year-round cold. Compared to most other times in the earth's history, we are in a cold period, and we will presumably stay in one until Antarctica migrates northward, probably some millions or tens of millions of years from now.

The existence of cycles is most convincingly explained by a number of predictable irregularities in the earth's relationship to its orbit and to the sun. We mentioned one of these in the introduction: the angle of the ecliptic, which defines the location of the Polar Circles and tropics. The angle changes from about 22 to 25 degrees and back again on a regular cycle of about 41,000 years. The intensity of the seasons is affected by this natural wobble, with the effect varying somewhat according to latitude. Other cycles are caused by variations in the shape of the earth's orbit and in the precession (another kind of wobble). When the theoretical effects of these phenomena on the amount of energy reaching the earth are plotted, they show a number of peaks and valleys that can be plausibly correlated with actual climatic changes. These climatic changes, in turn, would cause the advance and retreat of the ice sheets. Many unanswered questions in this area remain. For example, some evidence suggests that a triggering event may be needed to begin an ice advance. The release of large quantities of volcanic dust into the atmosphere has been suggested as an important one. Some scientists now predict that the next ice age will be caused by a nuclear winter caused by the dust and debris generated by nuclear war.

How is it that we are able to throw around precise dates for such distant times as 18,000 B.P., and how do we know that this was so much different from 15,000 B.P.? Such a study constitutes a major field in itself; it is one that has been revolutionized in the past three decades by radiometric dating, particularly radiocarbon (carbon 14) dating. (Recommended reading at the end of this chapter provides detailed information on this process.) Virtually any organic material derived from a plant or animal (including humans) that died within the past 35,000 to 50,000 years can be dated quite accurately by measuring the amount of radioactive carbon that remains in its tissue. Tens of thousands of samples from the latter part of the Quaternary have now been tested this way. Samples have come from frozen mammoths, Egyptian mummies, soil in the bottom of peat bogs, and stores of grain left behind as townspeople fled invaders. The result is a thin web of evidence supporting a reconstruction of worldwide events extending back through the last Ice Age (often called *Late Wisconsinan* or *Würm II*) into a warm period. (This warm period is not usually considered to be a true interglacial; it is sometimes called the *Mid-Wisconsinan Interstadial,* indicating a lesser warm period.) Finally, our radiocarbon chronology bottoms out sometime in an earlier cold period, still considered to be part of the last major glacial time. After 40,000 to 60,000 years or so, the proportion of radioactive carbon remaining in an organic sample is so minimal as to render an accurate assessment impossible. Back through the rest of the Pleistocene, we are still forced to rely on extrapolation, correlation of sediments with celestial events, and occasional bits of information from other methods of radiometric dating, such as potassium-argon dating.

To summarize, then, the Quaternary period has seen the culmination of a long downward trend in temperature and the onset of ice ages. These ice ages have occurred repeatedly. Each time the glaciers advance, they cause the "Arctic" to spread outward into what are currently temperate regions, and they cause huge portions of the Northern Hemisphere to be inundated by ice, creating conditions similar to those of present-day Greenland and Antarctica. The ice regularly retreats, bringing about conditions similar to those of the present, or, perhaps, sometimes a bit warmer. Within a few thousand years, the ice returns.

As suggested in Chapter 5, the advances and retreats are not usually either-or phenomena. A glacier may retreat a few kilometers, advance a bit, then stay stable for years. The ice always has an impetus to reach an equilibrium with the climate, and the climate is always changing. Every perturbation in the ice margin produces some bit of evidence, such as a line of recessional moraine. Together, a group of such bits of evidence ultimately acquires a name that in turn is applied to an event or time. The literature of the Ice Ages is strewn with terminology like *Valders readvance,*

Duvanny-Yar interval, and *Two Creeksian interstade.* Serious students of the Arctic and Quaternary will soon find their heads swimming with names. As confusing as this may be at first, students may eventually find that when they use the term *Duvanny-Yar interval,* for example, it brings with it an image of a herd of mammoths emerging from an Ice Age dust storm in central Siberia, perhaps into the field of fire of a tense group of hidden, javelin-bearing hunters. The Ice Age past is the key to the Arctic, and its events are still echoing down through time.

QUATERNARY PALEOGEOGRAPHY

At its most basic, geography studies the relationship between land and water. In the polar regions, it makes sense to add a third element, ice. *Paleogeography* looks at these relationships in times past and in the sequence of events leading from the past to the present. The relationships between the distribution of land, water, and ice are fundamental. In a sense the land is the passive member of the triad, inundated alternately by water and by ice as the climate changes. The nature of the terrestrial environment itself changes radically as the relationship between the oceans and the ice sheets changes. We'll be referring to these changes, or simply tacitly accepting them, throughout the rest of this book.

SEA LEVEL CHANGES ASSOCIATED WITH GLACIATION

Eustatic Changes

Glacial ice is ultimately derived from water evaporated mainly from the ocean, and changes in the volume of glacial ice therefore have a concomitant effect on the volume of the oceans. The total extent of glaciated terrain has varied by several million square kilometers repeatedly over the past million or so years. Since the average thickness of the continental glaciers can be assumed to have been over a kilometer, millions of cubic kilometers of water have been removed and replaced in the oceans each time the ice sheets advanced or retreated. It has been estimated that the melting of the present ice caps in Antarctica and Greenland would result in a raising of global sea levels by up to 25 meters, drowning many of the earth's major population centers. Eighteen thousand years ago, the volume of glacial ice was about four times the present amount, and it is generally estimated that seas were lowered 100 meters or so. Previous glaciations may have lowered the sea level even more, perhaps as much as 120 to 130 meters.

Changes in sea level that are related to the volume of ocean water are known as *eustatic changes in sea level*. Eustatic changes in sea level can be caused by changes in the volume of land ice or by other factors, such as the transfer of water to the earth's surface by volcanic activity. It is generally accepted that any significant occurrences of the latter type took place in the remote past and do not concern us in the Quaternary.

Eustatic changes in sea level, by definition, occur on a world-wide basis, so that their effects are felt far from centers of glaciation. The major effect of eustatic changes in sea level has been to cause the alteration of vast areas of the continental shelf from dry land to shallow sea, with resultant changes in the proportion of shallow seas to deep ocean basins. During a period of maximum glacial activity, the amount of ice-free land doesn't diminish all that much, whereas shallow seas are radically reduced in area. Eustatic changes in sea level during glacial maxima provided huge areas of ice-free land, even at high latitudes. The best known example is the Bering land bridge (see Chapter 13), but the North Sea plain and the Grand Banks could have been of great importance as *refugia* for animal populations retreating before the burgeoning ice. Equally important refugia and migratory routes for animals would have been land bridges in areas like Australia and New Guinea.

ISOSTATIC DEPRESSION AND REBOUND

The buildup of glacial ice on a land mass has another, more localized effect, which often affects sea level. This effect occurs because the continents are not rigid and fixed but rather are somewhat plastic and are afloat on a deeper-lying layer of semi-molten rock. An increase in the weight of a continent, which can occur when the ice load is increased through continental glaciation, actually causes the continent to sink deeper into the underlying layer. Among the less important repercussions of this phenomenon is the slight offsetting of eustatic changes in sea level, since the weight of the sea actually depresses the sea floor and reducing the amount of water reduces the weight.

The changes in land and sea level associated with ice loading come under the category of *isostatic changes,* or changes in the equilibrium of the earth's crust. Isostatic changes result from processes other than glaciation as well, such as the deposition of deep layers of sediments in a geosyncline, or downward flexure of the earth's crust, or through widespread volcanic activity and the formation of deep lava shields. Most examples of this type of isostatic change took place over long periods of time in the distant past, and we can ignore them here.

In terms of geologic time, isostatic depression and rebound occur quickly, but they often lag some thousands of years behind rapid glacial advances and retreats. Isostatic rebound is still occurring in several areas that were near centers of continental glaciation, as in the northern Baltic Sea and Hudson Bay. A good deal of new arable land is added to Finland each century.

Isostatic adjustments of the earth's crust are complex. Isostatic depression under an ice sheet results in a certain amount of bulge immediately outside the glacial borders, while the lands adjacent to depressed areas may sink somewhat as deglaciation progresses. The land may thus actually tilt slightly, altering drainage patterns and causing irregular changes in shorelines. In Denmark, for example, early postglacial archaeological sites on the Jutland peninsula are found at progressively higher elevations as one proceeds northward. On the other hand, no early postglacial sites were identified in southern Jutland for some time, until it was realized that they should be sought below current sea level, since the southern terrain had sunk as isostatic rebound occurred to the north. But another complexity comes into play: it results from the interplay of eustatic and isostatic changes.

The bases of continental glaciers often lie below sea level because of isostatic depression. For example, much of Greenland would be an enclosed, temporary sea if the ice cap were to melt suddenly. But if the ice melted, there would also be a eustatic rise in sea level; this would be followed by an isostatic rise in the land—or the two phenomena might keep pace! Changes in sea level associated with changes in ice loading, then, can radically alter shorelines and the general relationship between land and sea when the amounts of ice change repeatedly and rapidly, as they have during the Quaternary period. The classic example of this is in the case of the present Baltic Sea. In the last 10,000 years it has twice been a freshwater lake, twice a salt sea.

CENTERS OF GLACIATION

The early twentieth century finally put to rest the idea that there was a major land mass near the North Pole. With this discovery, or nondiscovery, also dissolved any lingering idea that the great ice sheets had radiated southward from a single center located near the North Pole. There is no way that glacial ice can form over a deep ocean. So it became obvious that the ice sheets had grown out of centers located far to the south, on the continents. This, of course, immediately raised a number of new questions: How many centers? Where were they? and (importantly) Were there differences in the times of expansion and retreat between the various centers?

We know that there were several centers of glaciation around the circumpolar North. The largest ice sheets, such as the Laurentide ice sheet (which covered Canada east of the Rockies and covered the northern tier of the United States), may have resulted from the coalescence of more than one original ice mass. Other sheets, such as the Cordilleran, resulted from the deepening and coalescence of many alpine glaciers and ice fields. Overall, there is some synchronicity in the regimes of nearby glaciers, but they don't all expand and contract simultaneously. The existence of separate centers of glaciation helps to explain some apparent anomalies, such as the unglaciated area of Alaska and Siberia, often called Beringia (see Chapter 13). Ice expanding from major centers was simply blocked by mountains or a combination of low accumulation and high ablation along the closest margin. (This is not, however, a complete explanation, nor is a satisfactory comprehensive explanation available at this time.)

The margins of shrinking glaciers tend to retreat toward the center, and the remnants of the glaciers persist longest over the center. Well after what we might call the official end of the Pleistocene, some 10,000 years ago, continental glaciers remained at low latitudes. Scandinavia lost its last major ice sheet only about 8,000 years ago. A mass of ice still sat on Labrador as recently as 5,000 to 6,000 years ago, about the time people in Egypt first began to think about pyramids.

In other areas, continental glaciers tended to break up into local alpine glaciers. If these lasted for a few hundreds or thousands of years, they often rejuvenated the smoothed and ice-scoured landscape by creating new cirques and glacial valleys.

IN THE WAKE OF THE RETREATING ICE

We have looked now at the advance and retreat of the oceans and the ice and in Chapter 6 identified a wide array of features that are left behind by a retreating glacier on a local scale. Expanding our perspective now, we will examine regional glacial geology as an ice age ends and continental glaciers retreat. In this realm, our uniformitarian explanations take on interesting twists. First, we must recognize that many glaciated landforms are the result of processes that occurred in the recent past but now have no exact counterpart. For example, there are now no mid-latitude continental glaciers, and there is no extensive loess deposition. But the evidence that appalling Ice Age dust storms happened is compelling, and the processes, although they no longer occur on this scale, can be visualized and studied in detail. This is particularly true since Ice Age events are so recent in terms of geological time, and their effects are plainly visible on the surface of the land. Also, we can study some past events more readily than we can their present counterparts, since the geomorphic events of current glaciation occur under an impenetrable mantle of ice. Any discussion of glacial geology and geomorphology necessarily oscillates between past and present events.

Awe-inspiring scenes and events were played out along the margins of the shrinking glaciers 15,000 or so years ago. We can imagine what would have happened to the ancestor of the Mississippi River if an ice-dammed lake the size of Lake Ontario drained completely overnight. Many geologists believe that the appearance of the terrain of much of Washington state was totally altered by a flood lasting only a few days.

In this chapter, we have looked at the creation of a blank slate in much of the Arctic and Subarctic at a time ranging from perhaps 5,000 to 15,000 years ago. It remains now to examine the repopulation of most of the far north with the organisms that have been able to march back onto the bare rock, sterile eskers, and old proglacial lake beds left behind by the retreating glaciers. Many of the colonizing organisms, both animal and plant, were veterans of many previous advances and retreats before the fickle ice. We know that many were lost forever, like the woolly mammoth and the saber-toothed "tiger." Other species may be making their first incursion into the Arctic in our time, after a training period on some mountain summit in central Asia or the Canadian Rockies. We'll turn now to the present environment and its inhabitants, then return for another look at Ice Age events in terms of these migrations and homogenizations of the arctic flora and fauna over the millennia.

SUGGESTED FURTHER READING

An extensive and rapidly developing literature is available on this topic. Additional titles are listed in Chapters 5, 13, and 14.

Bowen, D. Q. *Quaternary Geology.* London: Pergamon, 1978.

Bradley, R. S. *Quaternary Paleoclimatology: Methods of Paleoclimatic Reconstruction.* Boston: Allen and Unwin, 1985.

Denton, G. H., and T. J. Hughes, eds. *The Last Great Ice Sheets.* New York: John Wiley & Sons, 1981.

Imbrie, J., and K. P. Imbrie. *Ice Ages.* Hillside, NJ: Enslow Publishers, 1979.

John, B. *The Winters of the World.* Newton Abbot, England: David and Charles, 1979.

Chapter 8

Gateway to the Arctic:
The Northern Forest and the Timberline

TUNDRA, TAIGA, AND TIMBERLINE

In Lapland, the deep, dark Scandinavian forests of spruce and pine begin to shun the ridge tops and to thin out into scattered copses and groves along the valley floors. The rocky, glacier-scoured summits appear barren; only in ravines and other protected situations are there miniature woodlands of scrub birch and willow. On the spines and shoulders of the hills are bare rock, lichens, and, wherever a bit of soil has built up, mosses, grasses, sedges, and a variety of flowering herbs and dwarf shrubs. Similar areas in the higher mountains to the south, in Norway, are traditionally called *fjells,* a word we shall encounter again. The Finnish word for these open barrens and dwarf woodlands is *tundra.* Although the word connotes unfriendliness or even danger, tundra areas for millennia have been important summer pasturage for reindeer, so they also figure importantly in the lives of the nomadic Lapp herders.

The word *tundra* long ago spread into other languages, particularly English and Russian. Perhaps it has a numinous quality that transcends linguistic boundaries. It has been said that the shortest Zen *haiku* is:

tundra

In English, tundra has generally come to mean any treeless barren area beyond the limit of tree growth in the Arctic or in the higher mountains. The term *tundra* has tended to replace *barren grounds,* the term by which the treeless stretches of northern Canada were traditionally known. On the other hand, some scientists use the word *tundra* to refer to a particular type of vegetation: treeless, but rich in sedges, herbs, and dwarf shrubs, as opposed to the more barren fell fields. In the Soviet Union tundra is often used as a part of a proper name for a large area of treeless vegetation, so that one may hear of the Yamal Tundra, for example. In any case, the modern use of tundra emphasizes treelessness, ignoring the original Finnish use of the word for areas of sparse woodland and barrens near the timberline. Many people now use tundra or tundra biome essentially as a synonym for the terrestrial arctic regions.

Northern Russia also has large areas where the coniferous trees become increasingly sparse and the forest is interspersed with areas of scrub and treeless barrens and peatlands. The Russian word for this situation is *taiga;* it refers to conditions comparable to the Finnish use of *tundra.* The word *taiga* has also spread into English during this century. But in its English usage, the presence of trees has been emphasized rather than ignored, with the result that *taiga* is now commonly used for the immense stretches of boreal forest that cover much of Canada, Alaska, Siberia, and Scandinavia. Many scientists who work in the far north now limit taiga to the open woodlands that extend southward from the borders of the tundra on ridges and peatlands, and that tend to become more rare and discontinuous in the taller, denser forests of the lowlands of the Subarctic. These open woodlands are also sometimes known as forest tundra. In some older literature, the term *elfin forest* appears, but it has evidently lost out to the modern style of baldly descriptive scientific writing.

TIMBERLINE: THE FOREST-TUNDRA ECOTONE

Given a clear view of a range of high mountains anywhere in the cooler portions of the Northern Hemisphere, one will notice that the mountains show altitudinal belts or zones of differing appearance. The boundaries of these zones are often strongly defined and run for long distances at the same elevation. This is particularly clear on days when there has been snowfall above a certain elevation, rain below (among summer scientists, the material in the white zone inching down the mountain slopes in August or September is known as *termination dust).* The clear line between snow-covered and snow-free terrain is a result of temperature. It suggests that other, more permanently located boundaries are also related to temperature, which, in turn, in the mountains, is related to the lapse rate (see Chapter 2). We have already mentioned the relationship between the most prominent of these boundaries, the timberline, and the 10° isotherm for the warmest month of the year. We will now look at the nature of the northernmost forests and at the interaction and processes that are involved in creating the *tension zone* or *ecotone* between the forest of the Subarctic and the treeless tundra of the true Arctic.

The transition between mountain forest and a treeless alpine tundra on the mountaintops is often remarkably abrupt (see Figure 8–1). We might expect this, given the rapid drop-off of temperature with increasing elevation and the relative uniformity of soil and other environmental conditions on a mountain slope. This altitudinal timberline has a counterpart in the far north, known as the latitudinal timberline. The latitudinal timberline is often defined as the seaward or poleward limit of arborescent coniferous forest growth. The latitudinal timberline is a much broader zone of transition than the altitudinal timberline. The

Figure 8–1. Aerial view of timberline zone in the lower Noatak River drainage, northwestern Alaska. Here, dense spruce forest grows on well-drained slopes, but both valley bottom and ridge top are treeless.

trees thin out and become dwarfed, and the forest becomes patchy and discontinuous over a distance of some tens or even hundreds of kilometers (see Figure 8–2). Given that the main force behind this timberline situation is temperature, it makes sense that the latitudinal timberline is a broad zone. Temperature changes far less per unit of latitudinal distance traveled than for a comparable distance unit of elevation change. Over changes in latitude, additional complexities such as variations in exposure, drainage, soil type, microclimate, and often elevation as well must be taken into account. The idea of a true arctic timberline, in the sense of a narrow boundary separating the tundra to the north from the forest to the south, is misleading. The latitudinal timberline is a widespread area of great complexity and variability, markedly different in different parts of the circumpolar north. Within this zone lie the conditions that were originally encompassed by both the terms *tundra* and *taiga*.

In Soviet literature, this and the lower edge of the treeless zone are commonly referred to as the *hypoarctic*. It is tempting to adopt this term, since it downplays a distinction based on the somewhat capricious presence or absence of coniferous trees. In North America, however, we are deeply imbued with the idea that the terrestrial portions of the earth can be divided into biomes, large areas that are characterized by a particular vegetation formation, and division of the far north into two biomes, the tundra biome and the boreal forest biome, is traditional. Biomes are separated by a boundary area—an ecotone, or tension zone.

Figure 8–2. A timberline or forest-tundra situation in central Labrador. Scattered white spruce trees grow in a matrix of dwarf-birch scrub.

The boundary area between forest and tundra is timberline. An alternative and, in some ways, better point of view is the approach of C. Hart Merriam, one of the pioneers in the field of ecology in North America. Merriam's classification of northern life zones includes a treeless Arctic-Alpine Zone, a broad area of open forest and forest-tundra called the Hudsonian Zone, and a stretch of deep, generally closed northern forest called the Canadian Zone. Rather than belabor the point further, we will use the concepts of tundra and boreal forest as a convenient basis for further discussion. More of the shortcomings of treating these concepts as absolute realities will come out as we look further into the distribution, past and present, of the vegetation, flora, and fauna of the far north. On the other hand, the phenomenon of timberline is a real one, and the relationship between organisms and physical factors (like summer temperatures) is well demonstrated. In the shifting world of causality in ecology, it has provided a paradigm that is useful in other realms, including some we will look at in Chapter 9.

TREES OF THE NORTHERN FOREST

The northern forest of North America is very different from that of the Old World. Although scientists increasingly consider American and Eurasian populations of closely related organisms as single circumpolar species (for example, reindeer and caribou), it is still generally accepted that there are no tree species widely indigenous to the boreal forests of both hemispheres. On the other hand, genera such as *Larix* (larch), *Picea* (spruce), and *Populus* (cottonwood and aspen) have close relatives on opposite sides of the Bering Strait or Atlantic Ocean.

For many people, the term *northern forest* is synonymous with *northern* (or *boreal*) *coniferous forest*. The mental picture they summon is of an endless expanse of dark evergreen forest, dominated by the cone-bearing spruces, firs, and pines. Although, as we will see, this is a serious oversimplification, we will begin our look at the northern forest trees with the conifers, since they are both conspicuous and are the basis for the most commonly accepted definition of timberline.

In North America, the timberline conifer forest can almost be characterized by the single word *spruce,* whether in Alaska, Keewatin, or Labrador. Spruces are easily distinguished from their near relatives in the pine family (the *Pinaceae* include, among others, larches, pines, firs, and hemlocks). Spruces have single needles that are usually squarish in cross section (see

Figures 8–3 and 8–4). They are borne on small peglike pro-
trusions that leave a roughened surface on the bark of the twig or
trunk when they are shed. The cones hang down from the
branches and often remain on the tree for several years, while
individual seeds drop out from between the cone scales.

North American conifer forests near timberline generally consist of two species of spruce: white spruce *(Picea glauca)* and
black spruce *(P. mariana)*. The two species are distinctive in
their habitat preferences and appearance. White spruce is usually
a tall, vigorous tree found on well-drained to dry uplands and
along river bluffs and stream banks. Black spruce is typically a
species of peatlands and other low-lying, poorly drained areas, as
well as of some cold, moist, generally north-facing slopes. It is
often of narrow growth habit, bent, gnarled, or dwarfed. Where
the two species grow close together in habitats that approach
each other, more subtle characteristics may be used to tell them

Figure 8–3. Black spruce, one of
the two major species of spruce
(Picea) in the boreal forest of North
America. Black spruce *(P. mariana)*
is a narrow, rather straggly tree of
muskeg and cool moist slopes. Its
small cones, short needles, and the
fine rust-colored hairs on the young
twigs distinguish it from white
spruce (see Figure 8–4).

Figure 8–4. White spruce prefers dry slopes, riverbanks, and other areas of good drainage. Generally larger than black spruce, it is an important timber tree. The cones are larger and longer than those of black spruce and seldom remain on the tree for more than a year or so. Needles are longer than in black spruce, and there are no fine hairs on the young twigs.

apart. The definitive difference is the presence of tiny, brownish, fuzzy hairs along the twigs and new growth of black spruce and their absence on white spruce. (This characteristic loses much of its usefulness at the onset of the Age of Bifocals in the observer.) Although the appearance of a black spruce is suggestive of a tree at the thin edge of life, and it often invades tundralike areas of bog and muskeg, white spruce is usually the last tree at timberline. Here it is often found as scattered individuals and groves in protected spots and along watercourses.

The larches (*Larix;* see Figure 8–5) are an interesting and important group of circumpolar northern trees in the pine family. Like other conifers, they are represented by different species in each hemisphere. The most obvious feature of the larches is that they are deciduous conifers; although they are close relatives of pine and spruce, they lose their leaves each fall. This has a number of interesting implications. Larch forests are different in appearance from spruce forests in all seasons. In winter such

Figure 8–5. Larch. This American larch or tamarack *(Larix laricina)* is the only deciduous conifer in the North American north. It is common but of irregular distribution. In the forests of Siberia, other species of *Larix* are the major tree species over millions of square kilometers.

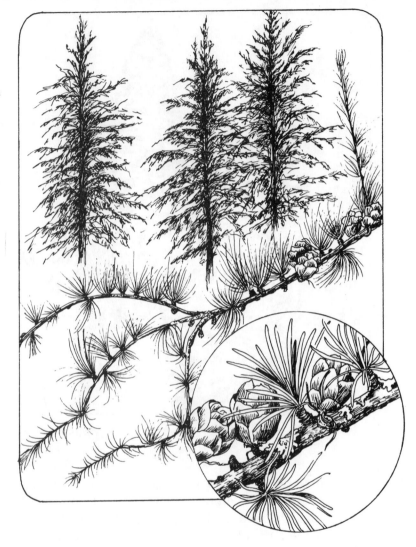

forests appear dead, since the shape and what might be called style of the leafless larches are much like those of other conifers. In spring the new leaves generally develop well after the ground is snow free and the air warm. Light can penetrate to the forest floor and allow the growth of herbs, shrubs, and mosses. Even during summer more light penetrates to the forest floor in larch forests than in evergreen forests. Larch "needles" are soft and of a pale grass-green in summer, perhaps because they have not needed to adapt to get through the harsh winter. In fall the leaves turn a brilliant gold, generally after the leaves of most other deciduous species are gone. Individual larch trees then stand out like candles against the background of the dark spruces.

The Amercan larch *(Larix laricina)* is found from Newfoundland to Alaska, but it has a rather patchy distribution. It is most often seen in boggy peatlands in association with black spruce, but its presence or absence is unpredictable. In Alaska, larch is often associated with layers of loess lying deep below the peat, but no convincing explanation for this correlation has been proposed.

Although many people think of the northern forest as a pine forest, true pines (*Pinus*; see Figure 8–6) are generally a minor component of the boreal forest in North America. New World

Figure 8–6. Two pines. Jack pine (*Pinus banksiana,* left) is an example of a two-needle pine. Related members of this group are found in various parts of the circumpolar North, although seldom at timberline. They are important pioneers on burns and disturbed areas such as glacial outwash. The five-needle pines such as the eastern white pine (*Pinus strobus,* right) are more common in temperate forests, but several species are important near alpine timberlines.

pines don't occur near the arctic timberline, although they may be seen at some alpine timberlines in the Subarctic. Lodgepole pine *(P. contorta)* grows widely near timberline in the northern Rockies, and jack pine *(P. banksiana)* reaches far northward in the boreal forest of central Canada. These species are well adapted to exceptionally well-drained situations such as eskers and other gravel and sand features left behind by retreating glaciers.

In Europe, several species of dwarf, scrubby pines grow in the higher mountains. As they reach their altitudinal limits, they become thick, creeping mats or impenetrable thickets, called *krummholz.* Similar vegetation, although involving different species, occurs elsewhere in mountainous regions, so the word has spread. In eastern Siberia, the timberline coniferous "tree" is a scrubby pine, *Pinus pumila.*

Firs *(Abies;* see Figure 8–7) are seldom a component of the arctic timberline forest in either hemisphere. An exception is the coastal region of Labrador. Inland in the forest-tundra regions of eastern Canada, balsam fir *(A. balsamea)* often is the timberline tree on mountain slopes. It is the main component of the notorious *tuckamoor* of Newfoundland. This is an extensive, impenetrable, subalpine scrub vegetation, similar to the *krummholz* of alpine regions of Europe. It is certainly at least partially responsible for confinement of human activities in much of Newfoundland and Labrador to the coastal regions. Firs are superficially similar to spruces, but they are easily distinguished from them by a variety of features, as shown in Figure 8–7.

TIMBERLINE FORESTS OF EURASIA

In Eurasia, the arctic timberline is nearly twice as long as that of North America, and it is much more complex. Instead of a single major species at timberline, such as white spruce in North America, one or more major timberline species replaces another as we travel eastward from Europe across Siberia. To make the situation more complex, there are areas in eastern Siberia in which the treeless vegetation at timberline is closely related to that of the dry steppes of interior Asia, rather than tundra as we usually think of it. Over extensive areas in Chukotka, in northeast Siberia, the timberline conifer is a shrubby pine *(Pinus pumila)* whose claim to qualify as arborescent coniferous forest growth is tenuous at best. Add to this situation a complex topography and an even more complex history of glaciation and climatic change

Figure 8–7. A typical fir, *Abies balsamea,* the balsam fir of Canada and the northeastern United States. Like pines, firs do not usually occur near the arctic timberline but are important in many alpine and coastal timberline situations. Balsam fir is often scrubby and is important in forming the infamous and impenetrable tuckamoor of Newfoundland and Labrador. Firs can be distinguished from other conifers by their flat needles, erect cones that shatter in fall to disperse their seeds, and usually smooth bark with numerous resin blisters.

and it is easy to see why Soviet scientists generally view the whole concept of timberline and a boundary between tundra and boreal forest biomes with a jaundiced eye. The addition of deciduous tree species such as birches and aspens is perhaps the final insult to the timberline concept in eastern Siberia, and we will also see a similar case in Alaska.

The timberline environment in Scandinavia has many similarities to that of eastern Canada. In both areas it is strongly influenced by the history of intense continental glaciation over ancient bedrock surfaces. Both Labrador-Ungava and northern Scandinavia are only marginally within the true Arctic. The inland areas are dominated by extensive areas of forest-tundra, and timberline is more of a coastal phenomenon than a strictly latitudinal one. In Scandinavia the timberline conifers are Norway spruce *(Picea excelsa)* and Scotch (or Scots to the purist) pine *(Pinus sylvestris).* These species are taxonomically and ecologily close to the white spruce and jack pine, respectively, of Canada. It is not surprising, then, that early timberline ecologists who were familiar with northern Europe felt at home in Canada. It was reasonable to hypothesize that a comparable timberline situation extended eastward across Siberia and westward across Canada and Alaska. As one travels into Siberia, however, spruce and pine become less and less common near timberline. They are replaced by Siberian larch (*Larix sibirica* and its close relatives) in Russia and western Siberia. These in turn give way to the widespread and aggressive dahurian larch (*L. dahurica*, sometimes called *L. cajanderi*) of the rolling uplands of Yakutia and the interior of Chukotka and Kamchatka. It has been suggested that the deciduous habit of larches allows them to adapt in some way to the intense continental winter cold of the deep interior of Siberia. Certainly, the northernmost forests of the world are the larch forests at the base of the Taimayr peninsula and in the Lena River delta, at about 72° to 73° north latitude.

In easternmost Siberia, larches fail to reach the shores of the Bering Sea, but *Pinus pumila* reaches to the base of the Gulf of Anadyr and the "conifer gap" across the Bering Strait is only a few hundred kilometers wide, from the central Seward peninsula to the base of the Chukchi peninsula.

DECIDUOUS TREES IN THE TIMBERLINE FOREST

Scientists have tended to downplay the importance of the nonconiferous deciduous trees of the far north, particularly with respect to the forest-tundra ecotone. One reason for this situation is again that much of the early research was done in northern Europe and particularly eastern Canada, where there are few broadleaved trees in the timberline zone. In much of western Canada, Alaska, and Siberia, however, broadleaved trees dominate immense areas of northern forest. Most of these trees are aspens, poplars, or cottonwood (the genus *Populus*) or the so-called whitebark birches (*Betula alba* of Eurasia, *B. papyrifera* of North America, and a wide array of somewhat distinct local species). The relationship between these trees and the more traditional conifers in the boreal forest is complex and often involves such factors as the fire history of a local area. The many species of woody broadleaved plants that straddle the distinction between trees and tall shrubs, deciduous counterparts of the *Pinus pumila* of eastern Siberia, often maintain a foothold well out into conifer-free tundra, further complicating the timberline picture. The most important of these plants are willows *(Salix)*, alders *(Alnus)*, and a thoroughly confusing array of scrubby dwarf birches.

One of the most interesting trees in the North American boreal forest is the balsam poplar, or black cottonwood *(Populus balsamifera,* see Figure 8–8). This tree grows throughout much of the far north and well southward into temperate regions. Near timberline it is commonly the largest of trees. Its trunk is often a meter or more in diameter and it may reach 30 to 40 meters in height. Its preferred habitat is generally along the shores of the larger rivers. Along the lower Yukon in Alaska, cottonwood forms pure stands of thousands of acres. It is particularly aggressive as a colonist on islands and river bars, and most stands in these situations appear to be of an even age and give the forest a flat-topped or crewcut appearance. Much of the colonizing ability of this species and its relatives comes from its ability to repro-

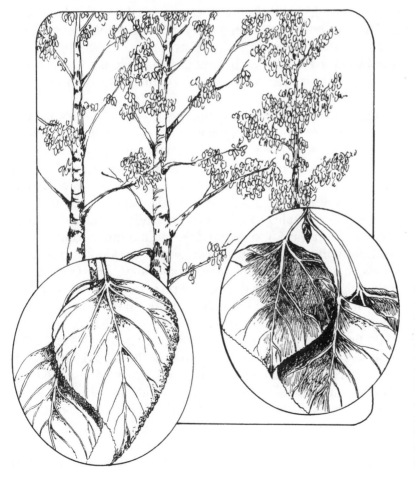

Figure 8–8. The genus *Populus* contains both cottonwood (*P. balsamifera,* left) and aspen (*P. tremuloides,* right), as well as many other species of poplar that grow throughout much of the world. Cottonwood is often the northernmost tree in North America and may range well beyond timberline as defined by conifers. Quaking aspen, with its ribbonlike petioles, or leaf stems, trembles in the slightest breeze. It is important in subalpine areas and as a pioneer in burns.

duce vegetatively from an extensive and fast-growing mat of spreading roots, which send up suckers. A poplar stand, then, is not really a group of individual trees, but rather a colony. This colony can far exceed in age the individual tree stems; in one sense it is essentially immortal. This ability to grow new trees vegetatively is particularly important in situations where worsening climate or other environmental changes may make the production or germination of seeds unlikely or impossible. The colony may persist for hundreds or thousands of years, sending up new shoots to replace those lost to fire, rot, windthrow, or insect damage. In Alaska, cottonwood stands extend as much as 50 to 100 kilometers beyond the conifer tree line. They probably can persist indefinitely as isolated relicts, waiting patiently for a few good years in which to produce seeds and establish new daughter groves. Increasing evidence suggests that these poplar stands provided the closest approach to forested conditions in unglaciated northern areas such as central Alaska during the height of the last glacial period. At present, they provide islands of what can only be thought of as forest conditions far out into areas that are shown on the map as tundra. Isolated stands of cottonwood have recently been found in Chukotka, making this species the only tree confirmed as occurring in both the Old World and the New.

Quaking aspen (*Populus tremuloides* in North America and the closely related *P. tremula* in Eurasia) is a close relative of cottonwood (see Figure 8–8). The North American representative of the circumpolar species complex is the most widespread tree in this hemisphere; it occurs from Mexico northward to near timberline in Alaska and all across Canada. Aspen tends to be a species of dry or at least well-drained uplands, and it is particularly common in the Rocky Mountains. On the other hand, in the northern part of the prairie provinces of Canada it forms pure stands on low-lying loess plains and other silty areas. Over broad areas, this aspen forest is the major type of boreal forest; conifers are sparsely scattered in bogs and uplands. In other areas, aspen is particularly well suited to rapidly colonize areas denuded by forest fire. Large portions of Alaska and the Northwest Territories support pure aspen stands as a result of fire. Like cottonwood, aspen can reproduce and spread rapidly by an extensive system of roots and suckers. But pure aspen stands are generally slowly colonized by spruce and other trees, and the forest may change more or less completely back to spruce over decades or centuries.

Aspen is distinguished from other trees by its pale, greenish bark, which is able to photosynthesize on warm days in spring and fall, when there are no leaves. The bark is covered by a white, waxy powder that sometimes becomes so thick as to make the bark a white nearly indistinguishable from that of white birch. The leaves of aspen are also distinctive. The petiole ("leaf stem") is flat, like a ribbon in cross section, rather than round. The flat petioles allow the leaf blades to tremble in the most minimal air movements; this is responsible for both the Latin and common names of the tree.

White birches (see Figure 8–9) of some variety are seldom far away in the northern forest, or in people's vision of it. Many people imagine northern forests made of columns of preternaturally pristine whiteness, growing along a northern water-

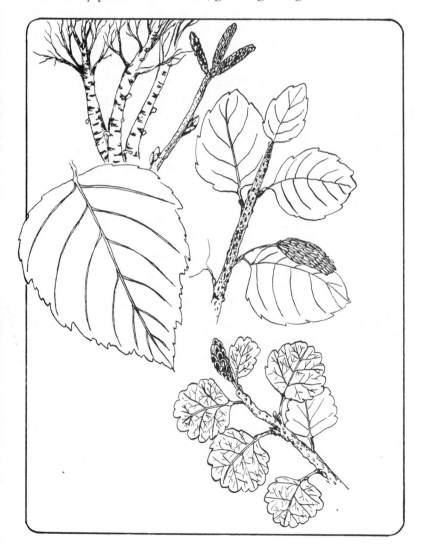

Figure 8–9. Birches. There are often hybrids (center) between the various whitebarked birches (such as *Betula papyrifera* of North America, above left), the scrub birches *(B. glandulosa),* and the dwarf birches *(B. nana,* lower right). Although typical specimens are easy to identify, intermediates abound in such intermediate environments as timberline.

course and waiting to be transformed into a canoe, basket, or the northern equivalent of parchment or clay tablet. In fact, the smooth, easily peeled bark is characteristic mainly of white birches of northeastern North America, where they are known as paper, or canoe, birches. Elsewhere in the circumpolar north, white birch bark tends to be less peelable and full of flaws, and the trees themselves are generally smaller and more gnarled and shrubby. The so-called white birches are actually a complex group of populations of one or several closely related species whose important features vary. The reason for this state of affairs seems to be that northern birches are able to adapt rapidly to changing conditions of climate and other factors, so that local races are constantly being created and then lost again into the general gene pool with the waxing and waning of glaciers and other northern events. Northern birches retain an ability to interbreed with even quite distant, at least in terms of appearance, relatives. Near timberline are commonly found hybrid swarms of birches that are clearly the result of interbreeding between white birches and one or more populations of the scrub or dwarf birches of the tundra (see Figure 8–9). In these situations, genetic reassortment results in birch shrubs with white bark, or trees with gray bark and the rounded, deeply toothed leaves of the tundra birches. Along with these hybrid appearances come hybrid ecological adaptations, so that it is often difficult to characterize a particular habitat as appropriate for northern birches. The more treelike types tend to be found in moist, cool woodlands, along streams, and on north-facing slopes of hills and ravines. The gray birch *(Betula populifolia)* of the eastern U.S. and Canada is a tree birch whose scrubbiness is probably the product of populations that became isolated during the last glacial episode and adapted to the sterile, acid soils found in bogs and glacial outwash plains. Gray birch has lately found an artificial haven in abandoned pasture and cutover woodlands, from which it shamelessly hybridizes with the pure white birch of the deeper forest. Somewhat similar situations are found throughout the circumpolar boreal forest region, particularly in the open forests that characterize the timberline zone.

Alders are a group of large, treelike shrubs and small trees found in and around moist, cool forest in many parts of the world. In the North, alders are circumpolar, with several species involved. Alders are related to birches and are somewhat similar to them in the appearance of their leaves, bark, and reproductive structures (see Figure 8–10).

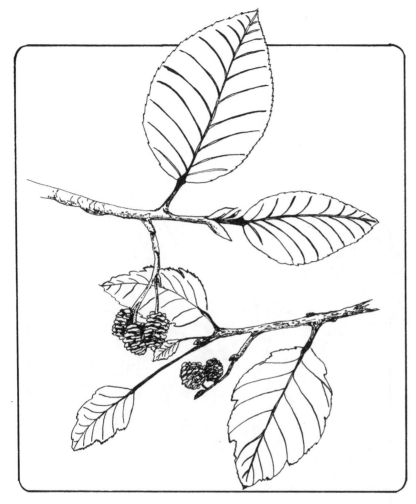

Figure 8–10. Alder. Related to birches and generally forming impenetrable thickets of tall shrubs, *Alnus* is a major element in many timberline forests and woodlands. Speckled alder (*Alnus crispa,* top left) prefers mountain and talus slopes while swamp alder (*A. incana,* lower right) colonizes river flats.

Alders are most common in moist areas such as river banks and marshes; they are also prevalent in snowbed communities and seepage areas on subalpine mountain slopes. Here they may form nearly impenetrable thickets. The trunks, upright when young, sag and lie half procumbent with age, so that an alder thicket resembles a pile of huge, rooted jackstraws. Sometimes the only way to pass through these thickets is along trails that are the regular travel routes of large bears.

Alder roots support colonies of nitrogen-fixing bacteria. These allow them to colonize barren areas of undeveloped soil such as outwash plains, talus slopes, and piles of tailings left by surface mining operations. A curious feature of alders is that they seem to generally need an abundant and continuous supply of water, but this must be in the form of stream flow or seepage; they cannot tolerate standing water and are thus seldom found in bogs and peatlands.

Willows (*Salix,* see Figure 8–11) are of fundamental importance in boreal forest, timberline, and tundra ecosystems. The dozens of species in the north range in size from small trees to plants that appear to be no more than a pair of leaves on the surface of the tundra. Later we will see that even these dwarf willows are most appropriately thought of as dwarf trees with

Figure 8–11. Willows. Dozens of species of willows *(Salix)* inhabit timberline forests as well as the true tundra. Shown here are a typical creeping willow (*S. arctica,* at top), a tall shrub willow of woodland and muskeg (*S. bebbiana,* center), and a true tundra dwarf willow (*S. glacialis,* at bottom). All willows are dioecious, with male and female flowers on separate plants. The male flowers are on the right, and the female flowers are on the left.

subterranean trunks and branches. But most willows in the vicinity of timberline range from knee height upward. While willows are widespread in northern environments, they are most prevalent in situations such as river flood plains, gravel bars, and sand and silt deposits formed by wind or stream action. They are also common in snowbed environments and in some bog and tundra areas. These situations are collectively called riparian willow thickets or stands, indicating the sometimes nearly total dominance of *Salix* shrubs. Within a given area the size of, say, arctic Alaska, perhaps six to twelve species of willow will make up riparian willow stands. Each species is likely to form pure stands under appropriate conditions and to participate in some mixed stands. It is difficult, then, to characterize a typical riparian willow thicket.

Riparian willows are important for a number of reasons. First, they provide an important food source for a number of animals and birds. The buds provide a staple for ptarmigan and hares in the winter, and the twigs are heavily browsed by moose, as they probably were in the remote past by woolly mammoths and arctic horses. The taller riparian stands are a true woodland in any sense of the word, yet they are found, often covering extensive areas, far beyond timberline as defined by conifer forest (see Figure 8–12). They are even known to occur locally on some of the southern islands of the Canadian arctic archipelago. Riparian willows are important in binding soils in unstable situations such as river bars and in dune fields and in windblown sand and silt exposed by thermokarst and drainage of thaw lakes. As important as these functions may be at present, it takes little imagination to recognize how significant willows might have been in stabilizing the environment in times past, when immense glaciers formed huge outwash plains, loess fields, and seasonally flooded river systems on a scale found nowhere today.

PLANTS AND ANIMALS OF THE NORTHERN FOREST FLOOR

As we will see in the next section, much of the northern forest is not forest at all, but various kinds of open woodland and treeless vegetation that grades more or less imperceptibly into what appears to be tundra at the timberline. This vegetation is similar enough to tundra to allow us to ignore its composition for the present and leave it for Chapter 9, on tundra. But the deep northern forest is a specialized habitat, and it includes a number

Figure 8–12. A riparian willow stand along the lower Colville River in arctic Alaska. Although over 100 kilometers beyond the accepted location of timberline, riparian willow thickets of this type grow as tall as 5 to 7 meters and constitute extensive arctic woodlands. They allow the penetration of typically subarctic animals, such as moose, deep into the tundra environment.

of organisms and features worth a brief examination before we leave the forest for the tundra.

In the amount of light available, the floor of the closed northern coniferous forest is comparable to that of the densest tropical rain forest. In the dimmest recesses of the forest, very little can grow on the ground and most living activity is in the canopy of the trees. The ground is a dry, springy mat of shed needles, with an occasional pale-green shoot of some especially shade-tolerant herb. With slightly more light, a thick cover of mosses develops, particularly where there is a good moisture supply. Many species and genera occur, the most important of which are called *feathermosses,* based on their appearance (see Figure 8–13a and b). *Hylocomium splendans* is the commonest species in many places. In wetter, more open areas, *Sphagnum* comes to dominate the forest floor and the forest shades into a peatland; this is examined in more detail below.

Many flowering herbs, grasses, and sedges grow on the forest floor as well. Ferns and their so-called fern allies—horsetails *(Equisetum)* and clubmosses *(Lycopodium)*—give an archaic look to the dim recesses between the dark trees. Most of the herbaceous plants in the northern forest are found southward into at least the cool temperate regions and even farther along the spines of the higher hills. They also extend northward into the treeless tundra, usually in snowbeds and other protected areas such as will be discussed in Chapter 9 under *mesic tundra*. Perhaps because of their ancient origins in temperate regions, a relatively small proportion are truly circumpolar in their range.

Wildfire and Insect Invasions in the Northern Forest

The boreal forest is an exceptionally unstable kind of vegetation. Radical changes take place in it frequently, usually as a result of forest fires or severe insect infestations. In either case, the dominant tree species—usually conifers—are destroyed, then slowly rebuild their populations, and die off again in a continuing cycle.

A typical northern forest, consisting of a more or less closed stand of conifers, is extremely vulnerable to wildfire. During the dry summer, the forest floor is a tinderbox, consisting of a layer of dry needles and desiccated peat and feathermoss. A fire can start in this duff layer through many means, lightning and human activities being the most likely.

Fires in the boreal forest are relatively unspectacular, seldom crowning, or blazing from treetop to treetop. More often, the fire is confined to the forest floor and underbrush layer, where it is a creeping, smoldering process that may last for weeks or months and engulf thousands of acres. In a dry summer, there may be several large fires in an area the size of interior Alaska, and the brownish-yellow smoke may form an acrid haze noticeable hundreds of kilometers away from the nearest fire. Control of these fires is relatively difficult, since they are often far from a road and have an extensive perimeter by the time they are discovered. Fire is increasingly understood to be an integral process in northern forest ecosystems, and fire fighting is increasingly seen as neither ecologically nor economically sound policy except when the fire threatens a village or commercially important forest stand. On the other hand, fire fighting has been an economically important activity in many northern communities for decades, providing a source of cash income for subsistence trappers and fishers. An important twist in this situation developed in Alaska 20 years ago when the United States government first began to hire women on fire crews. When this hiring worked out well, political pressure to continue to fight fires increased considerably, despite doubts about valid management reasons to control the fires.

The aftermath of a fire in the boreal forest ranges from a landscape of blackened stubs to a forest of slowly browning trees,

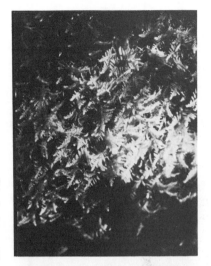

Figure 8–13. Two important mosses of the boreal forest. Feathermoss (*Hylocomium,* above) and related species are the major group of plants able to live on the deeply shaded forest floor of a closed boreal forest. The unique mosses of the genus *Sphagnum* (below) are the true peatmosses, and they are responsible for the major portion of the organic buildup in the extensive peatlands of northern regions.

their roots destroyed by the ground fire, with tops untouched. In either case, the forest is essentially destroyed (see Figure 8–14), often along with much of the top layer of soil. This destruction can be disastrous in areas that were once heavily glaciated, as in much of Canada. Here, even a smoldering fire can burn down to bedrock. Rains then wash away the remaining ash, and the bare rock may remain sterile and treeless for centuries.

Where soil or loose substrate remains, burned forests are rapidly colonized by an array of plants that are specialized for the invasion of disturbed areas. Among the most important of these are fireweed *(Epilobium angustifolium)* (see Figure 8–15), willows, and the common red raspberry *(Rubus idaeus)*. Fireweed and willows have light seeds with fluffy parachutes, ideal for wafting into a burn. Raspberries are well adapted for distribution by birds. Mosses, liverworts, and horsetails (*Equisetum* species), dispersed by their myriads of tiny, windblown spores, help fill in the bare areas.

For a decade or two after a fire, a typical burn is a dense stand of herbaceous vegetation, with increasing amounts of willow and other brushy species. This stage in forest development may well be the most productive part of the cycle. Revegetating burns provide both cover and browse for a wide variety of animals and birds, from moose on down to chickadees and voles. In time, though, certain of the longer-lived, taller species, such as aspen, birch, and cottonwood, generally grow tall enough to create a canopy, decreasing the amount of sunlight reaching the forest

Figure 8–14. Recent burn in a black spruce forest of northern New-foundland. The slow-burning, smoldering fire spread largely at the ground level and left dead trees standing. However, most of the vegetation and much of the soil have been destroyed and a new habitat for postfire colonizers has been created.

floor. The tall herbs begin to thin out. They are likely to be replaced by tougher, slower-growing vegetation such as heath plants (see Chapter 9). Mixed in with these will probably be a few spruce seedlings, sprouting from seeds blown in from a surrounding unburned spruce stand. A few decades later, the spruce will have overtopped the deciduous trees, which will begin dying from age, windthrow, and deepening shade. Ultimately, perhaps as soon as 50 years after the fire, but more likely several centuries later, the spruce forest will have returned, ready for the next round of fire.

This is a generalized picture; details vary from place to place in the circumpolar north. A couple of things stand out, though. First, the cycle is not only normal, it is also desirable, perhaps essential, to the health of the overall boreal forest ecosystem. A mature spruce forest is a relatively sterile environment for many of the mammals and birds we think of as typical of the northern forest. The ecosystem would stagnate and populations of animals such as moose would be in rough shape if it were not for turnover such as that caused by fire.

Second, the cycle affects all of the organisms of the forest ecosystem, and these plants and animals have developed a wide array of adaptations for the boom and bust cycles that have characterized their homelands for probably several million years. In some cases, such as snowshoe hares, vertebrate populations have developed their own population cycles of abundance and scarcity, apparently little related to forest productivity.

A tired old spruce forest without a fire to rejuvenate it is vulnerable to other threats, particularly insect attack. Because most boreal forest stands are essentially monocultures with little more species diversity than in a cornfield, any insect that feeds on the dominant plant species can rapidly build up a tremendous population density and thus also rapidly deplete the food resource. Moreover, unhealthy populations of host plants tend to have lost a certain natural defense against the insect infestations, so insect attacks spread, literally, like wildfire, and with much of the same effect.

The most devastating insect attacks are by the larvae of moths such as the spruce budworm (which much prefers fir to spruce), and the hemlock looper, an inchworm that also has a taste for fir. These insects can destroy virtually every mature tree in a forest over thousands of acres. They are a deadly economic threat in areas of the boreal forest that are used to produce lumber and paper pulp, as in Newfoundland and Quebec.

Various kinds of bark beetles are also important mortality

Figure 8–15. Fireweed (*Epilobium angustifolium*), one of the most important and spectacular colonizers of burned and disturbed areas in the circumpolar North.

factors in boreal forest stands. Depredations of bark beetles are generally less spectacular than the work of the defoliators, since bark beetles kill the tree by burrowing under the bark. They are most effective in stands that have been weakened by age, drought, attacked by fire or by other pests.

The overall effect of these instability factors on the northern forest is to create a patchwork or mosaic ecosystem in which plots at all stages of the cycle of maturity or recovery from fire, insect, and wind damage are represented over a limited area. Another feature of this patchwork is a vegetation type that has little or no tree cover, but that may equal or exceed the area of forested terrain over huge expanses of the boreal forest biome.

Peatlands

Peatlands, along with mosquitos and blackflies, are the most infamous features of the northern forest. The endless muskegs of Canada have been likened to a case of leprosy on the landscape—an evil-smelling, rotting mire that gobbles up roads in summer and becomes an eerie world of half-light and windigo ghosts in winter.

The bogs of Europe have a similarly unsavory reputation. Not only are they the subject of legends of witches and mysterious lights, but they regularly disgorge the well-preserved bodies of prehistoric human inhabitants of the region. More often than not these "bog people" appear to be the victims of murder or execution, either as a result of their misdeeds or for some ritual purpose.

Unenthusiastic commentaries on northern peatlands go back many centuries. In fact, there is some basis for suggesting that the Arctic remained as little explored as it was for as long as it did because it was protected by a seemingly endless belt of peatlands immediately to the south. Particularly in recent years, though, peatlands have been objects of both scientific and commercial interest. Among the results has been the evolution of a complex terminology only a little less picturesque than the terms for glacial features, and generally much more confused and confusing.

Peatlands are found throughout much of the world and have a history of at least 400 million years. All of the earth's coal is the result of metamorphosis of ancient peatlands. The type of coal is a function of the age of the peat deposits and the geological events that have transpired since they were formed. The vast majority of the area and, particularly, the volume of true peat deposits, however, are in the Subarctic and in cool temperate coastal regions. In addition, most of the earth's peat deposits are of geologically recent origin. They generally postdate the retreat of the last glaciers, some 10,000 to 15,000 years ago. Peat bogs continue to warrant their malevolent reputation in parts of Atlantic Europe, where they actively encroach on prime farmland. On the other hand, peat deposits have long been a source of fuel. They have recently become the object of increased commercial interest as energy sources and as sources of horticultural peat. Relatedly, concern about their overexploitation has also grown, although the peatlands "smeared across Canada like leprosy" cover well over a million square kilometers, and similar peatlands encompass comparable areas in northern Europe and northeastern Siberia.

Boreal peatlands are known by local names wherever they occur. Since there are differences, subtle and less subtle, between the peatlands of various regions, there is no general agreement on any one correct name. The peatlands of boreal North America are commonly called *muskeg. Aapamire, palsamire, strangmoor,* and *hochmoor* are European terms for specific types of peatlands, and their use has spread to other areas. The word *mire* (*myr* in the Nordic languages) is a broad term for peatland. It is sometimes interpreted to include fens, marshes, and swamps, which are generally richer wetlands of temperate regions, and which contain less organic matter than the boreal peatlands. A *bog* is generally considered to be a type of peatland particularly rich in organic matter, exceptionally acid, and poor in nutrients.

All peatlands share one attribute: the decomposition cycle of their ecosystem is inhibited, so that over time there is a buildup of organic matter in the environment. The quantities of this excess organic matter can be impressive, so that peatlands are often called organic terrain. The conditions that inhibit the decomposers invariably include a situation under which the organic horizon is normally saturated with water and a lack of oxygen (an anaerobic environment). Thus, to form and to continue to exist, a peatland needs an excess of moisture as a result of high precipitation, poor drainage, low evaporation, and low transpiration in various combinations. Cool temperatures, short growing seasons, and drainage impeded by glaciation or permafrost encourage peatland formation. By the same token, peatlands are rare or absent in tropical rain forests in spite of the heavy precipitation and great production of organic matter. Fungal and bacterial action simply destroy organic matter before it can build up as peat.

THE CLASSIC BOG

Bogs are often a conspicuous feature of the landscape in cool temperate regions such as northeastern North America. Mysterious and perhaps terrifying because of the seemingly bottomless pools of black water they often contain, bogs' unusual plant communities have long made them objects of interest. These often contain rare species of plants such as certain orchids or supposedly carnivorous plants such as sundews and pitcher plants (see Figure 8–16). Only relatively recently has an awareness developed that these temperate bogs are isolated outposts of subarctic peatland environments, stranded by the warming climate as the glaciers retreated.

Bogs were of particular interest to the originators of the new science of ecology early in the twentieth century, since they appeared to display the process of succession exceptionally well. In theory, bogs originated as lakes caused by the impeded drainage associated with glacial retreat. These lakes were then supposedly slowly filled with organic matter, until they were ultimately able to support forests. Although the accuracy of this scenario is now considered dubious for many cases, reliance on it did result in the careful study of bog processes over the past several decades.

A classic bog is formed by the ingrowing of plants from the edges of the lake over which it is forming. The most important plant in this process is usually a type of moss, *Sphagnum,* or peatmoss (see Figure 8–13b). Of the many species in this group, different species play different roles in the growth and maintenance of the bog environment. Some species of *Sphagnum* grow particularly well in association with the roots and submerged stems of certain shrubs. Together, the plants tend to form a tough, fibrous network of plant material, which floats on the surface of the pond. *Sphagnum,* because it is a moss, does not have true roots. The top of the plant grows indefinitely, while the lower portions continuously die off. This process allows the bog mat to increase in thickness and solidity. In time, it provides a solid footing for additional plant species to colonize, although open water may remain beneath the floating mat.

Special properties of the body of *Sphagnum* are crucial to the

Figure 8–16. Sundew (*Drosera rotundifolia,* above) and pitcher plant (*Sarracenia purpurea,* below), two insectivorous plants typical of boreal peatlands. The sundew captures insects with the sticky tentacles on its leaves. The pitcher plant, the provincial flower of Newfoundland, captures and drowns insects in its hollow, liquid-filled leaves. In both cases, the plant derives otherwise rare nutrients from the decomposing insect bodies.

maintenance of the bog. Much of the plant consists of large, thin-walled, hollow cells. These cells allow the plant to absorb large quantities of water, many times the weight of the plant itself. Because it is trapped, this water is not easily evaporated. Thus, a *Sphagnum* mat tends to preserve its water supply. In addition, evidence shows that *Sphagnum* actually increases the acidity of the bog environment. The highly acid conditions prevalent in most *Sphagnum* bogs tend to inhibit the growth of bacteria and fungi, further limiting organic decomposition.

NORTHERN BOGS AND PEATLANDS

The bogs along the southern edges of the boreal forest and in temperate areas are few and scattered. Because warm temperatures encourage rapid drying and active decomposition, bogs are limited to local situations in which conditions are peculiarly suitable. As a result, bogs are confined to the basins of the lakes and ponds they have superseded: They cannot outgrow these confines and invade dry land. In an area of glaciated terrain such as occurs in much of Canada and Scandinavia, bogs can be common and extensive simply because of the impeded drainage and dead-ice topography, which provide endless small ponds and depressions suitable for bog formation. In areas where precipitation is heavy and summers are cool and damp, there are mechanisms that allow bogs to burst their bonds and engulf the surrounding countryside. These mechanisms involve the near impermeability of saturated peat to water seepage, and the ability of *Sphagnum* moss to hold quantities of water for long periods of time, losing little to evaporation.

In the cool, damp conditions of northern mainland Canada and northern Europe, *Sphagnum* may continue to grow above the original water table. It can trap water and remain saturated, in essence creating its own raised local water table. This raising, in turn, encourages the growth of more peat on the surface of the bog and around its edges. In time, the bog swells and spreads over the surrounding terrain, following roughly the contours of the ground and creating a phenomenon sometimes called a blanket bog (see Figure 8–17).

In a blanket bog, all of the water found at the surface has fallen on it directly, as rainwater. No water has come in from the surrounding environs by means of seepage, since the water table lies above the surrounding terrain. A bog of this type is called an *ombrotrophic* bog—its root word is the same as for umbrella,

Figure 8–17. A blanket bog in New-foundland. The dense peat combined with high precipitation and low evaporation raise the water table into the accumulating peat. Over time, blanket peat spreads out from low areas over the surrounding terrain, drowning the land in sodden peat.

and refers to rain. In a bog of this type, the bog water will be exceedingly impoverished of nutrients and of many soil chemicals, since rainwater is, or used to be before acid rain, nearly pure and sterile. This odd and impoverished soil chemistry has important implications for the vegetation of the bog surface. Only plants with a high tolerance for acid conditions and low nutrient concentrations can survive. On the other hand, competition is reduced for those plants that can adapt to the bog environment, so a number of specialized plants are often found. These are often species adapted to capturing insects, like sundews and pitcher plants (see Figure 8–17). These so-called carnivorous plants actually derive only nutrients, primarily nitrogen, from their prey. They do not eat the insects as animals do to derive energy.

Much peatland lies within the permafrost zones, and permafrost and peatland interact, evidently in a number of ways. The southernmost occurrences of sporadic permafrost in lowlands invariably occurs within peatlands. We mentioned palsas and string bogs *(aapamire, strangmoor)* in Chapter 6 and there skirted the issue of the relationship between permafrost and various raised features found on the surfaces of peatlands, as we will continue to do since little is known of the processes by which these features are created or about their relative importance.

PEATLAND, WOODLAND, AND TIMBERLINE

Many timberline species of trees and shrubs do poorly, if they survive at all, in peatlands. Peatlands seem to be anathema to white spruce, and the line between white spruce forest and bog can look as though it were cut with a bulldozer (see Figure 8–18). Black spruce is much more tolerant of muskeg conditions. In some situations, it may cover a peatland surface with a dense, dwarf woodland, but nearby it may be sparse or completely absent. Simply stated, peatlands are largely unforested but, if they do have a tree cover, trees are likely to be dwarfed and scattered. Since well over half of the terrain in many timberline environments is often covered with deep peat deposits, the timberline

Figure 8–18. Relationship of forest and treeless peatland in interior Alaska. From the stream level, the terrain appears to be a continuous dense conifer forest, but this aerial view clearly indicates how extensive the unforested, tundralike peatlands are in the subarctic regions.

forest is often patchy and dispersed. From the air, it appears to be a mosaic of forest, woodland, and treeless vegetation, perhaps interspersed with uplands extending above the regional altitudinal timberline. These are among the factors that often make it difficult to delineate the poleward limit of arborescent coniferous forest growth, which the timberline is said to demarcate.

Peatlands near timberline are nearly identical in the plants that grow in them, whether they occur within the forest borders or some distance beyond the last tree. So, in one sense, peatlands are a form of tundra. If we approached our discussion of the boundaries of the Arctic from the point of view of a tundra dweller, we might suggest a *tundraline* rather than a *timberline,* and we would place it deep within the forests of central Canada. The plants that dominate peatlands seem to be unaffected by the presence or absence of a few trees. These plants are discussed in some detail in the Chapter 9.

Figure 8–19. Lichen woodland in interior Labrador. The sparse, stunted trees in this picture are flagged by the abrasive action of blowing snow. One or more mild winters provided a window during which the trees were able to send shoots above the level of heaviest snow damage.

One final vegetational phenomenon of the timberline environment needs to be mentioned: a type of open forest that tends to replace peatland forests on uplands and other well-drained situations such as old outwash plains and other gravel features. It is generally known as lichen woodland. Lichens are a type of primitive plant, discussed in some detail in Chapter 9 under polar deserts. Near timberline, the floor of many open forests is dominated by a continuous mat of a kind of lichen, *Cladonia rangiferina,* often called by the inaccurate name reindeer "moss." Lichen woodland can be extensive and provides a stable environment that can be important as wintering range for caribou and reindeer (see Figure 8–19).

SUGGESTED FURTHER READING

Additional titles listed at the end of Chapter 9 are also relevant.

Arno, S. F., and R. Hammerly. *Timberline: Mountain and Arctic Forest Frontiers.* Seattle: The Mountaineers, 1984.

Gimingham, C. H. *Ecology of Heathlands.* London: Chapman and Hall, 1972.

Larsen, J. A. *The Boreal Ecosystem.* New York: Academic Press, 1980.

Moore, P. D., and D. J. Bellamy. *Peatlands.* London: Elek Science, 1974.

Viereck, L. A., and E. L. Little. *Alaska Trees and Shrubs.* Washington, DC: Forest Service, U.S. Department of Agriculture, 1972.

Zwinger, A. H., and B. E. Willard. *Land Above the Trees: A Guide to American Alpine Tundra.* New York: Harper and Row, 1972.

Chapter 9

Tundra Vegetation and Zonation

THE extended discussion of timberline in the last chapter may have left the reader with the idea that the tundra beyond the timberline is a more or less uniform area of barren, treeless terrain extending from the limit of trees northward to the edge of the polar sea. But the Arctic is never as simple as it appears, and the nature of the tundra biome is no exception to this rule. In this chapter, we'll look at the vegetation patterns of the tundra, the more important plants that make up the vegetation, and some of the reasons that tundra vegetation is distributed in the way it is.

We saw the timberline as a conspicuous boundary marking the farthest limit of conifers' ability to colonize the far north. But we also saw that it was a climatic boundary, or more accurately, a visible sign of the interaction of a physical phenomenon, summer temperature, with the physiology of a small group of closely related plants, the spruces and larches. As evident as the timber-line is, the actual difference between forest and tundra near the timberline is mainly a result of the presence or absence of a few species. Among these species are the trees themselves, plus some plants and animals that are usually intimately associated with trees, such as woodpeckers and bark beetles. There is some validity in thinking of tundra near timberline as simply boreal forest vegetation with the trees missing! Another way to put this is to say that one major vegetation type of the northern environment, the conifer forest, drops out of the picture at timberline.

It would not be surprising, according to this view, to find additional vegetation types disappearing from the scene as climatic conditions became increasingly rigorous toward the northern limits of land. We might also expect that the further disappearances might be correlated with the summer temperature regime, similar to the timberline, 10°C July isotherm relationship. In fact, this is precisely the case. Tundra can be seen as consisting of a series of vegetation belts, similar to the timberline. As we go farther northward, the succeeding belts include fewer types of vegetation. There are also generally fewer species of plants; we would say in botanical terms that the flora is progressively *impoverished* or *depauperate* deeper in the tundra.

On a large area of tundra immediately beyond timberline we can expect to find an array of vegetation types. If the following list were compared to that of any other discussion of tundra vegetation, the main discovery to be made is that arctic scientists do not agree on what are the basic components of tundra. At least part of the disagreement is a semantic one; it concerns the level of differentiation of vegetation types. Our examination of tundra vegetation will be kept simple.

To begin with, tundra vegetation includes features familiar from Chapter 8's timberline vegetation discussions. Riparian willow thickets follow the rivers deep into the tundra. They form extensive quasi-woodlands along major rivers 100 or more kilometers beyond timberline. They also occur in situations that are not really riparian, such as warm, south-facing slopes, snowbed communities, and solifluction lobes. Isolated shrub willow thickets occur northward to the Arctic Ocean in several areas and are even found in some high arctic situations such as the Canadian arctic islands. The willows that form riparian willow thickets are often called shrub willows, to distinguish them from species that are lower growing, often creeping and prostrate, and occur deep into the Arctic. In the wild, though, there isn't always a clear distinction between the two types.

Alder thickets also extend well beyond the timberline, although they are seldom as extensive as willow. They generally grow on river bars and shores and on cool, moist slopes.

We will begin our discussion of tundra vegetation with a variety of closed vegetation types. This is the type of vegetation that scientists often call *tundra* to distinguish it from the more open, barren environments called *fell fields* and *rock deserts*.

Sedge Meadows

If there is such a thing as typical tundra, it is the sedge meadow. Almost any flat or rolling terrain in the low Arctic is dominated by a mat of grasslike sedge plants (Figure 9–1). Sedge meadows become more fragmented and less extensive in the more extreme northern areas, but even here they form the only greensward, the only relief from the sterile-looking exposed rock and gravel. On the other hand, sedge meadows are related to the vegetation of the open peatlands of the boreal forest and timberline regions. So, tundralike sedge meadows may extend across some 40 degrees of latitude, and are circumpolar in their distribution. As one might expect, given their abundance and broad distribution, sedge meadows are variable and can be subdivided into types. This should not blind us to their overall similarity, though, and we can usefully generalize about them. Perhaps the best generalizations are about the plants themselves, the sedges.

The vast majority of northern sedges, in terms of both species and individuals, fall into two closely related groups, botanically known as *genera* (the singular is *genus*). In biological classifica-

Figure 9–1. Sedge meadow on St. Lawrence Island, Bering Sea. The climate here is too cold to support tussock tundra. Instead, a moist tundra consisting of various sedges and nontussock-forming cottongrass stretches to the horizon.

tion, the genus is the category above *species,* and each genus may contain one, several, or many species. The two major sedge genera of the far north are rich in species. Since the difference species generally differ in their tolerances and requirements for soil, drainage, climate, and so forth, these differences account at least partially for the ability of sedge meadows to dominate such a broad range of environmental conditions.

The most important group of sedges is known as cottongrass, or arctic cotton (see Figure 9–2). The *grass* part of the traditional name is inaccurate, since sedges are not grasses, although they are somewhat similar in appearance and closely related to grasses. Cottongrasses all belong to the single genus *Eriophorum.* Their characteristic feature is a head or inflorescence of many tiny flowers. The petals of each individual flower are modified into long, straight, fine hairs. In aggregate, these appear as a globular tuft, like a gone-to-seed dandelion. The hairs are most commonly pure white, but in some species or populations may be buff or pale gray.

Nonbotanists often despair of telling the various species of *Eriophorum* apart. This is understandable if the specimen to be identified is, say, a fragment recovered from the rumen of a caribou, but it is easy to identify the common species if they are seen or collected in flower. If you make an effort to identify the species, you will quickly see that different *Eriophorum* species are found in different conditions and, in fact, define different kinds of sedge meadow.

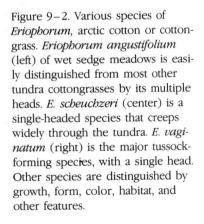

Figure 9–2. Various species of *Eriophorum,* arctic cotton or cotton-grass. *Eriophorum angustifolium* (left) of wet sedge meadows is easily distinguished from most other tundra cottongrasses by its multiple heads. *E. scheuchzeri* (center) is a single-headed species that creeps widely through the tundra. *E. vaginatum* (right) is the major tussock-forming species, with a single head. Other species are distinguished by growth, form, color, habitat, and other features.

If you find yourself face to face with a patch of cottongrass and wish or need to find out which species the plants belong to, there are two features to look at immediately (see Figure 9–2). First, determine whether the plant grows in dense clumps, or tussocks, with spaces between the individual colonies, or whether the plants form a continuous mat with no divisions between colonies. Second, look at the flowering portion to see whether each flowering stem has several heads, usually with each head drooping on a flexible stalk, or whether there are single, upstanding flower heads. If the plant is densely tufted, with single flowering heads, and if it occurs over broad areas of rolling terrain, it is probably *Eriophorum vaginatum.* This may be the single most abundant plant in the low Arctic, and it forms the basis for a type of sedge meadow often called tussock tundra. The other most common species of cottongrass has multiple heads, form mats rather than tussocks, and generally grow in flat areas with standing water. This will be discussed further under the topic of wet tundra.

Tussock Tundra

Tussock tundra is, to a greater or lesser extent, dominated by the tough, fibrous clumps of *Eriophorum vaginatum.* At a distance, tussock tundra appears to be a smooth, flat field, similar in appearance to a well-kept pasture. This perception is quickly dispelled when one tries to walk on tussock tundra. At their most virulent, tussocks are about the size of a human head (see Figure 9–3) and are connected to the ground by a narrow, flexible, but tough neck. The tussocks are not stable enough to bear an adult's weight but are firmly rooted to the ground and cannot be kicked out of the way. They are generally too densely situated to be stepped between. The interstices are usually filled with water or wet moss, and the moist, protected areas are perfect breeding places for mosquitos.

Tussock tundra can form a vegetation cover about as uniform as a cornfield, and the purest stands apparently rely on some special events comparable to cultivation for their continued integrity. Tussock tundra is the only type of tundra vegetation that is dense and inflammable enough to allow the spread of wildfire. In dry summers, thousands of acres of the dense, peaty mounds may smoulder for weeks in tundra fires. Generally, these fires kill any intervening vegetation such as willow and dwarf birch shrubs, but burn only the outer layers of the tussocks, removing a layer of dead stems and leaves. These fires actually rejuvenate the tus-

Figure 9–3. A classic tussock. The cottongrass *Eriophorum vaginatum* characteristically grows as a dense head connected to the ground with a flexible neck. This species is so successful in the low Arctic that it has been estimated that several trillion tussocks occur within Alaska alone. It might further be calculated that a predictably large number of mosquitoes accompany each tussock.

Figure 9–4. Tussock tundra with frost boils, seen from the air. Frost action seems to bring nutrients to the soil surface, apparently encouraging tussock growth and flowering.

socks, removing competition and probably making nutrients available. There is good reason to suppose that the "best" tussock tundra is the result of regular fires, probably occurring decades apart on the average. Tussock tundra also seems to be favored by intense frost action. Frost boils are often ringed by particularly healthy-looking tussocks, which give them a characteristic appearance in an aerial view (see Figure 9–4).

If a tussock field avoids fire and frost boils for long periods of time, the tussocks tend to become overgrown and covered with a layer of dead and decaying leaf bases and other detritus. This material seems to inhibit or smother the tussock, reducing the quantity of leaves and flowers. At the same time, a large tussock covered with dead material provides an excellent seedbed for other plants. In time, a mixed type of vegetation may develop, with various kinds of dwarf shrubs and other plants superimposing themselves on the underlying substrate of peaty tussocks. This phenomenon will be discussed further under shrub tundra.

Wet Tundra

Wet tundra is more widespread and less uniform than tussock tundra, and it is less dependent on a single species. Again, however, cottongrass is nearly always a major component, so we'll look at the relevant species of this group first. An extremely important species is the multiheaded, mat-forming *Eriophorum angustifolium* (see Figure 9–2). This species reaches its best development in flat, marshy areas, usually with standing water remaining over most of the summer. Low-center polygons provide the perfect habitat. This is generally not quite as uniform a vegetation type as tussock tundra, since the peaty ridges separating the polygons are slightly drier and usually support a variety of other plants. As the ground develops some slight relief and water tends to run off, *E. angustifolium* is often replaced by the mat-forming but single-flowered *E. scheuchzeri.* This species is often a very heavy flowerer, covering the tundra with a short, wiry, frosted-looking turf (see Figure 9–5). Where the marsh gives way to actual ponds another species, *E. russeolum* forms tussocks that are much more lush in appearance than those of *E. vaginatum.*

Cottongrasses are by no means the only sedge component of wet sedge meadows. In addition, a variety of true sedges, of the genus *Carex,* occur here. This group of plants is more difficult to identify than *Eriophorum.* Over a hundred species are known in Alaska alone. Figure 9–6 shows some of the characteristic features of this group of sedges and some of the most important

Figure 9–5. *Eriophorum scheuchzeri* in flower in a typical tundra environment, the arctic lowland near Barrow, Alaska.

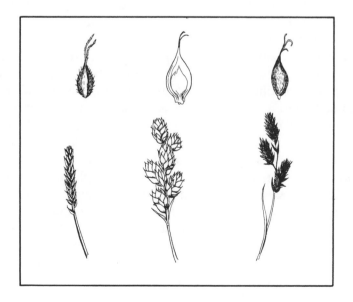

Figure 9–6. Inflorescences (aggregates of flowers) of several common species of *Carex,* or true sedge, common on tundra. On left is *C. scirpoidea,* with a single head. Center is *C. aenea,* with several identical heads. *C. atrofusca,* on the right, has both staminate (or pollen-bearing) and pistillate (or seed-bearing) heads in the same inflorescence. The nature of the inflorescence along with size, shape, and color of the *perigynium,* the flasklike structure enclosing the fruit (shown above the heads), are identifying features of many tundra sedge species.

tundra species. One species *(C. aquatilis)* approaches *Eriophorum angustifolium* in importance in many wet tundra areas throughout the Arctic. Other species are locally important in wet tundra, while many others occur in a wide variety of arctic habitats. Few of the vegetation types we'll mention are without one or more characteristic species of *Carex.*

In terms of sheer volume, or biomass, sedges far outweigh the true grasses in most tundra environments. Nonetheless, grasses are often abundant in both individuals and species in the tundra environment. Several species may be locally dominant. For example, a large, coarse grass called *Arctophila fulva* tolerates slightly deeper water than does *Eriophorum vaginatum.* If a low-center polygon contains a real pond, it may support a pure stand of this species. Grasses tend to be more important in local situations that are often lumped together for convenience under the term *mesic tundra.*

Mesic Tundra

Mesic tundra is the technical name for what might be called the rock gardens of the Arctic. Such tundra is also common in alpine areas; in fact, the so-called alpine meadows are essentially the same as mesic tundra. Mesic tundra comprises a variety of situations that provide an exceptional localized habitat and often allow a wide variety of otherwise-rare plants to flourish. The word *mesic* implies that the area is neither too wet nor too dry. This situation usually comes about because there is some water source: a spring, melting snowbed, or rivulet, and where there is some relief to allow for drifting snow or flowing water. Mesic situations also tend to favor small mammals, birds, and insects, and these may enrich the habitat in a number of ways.

Grasses are often important in mesic tundra. Many of the common tundra grasses are close relatives of lawn and field grasses familiar to temperate dwellers (see Figure 9–7). Bluegrasses *(Poa)* come in several species. Bluejoint *(Calamagrostis),* bent *(Agrostis),* fescue *(Festuca),* and brome *(Bromus)* are common. Grasses seem to be much more palatable and nutritious than most sedges, and they tend to attract grazing animals ranging in size from lemmings to mountain sheep and, in earlier times, probably bison and woolly mammoths. Thus, even relatively small proportions of mesic tundra may play an important role in the workings of the arctic and alpine ecosystems. Similarly, any change in conditions that favors the spread of, or

Figure 9–7. Some common tundra grasses. *Poa,* or bluegrass, (left) and *Festuca,* or fescue, (right) are common lawn grasses and are important in many mesic tundra areas as well.

causes the retreat of, mesic, grassy tundra can be reflected in major changes in animal populations and distribution.

Although grasses are often the green matrix of mesic tundra, mesic tundra's most conspicuous feature is its wildflowers. In terms of the total number of species and individuals of brilliantly flowering plants, probably nothing on earth compares with an acre or so of rich mesic tundra in a low arctic area. Over 100 species in flower simultaneously can be counted along a few hundred meters of lake shore at Feniak Lake, in the Noatak River drainage of northern Alaska, for example.

Snowbeds are a particular type of mesic tundra with special features. Snowbeds form when snow drifts deeply by filling a hollow or creating a cornice. The snow then lies late during the following spring. This shortens the growing season, but it also provides a steady source of moisture throughout the growing season as the drift melts. More important, it provides a comparatively warm, moist, protected environment for overwintering plants. Many snowbed species burst into flower within hours of being freed from drifted snow; some of our important cultivated plants, such as the early-flowering spring bulbs, are derived from snowbed species with this habit.

A related type of vegetation occurs on avalanche tracks, where any taller plants are scoured away by the moving snow. In mountainous regions, mesic tundra species may occur far below timberline under these conditions.

Because such a variety of species grow in mesic tundra, it is not possible to list typical plants. Many groups such as primroses *(Primula)* and gentians *(Gentiana)* are rich, important, and spectacular. One interesting feature of the plants of mesic tundra is that many of them are not circumpolar in their distribution patterns. They often appear to have originated in alpine areas and to have migrated into the Arctic secondarily and locally. So while wet tundra in Alaska may be indistinguishable from that of, say, northern Norway, the ancestors of plants in a nearby patch of mesic tundra might have been from the southern Rocky Mountains or the Alps.

A special type of vegetation best considered under mesic tundra inhabits many treeless oceanic islands such as the Aleutians. As earlier noted, the climate of many of these islands is hardly typical of the Arctic, and this is reflected in the nature of their equivalent of tundra. For example, some lowlands in the western Aleutians are covered by a nearly two-meter high growth of cow parsnip *(Heracleum lanatum),* an herb of the carrot family that resembles a giant celery plant. This growth is a favored resting habitat for the giant brown bears of the area, which may be first discovered by hikers at a distance of a meter or two in the dense, rank growth. At slightly higher elevations, most oceanic arctic islands are covered by a heathy shrub vegetation, a variation of the shrub tundra we'll look at next.

SHRUB TUNDRAS

Many low arctic areas are vegetated with a cover of shrubs, ranging in height from ankle high to a couple of meters. Three basic components of this shrub layer can usually be distinguished: willow, dwarf birch, and heath. Although the relative importance of these varies, we can use the most dominant group to characterize the vegetation type.

Riparian willows follow up the smallest tundra rivulets, generally becoming progressively lower in growth as the streams become smaller. Eventually, the heads of streams merge with the overall tundra, and low willow shrubs may spread out, particularly if the surrounding vegetation is old undisturbed tussock tundra. The result is a vegetation that is a hybrid between riparian willow and tussock tundra, combining many of the less pleasant features of each: notably, clouds of insects and rough walking.

We encountered dwarf birch in Chapter 8, where we mentioned that birch scrub of doubtful parentage was often an important component of the tree line environment. By the time we have left the trees a few kilometers behind, most dwarf birch is relatively pure blooded and has been reduced in stature to spreading shrubs no more than knee high. Dwarf birch is known by many scientific names (among them, *Betula nana, B. glandulosa, B. exilis*), probably because the influx of genes from the forest below favors the development of local populations or races. The shrubs usually have small, round, dark green leaves with prominent teeth along the edges; gray bark; and twigs that are often covered with warty protuberances that may exude a sticky substance, probably making the plants unpalatable for browsing animals. This resin is also very flammable; a tundra fire that rejuvenates the tussocks will usually eliminate dwarf birch, as the twigs blaze. Dwarf birch is brilliantly colored during the fall, often giving the tundra the appearance of a miniature maple forest.

Dwarf birch also invades old tussock tundra and may mix freely with willow and heath. It seems to be particularly well adapted to colonize dry upland ridges and situations such as karst-and-kettle topography. Pure dwarf birch tundra is particularly prominent in areas where glaciers have vacated rolling uplands relatively recently. (See Figure 9–8).

The heaths are members of a huge, worldwide family of plants known as the *Ericaceae,* or heath family (see Figure 9–9). This family includes such familiar plants as rhododendrons and azaleas, manzanita, heather, blueberry, cranberry, and mountain laurel. As huge and diverse as this family is, its members share

Figure 9–8. An extensive area of dwarf birch tundra, with an admixture of willow and a sprinkling of spruce trees, in central Alaska.

Figure 9–9. An array of typical
heath plants, all with circumpolar
distribution patterns in the low arctic and alpine regions. Top left, Labrador tea *(Ledum groenlandicum),*
top center, arctic bell heather *(Cassiope tetragona),* top right, Lapland
rosebay *(Rhododendron lapponi-
cum),* lower left, alpine bearberry
(Arctostaphylos alpina), lower center, tundra bilberry *(Vaccinium uliginosum),* lower right, alpine azalea
(Loisleuria procumbens).

many characteristics and adaptations. Many of these make the
group particularly well suited to colonize cold acid bogs and
tundra.

All heaths are more or less woody, and most are shrubs,
including many creeping, colony-forming types. They tend to
have small, thick leaves and are often evergreen. The roots are
shallow and particularly adapted to acid, boggy conditions. The
flowers are usually numerous, often spectacular, and provide a
major source of brilliance and color in many northern environments. Heathy shrubs are often the dominant form of vegetation
on the peatlands that surround the northernmost patches of
forest. In one sense their role in the Arctic is as a northward
extension of the muskeg and mire; the majority of species don't
extend north of the low Arctic, although a few are found in stony
uplands far beyond timber. Most of the heath plants are often
closely associated with *Sphagnum* moss. *Sphagnum* and heath
tend to invade tussock fields when moisture is abundant and fires
have not occurred for a long period.

The list of heath shrubs generally found in shrub tundra is
relatively short. The plants are easily identified, and, since they
are mostly circumpolar, the ability to recognize them is useful
anywhere in the North. Several of the most important are illustrated in Figure 9–9.

Labrador tea *(Ledum)* includes at least two populations that are
often considered as separate species, although they differ mainly

in the size of their leaves. *Ledum* has white flowers in clusters and looks like a miniature rhododendron. Its leaves are evergreen and have a white or orange feltlike fuzz on their undersurfaces. They are aromatic and give the tundra a spicy odor under warm summer sun. They can be used to make a tealike decoction. Labrador tea ranks with cottongrass as a predictable component of low arctic tundra.

The genus *Vaccinium* includes the blueberries, two species of which are common on the tundra. One, *V. vitis-idaea,* is actually a red berry, and it is also unusual among blueberries in that it has shiny, evergreen leaves. It is well known in Scandinavia as the lingonberry, but it occurs throughout the circumpolar North, in all but the highest arctic areas. It is sometimes so dwarfed as to hardly seem woody. A larger plant, the tundra bilberry *(V. uliginosum)* is a more typical blueberry, with deciduous leaves and blue-black berries. It produces vast quantities of berries over much of the tundra area and well south in mountains and bogs. Like many other circumpolar species, it includes a wide variety of races, and its classification is a fertile source of disagreement among botanists of the tundra flora.

Alpine bearberry *(Arctostaphylos alpina)* is actually a dwarf species of manzanita. It has large, wrinkled leaves, pale green, bell-shaped flowers, and large, black, tasteless berries. The leaves of this species turn brilliant scarlet in the fall. In mountainous areas, it often forms a belt of vegetation above a level dominated by dwarf birch; late August brings a zone of brilliant orange birch foliage, surmounted by a belt of deep scarlet, and this is often topped by white from rime or snow.

There are several species of bell heathers in the genera *Cassiope* and *Phyllodoce.* They are similar in that they have needle-like evergreen leaves and bell-shaped or urn-shaped leaves. These plants are more common on dry, rocky uplands than on typical shrub tundra. They are particularly prevalent in moist coastal mountain regions where they may form extensive heaths. One common circumpolar species *(C. tetragona)* extends far into the high Arctic, the northernmost of the heath shrubs. Its thick mats may sometimes be useful as an emergency fuel or kindling.

One of the most important dwarf shrubs in this group is not actually in the *Ericaceae,* although its differences from members of that family are only technical, and it might as well be considered as a heath. This is the crowberry, *Empetrum nigrum.* It is a dwarf, creeping, evergreen shrub with black or dark red berries. Humans find them at best only marginally edible, but these berries are an important source of food for some birds and mammals. *Empetrum* is often common on tundra, beach shores, stony uplands, and all but the most exposed situations throughout the Arctic.

Before leaving the various kinds of closed, sedgy, shrubby, and heathy tundras, a final mention is in order of the dwarf, creeping, white-flowered species of raspberry known technically as *Rubus chamaemorus.* It is called by a variety of names, including salmonberry and, in Newfoundland, bake-apple. The fruits are large, orange, and considered a delicacy by most northern people, although some southerners have difficulty in acquiring the taste, which is faintly redolent of seal oil. Salmonberry fruits sporadically on the tundra, but a good year sets all northern communities to serious berry picking. The berries can be so abundant as to stain the tundra a pink-flesh color, and one Eskimo dialect describes this situation with a word that translates as "man with no clothes on."

FELL FIELDS

In the Norse languages, the word *fjell* means stony mountain slopes; the word migrated to Scotland in Viking times and at some point lost its *j,* which is unpronounced anyway. We now apply the term *fell field* to any stony tundra area where vegetation is thin and discontinuous. On a moisture and exposure gradient, fell field tends to supplant heath tundra and tussock tundra in drier areas. Under the most rigorous conditions, it gives way to bare rock, talus, and gravel, which is in appearance, at least, devoid of vegetation.

One might also view fell field as a drier and less rich counterpart of mesic tundra. It is similar to this type of vegetation in that it is quite variable in the species that occur there. Many of the plants are the same as or related to the beautiful alpine species, and a close look may reveal that a fell field that appears barren is a rock garden.

In spite of the variability of fell fields, one group of plants is so typical that it is often almost a synonym for fell field: again and again the term *Dryas* fell field appears. *Dryas* is a dwarf, creeping, slightly woody shrub in the rose family. It has distinctive evergreen leaves and white or pale yellow flowers (see Figure 9–10). These are found throughout most of the circumpolar Arctic, with a wide variety of species and races. The flowers are commonly pollinated by bumblebees, and it can be disconcerting to see a

Figure 9–10. *Dryas.* One of the most characteristic of the arctic flowering plants, *Dryas* is a slightly woody, creeping, shrubby species that occurs on barren uplands throughout the circumpolar North, so that such barren uplands are often known as *Dryas* fell fields. Species can be distinguished from one another by their leaves. The leaves are tough and resistant to decay, and they often show up intact in deposits that are thousands of years old.

flower garden complete with buzzing bees at the foot of a glacier at 80° north. *Dryas* flowers are in the shape of a parabolic reflector; they follow the sun and are able to focus its rays on their reproductive structures to raise temperatures of these organs several degrees on a sunny day.

Fell fields also usually have a wide variety of heath plants, including many of those mentioned before, as well as some additional species. Perhaps the most common of these is one called alpine azalea *(Loisleuria procumbens)*; its evergreen leaves and pink flowers lie flat on the surface of the ground.

Another important denizen of fell fields is the arctic poppy (see Figure 9–11). Again, the final identification of the several closely related species is best left to botanists. Most arctic poppies are brilliant yellow, but they may also be pale yellow, white, or occasionally rose. These poppies are among the most fragile and delicate of flowers, yet they reach their peak in the most exposed situations and can often be seen poking through a snowdrift after a June storm.

POLAR STEPPE

Arctic botanists have begun to recognize a type of vegetation somewhat similar to fell field but that differs in several respects. It usually occurs on dry, fine-grained soil, silt, or sand deposits, rather than on gravel or rock and rubble. Vegetation cover is generally more complete, and the majority of the plants are herbaceous rather than woody. This steppe has a dry, turfy appearance, and it seems to have some kinship with the steppe of the dry uplands of northern interior Asia, such as Outer Mongolia and central Siberia.

This steppe is often dominated by a single group of grasslike plants, which are also common in temperate regions and are known as woodrushes *(Luzula)*. A close relative, *Juncus,* the true rushes may also be important, but they tend to prefer wetter areas. *Luzula* may be abundant enough to form a sparse turf by itself, or it may be mixed with a variety of grasses and sedges, poppies, and other herbaceous species.

Polar steppe, or luzula steppe, as it is sometimes called, often occurs on the tops of high-center polygons. It may be extensive in areas where ice-rich soil has resulted in a gently rolling topography with dry hillocks and ridges (see Figure 9–12). Over long enough periods of time, it may cover dune fields and drained lake beds.

Figure 9–11. Arctic poppies. Although they appear to be as fragile as tissue paper, these flowers occur on the most barren and exposed situations throughout the Arctic.

Figure 9–12. Dry, turfy vegetation, sometimes called luzula steppe. This is a common high arctic vegetation type, which often develops in semi-arid situations such as the tops of high-center polygons.

POLAR DESERT

The term *polar desert* usually describes barren areas of bare rock, shattered bedrock, and sterile gravel. These conditions are essentially an extreme form of fell field, with vegetation cover, at least of higher plants, reduced to near zero. Actually, this initial impression of barrenness is usually inaccurate. It is hard to find a square meter of polar desert that has no form of vegetation growing on it. By far the most important group of plants here are the lichens.

Lichens (pronounced *like'-unz*) are the foot soldiers or unsung heroes of the tundra environment. Lichens are in a sense a group of primitive plants, although it is more correct to think of them as a colony or association of two kinds of plants living together. The main body of a lichen is called a thallus; it consists of a dense, tangled mass of threadlike fungal material. This fungal matrix varies greatly in shape from one kind of lichen to another, but each kind has a characteristic form by which it can usually be identified. Encapsuled with the fungal strands are quantities of single-celled algae. These tiny green plants supply the colony with nutrients.

Most of the fungi that participate in the lichen relationship cannot exist without the algal component. This severely limits the sex life of the fungus, since it cannot reproduce sexually and at the same time provide a source of algae to offspring produced by spores. It solves the problem by bypassing its normal reproductive strategies and structures by producing various kinds of asexual propagules: little packages with a sprinkling of the algal cells included. This situation, cumbersome and unsatisfying as it may seem, works pretty well for the lichens, and they are widely distributed in virtually every terrestrial habitat on the earth, including the northernmost and southernmost lands in the world. The situation is less satisfactory for botanists who try to classify lichens, since sexual structures are the *sine qua non* for most plant classification systems. As a result, lichens are classified by a series of schemes based on shape, growth habit, color, reproductive structures, and often the chemical constituents of the plant.

Lichens are traditionally included in three groups based on growth habit (see Figure 9–13). Fruticose lichens look like tiny shrubs; they grow up from the substrate (or hang down from tree limbs) in filaments, columns, or branching structures. The so-called reindeer moss *(Cladonia)* of the lichen woodlands near timberline is a classic fruticose lichen. Foliose lichens have a flat, leaflike form, with a distinct upper and lower surface. Many foliose lichens are attached to the substrate by a central stalk, and these are sometimes called umbilicate lichens. Crustose lichens form a flat layer on a surface, often looking like a thick layer of cracked paint.

Lichens are primitive in that they do not have flowers, seeds, roots, leaves, or conductive tissue. On the other hand, they are chemically sophisticated. Many lichens produce complex organic

Figure 9–13. Lichens. A typical crustose lichen *(Rhizocarpon geographicum)* grows on the upper surface of the rock, while foliose lichens such as *Parmelia* (at left on rock) and *Umbilicaria* (on lower right of the rock) grow below. Several types of fruticose (shrubby) lichens grow on the soil around the rock. The tentaclelike lichens at the lower right are *Dactylina*. On the bottom left is *Cladonia rangiferina* (reindeer "moss").

acids that can etch or dissolve stone and allow the plants to gain a firm foothold on the bare rock that they often colonize. These lichenic acids are often useful in identifying the lichens; they develop brilliant colors in the presence of some chemical reagents. This same property is responsible for a long-standing commercial use of lichens, which can produce brilliant and long-lasting dyes. Lichens have long been exported from northern areas for this purpose. Although they have been largely supplanted by modern chemical dyes, they are still used to produce the color in some traditional fabrics such as Harris tweed.

Lichens are extremely slow growing. One familiar species, known as map lichen *(Rhizocarpon geographicum),* is a crustose species that in cold climates may take centuries to form a patch the size of a human hand. It has been useful in dating the time and rate of glacial retreat in arctic areas such as Ellesmere Island; the larger the lichen colony, the longer the time since the ice left. The slow growth of lichens also causes them to effectively concentrate any airborne pollutants. Lichens are extremely susceptible to sulfer compounds, and most lichens disappear completely from areas where this form of air pollution occurs. In the 1950s, when atmospheric testing of nuclear weapons was still being carried out, the slow-growing surfaces of reindeer lichen tended to concentrate radioactive fallout. The reindeer ate the lichen, and several groups of indigenous people ate the reindeer. Some of these people, who may well never have heard of nuclear weapons, proved to have markedly elevated levels of radioactivity in their bodies. The problem has recurred recently in Lapland as a result of the Chernobyl accident.

In many arctic environments, the number of species of lichens in a given area is greater than the number of species of higher plants. In terms of the total amount of living material (or biomass), lichens are often much more significant than higher plants in polar deserts, bare rock, and fell fields. Lichens can also be a major component of other tundra vegetation. They inhabit the bare soil between tussocks if it is not too wet, and some species even colonize other tundra plants. Most areas of rock desert seem to be expanses of dark gray, but a close look at the rocks oftens shows that they are some other color beneath the nearly continuous coating of dark lichens. This is often particularly evident in a snow-filled corrie. As the summer progresses, more and more bare rock is exposed by melting snow until, in an exceptionally warm summer, rock that is exposed only at intervals of many years may appear at the edge of the retreating snow. This rock will normally be devoid of lichens, and it will generally contrast strongly with the surrounding snow-free area.

Since lichens colonize bare rock and gravel, and since they have the ability to break down rock surfaces chemically, it has long been accepted that they are intimately involved in the building of soils in barren areas such as those left behind by retreating glaciers. Recent studies suggest that lichens' role in these processes may be overestimated, but there is no question that they are generally the first group of macroscopic organisms to reclaim habitat vacated by glaciers.

Although the role of higher plants in polar deserts appears minimal, the actual number of species is often quite large. Polar desert is really an extreme form of fell field and, if it has protected areas, or areas where soil and moisture are abundant, these will often develop patches of richer vegetation—fell fields, or mesic tundra.

No plants are entirely confined to the polar desert, but a number of plants tend to be squeezed out by the vigorous, weedy growth of the tundra but really come into their own in the otherwise bleak wastelands of bare rock and fell field. Other than some species of grasses and sedges, perhaps the most important are some members of the saxifrage family and mustard family (see Figure 9–14).

Figure 9–14. Four saxifrages. *Saxifraga cernua,* top left, is a white-flowered species with small red bulblets, which look like kidney stones, in the axils of the stem leaves. To the right is *S. hirculis,* a yellow-flowered plant of seepage areas and wet tundra. Lower left is *S. oppositifolia,* whose bright purple flowers are abundant on the earliest bare ground in the high arctic spring. On the lower right is *S. flagellaris,* named after the whiplike reproductive tendrils that help it form mats in exposed barrens in some of the lands nearest the North Pole.

Saxifraga means *stonebreaker* in Latin, but its name has nothing to do with any ability of the tiny plants to do away with the rocks of the polar desert. Many saxifrages reproduce by dropping off tiny pink buds, as well as seeds. This relatively common reproductive strategy among arctic plants is known as *vivipary*. In saxifrages, the buds supposedly look like kidney stones, and early herbalists and physicians believed that this was a sign that they were useful for treating that malady and so named the genus after this supposed ability. With the demise of this doctrine, saxifrages' only claim to fame is to brighten up the barren fell field environment with a variety of white, pink, and yellow blossoms, sometimes the only color to be seen other than the ubiquitous lichens.

The mustard family also includes tiny, brilliant tundra flowers; they are distinguished from saxifrages by their petals in groups of fours. These may be white, yellow, or occasionally pink or purple.

The carnation family, which includes such familiar garden weeds as chickweed, is also represented in some of the bleakest and northernmost polar deserts. The most familiar arctic representatives of this family are indistinguishable from those in temperate gardens. Other familiar tundra wildflowers include buttercups and forget-me-nots!

DISTRIBUTION OF FLORA
AND VEGETATION IN THE ARCTIC

We should begin here by defining *flora* and *vegetation*. The flora of an area is the array of species of plants found there, while the vegetation is the overall aspect of the plant cover, as in several examples above. Thus, two examples of fell field *vegetation,* which may appear to be identical, may yet have very different *floras.* On the other hand, many of the same plants may occur in two distinct vegetation types, such as wet tundra and fell field. However, vegetation is seldom spread uniformly over even a small area. An area that overall is best characterized as fell field may well have a bit of marsh, possibly even a patch of forest in it. Each of these will cause an increase in the total flora of the area. This means, too, that a fell field near timberline will be different in its flora from an area of similar vegetation in the high arctic islands.

People who classify vegetation generally develop a hierarchical system, in which each major type (for example, fell field) includes subtypes. Our classification of sedge meadows followed this plan, since they are so widespread and variable, but we could have carried the process several steps farther. A sophisticated system of classification of the vegetation of Alaska, for example, recognizes hundreds of different units of classification. The smallest units tend to be dominated by one or a few species, so they are often named in terms of the species (for example, *Dryas* fell field). So, at lower levels, flora and vegetation tend to run together.

As we travel northward into the Arctic from timberline to the northernmost arctic islands, both the vegetation and the flora change. Certain vegetation types, like forest, disappear totally, so that all the species that occur only in forest cease to be components of the flora. On the other hand, other vegetation types become more widespread; polar desert dominates most of the Canadian high Arctic. But the floristic components of polar desert on Ellesmere Island are quite different from those in an area of similar-looking vegetation in, say, northern Labrador. Generally speaking, the more extensive, more northern polar desert of the high Arctic has many fewer species, and thus much less diversity and fewer subtypes, than similar-looking areas to the south. The reason for this is analogous to the timberline situation discussed in Chapter 8. At timberline, a conspicuous part of the flora drops out of the picture. In fact, this floristic component defines a vegetation type: boreal forest. So, timberline functions as a boundary for both flora and vegetation.

There are many "timberlines" to be crossed in a journey northward from the forest edge to the polar coast of the high Arctic. If we see the northern terrain as covered by a mosaic of vegetation types, forest, tundra, fell field, and so forth, the mosaic becomes simpler as we go northward and lose plants. Before timberline we lose pines and firs; at timberline we lose spruces or larch. A few tens of kilometers farther and we lose alder scrub; then riparian willow thickets disappear. We then have sedge meadow of various kinds, some dwarf scrub composed of birch, willow, and *Ericaceae,* broad areas of fell field, and, probably in localized areas, mesic tundra and polar desert. In fact, we are describing a typical example of what would commonly be called low arctic tundra, the treeless vegetation typical of continental areas along the northern borders of much of Eurasia and North America, but generally some distance inland from the actual coast. This corresponds to the area called zone 4 in Figure 9–15.

As we continue toward the coast or out onto the islands, more *timberlines* occur. These are often rather subtle, but they become quite evident under closer examination. For example, one of the

Figure 9–15. Circumpolar zones 1 through 4. Zone 4 begins near timberline and encompasses most of what has traditionally been called the low Arctic. Zone 1 encompasses the most extreme and depauperate high Arctic, or polar desert environment.

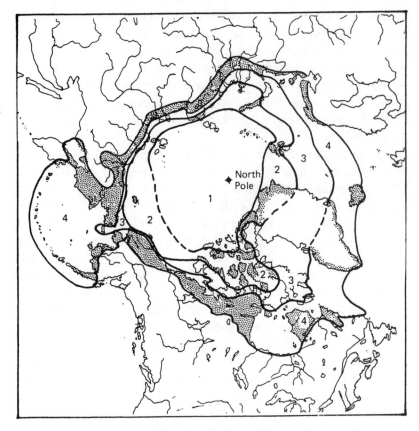

most interesting features of the tundra around Barrow, in northernmost Alaska, is the total absence of tussock tundra. Why is this? *Eriophorum vaginatum,* the tussock-forming cottongrass, has a northern limit that is just as clearly defined as that of spruce, although it is farther to the north. Some distance beyond timberline in Canada, Alaska, or northern Siberia is a *tussock line,* marking the circumpolar disappearance of both *Eriophorum vaginatum* and tussock tundra. At a virtually identical location is the northernmost limit of dwarf birch and of Labrador tea, so some kinds of dwarf scrub also disappear. These lines mark the northern edge of zone 4, the traditional low Arctic. We are now left with wet tundra, fell field, and polar desert, and a pretty good remnant of the many subtypes of mesic tundra.

Farther north we lose more groups of plants. Most ferns and horsetails are now gone, and almost all of the *Ericaceae.* The few woody plants left are mainly willows and can hardly be considered shrubs, as their twigs lie flat on the ground or under the surface. We are now in the traditional high Arctic: Svalbard,

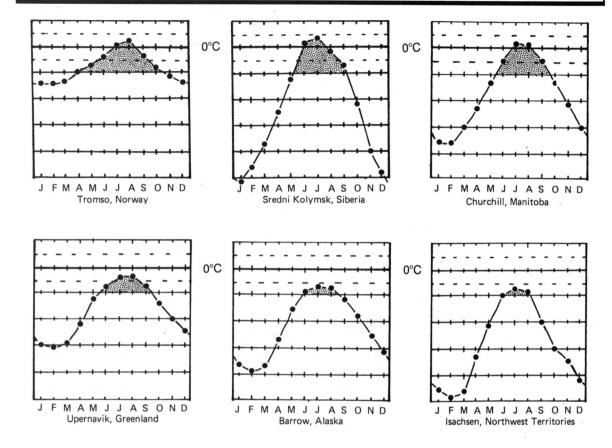

0°C   0°C

J F M A M J J A S O N D
Tromso, Norway

J F M A M J J A S O N D
Sredni Kolymsk, Siberia

J F M A M J J A S O N D
Churchill, Manitoba

0°C   0°C

J F M A M J J A S O N D
Upernavik, Greenland

J F M A M J J A S O N D
Barrow, Alaska

J F M A M J J A S O N D
Isachsen, Northwest Territories

Novaya Zemlya, Ellesmere Island, or north Greenland. This is mostly the area called zone 2 in Figure 9–15.

Finally we come to an area in which polar desert is virtually all that is left. Bits of wet sedge meadow may occur here and there in protected hollows, and some bluffs and raised beaches may have a thin *Luzula* steppe. Even the most dwarfed woody plants (like *Dryas*) have been left behind, and we are in the extreme Arctic, zone 1.

As we did with the timberline, we can correlate these zones and boundaries within the Arctic with climatic factors; summer temperature is clearly the most important. Figure 9–16 shows diagrammatically the climate of several arctic stations typical of the various zones. While the zone boundaries cannot be precisely linked to any specific isotherm (among other problems, not enough weather stations exist), the relationship between short, cold summers and increasingly bleak and impoverished vegetation is clear.

Figure 9–16. Climatic diagrams from stations within the floristic zones of Fig. 9–15. Mean monthly temperatures vary by only a few degrees between stations; duration of temperatures above freezing controlls the distribution of plant species whose ranges define the zones. Tromso and Sredni Kolymsk are near timberline at the lower edge of zone 4. Churchill Manitoba is in central zone 4, while Upernavik is a typical zone 3 station. Barrow lies within zone 2, while Isachsen, deep in the Canadian high Arctic, has only two months in which temperatures average barely above freezing, typical of zone 1. Only about 30 species of flowering plants, all herbaceous, grow in the immediate vicinity of that station.

If any more support were necessary to show the relationship between summer temperature and arctic vegetation, some of the best is supplied by the recognition of what have come to be called heat oases. Certain places in the high Arctic have unusually warm summers, by virtue of a continental climate, protection from cold winds off the ocean, a southern exposure, or some combination of factors. Even in the most isolated areas, these heat oases tend to support islands of vegetation characteristic of a more southerly zone. For example, the inner fiord district of Spitzbergen was once believed to have escaped glaciation during the last Ice Age because so many unexpected plants grow there. A more parsimonious explanation is simply that an array of more southerly (lower zone) plants have been able to colonize this relatively warm, protected site in the few thousand years since the glaciers vacated it. Many similar sites have been found in parts of the Canadian Arctic as exploration has progressed.

It is obvious that this zonation and progressive impoverishment of the vegetation northward in the Arctic have a major effect on what animal species can live on the tundra. In some cases these relationships seem to be pretty simple: woodpeckers or red squirrels are not found beyond timberline. Others are more complicated and depend on a variety of interlocking factors. Chapter 10 will examine the animal inhabitants of the tundra and at least the rudiments of their interrelationships with plants and other features of the tundra environment.

SUGGESTED FURTHER READING

Several *floras,* or systematic treatments of the higher plants inhabiting an area, are listed. One or more of these would be indispensable for any serious attempt to identify the local plants of any given arctic area. Fortunately, much of the tundra flora is circumpolar in its distribution, so a flora of, or guide to, one region can be useful elsewhere. Following the floras, recent general, but rather technical, works on the tundra biome are listed.

Floras

Böcher, T. W., K. Holmen, and K. Jakobsen. *The Flora of Greenland.* Copenhagen: P. Haase and Sons, 1968.

Hultén, E. *The Circumpolar Plants I.* Stockholm: Almqvist and Wiksell, 1964.

————. *Flora of Alaska and Neighboring Territories.* Stanford, CA: Stanford University Press, 1968.

Porsild, A. E. *Illustrated Flora of the Canadian Arctic Archipelago.* Ottawa: National Museum of Canada Bulletin #135. 1957.

Porsild, A. E., and W. J. Cody. *Vascular Plants of Continental Northwest Territories, Canada.* Ottawa: National Museums of Canada, 1980.

Tolmatchev, A. I., and B. A. Yurtsev. *Flora Arctica URSS.* Leningrad: Nauka. (Published in Russian in a series of fascicles.)

Welsh, S. L. *Anderson's Flora of Alaska and Adjacent Parts of Canada.* Provo, UT: Brigham Young University Press, 1974.

Additional Literature

Bliss, L. C., O. W. Heal, and J. J. Moore. *Tundra Ecosystems: A Comparative Analysis.* Cambridge, England: Cambridge University Press, 1981.

Brown, J., P. C. Miller, L. L. Tiezen, and F. L. Bunnell. *An Arctic Ecosystem: The Coastal Tundra at Barrow, Alaska.* Stroudsburg, PA: Dowden, Hutchins, and Ross, 1980.

Chernov, Yu. I. (trans. D. Love, 1985). *The Living Tundra.* Cambridge, England: Cambridge University Press, 1980.

Walker, M. *Harvesting the Northern Wild.* Yellowknife, Canada: The Northern Publishers, 1984.

Chapter 10

Tundra Animals

THE middle of the twentieth century was a time of renewed interest in the Arctic. While much of this interest was, sadly, based on the recognition of its strategic military significance, basic scientific curiosity also played a part. Coincident with the new round of arctic studies was a revolution in the burgeoning science of ecology. This revolution resulted from an increased awareness of the importance of the relationship between organisms and ecosystems: a recognition of the importance of competition, parasitism, symbiosis, and so forth. Ecologists became aware that the flow of energy through ecosystems is a function of the interactions of organisms. Models of these systems of interaction soon became dauntingly complex, a complexity increased by the first generation of computers available to ecologists.

The Arctic appeared to be an ideal place to study a real world ecosystem in terms of energy flow. The tundra biome is a system in which everything seems simplified, honed down to the bare essentials, with all but the strongest players eliminated by the bleakness and rigor of the natural environment. In this view, the

Arctic was a living laboratory in which ecological theory could be tested within the constraint of many natural controls, before turning the theory loose on the riotous complexity of a coral reef or a tropical rain forest.

Like any scientific hypothesis worth talking about, this idea turned out to be an egregious oversimplification with a kernel of truth in it. We can, in fact, easily get a handle on the tundra ecosystem. In comparison to, say, temperate forest, the tundra biome eliminates the entire canopy of forest trees, the understory of shrubs and vines, and most of the forest floor plants that compete for the limited sunlight filtering through the leaves. It does away with the cold-blooded terrestrial vertebrates, reptiles, and amphibians, since they cannot survive the long, frozen winters or burrow into the permafrost. The majority of standard temperate soil organisms are absent, unable to survive in the thin active layer during the short summer or to colonize bare, ice-scoured bedrock.

One way to visualize this situation is to examine the ecological niches of the various organisms that make up a community in the tundra, or elsewhere. The niche of a species is its role in the play of the ecosystem. The more species, the more roles and, in theory, the more complex and richer the fabric of relationships in the ongoing play. While it is an open question whether there can be such a thing as an open niche—a role without a player— we can generally think of the number of niches as equivalent to the number of species in the ecosystem. Since the web of interaction between species involves many other species, each additional niche in an ecosystem dramatically increases the complexity of the system. The smallness of the number of players in the arctic ecosystem supposedly reduces the complexity of the web of relationships to terms that make study of that system more manageable.

We have already looked at many of the players in Chapter 9: the plants. Over the objections of many botanists, however, we might think of the plants as being more analogous to stage properties than to the players themselves. In theater, the bowl of fruit on the table or the termites in the floorboards generally have a subservient role to the human (or at least vertebrate) actors. Without straining the metaphor any further at this point, we will begin our survey of the more conspicuous members of the arctic ecosystem. Later we will consider the interplay of these organisms among themselves and with others we have already discussed, and then reexamine the question of how subtle and complex these interactions are.

PRIMARY CONSUMERS

Primary consumers are organisms, generally animals, that derive their livelihood directly from plants. In the tundra environment these range from large vertebrates such as caribou to small ones such as lemmings, and to invertebrates such as mosquitoes, which (contrary to appearances) derive most of their energy from sucking plant juices. The number of species of conspicuous and important primary consumers on the tundra is sharply limited, and we can look at them in some depth. Since relatively few tundra birds are primary consumers, we will treat them with the remainder of the avian fauna in Chapter 12. The insects and other invertebrate primary consumers of the Arctic could easily fill a book of their own. Since this is not that book, we will give them a few paragraphs at the end of the section on mammalian herbivores in this chapter.

Caribou and Reindeer

Not many decades ago, it was fashionable to distinguish many species among closely related populations of large animals, such as caribou and reindeer. Until the 1950s, caribou were not only classified separately from reindeer, but several species of caribou were recognized on the basis of size, color, distribution, and similar factors. Fortunately, scientists have gotten away from this "splitter" concept, and we recognize all the races of caribou-reindeer as part of a single species, *Rangifer tarandus* (see Figure 10–1); reindeer in Eurasia, caribou in North America. The races are no more distinct than races within the human species. In fact, one of the difficulties of early attempts to herd domestic reindeer in North America was the what might be called kidnapping of reindeer by wild caribou herds, indicating that the reindeer and caribou considered themselves to be all in the same species.

Caribou are members in good standing of the large group of generally grazing mammals called ruminants. Ruminants characteristically have cloven hooves, a complex digestive system including a multichambered stomach, the first chamber of which is a rumen in which partially chewed food is held and undergoes early stages of digestion through the action of microorganisms. Food is regurgitated from the rumen and chewed as a cud in ruminants, such as deer, cattle, and sheep.

Caribou belong to the deer family, *Cervidae*. Deer differ from other ruminants in that they have antlers rather than horns.

Figure 10–1. Reindeer: the Eurasian equivalent of the North American caribou, and the dominant large herbivore in the modern tundra environment.

Antlers are formed of true bone instead of having only a bony core and are normally shed and regrown each year. Caribou differ from other deer in that both males and females, rather than only male animals, have antlers. Furthermore, the antlers on the does are shed much later in the year than those of the bucks, so that in winter, the antlered animals are female.

Throughout the circumpolar north, caribou are the common denominator among all large tundra animals. They range northward to the limit of land in Greenland and the various arctic islands (humans have introduced them to some of these). They originally ranged south as far as the northern tier of the United States and good-sized populations are still found in some forested portions of southern Canada. These so-called woodland caribou tend to utilize ridge tops and various types of barren ground and muskeg within the boreal forest region.

Caribou are generally larger than the woodland deer of temperate regions, but smaller than the largest cervids such as moose. An average cow of a small race would weigh less than 100 kilograms, while a typical bull of one of the larger races would weigh over 200 kilograms. (As if the nomenclature of caribou were not complex enough, caribou are *bull* and *cow,* while reindeer are *buck* and *doe.*) With this much variation in weight, it is difficult to say what is an average size for caribou; they appear a good deal smaller and much lighter and longer-legged than a domestic cow. They tend to have an overall ungainly appearance, with long legs, large hooves, long necks, and a long, square-looking head. In large bulls, the antlers may stand up as much as a meter above the line of the back, giving a top-heavy appearance.

Caribou and reindeer are quite variable in color, both from place to place and season to season. Northern populations tend to be pale brown to nearly white during the whole year; so-called woodland caribou appear dark brown during the summer, with the legs particularly dark. In common with many other domestic animals, some reindeer have a piebald coat. Caribou molt in spring and early summer, presenting a scruffy appearance with ragged tufts of fur and bare skin. A new coat of fine, dark summer hair grows rapidly throughout the summer. As winter approaches, a layer of thick, coarse, light-colored guard hairs appears and begins to protrude beyond the dark summer hair, lightening the color of the animal. In bulls, this also forms a white gorget at the throat, giving them a formal, regal appearance. The guard hairs are hollow and provide superb insulation. Winter caribou fur feels like a layer of dense upholstery a couple of inches thick. Skin from the legs is used by most northern natives for clothing. The body fur is too thick for clothing but is perfect as a ground pad and mattress. The hollow fur also makes caribou extremely buoyant; this, combined with their large, flexible hooves, allows caribou to swim rapidly and for long distances. On the other hand, the fur does not wear well, since the thick, hollow hairs are brittle and break away. Shed caribou hair is ubiquitous where the animals are butchered and cooked, and it is usually at least a minor component of any meal of caribou meat. The fur is also such good insulation that a caribou carcass will begin to spoil from its own body heat even with air temperatures far below freezing.

Caribou hooves are perfectly adapted for travel on snow and soft, marshy round. The hooves are not only large, but the toes can spread wide apart, while the dewclaws of the forelegs are large and provide additional surface. During winter the edges of the hooves become sharp and provide good traction on slippery surfaces, and are useful for digging through snow (or *cratering*) for buried food. Caribou can run very rapidly if pursued, but their normal gait is an unhurried amble that nonetheless takes them over the horizon before an observer realizes they are gone. Walking caribou can often be heard before they are seen because of an odd clicking sound their hooves make. This sound seems to result from an interaction of bones and tendons, but no one is altogether certain how the sound is produced.

Caribou and reindeer feed on a variety of tundra plants and can alter their diet to fit what is available: willow buds, newly

emergent cottongrass spears, or, whenever available, mush-
rooms! During winter they are often strongly dependent on
fruticose lichens, which they paw from under the snow or take
from the branches of trees if the animals are wintering within the
forest. Like many northern animals, they are able to store quantities of fat when conditions are right, so that their weight and
appearance may change markedly from season to season.

Caribou are comparatively slow reproducers, at least by
temperate standards. Cows are most commonly three years old
when their first calf is born. While they usually breed each year
thereafter, only a single calf is normally produced each year. In
many caribou populations, calving occurs in high, exposed calving grounds, usually in June. The concentration of animals probably helps to keep predation down. Many calves are lost to late
snowstorms and general bad weather conditions, although they
are precocial and ready to travel within a short time of birth. By
late summer the calves are largely independent and the cows
ready to breed again. By the end of the breeding season, all of the
animals have begun migration, with many tundra populations
moving down into the forested regions. The northernmost races
live out their lives on the tundra; their movements seem more in
the nature of wanderings than true seasonal migrations.

One factor in caribou seasonal and daily movement is the
presence of mosquitoes and other parasites. For an animal that
lives in a barren and pristine-appearing environment, the caribou
is subject to an amazing array of attacks from insects. Warble flies
burrow through the skin of their backs, sometimes producing
100 or more larvae that feed on the animal's flesh before emerging through the skin. Nose bot flies live in the animals' throats
and nasal passages. Summer caribou can be heard coughing and
wheezing across the tundra in reaction to these insects. Black
flies and mosquitoes form clouds around the animals; herds and
individuals commonly stick to windy ridge tops and late-lying
snowfields to avoid these pests as much as possible. All in all,
caribou during the summer often present a pitiable sight; they
must welcome the first sharp frosts.

Although they seem to epitomize the faceless herd, caribou
behavior can be endearing. Caribou are extremely curious and
can often be lured to close range by some unusual sight or
movement. The rutting behavior of young and even mature bulls
seems more in the spirit of good-natured competition than war-
fare; pairs and small groups of bulls are often seen together
acting like cronies.

In their numbers, caribou so far surpass all other large mammals of the tundra environment as to make other grazing species almost negligible in most areas. While this was evidently not true as recently as the last Ice Age, most of the other large tundra herbivores have become extinct within the past 10,000 or so years. Another herbivore that survives, although just barely, is the muskox.

Muskox

Muskoxen are odd and archaic-looking animals (see Figure 10–2) whose Latin name, *Ovibos,* indicates their presumed intermediate relationship to both sheep and cattle. Muskoxen are yaklike animals witn true horns that sweep across the forehead as a bony shield, curve down in back of the eyes, and then hook back upward as lethal pointed weapons. Combined with the animal's powerful physique, these horns are so effective as protection against predators that muskoxen will stand their ground against their natural enemies. This overconfident behavior rapidly led to their near extinction when the rifle was introduced into the tundra of North America. Muskoxen had died out of Eurasia long before; perhaps their habits were similarly inappropriate against spears of early northerners.

Muskoxen are short-legged, hump-backed, huge-headed animals that look as though they might be a polar version of bison. Perhaps their most characteristic feature is their immensely long hair. Individual guard hairs are often well over half a meter long; the hairs extend down from the animal's body as a fringe or skirt, accentuating the overall squat appearance. The fur is good protection from cold and injury, but it can be a problem in areas of heavy snowfall and freeze-thaw cycles. Muskoxen have been found frozen, apparently killed by buildup of ice in their fur, and have perhaps actually been frozen to the ground! It may be that the colder, drier climate of the Ice Ages was more to the muskox's taste, and its decline over the last few millennia may be associated with climatic change.

Figure 10–2. Muskoxen. The archaic-looking animals were nearly eliminated from the tundra environment because they stood their ground to armed hunters as they did to wolves.

Muskoxen also seem to be somewhat less adaptable than caribou in their winter food requirements. They evidently need something more substantial than lichens and may have trouble finding enough food to stay alive if the snow cover is heavy. Muskoxen are relatively slow breeders, probably more so than caribou. Contrary to much published information, however, they do breed at a relatively young age and probably can and do produce single calves at yearly intervals, rather than in alternate years. This means that muskox populations can recover or expand reasonably quickly, and some groups seem to be doing so. At the turn of the century, muskoxen were confined to north and east Greenland, some islands in the Canadian Arctic, and portions of the North American mainland west of Hudson Bay. They are now living in parts of Alaska, where they were killed off only within historical times, and they are being successfully introduced back into Eurasia.

Efforts to domesticate muskoxen have met with some success. The economic justification for these attempts has not been for meat and hides, but for the soft, thick underfur produced by the animals, called *quiviut* in Inupiat (the Eskimo language). Probably nothing more absurd could be imagined than a sheared muskox; fortunately, muskoxen need not be sheared since the fur is shed naturally. As the individual hairs loosen they are held in by the long guard hairs and can be separated from the animal in sheets. These can be removed by human hands if the person has good relations with the muskox. *Quiviut* is usually knitted; it is finer and lighter than such other wools as vicuna. As might be expected, it is also extremely expensive.

Moose

Moose are another circumpolar species of deer. The identical animal is known as elk in Eurasia; it is not to be confused with the American elk, or *wapiti,* which is more closely equivalent to the red deer of the Old World. Moose are most characteristically animals of the timbered country of the Subarctic, rather than of the true tundra. Known in Latin as *Alces alces,* moose are the largest living member of the deer family and the largest land animal currently living in the Arctic (see Figure 10–3). Like most other wide-ranging, circumpolar species, moose include a number of races, and there is a good deal of variation in size from place to place. Big Alaskan bulls may weigh 600 to 700 kilograms and have an antler spread of over two meters. Even a small cow

Figure 10–3. Moose, the largest and most ungainly looking of the northern herbivores. They are common near timberline, but usually found only along rivers in the true tundra.

would normally top 300 kilograms; as might be expected in an animal this size, data on live weight is scarce.

Moose, like caribou, have dense fur, with the individual guard hairs hollow and giving buoyancy in water. There is little color variation from animal to animal, time to time, or place to place; moose are pretty much invariably dark chocolate brown, the exact shade often depending on whether the animal is wet or dry. The legs are long, the hooves large, but smaller in proportion than those of caribou. Bulls in particular have a large hump on the shoulder; from it, the back tapers down to low and rather slender hindquarters. The most distinctive features of moose are on the head. The antlers occur only on bulls; they are large and flat, or palmate, with individual tines projecting from a bowl-shaped central portion. The snout is long and might be called roman; the lips are large and flexible. At the throat is an appendage of skin and flesh known as a bell; this may reach a length of half a meter or so in large bulls.

Despite their larger size, moose generally reproduce somewhat more rapidly than caribou. Twin calves are common and calf mortality under most conditions probably is somewhat lower than in caribou. Moose populations tend to fluctuate widely in size but are able to recover from low points fairly rapidly if given the chance. Moose populations tend to disappear and reappear in some areas along the margins of their normal range. Moose populations in Alaska have spread out throughout the Arctic in the mid-twentieth century. There are substantial year-round populations of moose well over 100 kilometers beyond the conifer timberline, and an occasional individual appears on the streets of Barrow, at the northernmost tip of Alaska. These arctic-fringe populations seem to fluctuate over decades or centuries. Few moose were seen in the Brooks range before 1950, but a good deal of evidence suggests that they had lived there a hundred or more years ago.

Moose are not truly arctic animals in that they do not spend much time on the open tundra. Their range beyond timber is closely correlated with the presence of rivers and extensive stands of riparian willow. Moose are largely browsers on brush, although they also eat a good deal of aquatic vegetation when ponds are unfrozen. In Labrador-Ungava, where the terrain is largely glaciated bedrock and lichen woodland, moose are found only deep within timbered country.

Sheep and "Goats"

Wild sheep seem to have had their origin in the high, dry, plateaus of central Asia. From there they migrated into North America across the Bering land bridge and down the Rocky Mountains. They have never spread out across the North American Arctic, and they are thus not circumpolar in their distribution. Neither are they true tundra animals, since they are seldom seen in lowlands. However, wild sheep (mainly the Dall sheep, *Ovis dalli,* shown in Figure 10–4, and its Asian relatives) are significant members of the arctic mountain ecosystem in places such as the Brooks Range of Alaska.

Figure 10–4. Dall sheep, the classic white sheep of the mountains of Alaska and the northern Yukon Territory. It has traditionally been one of the most sought after big game animals in North America.

The so-called mountain goat of North America is more closely related to Eurasian antelopes than to true goats. It is a species of the alpine tundra rather than of the true Arctic. The same is true of Old World animals such as the chamois.

Small Mammal Consumers

With a couple of exceptions to be mentioned later, all of the tundra herbivores smaller than caribou are rodents, and most belong to a particular subfamily of mouselike or hamsterlike animals called *microtines*. In the Arctic the most important of these are the lemmings and the voles (not to be confused with moles, which are not rodents, and, because they are burrowing animals, are not normally found in the Arctic). Lemmings belong to the genera *Dicrostonyx* (collared lemmings) and *Lemmus* (brown lemmings). A third genus, *Synaptomys* (bog lemmings), ranges into the southern edge of the tundra in some areas. The voles include the genus *Microtis* and also the redback voles *(Clethrionomys)*. Voles generally have a noticeable tail, whereas lemmings have little more than a furry stump. In total length, all of these animals are roughly the same, 140 to 160 millimeters, but the voles, with their longer tails, are somewhat smaller in body size. A typical redback vole might weigh 30 grams, a brown lemming as much as 80 grams.

The collared lemmings are the prettiest microtines; they have a richly varied summer coat with patches of white, buff, and chestnut. They are also the only arctic rodents that turn white in winter. The other tundra microtines are pretty much a uniform brownish or grayish summer and winter, although the redback vole has darker, mahogany-colored fur on its back.

Tundra microtines all eat dried grasses and sedges, fresh sprouts, seeds, tubers, and a good proportion of insects and grubs. None hibernate; they are too small to store enough food within their bodies to last throughout an arctic winter, even if they were able to find a year-round unfrozen place in their permafrosted environment. One might ask why they do not all put on a protective coat of white during the winter. The answer is that because they remain under the snow cover throughout the entire winter, burrowing through the subnivean space and finding both a source of food at the ground surface and protection from predators, camouflage is therefore unnecessary.

One might also wonder how several closely related species of similar size, habitat, and food requirements could survive in the same location. The answer is in subtle differences in habitat preference. Collared lemmings tend to like drier sedge meadows and tussock tundra, while brown lemmings more often evidently prefer the ridges between low-center polygons. *Microtis* species seem to prefer dry situations such as stream banks and miniature ridges, while redback voles often are found in rough, stony areas. It is probably safe to say that lemmings are more abundant near the coast, and voles inland. But all species known in a particular area may occur within a few meters of each other, partitioning the various resources in such a way as to minimize competition, at least under typical conditions.

The real confusion in the microtine population situation occurs in so-called lemming years. These are times when the populations of one or more species undergo an explosion. Signs of the early stages of these buildups are fairly subtle and might well not be noticed by the casual visitor to the tundra. At a certain point, though, the land seems to come alive with lemmings. Apparently, once a certain density of individuals is reached, social behavior is radically altered. The animals become more aggressive and territorial, so that many individuals are driven from their native haunts. Reproductive rates, which can be amazingly high even in normal circumstances, also rise. The result is a seemingly sudden appearance of large numbers of animals, who often seek to avoid already congested habitats by migrating. Even allowing for the expected exaggeration of legend, lemming migrations can be awesome. The animals are everywhere, seem to be fearless, and invade tents, cook shacks, and anything else in their paths. High populations of one species also tend to break down the local distribution patterns of the various species, so that partitioning of habitat and other resources among species is masked.

Among the most persistent parts of the lemming legend is the idea that the advancing hordes are suicidal and will throw themselves into oceans in mass drownings. This perhaps follows from the fact that lemmings are good swimmers, as might be expected of an animal whose native habitat often consists of more ponds, rivers, and marshes than dry land. At the same time, from a lemming's vantage point, it is difficult to judge the size of an intervening body of water, particularly when swarms of your relatives are pushing from behind. There is no reason to suspect that the swimmers don't have at least some belief that they will reach the far shore.

Explosive population expansions of microtines are generally followed by equally abrupt declines. The summer after a lemming outbreak, the tundra may seem to be nearly lifeless. Only abandoned runways and tunnels and little piles of bleached droppings testify to the crowds of the preceding year.

In their role in the tundra environment, microtine rodents are of at least equivalent importance to the caribou or reindeer. One of their most conspicuous roles is as a source of food for a broad array of predators, ranging from grizzly bears to eagles to freshwater fish. Microtines are sort of a funnel for transferring the solar energy fixed by the arctic plants to many of the larger animals of the tundra. This becomes particularly evident in relation to the cycles of microtine population expansion and decline. Any predator that depends on a resource as unstable as lemmings must have some specialized adaptations to allow it to survive lean years, then capitalize on the years of bonanza. We see this situation particularly well developed in the case of some of the tundra predatory birds, such as owls and jaegers (see Chapter 12).

Other Arctic Herbivores

Several larger rodents are common inhabitants of tundra and timberline situations. Many of these animals have recently colonized the far north from the grasslands and alpine regions of more temperate latitudes. For example, the marmots, a group of large ground squirrels including the familiar woodchuck or groundhog of eastern North America, have populations extending into the Arctic.

Smaller ground squirrels occurring in the Arctic are relatives of the many prairie squirrels. They belong to the genus *Spermophilus* (meaning seed lover); in older literature they are called *Citellus*. Arctic ground squirrels are among the very few true hibernators among arctic vertebrates. Hibernating in cold regions is a major undertaking: it entails finding a suitable place for a burrow in a permafrosted environment, and developing physiological adaptations to allow the body to remain torpid but alive for six months or more of winter. Ground squirrel burrows are rather elaborate. They are often found as fossils, sometimes complete with a mummified occupant whose bodily resources ran out before the end of winter.

Other rodents reaching the edge of the Arctic are beavers and, in North America, porcupines and muskrats. Beavers may be important in altering and maintaining some aspects of the timberline environment, since they cause regular flooding of small drainage basins. They seldom occur on the tundra.

Porcupines in the North are closely associated with spruce

forest, but they sometimes are found wandering through alpine brushland. Even the smallest, most isolated groves of white spruce forest at the timberline in northwestern Alaska show evidence of porcupine work. Porcupines originated in South America and colonized the North relatively recently. They have not yet crossed the Bering Strait or Atlantic Ocean.

Muskrats also reach the edges of the tundra, inhabiting marshy ponds in low arctic areas such as western Alaska. Their presence is indicated by small mounds of vegetation made into lodges. Muskrats are important furbearers in the boreal forest region, and they have been introduced to Eurasia.

One final herbivorous mammal of the tundra doesn't fit into any of the categories we have discussed. This is the tundra hare, *Lepus arcticus,* sometimes divided into two or more species. Hares and their close relatives, rabbits, are not rodents. Their chisel-shaped incisor teeth are the result of convergent evolution, and a close look at a hare skull and skeleton will show how distinct it is from that of a rodent. The arctic hare is one of the characteristic mammals of the tundra environment; it is particularly prevalent in the higher Arctic, and is abundant in places such as Ellesmere Island. Since arctic hares may weigh as much as 5 or 6 kilograms, it is hard to classify them as small mammals; among the dwarf shrubs and grasses of the tundra they seem more like small kangaroos.

Arctic hares are white during the winter, and the high arctic populations may stay white year around. Elsewhere, they develop a gray summer coat with elegant light and dark markings. Arctic hares are able to run in a standing position, using only their hind legs, simultaneously. Since the animals are often gregarious, groups are sometimes seen all standing erect and hopping rapidly away. This activity may be more a social event than anything else, and many travelers to the Arctic have reported seeing dancing hares.

In the vicinity of timberline, the arctic hare is replaced by the much smaller varying hare or so-called snowshoe rabbit. This is a much smaller, slenderer animal that can also be distinguished by its brown, rather than amber, eyes. Varying hares are also white during the winter but are brown in summer. They are common and important members of the ecosystem of the forest edge. Like lemmings and voles, their populations are highly variable and perhaps cyclical.

Another harelike animal of mountainous regions that ranges into the Arctic is the pika *(Ochotonus)* (see Figure 10–5). Pikas look more like rodents, with a round body, short legs, and small

Figure 10–5. Pika. These animals of the mountains of Eurasia and western North America look like lemmings but are actually related to hares. Their distinctive whistle and their haystacks are common features of alpine *felsenmeer.*

ears. They are somewhat colonial and live in rocky areas, where they make burrows under boulders and in talus. Pikas store food for the winter in the form of dried grass, and each burrow has what looks like a haystack drying in front of the entrance during late summer. Pikas have a piercing call that can be heard constantly in a colony; the animals are nearly as difficult to see as they are easy to hear. A watcher gains the impression that they are able to follow one's eyes and that they dive behind a rock just as that gaze is about to fix on them.

INVERTEBRATE HERBIVORES

Insects form a whole subworld in any ecosystem, and many of the interactions of this realm remain unknown in even the most accessible and closely studied places. Many insects are primary consumers. Others are secondary consumers or predators, while some participate in a variety of complex relationships as parasites, or are part of the breakdown cycle of scavengers and detritus feeders. Many insects shift roles at portions of their life cycles. Others shift habitat and are part of the aquatic ecosystem at some times of their life cycle, land-dwellers in another.

Among the most important insect groups in the tundra ecosystem are springtails *(Collembola)*, beetles *(Coleoptera)*, moths and butterflies *(Lepidoptera)*, bees *(Hymenoptera)*, and a tremendous array of flies and mosquitoes *(Diptera)*. Other groups such as grasshoppers *(Orthoptera)* and ants *(Hymenoptera; Formicidae)* are nearly absent in the Arctic. When they do occur, it is usually in relict situations, such as isolated cottonwood groves beyond the coniferous timberline.

Although insects are abundant in the Arctic, the number of species is low, usually only a fraction of that typical of temperate areas. Few species are endemic to (found only in) the Arctic, and there are surprisingly few specialized adaptations for dealing with arctic conditions. On reflection, this should not be surprising, since the major climatic difference between the Arctic and cool temperate regions is the relative length of the seasons. Among the more important adaptations is often a lengthening of generation time, which makes sense under some conditions of short growing season and low food supplies. The most extreme example known is that of moths of the genus *Byrdia,* which may remain in the larval (caterpillar) stage for more than a decade in the high Arctic.

Many herbivorous arctic insects feed mainly on simple, unicellular plants such as diatoms and other algae. Algae feeders include many *Collembola,* and the aquatic larval stages of such common insects as mosquitoes and midges. Other groups, such as beetles, are more dependent on the higher plants, on which they can graze with their powerful mouth parts. Bees store honey and pollen, as they do in temperate regions. Bumblebees are among the most conspicuous insects in even the highest arctic regions. When *Dryas* flowers and poppies open on the first bare patches, they are almost instantly visited by large, ungainly bees. Bees are generally the most important pollinators of tundra plants.

From the traveler's point of view, one group of arctic insects is so conspicuous as to obliterate all others from consciousness. These are the mosquitoes and their close relatives, the blackflies. Although there is no question that mosquitoes are ravenous for blood, the truth is that all mosquitoes are plant eaters for most of their life cycle. Only females are bloodsuckers, and the blood meal is a part of the breeding cycle, rather than normal metabolism. In fact, some species have evolved away from the necessity for a blood meal. Such insects continue to be attracted to warm-blooded animals but seldom bite. Nonetheless, biting in-sects are quite possibly the most unpleasant aspect of the tundra environment during summer, both for humans and for other warm-blooded animals from baby birds to caribou. Many species of the insects are involved, and they generally occur in waves as the summer progresses, with one type replacing another.

On the other hand, the clouds of mosquitoes provide an exceptionally high-quality protein and energy source for many of the smaller tundra predators, particularly birds. The tremendous migrations of shorebirds and waterfowl into the tundra environ-ment each spring would probably never have come into exist-ence without the massive production of insects.

Among the more bizarre roles of biting insects is as pollinators of one of the few tundra orchids, which is specialized for mos-quito pollination. The pollen is produced in a pair of tiny sacks held together by a cliplike structure that fastens to the mosquito's leg. For a few days in late June, these tiny yellow *pollinia* can be seen attached to a significant proportion of the mosquitoes in northern Alaska as they go about their rounds.

OTHER INVERTEBRATES

In addition to insects, the tundra environment contains a broad array of other invertebrates. Various species of mites are com-mon on plants. They are preyed on by their relatives, spiders, which also feed on many insect species.

Overall, though, the representation of invertebrates is relative-ly low, and many major groups are missing or are poorly repre-sented. Snails and slugs are found in few places, and then only along the arctic borders. Earthworms are rare or absent, as might be expected in permafrost. On the other hand, there are many individuals, and presumably many species, of groups such as roundworms.

MAMMALIAN PREDATORS

Predators are the *secondary consumers,* animals that eat other animals and thus derive their energy from the sun indirectly through at least two stages. At the outset, it is worth mentioning that many arctic animals are omnivorous, or are facultative preda-tors. Microtine rodents are basically herbivores, but will eat any insects they come across, and they have been observed preying on baby birds. They also sometimes scavenge carcasses of larger animals; they are particularly fond of shed antlers, which are probably a useful source of calcium. Caribou have been seen eating meat on many occasions. On the other hand, predatory species such as brown bears are often largely herbivorous. This ability to utilize a variety of resources as they happen to be available is one factor that calls into question the idea of the simplicity of the arctic ecosystem. The food webs obviously shift from season to season, from year to year in ways that are at least as unpredictable as lemming cycles.

Wolves and Other Canids

If the caribou is the most conspicuous primary consumer on the tundra, the wolf is just as clearly the dominant predator throughout most of the circumpolar north. All northern wolves are now classified under a single species, *Canus lupus*. There are many subspecies, varying mainly in color and size. Most northern wolves are large, though. In spite of their rangy build, they generally weigh more than all but the largest of domestic dogs, which are descended from wolves. Otherwise, wolves differ so little physically from domestic dogs that the skulls and other skeletal materials can overlap those of some breeds, such as German shepherds. The physical appearance of wolves is so well known by now that little description is necessary. Wolves range in weight from about 30 kilograms for smaller females to perhaps as much as 70 kilograms or more for large males. The animals look like large, slender dogs; the nose is longer and more pointed than in a husky or malamute. The fur is dense, generally in various shades of gray or grayish buff, but sometimes nearly white, particularly in more northern regions. The neck and shoulder fur is often long and dense, forming a ruff.

The main differences between wolves and dogs are behavioral. The wolf breeding season is closely timed to the seasons, unlike that of dogs. Male wolves are much involved in nurturing the pups, again in contrast to dogs. Wolves are considered by many to have the most complex social behavior of any nonprimate animal. It has been suggested that until sometime during the last Ice Age wolves and humans were roughly equal in the sophistication of their social system, and that it may have been nip and tuck as to which species would begin to domesticate the other.

Wolves have become such a staple in recent popular nature writing that extensive discussion of wolves here would be redundant. On the other hand, massive quantities of misinformation have been spread and sweeping generalizations that won't stand even cursory scrutiny have been made.

Wolves are strongly carnivorous and will feed on any fresh meat available, from lemmings and mice to moose. They are particularly well adapted for running down large animals in open country or woodland, often using team effort. The current popular idea is that wolves are closely attuned to their environment and food supply, and that they serve a profoundly meaningful purpose in the overall scheme of things by culling the lame, sick, and generally maladapted from the herds of herbivores. There is a good deal of truth in this view. Wolves have clearly been around for hundreds of millennia. They worked their way through all of the Ice Ages, probably changing their staple food from species to species as one type of prey became extinct and another arose. The fact that many potential prey species did become extinct is probably unconnected to the role of wolves, or predators in general, but we can't be altogether certain of this. The idea that wolves are self-limiting population controls on game animals depends on the idea that wolves are unable to successfully prey on healthy individuals, and that they will turn to other food sources and probably diminish in numbers if game herds begin to shrink (or if all the lame and halt have already been consumed). Again, there is some factual support for this concept. Wolf reproduction does fall off when prey populations diminish, and wolves often make unsuccessful efforts to capture healthy prey. The overall evidence strongly suggests that wolves and prey species can maintain a healthy relationship indefinitely if the overall environment is stable and healthy.

Problems seem to arise, though, when populations of game animals are brought under pressure by unusual circumstances, such as excessive hunting by humans. It appears that a population of healthy, hungry wolves faced with a sudden dearth of prey animals may very well do an effective mop-up operation on the remnants. This idea has had serious repercussions for wildlife management policy all across the North. The question is: If game populations are allowed to get more than so far out of balance, is it necessary to manage (kill) wolves until the prey species can regain equilibrium? This idea is anathema to the newly wolf-conscious public, but it is vigorously supported by many wildlife biologists.

Most of the earlier, seemingly endless controversy over wolves' danger to humans has been laid to rest over the past couple of decades. It has evidently been impossible to document any instance of a serious, sustained attack on humans by wolves. Even the old stories of wolves snapping at the inhabitants of sleighs crossing the frozen wastes of Russia seem to be fiction. Wolves, like killer whales but unlike bears, seem to have some inhibition against attacking humans, even when they might get away with it.

Other Canids

Canids are members of the wolf or dog family, which also includes foxes and coyotes. Along with the gray wolf, at least three species occur in the Arctic.

The red fox *(Vulpes vulpes)* is more familiar in the context of chicken coops and hunt clubs, but it is an important member of the circumpolar fauna. Northern red foxes are quite variable in color, with some individuals being gray or nearly black. As in temperate regions, these foxes are largely predatory on microtines and other small mammals; they are opportunistic and may feed heavily on birds' eggs and young in season, or whatever else is available.

The arctic fox *(Alopex lagopus)* is a markedly different animal that replaces red foxes along the coast and in higher arctic regions. Arctic foxes are generally somewhat smaller than red foxes, with shorter legs and muzzles, and smaller ears. During the summer they are shades of gray, but they become pure white in winter, with soft, dense fur. Because of the quality of their pelts, arctic foxes have been the staple of the trapping industry in the Arctic when long-haired furs are in fashion.

The arctic fox (see Figure 10–6) is a combination hunter of small animals and scavenger. In the latter role, it is often closely associated with polar bears. Foxes may follow the bears for miles out onto the pack ice, cleaning up the remains of seals. Arctic

Figure 10–6. Arctic fox. This nearly full-grown kit will develop a white coat for the coming winter.

foxes tend to concentrate near the coast and feed on marine mammal carcasses that may drift ashore. A single whale can support several foxes for months, so a beached whale carcass is often a gold mine to trappers. Arctic foxes are also associated with bird colonies as predators and scavengers. They are commonly found on offshore islands because of their tendency to travel on pack ice, and they may be the only mammalian predator on some islands. Arctic foxes and, to a lesser extent, red foxes, were introduced by humans on isolated islands such as the central Aleutians. The idea was to throw a few foxes ashore, leave for a few years, then come back and harvest a bumper crop of fine pelts. Unfortunately, many island dwellers such as sea birds are extremely vulnerable to fox predation. Subsequent efforts to defox these islands have had some success.

Coyotes *(Canus latrans)* are small, rather solitary wolves traditionally found mainly in the North American west. Their range extends into the Arctic in Alaska and western Canada. Relatively little is known about their role in the tundra environment, but they do not appear to be common in most places. In eastern North America, a large canid with characteristics of both coyotes and timber wolves has appeared recently and increased rapidly, mainly within the boreal forest region. There is some question as to what the ancestry of this animal, sometimes called the "new wolf," is, what its role may be, and how widely it will spread.

In a few cases, feral dogs can affect the polar ecosystem. In most native villages the dogs are kept tied. Free-roaming dogs are dangerous to people, particularly children, and can damage food supplies, such as drying fish, or equipment such as boats or clothing made of untanned skin. Few escaped animals make it in the wild. There have been cases, however, in which dogs left on islands did serious damage to native animals. One pack of dogs survived at least one antarctic winter in a penguin colony, with predictably devastating results for the penguins.

Bears

As we said in Chapter 1, bears have always had a special connection with the North in people's minds, and the word *arctic* is derived from the Greek for bear, *arctos.* Northern bears fall into three groups: black bears, brown or grizzly bears, and polar bears. They differ greatly in appearance, range, and preferred habitat, less in behavior.

Black bears are animals mainly of the forest. They have sharp, curved claws; smaller individuals are good tree climbers.

Although they are variable in color, they can usually be told from grizzly bears by their darker fur and by what might be called their roman-nosed profile. Black bears stay mainly inside timberline; they scavenge, kill small animals and an occasional deer, and eat a great deal of vegetable food. They are also the classic garbage dump bear. Black bears enter a torpid, semihibernating state during winter. They store a good deal of fat on their bodies during fall, so their weight is quite variable from season to season. A small female in spring might weigh 75 to 100 kilograms, while some large, fat males have been weighed at over 300 kilograms.

The brown bear *(Ursus arctos)* is the typical bear of mountains and tundra. It is circumpolar in its distribution, although not currently found in Canada east of Hudson Bay. Coastal Alaskan races of brown bears are known for their great size and their tendency to congregate at salmon streams. Among the largest of all are the race found on Kodiak Island and known, appropriately, as Kodiak bears. These were once considered to be a separate species, along with some 25 other races of brown bears in western North America.

A typical tundra brown bear is light brown in color (blond), but there is a good deal of color variation. It has long, thick, straight claws and a dished or concave face. Size is variable, but most races of brown bears average considerably larger than black bears. Some large male Kodiak bears may weigh 500 kilograms or more.

For an animal as large and conspicuous as the brown bear, it is surprising how little is known about its feeding behavior, diet, and general role in the tundra ecosystem. It was long an article of faith that bears seldom preyed on large mammals such as moose or caribou and instead scavenged on wolf kills and other carrion. Bears are amazingly fast, agile, and strong, though, and there is no question that they can and do kill caribou and moose at least occasionally. Their main mammalian prey is ground squirrels and other rodents, but they eat a wide variety of other animal and plant material. Coastal brown bears depend mainly on migrating and spawning salmon during much of the year.

Brown bears are long-lived, slow maturing, and generally slow breeding. They can stand relatively little pressure from hunting or habitat destruction, and they have long since become extinct throughout most of their nonarctic range.

Most brown bears have the good sense to stay out of the way of humans if they can do so without inconveniencing themselves. Bears' moods and etiquette are unpredictable at best, though, and unfortunate (for both parties) encounters occur regularly. Most human/bear problems involve some sort of annoying incident, but occasionally they seem to be a straightforward predator/prey situation.

Polar bears are very different from brown bears in appearance, range, diet, and behavior, but the two species are genetically close relatives and they commonly interbreed in zoos. It has been suggested that polar bears are among the newest species of mammals on earth and that they developed from an isolated arctic coastal population of brown bears possibly as recently as the last Ice Age. Polar bears are now generally recognized as the largest of all terrestrial carnivores. The largest brown bears have larger skulls, which impresses the keepers of trophy records, but the polar bear is, on the average, longer, taller, and heavier. Polar bears are all white except for the tip of the nose, claws, and the dark flesh of gums and tongue. Physically, they differ from brown bears in that they have longer necks, smaller heads, and somewhat sharper teeth, better adapted to a meat diet.

Polar bear behavior is centered around their way of life, which consists mainly of hunting seals. Polar bears almost never travel more than a few miles inland. They are often seen on pack ice far offshore on the open ocean, and they may swim across long stretches of open water, although their pace is slow. Because they travel on drifting pack ice, polar bears sometimes show up as far south as Newfoundland. Otherwise they are circumpolar around the shores of the Arctic Ocean, the channels of the Canadian Arctic, and far south into Hudson Bay and even James Bay.

Male polar bears are active throughout the year, generally following the shifting pack ice. Females den up during the winter and the cubs are born during this torpid period. Twins are usually born and are tiny and helpless, but grow rapidly throughout the denning period, then remain with their mother for a couple of years. Polar bears are generally solitary but may congregate at denning areas such as Wrangel Island in the USSR or near Cape Henrietta Maria in Manitoba. Males seem also to have certain concentration points, as along the west shore of Hudson Bay, and the coast of Banks Island.

The Weasel Family

Many northern carnivores belong to the weasel family *(Mustelidae),* including weasels, or ermine (see Figure 10–6); minks; otters; martens; fishers, or sables; and wolverines, or glutton. Skunks, which generally don't reach the vicinity of timberline, are also mustelids. The mustelids are generally smallish, rather nonspecialized carnivores, but they vary in size and habits.

The two common tundra species of weasel are the least weasel *(Mustela rixosa)* and the shorttail weasel, or ermine *(M. erminea)*. Both are long, slender, lithe animals, well adapted to the hunting of small tundra rodents. Both species have white pelage, or hair, in winter, brown in summer. The ermine has a black tail tip, while the smaller least weasel lacks this feature. As in most mustelids, there is a good deal of variation in size, with the female being considerably smaller than the male. The least weasel has the distinction of being the smallest member of the order *Carnivora*.

Weasels have elongated, cylindrical bodies; these allow them to follow their prey into burrows in the snow or ground. They are fierce and fearless, and they will attack prey that is a good deal larger than they are, such as varying hares. Both species are common and widely distributed throughout the circumpolar north. Their abundance is closely tied to the cycles of microtine rodents.

Minks *(Mustela vison)* are larger than weasels and are generally more aquatic. They are animals more of the boreal forest than the tundra but are common in some tundra areas such as the Yukon-Kuskokwim delta of Alaska.

Otters (*Lutra canadensis* and related Eurasian species) are large, long-tailed, web-footed aquatic mustelids. They feed on fish, muskrats, and sometimes beavers. They are valued highly for their fur but are relatively few in number and seldom occur in the true Arctic. We'll discuss their larger relative, the sea otter, under marine mammals.

Martens, sables, and *fishers* are names given to several species of forest mustelids that do much of their hunting in trees. All being to the genus *Martes*. For obvious reasons, they do not range beyond timberline. They are relatively common in the boreal forest, and they are highly valued for their fur.

Among the most important of the tundra mustelids is the wolverine, or glutton. It is a circumpolar species *(Gulo gulo)* that is the largest terrestrial member of the weasel family. It is found throughout the boreal forest and tundra area, but it is solitary, wary, and sparsely distributed. Wolverines have a fearsome reputation. Although they seldom weigh more than 20 to 25 kilograms, it is claimed that they will drive bears and wolves from a kill, and that they can successfully attack animals as large as moose. Allowing room for exaggeration, there is no question that wolverines are powerful predators. Their main prey, though, are probably rodents, smaller carnivores, and a healthy dose of carrion.

Wolverine fur is dark brown with a lighter fringe along the sides and flanks. The fur has a natural ability to resist frost deposition from breath, so it is in demand for the trim around the hoods of parkas. Even a healthy wolverine population is sparse, so trapping can endanger the species over a broad area. The animal also has a deserved reputation for raiding traplines and cabins, and trappers thus have a long-standing vendetta against wolverines.

The Cat Family: Felidae

Cats belong to a group of predators very different from the wolves, bears, and mustelids. They are much more animals of temperate and tropical regions, and no living species are true tundra dwellers. The closest to an arctic cat is the lynx, represented by closely related species in the Old and New Worlds. The lynx is a medium-sized cat, weighing 10 to 20 kilograms, or two or three times as much as a large house cat. Lynxes have long legs, tufts of fur on the ears, a mottled gray or buffy coat, and, their most conspicuous feature, a short, bobbed tail. This gives the lynx's more southerly American relative, the bobcat, its name. The lynx is an animal mainly of the boreal forest, where it preys primarily on hares. In some areas the predator/prey relationship between lynx and varying hares is so close that lynx populations regularly crash immediately after hare populations decline.

In Asia, the Siberian tiger occurs within the taiga and some areas of alpine tundra. North American scientists have remarked on the eerie feeling of being in a familiar-seeming boreal forest in Siberia but realizing that there are tigers lurking, as well as the more familiar small forest animals.

The snow leopard is a beautiful, fascinating, and poorly known cat of the alpine tundra of the high Himalayas but doesn't reach the Arctic.

INSECT EATERS: SHREWS AND BATS

Mammals generally leave the invertebrates for the birds, but shrews can be remarkably common in some tundra areas, and bats range northward to the fringes of the tundra during summer.

Several species of shrews often occur within the same general habitat type. For example, dusky shrews *(Sorex obscurus)*, arctic shrews *(S. arcticus)*, and cinereus shrews *(S. cinereus)* are found more or less together in northern Alaska. Little is known about how they share resources, or, indeed, how they survive in the arctic environment. Shrews are famous for their exceptionally high metabolic rates and their need for quantities of high-quality food. The animals are able to live throughout the year presumably on insect larvae, some small mammals, seeds, and some carrion. Their populations are known to vary cyclically.

Overall, the literature on the role of shrews in the tundra environment is remarkably slim. There is little reason to believe that these animals have any massive impact on the overall ecosystem, but they do pop up in surprising numbers and probably hold interesting secrets for scientists to ferret out.

Bats occur only rarely within the Arctic. They may occasionally be seen in the vicinity of timberline, hawking insects over marshes and thaw ponds.

SUGGESTED FURTHER READING

Again, the literature is voluminous and often highly technical. Much of it is found in journals, such as the *Journal of Mammology* and *Journal of Wildlife Management*. Among the works on the following list are several recent ones with good bibliographies.

Calef, G. W. *Caribou and the Barren Lands.* Ottawa: Canadian Arctic Resources Committee, 1981.

Chapman, J. A., and G. A. Feldhamer, eds. *Wild Mammals of North America: Biology, Management and Economics.* Baltimore: Johns Hopkins University Press, 1982.

Finerty, J. P. *Population Ecology of Cycles in Small Mammals: Mathematical Theory and Biological Fact.* New Haven: Yale University Press, 1980.

Irving, L. *Arctic Life of Birds and Mammals.* New York: Springer Verlag, 1972.

Merritt, J. F., ed. *Winter Ecology of Small Mammals.* Special Publication no. 10. Pittsburgh: Carnegie Museum of Natural History, 1984.

Morgan, A. H. *Field Book of Animals in Winter.* New York: G. P. Putnam's Sons, 1939. (This little-known work is unique, hard to find, and well worth tracking down, although dated.)

Olson, R., R. Hastings, and F. Geddes, eds. *Northern Ecology and*

Resource Management. Edmonton: University of Alberta Press, 1984.

Pruitt, W. O. *Animals of the North.* New York: Harper and Row, 1967.

———. *Boreal Ecology.* Institute of Biological Studies in Biology, no. 91. London: Edward Arnold, 1978.

Rearden, J. *Alaska Mammals. (Alaska Geographic* 8:2). Anchorage: Alaska Geographic Society, 1981.

Remmert, H. *Arctic Animal Ecology.* Berlin: Springer Verlag, 1980.

Schmidt, J. L., and D. L. Gilbert. *Big Game of North America.* Harrisburg, PA: Stackpole Books, 1978.

Stonehouse, B. *Animals of the Arctic: The Ecology of the Far North.* New York: Holt, Rinehart, and Winston, 1971.

Chapter 11

Cold Seas, Shores, and Inland Waters

THE ways land and water meet in the Arctic have few counterparts elsewhere in the world. Arctic coasts, riven by ancient
glaciers, are often sinuous and convoluted. There may be ten
times or more the actual linear coastline that shows on a map.
Coves, bays, channels, skerries, fiords, estuaries, and lagoons
combine to form an almost endlessly complicated shoreline.
When the Vikings came to a long, straight beach along the coast
of Labrador, they called it *Wonderstrand.* These denizens of the
glaciated coasts of the North Atlantic had never seen anything like
it before.

Water and land also combine in complex ways inland from the
seacoast. Arctic lowlands are often more than half covered by
lakes, the result of the endless play of ground ice buildup and
thermokarst. Even the dry land parts of many tundra regions
qualify as wetlands by most standards. The underlying permafrost

blocks percolation, the buildup of polygon ridges traps snow-melt, and the cool days slow evaporation (see Chapter 6).

The interplay of land and water is a temporal as well as spatial phenomenon. Change in the relationship of land and water occurs constantly, often rapidly and in plain sight. Thaw lakes are created and drained; the braided streams of outwash plains are constantly shifting. Bars and cutoff lakes in the larger rivers make the North a chartmaker's nightmare. Some of the largest lagoon systems in the world occur along arctic coasts. They may shift from fresh to salt water as barrier beaches are breached by storms or offshore islands coalesce. Silt-laden arctic rivers build huge deltas, full of shifting channels, irregularly invaded by salt water during *storm surges.*

Over longer periods, the boundary between land, sea, river, and lake is even less stable. The shallow seas drain away as glacier ice builds up on the land, leaving islands and sea cliffs isolated miles deep in the interior. Wave-cut cliffs form on the lands depressed by loads of ice; then, a thousand years later, they are towering headlands with old beaches on their summits. An ice tongue abandons a fiord, leaving a new bay large enough to anchor a major fleet.

We saw in Chapter 2 that the terrestrial Arctic is best defined by climate, and that the low summer temperatures that keep the forests at bay are largely the result of the cold sea winds. If we leave the sea very far behind, we find ourselves in the timbered country of the Subarctic. On the other side of the coin, many arctic seas are shallow; fringes of the continental shelf that at this moment in geological time are under water but that owe much of their character to the land. Many arctic seas are less salty than their temperate counterparts, the result of the influx of major rivers into landlocked seas. These rivers also bring silt and nutrients, often with profound effects on the inhabitants of the polar seas. The difference between high and low tides in the Arctic Ocean and its offshoots is much less dramatic than in other oceans. Changes in water level are more related to storms than to true tides, and they can be violent and unpredictable.

The cover of ice on polar waters further blurs the boundary between marine, aquatic, and terrestrial environments. In winter, lakes become roadways, rivers virtually disappear as all sources of liquid water freeze, and the sea surface copies the land, becoming a home for foxes and bears. On the other hand, the actual shoreline may become truly a no-man's-land, scoured of all life by the scraping and scouring of the pack ice come ashore, perhaps as the fearsome *ivu* (see Chapter 3).

The indefiniteness of the distinction between land and water has a profound effect on the organisms that live in the Arctic. Consider the disadvantage to any animal that cannot fly or swim! At the same time, the situation has many advantages, not the least of which is a result of what ecologists call *edge effect*. The edge effect recognizes that the boundaries between two distinct ecosystems often provide an exceptionally rich environment, allowing a blending of faunas and floras from both sources. The edge effect also spurs evolution, rewarding adaptability. We have mentioned several times arctic organisms' flexibility in withstanding seasonal climatic changes, changes in food resources, and other changes. This flexibility is a function, too, of the dominance of the edge effect in the far north, most particularly in the case of the land/water ecotone.

THE POLAR SEAS

The Arctic Ocean and its related bays, seas, straits, and other offshoots have loomed as a powerful and somewhat mysterious presence throughout our discussion of the Arctic. Whether we talk about climate, glaciers, sea ice, geographical definitions, or even human history, it is impossible to ignore the presence of the polar seas, and usually equally difficult to assess precisely the nature of their overall influence on the environment. It is tempting to tie threads together to set the role of the polar seas in an overall perspective, but, in practice, it doesn't work. We'll say a few more words here and suggest to the reader that the physical and biological oceanography of the Arctic is a growing field, rich in highly technical publications, but even richer in its tremendous array of unanswered questions. Some of these, such as those on the role of the Arctic Ocean in global climatic stability or change, or on the problems of environmental pollution, are of fundamental importance.

The Arctic Ocean contains two deep basins, separated by a ridge (the Lomonosov ridge) that runs from Greenland to Siberia, directly over the North Pole. It also has several million square kilometers of continental shelf, mainly north of Siberia, and sea floors of intermediate depth in areas such as the Barents Sea. For the origin and dispersal of water masses, the major contact between the Arctic Ocean and temperate oceans is with the North Atlantic, through what is sometimes called the Fram Strait, running between northern Greenland and Svalbard. It has been calculated that the total transfer of water (warm water in, and cold water out) through the Fram Strait is 7 million cubic meters per second, several hundred times the average flow of the Mississippi River at its mouth. The effect of this exchange of water and heat on ocean currents and on global climate is immense. Although the flow of fresh water by rivers into the Arctic Ocean is a more modest 90,000 cubic meters per second, it represents the drainage from an area roughly the size of the North American continent. The potential of this as a source for injecting industrial pollutants into the arctic environment is equally enormous.

We have already considered some aspects of the environment of the Arctic Ocean and other cold northern seas in the discussion of sea ice (see Chapter 3), and we'll talk more about biological features later in this chapter and in Chapter 12. It's worth pointing out though, that we are necessarily leaving major gaps, not only in physical oceanography, but in areas such as marine invertebrates and algae. We'll leave similar gaps in our discussion of freshwater environments. Because many of the phenomena encountered in these areas are not easily observed without special equipment and a good deal of time and training, they are not easily accessible to the average student or naturalist to whom this book is directed. It is also true that they have been studied so little that it may be premature to make generalizations. By no means can their importance be measured by their rather minimal treatment here.

PONDS, LAKES, AND RIVERS

In lowland parts of the Arctic, the vast majority of lakes and ponds are thaw ponds (see Chapter 6). Although there are plenty of exceptions, most thaw ponds are about 1.5 to 2 meters deep, and most freeze to the bottom each winter. There is a simple gauge, usually accurate, of whether or not the pond freezes completely: the presence or absence of fish. Contrary to some rumors, fish cannot stand being completely frozen (not even the blackfish, see below, is an exception). Even if the presence or absence of fish can't be established by direct observation, a good clue is the size of the *Daphnia* or other free-swimming invertebrates in the pond. The larger species are generally rare or absent if there is any predation from fish.

Because of their unstable shores and bottoms, thaw ponds usually have little vegetation of higher plants. Water lilies, most pondweeds (*Potamogeton* species), and other plants with floating leaves tend to drop out roughly in the vicinity of timberline, leaving most arctic ponds with a sterile appearance. Where there are shallow, muddy shores, a few species of higher plants such as horsetail (*Equisetum* species) may grow. In general, though, the dominant life in thaw ponds consists of algae, mainly of unicellular floating species, and invertebrates. In comparison to small ponds in temperate latitudes, even the list of invertebrates is short and full of glaring omissions. But there have been so few studies of tundra ponds that any careful look at a tundra pond's fauna is likely to turn up something unexpected, particularly in the case of insect larvae.

Many of the larger tundra lakes have been formed by processes other than thermokarst. They may be tarn lakes, or the result of more general glacial erosion; they may be old proglacial lakes, dammed by moraine; or they may be oxbow lakes left by meandering rivers. Most larger lakes are too deep to freeze to the bottom, and are connected to other lakes and stream systems. As might be expected, most contain fish populations. The larger upland lakes tend to be clear, cold, poor in nutrients, and comparatively unproductive. They are generally comparable to oligotrophic lakes of cool temperate regions.

Arctic rivers have a number of features that tend to distinguish them from their more temperate counterparts. To begin with, most of the larger arctic rivers are, in a sense, exotic rivers, in that their origins are outside the tundra zone. Rivers such as the Mackenzie, Lena, Ob, and Kolyma all originate in continental areas far to the south of their mouths. Even more east-west flowing rivers, such as the Yukon and Anadyr, originate in timbered country before reaching the tundra. The larger rivers reaching the Arctic, then, tend to bring warmer water from the interior of the continents to the north. The effect on the climate is enough to affect the location of timberline. Conifer woodlands reach essentially to the shores of the Arctic Ocean at river deltas, causing breaks in the circumpolar distribution of tundra. At the same time, the warm waters, nutrients derived from a more temperate environment, and, more recently, industrial pollutants have a significant effect on the arctic environment.

Because they originate deep within the continents, many large northern rivers undergo breakup in their upper reaches while their mouths are still solidly frozen. This can result in enormous ice buildups, dams, and flooding in late spring and early summer.

At least some of the tributaries of most northern rivers are likely to be glacier-fed streams. This results in extreme turbidity in most of the larger rivers. Turbidity reduces light penetration, limiting vegetation growth and visibility for animals. Another result is a rapid buildup of sand and silt bars and extensive delta deposits. These in turn create meanders, sloughs, and cutoff lakes. Where the larger rivers cross flat country, they generally create huge areas of shifting channels, sloughs, thermokarst ponds, bogs, marshes, and virtually every type of wetland environment possible under a cold climate regime. While these areas are forbidding to humans, they are tremendously productive of wildlife of all kinds, most particularly waterfowl and biting insects (see Figure 11–1).

Seasonality affects arctic rivers and streams in other ways as well. Many smaller rivers freeze to the bottom or have only occasional pools deep enough to remain unfrozen and sustain fish. In winter, stream flow may be so curtailed that even larger rivers essentially cease to flow. The Colville River of arctic Alaska becomes little more than a series of isolated pools in winter. On the other hand, overflow from springs and other sources may result in deep deposits of overflow ice or *aufeis* (see Chapter 3).

An arctic river is a complicated and hazardous place for living things, particularly on a year-round basis. On the other hand, there are great advantages to being able to use the river habitat. This is particularly true in the upper reaches of tributaries. Here the cold, fast-moving water is rich in dissolved oxygen; in some seasons there are myriads of insect larvae and other invertebrates that are potential food sources. This situation presents great advantages to organisms such as fish that can utilize the resources on a seasonal basis. And this brings us to what has traditionally been one of the most important commercial resources of the cold regions: fish. Before we turn to aquatic and marine organisms, though, we will briefly examine coastal vegetation.

COASTAL AND AQUATIC VEGETATION

The foreshores of the arctic seas are notoriously poor in vegetation. Heavily ice-affected shores don't favor plant growth, and long stretches of the coasts of arctic Canada and Siberia are almost perfectly barren. Strand, or beach, plants of the Arctic often have their otherwise circumpolar distribution patterns interrupted for hundreds of miles along such shores.

Most vegetated arctic beaches, barrier islands, and dunes are dominated by a rugged, coarse grass called lyme grass *(Elymus arenarius)*. A few other sand- and salt-tolerant species may be interspersed. Backshores and the sides of beach ridges rapidly

take on the appearance and flora of dry tundra and fell field. Sedge meadows fill the channels and hollows between beach ridges and dunes.

Some arctic lagoons support huge stands of a marine flowering plant called eelgrass *(Zostera marina)*. Eelgrass beds are of critical importance to many species of migrating waterfowl. The densest eelgrass stands occur in lagoons on arctic coastal fringes at lower latitudes, not on the shores of the Arctic Ocean itself. The floors of arctic lagoons are mainly bare mud, with perhaps a thin coating of algae.

Figure 11–1. The lower Colville River as it crosses the arctic lowland of northern Alaska. The tremendous expanse of unstable bars and dunes is typical of arctic rivers. Water is high in this summer photograph, but river flow nearly ceases in winter.

ARCTIC FISHES

Fishes are found in most fresh and salt water environments in the Arctic. In the Arctic Ocean itself the number of species is small, as is the case in lakes in various high arctic areas. The number of species increases rapidly in the lower Arctic, particularly in coastal regions where the terrestrial environment is classified as arctic, but where the waters are more subarctic or temperate.

Anadromous fishes are those that spend a major portion of their life at sea but return to fresh water to spawn. In most anadromous species, the young spend from one to several years in the safer environs of freshwater streams and lakes before returning to the sea. (Catadromous fishes reverse the process; the only familiar example is the common freshwater eel.)

The majority of arctic fishes that live part of their lives in fresh water are anadromous, and in numbers of individuals, biomass, and commercial and sport importance, these species dominate the arctic aquatic environment. On the other hand, anadromy is not quite the clear-cut phenomenon it would seem to be. Many species contain both anadromous and landlocked freshwater populations, as is true of the Atlantic salmon and its relatives. The landlocked populations tend to live in large lakes and spawn in streams, though, so their habits are similar except for the salinity of the water. Many purely freshwater species also migrate between lakes and streams. There are also marine species that prefer or need estuarine waters of low salinity in which to spawn, such as some flounders and sculpins. Finally, some fishes thought of as purely marine, such as herring, are occasionally found in brackish estuaries and even in freshwater rivers. The ability to tolerate changes between fresh and salt water is present in a wide variety of fishes; and the degree to which this ability is utilized varies accordingly.

Primitive Fishes

A number of archaic types of fish are found in various locations throughout the world, and a few are found in arctic or subarctic waters. Several species of lamprey occur around the periphery of the Arctic Basin. These are primitive, jawless fish, often parasitic on other fish. Most species are anadromous and spend several years as larval stages in rivers and streams before moving into larger rivers, lakes, and the ocean.

Sturgeon also occur in some arctic areas, particularly as anadromous fish using the Siberian river systems. Sharks are generally rare in arctic waters, but the large basking sharks are common enough in Greenland waters to have supported a commercial fishery.

Herring

Herring range into polar waters in the North Atlantic and Bering Sea region. Some species are anadromous, others spawn in shallow marine environments. Herring occur in large schools. They are important as commercial fish and also as food fish for many larger fish and for humpback whales, which have well-developed strategies for catching them. Other herringlike fish include alewife and shad, which barely range into cold waters.

The Salmonids

By almost any standard, the salmonids include the most important fishes in polar waters. The family *Salmonidae* includes three subfamilies, sometimes considered as separate families. The *Salmoninae* includes salmon, trout, and charr (or char), many of which are anadromous, though some are confined to fresh water. The *Coregoninae* are the whitefish, most of which are freshwater fish. The *Thymallinae* include only the grayling.

The Atlantic salmon, brown trout, and rainbow, or steelhead, trout are all closely related and are classified in the genus *Salmo*. The various species in this group usually have both sea-run and landlocked populations. Most species range only into the southern border of the cold regions, but Atlantic salmon are found in the arctic borders of the North Atlantic; they are fished extensively in Greenland waters, apparently to the detriment of breeding stocks of various other coasts. Efforts at restocking and at raising the fish commercially are probably helpful. The Atlantic salmon differs from the Pacific salmon in that it does not undergo such drastic physical changes before spawning, and it does not necessarily die after spawning, but may return to sea. During the spawning runs, the Atlantic salmon is the most prized of all sport fish, at least in the Atlantic region.

The arctic charr *(Salvelinus alpinus)* is the most northern of all freshwater or anadromous fish. It breeds in ice-choked lakes and streams north into the Canadian high Arctic and all along the arctic coast of Eurasia and Alaska. Charr are superb sport and eating fish, but they grow slowly in their cold waters, so populations must be carefully watched. The range of charr has been much affected by glaciation, and isolated populations are found in lakes as far south as southern Canada. The famous golden trout of some lakes in New England are apparently derived from these charr.

Lake trout are related to charr, but they are found naturally only in North America, and only in freshwater lakes. They are found in cold, deep water lakes far into the Arctic. They are comparable to charr as sport fish, and also are slow-growing and easily overfished in northern lakes. Brook trout are found in eastern North America north into arctic Quebec and Labrador. Their western counterpart, which is often anadromous, is the Dolly Varden, found north to arctic Alaska and Siberia.

Pacific salmon belong to the genus *Oncorynchus,* and this group occurs only in the North Pacific, where five species are found. All of them range north to the Bering Strait, some extending as far as the Mackenzie and Lena Rivers. The center of abundance of all species, though, is farther south, in the southern Bering Sea and North Pacific.

Almost all Pacific salmon are anadromous, to the extent that they are apparently unable to complete their life cycle without going to sea; there are few landlocked populations comparable to Atlantic salmon. As they return from the sea, Pacific salmon are generally silvery or deep bluish in color and resemble Atlantic salmon. As they ascend the rivers, however, they undergo a series of changes in color and shape that transform them into most bizarre-looking fish. These changes are species specific and sex specific; the males, for example, develop grotesquely hooked jaws, enlarged teeth, and humped backs, which in the case of the pink salmon *(O. gorbuscha)* are enlarged to the point of absurdity. The fact that the fish change their appearance so radically is probably responsible for each species having two or more names. The red, or sockeye, salmon *(O. nerka)* is appropriately named, since it is an overall brilliant cherry red in spawning color. Fresh from the sea, though, it is silver with a rich blue back, so is appropriately known as the blueback. The red salmon also has the distinction of spending an intermediate phase in its life in large lakes before going to sea. This means that drainage systems containing large, deep lakes are at a premium for this species, and this in turn means that the distribution and success of the species are closely associated with the glacial history of the area. Although extremely abundant now, it may have been a rare species at the height of the last glaciation. This lake-dwelling habit has resulted in the rise of landlocked populations, known as kokanee salmon.

Once Pacific salmon have spawned, they invariably die. Millions of individuals become instant carrion at the upper reaches of the spawning streams. The fish are in such poor condition, and the number of carrion eaters in the far north is so low, that the spent fish simply rot along the stream banks.

Pacific salmon are a unique part of the northern ecosystem, since they bring resources essentially marine in origin far into the interior. Terrestrial organisms such as brown bears are highly dependent on the salmon runs, which may last for several months in parts of Alaska. Individual bears could never reach their immense size nor bear populations their levels of abundance without the salmon resource. But salmon are something like lemmings in that their populations are quite variable from year to year. A year of successful spawning will generally result in a good run two to four years later. Human intervention has a clear relationship to salmon abundance and breeding success. This human intervention consists not only of fishing pressure and escapement (the number of breeders that are allowed to get through the barriers of nets), but also of pressure on the spawning grounds. The eggs are deposited in the gravel bottoms of clear, fast-moving, silt-free streams, where the critical factor seems to be an abundance of oxygen for the developing embryos. The slightest amount of silting, from upstream construction, for example, can wipe out practically every egg in the stream. This, in turn, can mean no returning spawners several years later.

In addition to the red salmon mentioned above, pink salmon and chum, or dog, salmon are the most abundant species. These are both comparatively small salmon, whose flesh is not highly regarded. Both, however, have been important as subsistence food, and both are fished and canned in quantity now. Dog salmon is often marketed as *keta salmon,* from its Latin name, *O. keta.* Both these species are most common in small streams near the coast.

Silver, or coho, salmon are less abundant but more desirable as sport fish. They have been transplanted into other cold water areas such as the Great Lakes, where they flourish but do not usually breed.

King, or chinook, salmon are the largest and most highly prized of the Pacific salmon. They travel long distances up rivers, are strong fighters, and are excellent eating. Much of the commercial harvest is by hook and line near the river mouths, where the fish are in good condition and can be sold fresh or frozen for high prices.

Whitefish, Ciscos, and Inconnu

Although closely related to the salmon and trout family, whitefish are different in appearance, and most spend their entire life in fresh water. They are silvery fish with large scales, and generally smallish mouths and small teeth. Most species live their entire lives in fresh water, some in streams, more in lakes. Whitefish generally do not take bait, so are fished with nets and used commercially or for subsistence.

There are many species of whitefish classified in the genera *Coregonus* and *Prosopium*. They are often difficult to identify or classify, and there is no general agreement on the delineation of all species or such factors as their individual ranges. Whitefish are important commercial species in many large, cold lakes throughout the circumpolar north and south to places like the Great Lakes.

An exceptional whitefish is the inconnu, or sheefish, *Stenodus leucicthys*. This is a large, anadromous fish of the Bering-Chukchi Sea area, extending to much of Siberia and northwestern Canada. It is prized for sport, eating, and subsistence uses. It is also taken commercially and would probably be more heavily utilized if its range were not so far north.

Grayling

The grayling *(Thymallus arcticus)* is a purely freshwater fish of northern North America and Siberia. Related to trout and whitefish, it is small in size (generally weighing less than 1 kilogram) and characterized by its immense dorsal fin. Grayling are generally found in clear lakes and swift streams. They are ravenous surface feeders and so are beloved of dry fly sport fishers. Although they are common, they can be rapidly fished out by sport fishing. They are of little or no commercial significance, but they have some subsistence value, and can be important survival food.

Pike

The pike family *(Esocidae)* includes several species of large, elongated, voracious fishes of lakes and slow-moving rivers. The northern pike *(Esox lucius)* is the major northern species, with a circumpolar range extending northward to the shores of the Arctic Ocean. It is highly regarded as a sport fish, caught in some quantities commercially, and is also cursed for being highly predaceous on more desirable species and too bony and muddy-tasting to eat. It is sometimes considered to be a useful predator, keeping populations of smaller fish under control. In some arctic lakes, pike populations build up to unhealthy levels, resulting in quantities of stunted fish.

Other Fresh Water Fish

There are relatively few other truly freshwater fish in the Arctic. Although virtually none occur at the highest latitudes, the number increases rapidly at the lower edge of the tundra zone and a number of generally temperate groups range into the lower reaches of the Arctic. These include, for example, a few species of the huge family of minnow, carp, and dace *(Cyprinidae)* and some members of the perch family *(Percidae);* on the other hand, such familiar warm water groups as the bass and sunfish and catfish are totally absent from the far north.

An unusual fish is the blackfish *(Dallia pectoralis)* of the *Umbridae* or mudminnow family. It is a small fish found only in Alaska and eastern Siberia, and renowned for its ability to withstand low temperatures, even freezing, and the virtual absence of oxygen in ice-covered or stagnant water. This fish's ability to survive has, in the process of becoming legendary, been exaggerated. Complete freezing will kill it, but a thawed blackfish may survive for some time. The fish is seldom more than 10 centimeters long so is of little use as human food, but it has been caught for dog food and survival food.

Some fish groups that are typically thought of as marine include freshwater representatives. For example, the burbot, or lingcod, is a more or less typical codfish that never leaves fresh water and is an important food fish throughout much of the circumpolar north. There are also freshwater sculpins *(Cottidae).* Fishes typical of inshore and estuarine waters, such as smelt and sticklebacks, have species that are anadromous or even confined to fresh water.

MARINE FISH

Arctic marine fish are of numerous species and are important for many reasons, including as commercial catches. Most of the important species occur in the North Atlantic and Bering Sea and become rare or absent in the Arctic Basin itself. There are few, if any, commercial fisheries within the waters considered by oceanographers as truly arctic, and little is known regarding the fish populations, other than that they generally have no commercial potential. The subarctic seas, on the other hand, contain the most important and valuable fisheries in the Northern Hemisphere. The Grand Banks, off the eastern Canadian coast, played a greater role in the economics of New World colonization than did the gold of Mexico, a role based mostly on its codfish. For centuries a quintal (one hundred pounds) of dried cod was practically a unit of legal tender in the North Atlantic economy. Cod is still so much a part of the Newfoundland environment that the words *cod* and *fish* are interchangeable there. Any other species of fish is called by its own name.

Codfish were perhaps the first important product of the polar North Atlantic, and they were the reason for much of the early exploration of the arctic shores of Greenland and eastern Canada (see Figure 11–2). They are still of tremendous importance to the commercial fisheries of Norway, Iceland, Canada, and Greenland. Pollack and haddock are cod relatives that have been increasingly heavily fished in recent years. Since the 1960s, Bering Sea pollack have become one of the major commercial fish species. Among their other uses, they are the raw material for the artificial crab meat that has become a common item in the fish market.

Various species of flatfish, such as sole, flounder, and halibut, have become increasingly important as seagoing freezing plants and rapid transportation have changed the northern fishing industry. More recently, fish such as lumpfish, wolffish, and grenadier have also taken a larger role.

A particularly important coastal fish is the capelin *(Mallotis villosus),* a small, silvery fish related to smelt, and, more distantly, to salmon and whitefish. Capelin are extremely abundant, schooling fish found throughout much of the maritime circumpolar North. They are among the major prey species of a tremendous array of denizens of the northern marine ecosystem. A puffin's beakful of fish is likely to contain capelin, as is the contents of a cod's stomach. Humpback whales fish for capelin. Humans, though, have traditionally had relatively little to do with capelin, since the fish is seldom much more than 15 or 20 centimeters long. A few Newfoundlanders have always collected them as they arrived on the beaches to spawn, and they have been used for fertilizer, dog food, and occasionally been smoked for human use. In the 1980s, however, capelin roe became tremendously popular, particularly in Japan, and a fishery for the species was established. Fishing pressure soon became so intense in Newfoundland waters that regulation was necessary.

MARINE MAMMALS

In the 70 million or so years since mammals became the dominant vertebrates on the earth, offshoots of some groups have returned to the sea. Sometimes the land-dwelling ancestor is easily identified, as in the case of the sea otter. The roots of the seals are more deeply buried in time, but probably involve bearlike and weasellike animals. Whales first went to sea as early as the Eocene, the dawn of the Age of Mammals. What affinities their ancestors had to any modern mammals remain a mystery.

For an air-breathing vertebrate to go to sea is an initiative in many ways comparable to growing wings and taking to the air. The sea is a medium that allows movement in three dimensions, and being able to "fly" effectively in the water opens up vast possibilities of access to food resources. There are other advantages, such as being able to generally ignore the force of gravity and grow to whatever size is convenient. Marine mammals can also take advantage of the dense medium of water to develop methods of communication and echolocation (or *sonar*) that have no counterpart on land. On the other hand, there are definite disadvantages to being a warm-blooded, air-breathing organism in the sea. Heat loss is always a potential problem, not to be solved without costly evolutionary or behavioral compromises. Marine mammals are in, but not of, the sea, and they must never be more than a few minutes away from the edge of the sea: its interface with the atmosphere. This becomes particularly a problem in giving live birth, and most marine mammals become terrestrial for a time as birthing approaches; whales are the main exception among arctic marine mammals. Access to air in combination with ice cover is also a problem for marine mammals.

Given the specialized requirements mammals have in living in the sea, it is not surprising that there are many examples of evolutionary convergence. Locomotion in the dense medium of water puts a premium on streamlining, so most marine mammals are elegant and sleek in water, although often graceless on land. Heat loss control is easier in a large body; most marine mammals are much larger than their terrestrial counterparts and are often immense. There are no small mammals, no seagoing mice, in the marine environment. Fur is of comparatively little use for keeping warm in water, and most of the larger and more highly adapted marine mammals have phased out dense fur. Much more effective is a layer of blubber under the skin. Marine mammals can control blood flow through this blubber, letting it act as insulation most of the time and as a radiator in times of heavy exertion. But blubber's effectiveness is closely related to its thickness, and an animal must be large to carry a thick layer of blubber. Fur seals and sea otters are comparatively small and at least partially dependent on fur, with some interesting behavioral consequences.

By terrestrial standards, marine mammals are able to go without breathing for long periods of time. This is the result of several interlocking adaptations. The most important of these adaptations is the ability to store oxygen in muscle tissue and to channel oxygen supplies to vital organs while building up oxygen debts in other parts of the body. This channeling is related to the mammalian diving response, which evidently allows children to sometimes survive immersion in cold water for periods of time that, according to common sense standards, should kill them. The muscles of all marine mammals are rich in myoglobin, a compound related to the hemoglobin of blood, and which shares hemoglobin's ability to store oxygen. The oxidation of myoglobin makes the flesh of marine mammals turn nearly black when it is exposed to air. This is why seal or whale meat drying on a rack in an Eskimo village looks like strips of rubber tire.

One factor *not* involved in marine mammal breathing is large lungs for storage of air. Not only would the buoyancy of air in the lungs work against diving, it would also lead to the dissolving of nitrogen in the bloodstream under the pressure of deep water, and its release as bubbles as the pressure diminished on surfacing. This transformation of nitrogen causes the *bends*, so much feared by human divers, who must carry their oxygen to the depths in the form of a gas.

Not only does the support of the sea allow marine mammals to reach large size, but it also does away with the need for the skeleton, ligaments, and musculature required to overcome gravity. Marine mammal skeletons are frail by terrestrial standards. Butchering a seal is much easier than butchering a caribou, since the joints separate easily. The skeleton of a marine mammal disarticulates rapidly after natural death as well, so that marine mammal fossils tend to be fragmentary; this is one reason why marine mammal ancestry isn't well known. Even the huge bones of whales are mostly spongy and soft and when dried are light in weight. The skull of a seal is sometimes almost paper thin. For this reason, seals are easily killed by a blow to the head. It is for this reason, rather than out of intrinsic cruelty, that sealers kill seals with clubs.

Another advantage to being supported by water is that pregnancy is relatively easy for a marine mammal. This translates into long gestation periods and large, well-developed babies. There are many advantages to being born in a relatively mature state in an environment as full of dangers as the sea.

In the Arctic, marine mammals are tremendously important to the environment, much more so than in other parts of the earth. This is related to the richness of arctic seas, with their many upwellings of nutrient-rich water and to the high oxygen content of cold water. Also, the closeness of land or ice to the sea, the shallowness of the extensive continental shelf, and many other factors contribute to the edge effect we have so often noted in the arctic environment. Some of the arctic marine mammals are migratory and leave for warm waters; the gray whale is an example. Others stay in or near the ice year round, or follow the advancing and retreating edge of the pack ice through the seasons. By far the most important marine mammals are the whales and the seals, but we will discuss others of interest at the end of this section.

Whales

Only a relatively few species of whales occur within the truly arctic waters as narrowly defined by oceanographers. Thick pack ice is obviously a serious deterrent to even a large whale, and few wander widely within the Arctic Basin. Many more are found within the fringes of the Arctic, often along tundra-covered shores.

Whales are divided into two distinct groups, called the toothed whales (order Odonticetae) and the baleen whales (Mysticetae). Although superficially similar, these groups are so distinct that they may well have diverged before their ancestors ever left the land.

Baleen whales have no visible teeth (although tooth buds occur in the embryos). Their upper jaws have grown into great archlike structures from which hang a series of plates of material similar in composition to horn or fingernail. These plates of baleen overlap in a fashion similar to a partially closed venetian blind. Their inner edge is composed of overlapping fibers that create a mesh and turn the whale's mouth into an effective approximation of a trawl net. Baleen whales are, then, gigantic filter feeders, well adapted to sifting out small fish and crustaceans from dense schools. The water taken in with the food organisms is forced out through the baleen by the huge tongue, and the residue is swallowed. The effect of a large mammal feeding on such small organisms is the bypassing of several steps in the normal oceanic food chain, allowing a large biomass of whale to occur in an undisturbed marine environment.

Most baleen whales are large, and many are truly immense.

The blue whale is probably the largest animal ever to exist on the earth; it may reach 30 meters in length and weigh nearly 100,000 kilograms. Baleen whales are divided into three families. The bowhead and right whales are stout, placid, slow-moving whales, while the rorquals are slender, swift, and sleek. Gray whales are a sort of nonspecialized baleen whale, considered more primitive than the others.

As the Latin name *Balaena glacialis* suggests, the bowhead whale is truly a whale of the Arctic. Each year herds cruise northward through the Bering Strait toward summer feeding grounds deep within the Arctic Ocean. The whales are seldom far from ice, and live mainly around open leads and *polynyas,* although they calf in more temperate seas. The bowhead is nearly one-third head; the jawbones may be 5 meters long and the baleen plates may be 4 meters long. Eskimo whalers can use a single piece of bowhead baleen as a toboggan. Bowheads are rotund and slow moving, with thick blubber. They can be hunted effectively from small, open boats, and they float when killed. These attributes gave their close relative, the right whale, its name, since these were the *right* whale to kill. There is archaeo-logical evidence that bowhead whales were hunted by Alaskan natives over 3,000 years ago, and they have probably been a staple part of Eskimo culture from its beginning. This type of subsistence existence was seriously compromised by the whaling industry, which delighted in bowhead whales and rapidly nearly wiped them out, first from the Barents Sea, then the Davis Strait–Baffin Bay seas, and later from the Bering and Chukchi Seas. Bowhead whale management continues to pose problems, which arise from the conflicting interests of native hunters, petroleum interests, and conservationists.

The rorquals include the huge blue and fin whales and several smaller species. The humpback is a somewhat aberrant member of the group. Most rorquals are whales of the open ocean and seldom are found within the pack ice, although they tend to feed in the cold, rich waters of the polar regions. When seen from ship or some promontory, they are usually visible only as a distinctive spout and a long, arched stretch of gray back. They look some-thing like a huge wheel rolling slowly through the ocean, with only a bit of rim showing momentarily above the surface. Humpback whales are more common inshore and are often seen around the arctic fringes, as in Newfoundland and the Gulf of Alaska. Humpbacks are distinguished by their long, armlike flip-pers (about one-third of their 15-meter or more length) and by their eerie, ethereal songs that have become well known since the early 1970s. Humpbacks tend to occur in groups, and they seem playful (frisky, if the word can properly be applied to a whale). They are the best known of the large whales and are often approached closely by whale-watching expeditions or excursions.

Gray whales are currently found only in the Pacific, although it seems likely that an Atlantic population existed into historical times. These whales were nearly wiped out by hunting but have since recovered. They are common in spring in the North Pacific and Bering Sea.

Toothed whales are generally smaller than baleen whales. They include the various porpoises and dolphins, some of which are only a couple of meters long and roughly the bulk of a human. Larger species include the killer whale, up to 10 meters and several tons, and the sperm whale, which reaches 20 meters and is comparable in size to all but the largest baleen whales. Toothed whales fill a broader range of ecological niches than baleen whales and are found in most oceans, shallow seas, and a number of large rivers. They are common in cold waters, but only a few species reach the fringes of the Arctic. Among the toothed whales are some of the most bizarre, as well as some of the least known, of all mammals. For example, in one species, the strap-toothed whale, the two teeth in the lower jaw of the male grow over the outside of the upper jaw and meet in the middle, essentially forming a muzzle that hardly allows the mouth to open. This and several related species of bottlenose, or beaked whales, probably reach the edges of the pack ice, but their ranges and life cycles, as well as their strange adaptations, are still almost entirely mysteries.

Toothed whales have developed sonar to such an extent that they are often able to survive perfectly well if deprived of vision. The full nature of this echolocation and communication system is only now being partly unraveled scientifically. It seems to involve the enlarged "melon" of tissue that commonly occurs on the forehead of toothed whales. It also seems likely that the large and complex brains of these animals have developed in relation to these unusual abilities. There is also evidence that some toothed whales may be able to broadcast a jolt of concentrated sound waves of such power and intensity as to stun prey fish.

The most arctic of toothed whales is the narwhal, which also has one of the strangest and most mysterious features of any mammal. The narwhal is a smallish whale, seldom more than about 4 to 5 meters long. Its mottled gray color gave it its name: *corpse-whale* in Norse. In the male narwhal, one incisor tooth (not the eyetooth) has become elongated into a tusk that can approach the length of the entire body. The tusk is straight, sharp-pointed, and twisted. It is identical in appearance to the horn of unicorns shown in medieval prints and tapestries, and it is a pretty sure bet that the narwhal is involved in the origin of unicorn legends. Narwhal tusks were worth roughly their weight in gold in medieval Europe, and they may have been one of the first exports from the polar regions. Narwhals are found in loose herds or family groups and can sometimes be seen from shipboard in the waters of places such as Greenland and the Canadian Arctic. Their biology, including the function of the tusk, is comparatively little understood.

The *belukha,* or beluga, whale is a relative of the narwhal. Its name means *white* in Russian. The former spelling is now preferred, to distinguish the whale from the beluga fish, a sturgeon that is famous as the source of the best caviar. Belukha whales follow the pack ice and are often seen in open leads with bowhead whales. They are born gray but become pure white at maturity. They cruise the shallow waters of bays and estuaries in groups of as many as several dozen, feeding mainly on fish. Belukhas are easily hunted from small boats and are an important source of food for some coastal communities.

Pothead, or *pilot, whales* are somewhat larger whales (up to about 7 meters). As their Latin name, *Globicephala,* suggests, they have a very large melon, which gives them a beetle-browed appearance. The skin is black. Pothead whales are found mainly in cold, ice-free, subarctic waters, where they may occur in herds of up to 100 or more individuals. These animals are famous for their strandings, in which dozens of them appear to become confused and ground themselves on beaches where they soon die of suffocation. Attempts to save them by driving them to sea usually fail, as the animals will often return to the beach again. While no one knows why this behavior occurs, it has been used in developing methods for hunting potheads. As late as the 1960s, this species was harvested in Newfoundland to be shipped south as food for commercial mink-raising operations. The raising of public consciousness about marine mammals has effectively ended the hunt.

Possibly the most profound change in public attitudes toward an animal has occurred in relation to the *killer whale,* an important species of polar and subpolar waters. Not long ago it was routine to shoot at killer whales when they were seen from ships, and the stories of their viciousness and danger to humans were truly bloodcurdling. Now they are studied within an inch of their lives, kept in major aquaria, petted by small children, subject to rigorous protection, and generally regarded as good and even lovable citizens.

The basis for killer whales' fearsome reputation is easily understood. They are arguably the most powerful predator on earth, at least a couple of orders of magnitude larger than the wolves with which they have occasionally been compared. With their bold black-and-white pattern and a dorsal fin as tall as a person (on the males), they are visible, recognizable, and make a vivid impression wherever they occur. Their impressive teeth clearly support their reputation, as do the generally exaggerated reports of the contents of the stomachs of whales killed before saving them became fashionable.

Along the Pacific coast, killer whales seem to feed mainly on salmon. But they have been observed in many places killing and eating marine mammals; they are known to attack the large baleen whales. One awesome series of photographs taken in southern Argentina shows killer whales sending huge sea lions literally sailing through the air from a flip of the whale's tail. Although it is possible that an occasional killer whale in the Antarctic may have mistaken a person on an ice pan for a penguin and had a try at him, there is no documented case of the whale attacking humans. Just why this should be is unclear, since there is little reason to suggest that humans would be any less nourishing or palatable than seals.

Seals

Like whales, seals are separated into two major groups. These are the *Otariidae,* sometimes called eared seals, and the *Phocidae,* true, or hair seals. The phocid seals give the impression of having become much more closely attuned to a marine existence than the otariids. They are particularly well adapted to living in cold seas and to dealing with pack ice. Probably the most important difference between the two groups has to do with their modes of locomotion. In the phocid seals, the hindlimbs have been reduced to a pair of flippers, not much different in appearance from the flukes of a whale. The animal swims by sculling with the after part of its body. The forelimbs are relatively short and act mainly as fins for steering. The forelimbs also have powerful nails that are useful for scraping away ice from breathing holes. The specialized hindlimbs are permanently set in a backward-pointing position and can't be reversed to act as feet on land. A phocid seal on land or ice has to move by a wriggling motion, helped by the powerful front flippers. Other characteristics of the phocid seals are the compact, spindle-shaped body, a thick layer of blubber, a coat consisting only of coarse guard hairs, and no external ears.

Otariid seals are most common in cool temperate waters. They are seldom found near sea ice, and never in heavy pack ice. (The walrus, which is on the fringe of this group, is an ice-dweller.) Otariid seals include fur seals and sea lions. One species of each occurs in the Bering Sea region and thus reaches into the area we are concerned with. There are no otariids in the North Atlantic or the Arctic Ocean proper, with, again, walrus excepted.

The hindlimbs of otariid seals are highly modified but clearly show their affinities to the legs of land mammals. The foot is a large, fanlike flipper that can serve as a heat radiating mechanism when the animal is on land, so it is often waved in the breeze. The foot can be rotated to point forward, and the animal can run, or at least shuffle, on all fours. The forelimbs are long and paddle shaped, and they provide much of the power for swimming. Otariid seals have small external ears, actually little more than conical bits of bare skin and flesh. The smaller species, generally called fur seals, have well-developed underfur. In fact, their pelts are among the finest furs, and fur seals in both the Northern and Southern Hemispheres have suffered mightily as a result.

Another factor that works against otariid seals in their relationship with humans is their tendency to breed in tremendous concentrations in a few colonies. The northern fur seal of the Bering Sea confines most of its breeding activity to St. Paul Island in the Pribilofs, with a few much smaller colonies on St. George and on the Aleutian and Commander Islands. It is hard to find a greater concentration of animal life than on St. Paul during breeding season, and equally hard to find an animal more vulnerable to humans. Otariid seals tend to be harem breeders, with a few dominant males amassing large groups of females. Adult males are several times larger than females. The younger males must wait for years before they can break into the system, and many never make it. This means, at least theoretically, that a large proportion of the young males could be harvested for their furs without damaging the population. Whether this is true in a long-term, evolutionary sense remains a moot point. Another peculiarity of the breeding biology is delayed implantation: the fertilized ovum does not attach itself to the uterine wall for several months. This results in a long gestation period, so that the pupping and breeding season occur at the same time each year.

Sea lions are larger and less colonial than fur seals. Their fur is coarser and in little demand, and they have never been decimated in the way that fur seals have. They do tend to become entangled in fishing nets. With increased fishing in the Bering Sea and North Pacific, this mortality could have an effect on the populations of Steller's sea lion, the northern representative. At present, there are many breeding colonies of this species throughout the Bering Sea and North Pacific.

It is now generally accepted that eared seals have an ancestor somewhere in the line of bears. They are clearly quite closely related to land carnivores in appearance and behavior.

The walrus (see Figure 11–2) differs from typical eared seals in a number of ways and has often been classified in a separate family, the *Odobenidae*. Walrus have no external ears, but their hindlimbs are rotatable. The most unusual feature of the walrus is the greatly developed canine teeth, which may become tusks nearly a meter in length. The whiskers are also strongly developed and have the consistency of long, thick, curved toothpicks. Walrus are bottom feeders, eating mainly clams. They apparently root around in the shallow seas of the continental shelf, mainly with the stiff whiskers. They remove the clams from their shells by some sort of suction mechanism that must be very effective, since walrus stomachs are usually filled with many pounds of shucked clams. These are eagerly sought by Eskimo walrus hunters and eaten on the spot. Oddly enough, the tusks don't seem to be used for clam-digging. There are many questions on their function; they seem to be useful for helping the animal haul out onto ice pans. Eskimo walrus hunters fear that a

Figure 11–2. Walrus. These large northern seals spend most of their time at sea or on ice pans but sometimes come ashore in large numbers at traditional hauling grounds.

walrus may hook its tusk over the gunwales of a boat, with unfortunate consequences for the hunters, since the animals may weigh well over 1,000 kilograms. This doesn't happen often, however.

Some walrus seem to learn to attack and eat seals. Certain individuals have tusks that are yellowed from blubber and covered with deep scratches, apparently from the seal's teeth. Seal-eating walrus were regarded as a folk tale until recently, but the behavior does seem to occur.

Walrus occur in the North Atlantic, the North Pacific–Bering-Chukchi Sea area, and a separate population occurs in the Laptev Sea north of Siberia. The differences between populations are no more than racial, and all are now considered to be the same species. The Atlantic walrus once was found as far south as Nova Scotia and the Gulf of St. Lawrence but is now seldom seen south of Ungava Bay and the Davis Strait. Walrus are plentiful in the Bering Sea. In spite of hunting pressure, they increased rapidly in the 1970s and 1980s. During this period, they extended their range southward toward the Aleutian Islands and reoccupied hauling grounds that had been unused for years. The Pacific walrus is heavily hunted by the indigenous peoples of the Pacific Arctic. Walrus are a source of meat, and their ivory tusks have given rise to an important industry and art-form: the carving of ivory artifacts. Walrus hides are also used in a variety of ways (see Figure 11–3). They cover the skin boats, or *umiaks,* still widely used in the Bering Sea, and they can be made into cordage, buckets, and so forth. A particularly bizarre walrus product is the *oosick,* a bone found in the penis of the animal and sometimes 60 or 70 centimeters long. These are sold to tourists as is, or sometimes fashioned into cribbage boards or similar works of art.

The phocid seals are the most widespread and abundant marine mammals in the Arctic. All species of this group are highly adapted for life in cold waters, and several are found deep within the polar pack year around. Phocid seals are also found in great numbers in the Antarctic, but most of the antarctic species are only distantly related to those of the North.

In their social behavior, phocid seals range from solitary to gregarious, although none breed in colonies in any way comparable to those of fur seals. The most familiar species in most areas outside the Arctic Basin is the harbor seal, also called the common, or spotted, seal. Harbor seals range southward to the densely populated temperate shores, and some probably never

Figure 11–3. Women preparing a walrus skin for an *umiak* cover. The skin is being split so that the cover will be twice the size and half the thickness of the original hide.

see sea ice. More northern populations breed and pup in pack ice and range into the fringes of the Arctic Ocean.

The harbor seal is a small seal, generally less than 2 meters long and weighing less than 100 kilograms. Its coat of coarse hair is generally a silvery grayish or buff color, mottled with darker spots. It is used by native peoples for clothing and other uses where a relatively thin, flexible skin is appropriate. It is some- times bleached and the hair removed, leaving a creamy-white hide like thick parchment, good for decorations or drawing. Like other hair seal hides, it has had little commercial significance, but has recently come into some demand for fashionable footwear. Harbor seals are mainly fish eaters and are often considered to be competition by commercial fisheries. Until the 1960s, the state of Alaska paid a bounty on them.

Harbor seals haul out on rock ledges, particularly on mud flats, where they may be seen in groups of 100 or more. When they are disturbed, they can make their way to water with surprising speed, then often stay around showing a great deal of curiosity.

The ringed seal is a close relative of the harbor seal. It is about the same size and similar in color, although generally more buff colored. The spots on its coat have hollow centers, looking like rings or links of a chain. Ringed seals are truly circumpolar, reaching the northernmost coasts and the open polar seas. In fact, their range hardly extends south of the Arctic Basin. With the necessarily close association with pack ice, the ringed seal has developed a number of behavioral features that adapt it to this regime. It keeps open breathing holes in the pack, and these may enlarge into snow-covered chambers in which the animals may haul out and even give birth. Both humans and polar bears have learned to hunt at these holes. The chamber has a hole leading to the snow surface, and Eskimo hunters may place a feather over the hole. When a seal surfaces, the change in air pressure disturbs the feather, and the hunter strikes with a harpoon. A good deal of speculation and work has gone into trying to find out how the seal can locate its breathing hole in the rough undersurface of the moving pack, but no clear answer has yet emerged.

The ringed seal was widespread during the Ice Ages, and its range changed with changing climate and ice conditions. Isolated populations are now found inland in such places as the Caspian Sea. Lake Baikal, located deep in central Siberia, contains seals that are closely related to the ringed seal and that may have dispersed to the lake at some earlier time, perhaps by following the Yenisei River.

The harp seal is a widespread phocid of the North Atlantic sector. It ranges southward along the edge of the sea ice and pups in great numbers off the coast of Greenland and Newfoundland. Its young are the main species of the famous seal hunt at "the front," the extensive area of spring pack ice off eastern Newfoundland, in the western North Atlantic. The whitecoats, still wearing their natal fur and unable to swim, are clubbed and skinned by the thousands. Mature harp seals have a bold, dark gray and white coat.

The Bering Sea counterpart of the harp seal is a bizarrely marked species called the ribbon seal. Its pelt has broad bands of pale yellow on a dark background. This is a little-known seal, apparently spending most of its time out at sea. It occasionally shows up in large concentrations near the Bering Strait. It is not harvested commercially.

The bearded seal is the other denizen of the Arctic Ocean, with a range similar to that of the ringed seal. It is a much larger animal, reaching a length of 3 meters and weighing as much as 300 kilograms or more. Bearded seals are solitary animals. They seem to be bottom feeders, and their name derives from the coarse whiskers that are comparable to those of walrus and probably serve a similar function. The pelt of bearded seals is a uniform or two-toned pale grayish or buff. The skin is in demand by Eskimos, since it is intermediate in thickness between that of smaller seals and walrus. It is useful for covering smaller boats and is the preferred material for making the soles of footgear (*mukluks* or *kamiks*). In the Bering Sea, it is known as the mukluk seal or simply the mukluk.

The gray seal is a large, gregarious seal of the temperate North Atlantic, reaching the southern fringes of the Arctic in areas such as Iceland. It has a long, arched nose and is easily distinguished from the harbor seal. Its profile gives it the name horsehead seal.

The hooded seal is another large seal of the North Atlantic sector. It is distinguished from all other arctic seals by its inflatable nasal passages, which indicate its relationship to the huge elephant seal of the antarctic and temperate Pacific regions. The hooded seal is generally seen on sea ice, sometimes in association with the harp seal. It is also hunted at the front. Here it congregates in large numbers for pupping and breeding.

OTHER MARINE MAMMALS

Besides the polar bear, discussed in Chapter 10, two other species occur, or did occur, in the mammalian fauna of the polar seas or at least the North Pacific fringes.

Steller's seacow was the only cold water representative of a widespread group of marine mammals called the *Sirenia* (from their supposed similarity to mermaids) and including manatees and dugongs. Steller's seacow was narrowly confined to the western Aleutian and Commander Islands, where it was discovered by Vitus Bering when he was shipwrecked in the mid-1700s. The seacow was a huge, placid beast that fed on seaweeds in the shallow waters around the islands. It had no teeth but was nonetheless able to grow to 6 meters or more in length and weighed several tons. The animals were easily killed, and it is claimed that their meat was comparable in quality to fresh beef. Within 25 years of its discovery, the species was totally eliminated, largely to feed hunters who were busily decimating the fur seal and sea otters. Occasional rumors from the Soviet Union suggest that individuals of this species have been sighted recently, and it is remotely possible that an isolated population could have survived in these cold and stormy seas, but it is probably too much to hope that Steller's seacow is still with us.

The sea otter came very close to suffering a similar fate, but enough breeding stock did survive to set off a successful repopulation of much of its former range. The sea otter is a large relative of the land otter, weighing as much as 40 kilograms. This is still small by marine mammal standards and doesn't allow for the development of a very thick blubber layer. Consequently the sea otter depends more on its fur for temperature control than any of the larger sea mammals. As a result, its fur is of incredibly fine quality; it is often considered to be the finest fur in the world.

The center of the sea otter's range is the Aleutian Islands; the presence of sea otters was largely responsible for the rash of Russian activity that began in this stormy and fog-shrouded area before 1800 and ultimately extended down the coast as far as California. Sea otters were nearly wiped out, as were the native Aleuts who were essentially enslaved as hunters of the otter and fur seals.

The sea otter is an endearing animal that spends a good deal of its time floating on its back and eating sea urchins, often using a rock balanced on its chest as an anvil for cracking the shells and a smaller stone as a hammer. They may even sleep in this position, anchoring themselves in place with a strand of seaweed so as not to wash out to sea.

The sea otter's dependence on its fur presents a problem in relation to oil spills. If the otter's fur is soiled, it loses its ability to hold a layer of air against the skin, and the animal then soon dies of hypothermia. Sea otters spend a great deal of their time grooming but are unable to deal with a heavy coating of oil.

SUGGESTED FURTHER READING

A tremendous amount of technical information, mostly published in various periodicals, is available on material covered in this chapter. Most of the following recent volumes contain basic information about the polar marine and aquatic environment and its inhabitants, as well as useful bibliographies.

Dunbar, M. J., ed. *Polar Oceans.* Calgary: Arctic Institute of North America, 1977.

Haley, D., ed. *Marine Mammals of the Eastern North Pacific and Arctic Waters.* Seattle: Pacific Search Press, 1978.

Heintzelman, D. S. *A World Guide to Whales, Dolphins, and Porpoises.* Tulsa: Winchester Press, 1981.

Hobbie, J. E., ed. *Limnology of Tundra Ponds.* Stroudsburg, PA: Dowden, Hutchinson, and Ross, 1980.

Katona, S. K., V. Rough, and D. T. Richardson. *A Field Guide to the*

Whales, Porpoises, and Seals of the Gulf of Maine and Eastern Canada. New York: Charles Scribner's Sons, 1983.

Morrow, J. E. *The Freshwater Fishes of Alaska.* Anchorage: Alaska Northwest Publishers, 1980.

Rey, L., ed. *The Arctic Ocean.* New York: John Wiley & Sons, 1982.

Ridgway, S. H., and R. J. Harrison, eds. *Handbook of Marine Mammals. Vol. 1: The Walrus, Sea Lions, Fur Seals and Sea Otter. Vol. 2: The Seals.* New York: Academic Press, 1981.

Scott, W. B., and E. Crossman. *Freshwater Fishes of Canada.* Ottawa: Fisheries Research Board of Canada, 1973.

Watson, L. *A Sea Guide to Whales of the World.* New York: E.P. Dutton, 1981.

Chapter 12

Birds of the Arctic

WE have saved our discussion of birds until now because the birds (or *avifauna*) of the Arctic epitomize so many of the concepts we have dealt with so far, while simultaneously seeming to transgress many of the rules and generalizations we've made. Many birds straddle the border between marine or aquatic and terrestrial ecosystems. They may feed in the water and breed on land, or they may be terrestrial organisms in June and marine in August. Others may be important players in the activities and energy flow of the tundra ecosystem in one portion of the year and totally absent a few weeks later. Or they may spread their favors around the Arctic, at one location, habitat, or niche at one time, filling a very different role later.

In summer, birds are the most conspicuous element of the tundra fauna, possibly excepting mosquitoes. In winter, they are virtually absent. Many birds that are familiar to ornithologists from the temperate regions occur on the tundra, but they are often so different in appearance and behavior as to be nearly unrecognizable. On the other hand, there are a few old favorites. Anyone who has ever wondered what happens to the masses of robins that pass through suburban North America each spring and fall will find the answer in the Arctic, where robins are often among the most common birds.

LOONS AND GREBES

People often think of loons as denizens of the northern forest, but they are generally more common in the Arctic. All four species of loons are circumpolar; they are known as divers in English-speaking Europe. Loons are large, heavy-bodied birds, with proportionately small wings and with solid, heavy bones. Once in the air they are fast and efficient flyers, but they have difficulty taking off and need a large area for a runway. This requirement controls the distribution of the birds as a group and as individual species; the smaller loons can get by with smaller lakes. Loons' feet are set far back on the body and are ideal for propelling the slender, streamlined body through the water, but they are pretty much useless for walking. As might be expected, loons never leave the vicinity of water; they breed along the shores of ponds and slow rivers, live mainly on fish, and winter along the seacoast. In winter they look like big, low-slung, dull gray waterfowl, but their summer plumage is spectacular and distinctive from species to species. Loons are seldom shot for food even in the bush, but they are often taken accidentally in fish nets as they dive for prey.

The common loon is the familiar species of the northern forest, reaching the southern fringes of the tundra. Beyond timberline it is replaced by the very similar yellow-billed loon, which, as the name implies, differs mainly in that its bill is pale colored and slightly upturned. The yellow-billed loon is something of a mystery bird to southerners, since it winters near the edge of the pack ice and is seldom seen in temperate latitudes. It is regarded as rare even in the Arctic, but this supposed rarity is more a function of its preference for large lakes such as occur in the more inaccessible and mosquito-ridden parts of the tundra.

The arctic loon, or black-throated diver, is a smaller bird. Its stout, straight bill, black throat, and pearly gray head are distinctive (see Figure 12–1). These loons are abundant from the open forested areas well into the Arctic.

Figure 12–1. Arctic loon, known in Europe as the black-throated diver. One of the smaller loons, this species is a common inhabitant of tundra and timberline ponds.

Red-throated loons are similar in size to arctic loons, but much more slender and gangly looking. The bill is slender and up-turned, the throat brick red. Red-throated loons breed northward roughly to the limit of land. They can negotiate smaller ponds than the other species and so are more evenly distributed and may occur in upland areas. Red-throated loons also seem to fly more than other species. They have a disheveled, humpbacked appearance in the air, and they often give voice to a dull, hoarse quack as they fly.

Grebes are somewhat similar in appearance and habits to loons but are not closely related. Grebes are more typically boreal forest than tundra inhabitants, but the horned grebe and red-necked grebe are seen in arctic and timberline situations.

THE ALBATROSS GROUP

A well-defined group of seabirds is the order Procellariiformes (called Tubinares in older literature). These birds range in size from storm petrels, not much larger than sparrows, to albatrosses with wingspans of nearly 4 meters. All have distinctive nostrils that are tubular structures located on the top or sides of the bill (see Figure 12–2). Almost all breed only on islands, and all are birds of the open sea, migrating great distances and coming within sight of land only to breed or for shelter from storms. Tube-noses are most abundant in the far reaches of the Southern Ocean. A few species breed in the Arctic and a few others show up as migrants from the antarctic winter.

Ornithologists do not agree on the function of the tubular nostrils. It has been suggested that they are involved in the excretion of salt, allowing the birds to drink salt water. But birds without these structures also can exude concentrated salt solutions through their nostrils. A more plausible explanation is that they have some role in distributing oil to the feathers for preening.

The northern fulmar is the only tube-nose that breeds widely in the Arctic, although not within the Arctic Ocean itself. Fulmars are a bit smaller than herring gulls; they are variable in color, but generally range from pale to dark gray. They are easy to distinguish from gulls once one is familiar with them, although the differences are not easy to describe. Fulmars have a solid, thick-necked aspect; they fly with stiff wings, seeming to scale across the waves. The difference between a fulmar and a gull in flight has been compared to the difference between a projectile and a

Figure 12–2. Fulmar. This is the only member of the albatross order (Procellariiformes) regularly breeding in arctic waters. The tubular nostrils are an identifying feature of this group.

kite. Fulmars are unusual among the smaller tube-noses in that they generally nest in the open, rather than in burrows. They are tough and aggressive, and even the larger gulls and skuas seem to leave them and their nests alone. Fulmars nest in large colonies, often with other cliff-nesting seabirds, where they generally occupy the higher parts of the cliffs. Away from the nesting colony, they are usually seen only at sea.

Storm petrels are small seabirds; they are usually dark gray or black, often with a white patch at the base of the tail. They breed in a few peripheral arctic areas such as the Aleutians and the Faeroes. One species, Wilson's petrel, breeds in the Antarctic but migrates into the Northern Hemisphere in great numbers, sometimes reaching arctic waters. Except when they are driven ashore by storms, storm petrels are seen only at sea. They often follow ships, feeding on small organisms stirred up by the wake.

There are many species of medium-sized tube-noses, usually called shearwaters, or petrels. The majority of species breed in the Southern Hemisphere, but they range widely over the oceans of the world. Two dark-plumaged species, the sooty shearwater and the short-tailed (also called slender-billed) shearwater may be abundant in arctic waters. Several other species are more or less common over the North Atlantic and North Pacific. They look like more slender, graceful fulmars.

Albatrosses are mainly wanderers to arctic waters, although one species was known to breed on the Aleutian Islands in earlier times. Albatrosses look like huge shearwaters, larger than any other seabirds except gannets. They are seldom seen from shore.

THE PELICAN FAMILY: CORMORANTS AND GANNETS

Birds in this group typically have patches of bare, bright-colored skin at the base of the bill. Cormorants are large, dark-plumaged sea and coastal birds. They are fish eaters and nest on cliffs and sea stacks throughout much of the world as well as on trees in more temperate regions. Cormorants have a rather loose-jointed, gangly, unkempt look; this probably gives them their other common name, shag. Cormorants are also peripheral arctic birds. They nest in the North Atlantic sector and into the Bering Strait region, but they are seldom seen within the Arctic Ocean proper. One species, the red-faced cormorant, breeds only in the southern Bering Sea. The pelagic cormorant (see Figure 12–3) is more

Figure 12–3. Pelagic cormorant. The common breeding cormorant in the North Pacific–Bering Sea region, it is replaced by related species in other parts of the lower Arctic.

widespread in the North Pacific zone. The great cormorant is the main species at higher latitudes in the North Atlantic.

Cormorants are generally found nesting with other cliff-nesting seabirds, particularly alcids. Their numbers in a colony are usually relatively small and they occur in scattered patches.

Gannets, although related to cormorants, look very different. Large, graceful flyers, they look more like waterfowl or albatrosses. Most members of this group are tropical, but one species, the gannet or solan goose, nests in several large colonies in the North Atlantic, on the periphery of the Arctic. Gannets are about as thoroughly colonial as any seabirds. If they nest in an area at all, they are likely to occur in tens of thousands as they do on Bonaventure Island in Quebec, Cape St. Mary's in Newfoundland, and St. Kilda, off the Hebrides. Mature gannets are easily identified at sea. They are larger than gulls, have a long, pointed tail, and are pure, brilliant white with black wingtips. Immature gannets are brown or piebald, but otherwise identical to adults. Gannets have been a major source of food for North Atlantic people for millennia. Eggs, young, and adults were all taken by intrepid climbers on the sea cliffs long before rock climbing became a sport. An old Atlantic name for gannets is solan goose or sule, and many wave-beaten islets and sea stacks have names—Sule Skerry, for example—that reflect the gannetrys they support.

We tend to think of pelicans as birds of warm seas, but the white pelican breeds northward nearly to timberline in the Canadian Northwest Territories.

One group of water birds missing from the far north is the long-legged waders, the herons and the similar but unrelated storks. Arctic marshes and lagoons look empty to temperate zone bird-watchers, with at most an occasional great blue heron near timberline.

WATERFOWL

Waterfowl—ducks, geese, and swans—are as much a part of the summer tundra ecosystem as are caribou. In fact, they are more numerous, generally more conspicuous, and in terms of total weight (or biomass) might well surpass caribou. During the winter months, though, they vacate the tundra entirely. Most species travel deep into the temperate regions, while a few stay near the edges of the pack ice.

One reason that waterfowl are so significant in the Arctic is that many different species are involved, so that a wide variety of ecological niches are filled and competition is reduced. Roughly 30 species nest at timberline and northward in North America. Most of these species are either circumpolar or are replaced by closely related birds in Eurasia.

Swans

Swans are the largest and, with their white plumage, the most conspicuous of waterfowl. Most wild swans are highly migratory and are tundra breeders, although they are familiar in the temperate regions on their wintering grounds. The North American whistling (or tundra) swan and its close Eurasian relative, Bewick's swan, are by far the most abundant species. In each hemisphere, there is a larger, rarer species (whooper swan in Eurasia, trumpeter swan in North America) that breeds locally in or near the Arctic.

With their long necks, swans are perfectly adapted for feeding on plants growing on the bottoms of shallow tundra ponds and meandering rivers. In some tundra areas, there seems to be a pair of swans for each thaw pond; conducting a census of them from low-flying aircraft is a piece of cake!

Geese

Geese occur in virtually every corner of the Arctic, migrating across the timberline in long skeins every spring, spreading out to the shores of the Arctic Ocean, sometimes crossing from one hemisphere to the other, filling the coastal lagoons in late summer as they change plumage and gain strength for their fall migrations, and producing hundreds of thousands of young each year.

Gray geese are the ancestors of the familiar barnyard geese; they include several closely related species or races spread around the circumpolar north. The white-fronted and graylag are probably the most familiar. They generally nest in open, grassy or marshy tundra areas, usually near the shores of lakes and ponds.

Canada geese are the most familiar geese of North America. While many breed in the Arctic, they have also established resident feral populations in many temperate regions; they winter in tremendous numbers along the Atlantic seaboard, mainly in cornfields and meadows; they are highly prized by hunters, and hunting is carefully regulated. The popularity of Canada geese as game for wealthy urban hunters provided impetus for the early research on the biology and management of arctic wildlife. Many of the birds shot by Washingtonians in the Chesapeake Bay had migrated from Alaska a few months earlier.

Canada geese exist in many races, which differ from each other mainly in size, proportions, and darkness of the plumage. Some, such as the Aleutian Canada goose, are nonmigratory and little known outside of their native area.

Surprisingly, Canada geese are strictly a North American species, but they have been successfully introduced into parts of Europe; why they have never crossed the North Atlantic or Bering Strait under their own steam is an interesting question, whose answer may have to do with the presence of the closely related barnacle goose in Europe.

Also related to the Canada goose is the smaller brant, a circumpolar species nesting far into the high Arctic. The darker race of western North America was once considered to be a separate species. Brant are more coastal than Canada geese. During much of the year their preferred food is a marine flowering plant called eelgrass, which is abundant in shallow lagoons such as occur along the Alaska peninsula. Brant may occur in huge concentrations at eelgrass beds during fall migrations. Their dependence on eelgrass is also a weak link in the brant's life cycle, since eelgrass beds are subject to a periodic blight that decimates them and that, in turn, may cause serious reductions in brant populations.

Snow geese are pure white geese with black wingtips, breeding mainly along the shores of the Arctic Ocean and on some of the high arctic islands. They are often seen in immense flocks on resting areas during migration. Some snow geese wintering along the Atlantic coast of North America actually breed in eastern Siberia, migrating all the way across North America twice each year. Not all snow geese are white. A genetic color phase known as the blue goose has gray plumage. It was once thought to be a separate species, but it has been shown that a so-called blue goose may have white snow goose parents. The emperor goose, found only in the Bering Sea during summer and winter, looks somewhat like a blue goose. A small white goose similar to the snow goose, known as Ross's goose, has a limited breeding area in western Canada.

Ducks

Ducks actually include several groups of smaller waterfowl; most differ from geese and swans in that males and females have distinctly different plumage, at least during most of the year. Bird-watchers in the temperate zones traditionally separate ducks into *puddle ducks* and *diving ducks,* based partly on behavior (dabbling as opposed to diving), but also on habitat: shallow water versus deep water. These distinctions are not so clear on the northern breeding grounds. Scoters, diving ducks usually seen out to sea in winter, are common in tundra freshwater ponds in summer. Although many species of ducks breed south of the Arctic, they are also common within the tundra zone. Even such common species as the mallard and pintail have tundra nesting populations.

Mallards and pintails are typical puddle ducks, breeding mainly on small ponds of fresh water throughout the circumpolar north. Teal are related ducks, much smaller in size, and are found in tiny ponds and sloughs. Several species of related teal are found in similar habitats around the circumpolar north. Wigeons are slender puddle ducks, slightly more partial to seashore conditions and larger ponds and lakes. There is a Eurasian and an American species. The black duck is an eastern North American counterpart of the mallard, breeding northward to the Labrador coast.

Goldeneyes and buffleheads are bay ducks during winter but usually inhabit tundra and forest ponds and river shores in summer. The same is generally true of the light-bodied, dark-headed ducks sometimes known as pochards, and including scaup, tufted ducks, and others. Scoters, as we mentioned before, breed in freshwater ponds and rivers; they are large, ponderous, black-plumaged ducks that winter at sea and in large bays.

The most truly arctic ducks are the eiders and the oldsquaw, or long-tailed, duck. Eiders are large, heavy ducks, as large as some geese. Two species, the common eider and the king eider, breed along most arctic coasts, with the king eider tending to replace the common at higher latitudes. In some areas eiders are colonial nesters. Even where nests are more scattered, the females and young tend to congregate into large flocks. Colonies of eiders are the source of eiderdown, which is collected from the nests after the young have left. This is probably the finest of all down, although not much is available.

Eiders feed mainly on shellfish; they dive to the bottoms of shallow bays, estuaries, and ponds. In winter they congregate in flocks sometimes numbering tens of thousands, usually at about the southern fringe of pack ice. Eiders are an important food source for many coastal arctic communities. At Barrow, Alaska, they cross the narrow spit of Point Barrow in more or less continuous flocks during early August, and a special temporary duck camp has traditionally been set up at the base of the spit.

In addition to the two circumpolar eider species, the spectacled eider and the bizarre Steller's eider are found in the North Pacific–Bering Sea region. Soviet scientists have recently suggested that the Steller's eider is a close relative of the extinct Labrador duck, a mysterious species of waterfowl that became extinct, apparently with little help from human hands, during the nineteenth century.

The oldsquaw is a much smaller, more slender, and graceful duck of the arctic coasts. On the water it is a light-colored duck with a long, spikelike tail. In flight it appears darker because of its dark wings. Oldsquaws are very vocal on their wintering grounds in the colder ice-free seas; this has given them their American name. Oldsquaws go north roughly to the limit of land; they breed along the shores of tundra ponds and the sea itself.

The harlequin duck is a small, dark, rather odd-looking but handsome duck. It seems to have a preference for rough or fast-moving water. Inland it is found breeding along swift-moving rivers. At sea it tends to frequent tide rips, channels, and surf at the base of sea cliffs. Seldom common, it may be seen in small flocks in these special areas. Even in winter, it seldom goes much south of the arctic coasts.

RAPTORS AND OWLS

Raptors include several families of closely related birds known as hawks, falcons, buzzards, and harriers. In the bird world, they fill a role roughly equivalent to that of wolves, foxes, weasels, and wildcats; in fact, they overlap these mammals ecologically in that they often prey on small mammals such as lemmings. Owls are not closely related to raptors in an evolutionary (or taxonomic) sense, but they fit into the same predatory pattern in the tundra environment. Another group that occupies similar ecological niches includes the gulls and skuas, or jaegers, which we'll look at later in this chapter.

Falcons

Falcons are fast-flying, powerful, graceful, predatory birds. They tend to prey on other birds, although they may take mammals as well. They are distributed throughout the world, and several species are found in the Arctic. Like most animals that are secondary, or even tertiary, consumers, they are seldom numerous. This means that the loss of even a relatively few individuals can have serious effects on the overall population. Animals this far up the food chain also can suffer from their prey's tendency to concentrate certain environmental pollutants. These may reach critical levels in predators, as happened in the case of ospreys, peregrine falcons, and bald eagles with DDT and related compounds. The Arctic and Subarctic have been extremely important in providing relatively safe and unpolluted breeding grounds for some of these species when they were virtually eliminated from many temperate regions.

The gyrfalcon (see Figure 12–4) is the largest of all falcons, and it is almost entirely confined to the Arctic as a breeding species. It may occasionally show up far to the south during some winters, often prompting local population explosions of bird-watchers. Gyrfalcons vary in color from slate gray to nearly pure white, with the white color phase particularly common in Greenland. A typical gyrfalcon is about the size of a large seagull, and in flight has a gull-like grace, though with more speed and power. Gyrfalcons nest on cliffs and ledges, generally inland. They feed on ptarmigan, waterfowl, smaller birds, and small mammals.

Gyrfalcons have long been in demand for the sport of falconry. They were shipped from northern Scandinavia and Greenland as early as the Middle Ages. On at least one occasion in the mid-twentieth century, history repeated itself as the gift of a Greenland falcon paved the way to obtain permission to carry out an archaeological dig in the Middle East.

In spite of demand by falconers, gyrfalcons have never suffered population declines like those of their smaller cousins, the peregrines. This seems to be mainly because gyrfalcons don't migrate into temperate regions and so don't run afoul of DDT in high concentrations.

Peregrines are also circumpolar falcons, ranging from warm regions well up into the tundra zone. More migratory than gyrfalcons, they have been wiped out of many temperate areas by pollution. Arctic populations were less affected, and birds brought from the North are being used to help re-establish temperate populations as DDT is slowly eliminated from the environment.

The peregrine is also known as the duck hawk and does prey on waterfowl, as well as other birds. Peregrines are even faster and more vigorous flyers than the larger gyrfalcons, and they take much of their prey by diving (or stooping) on them as they are flying and literally knocking them out of the sky. Peregrines are

Figure 12–4. Gyrfalcon. The largest of all falcons, the gyrfalcon is often considered the most spectacular predatory bird of the circumpolar North.

smaller and generally darker than gyrfalcons. At close range they are easily distinguished: the peregrine has strongly defined dark mustaches on the side of its face.

Northern peregrines nest on cliffs and bluffs, like gyrfalcons, but they are more partial to rivers. Until it became illegal to capture them, they were easy marks for falconers, since they could often be approached by boat.

Merlins are small, gray falcons that look like chunky peregrines with less-defined markings. They are circumpolar and found throughout the low Arctic, although they are seldom common. They apparently feed mainly on smaller birds and are strongly migratory.

The kestrel and its American relative, sometimes called the sparrowhawk, are small falcons, more slender and graceful than the merlin. They also occur in the low Arctic, where they prey on small birds and insects. They are often quite common. A few other species of falcon may be found within the boreal forest in Eurasia and America.

True Hawks

In Europe the term *hawk* is used for only a few species of short-winged, long-tailed raptors that are well adapted to catching other birds on the wing by rapid maneuvers in dense woodland and brush. Two species reach northward to timberline throughout most of the circumpolar north. These are the goshawk, nearly as large as a gyrfalcon, and the much smaller sharp-shinned hawk, not much larger than a robin. Both are common and are often seen dashing through openings in the forest. They are both slate-gray in color as adults, brown when younger. The goshawk is most likely responsible for the patches of grouse feathers that are often seen on the forest floor.

Eagles and Other Buteos

Buteos are large, broad-winged birds, known as eagles and buzzards in Europe, eagles and hawks in North America. They are particularly well adapted for soaring on rising columns of heated air, or thermals, and on updrafts associated with mountains and ridges. As would be expected, they are most common in continental areas where the sun warms the land surface, and in uplands.

The most important tundra buteo is the rough-legged hawk, or buzzard (see Figure 12–5). It is roughly the size of a raven but more slender, with long wings and tail. Although generally a buff

Figure 12–5. Rough-legged hawk. One of the major predators of microtine rodents in the low Arctic during summer. In winter, it is a familiar species in temperate regions.

or brown color, roughlegs are quite variable. They generally have light-colored "windows" in the wings and light feathers at the base of the tail, giving them a two-toned appearance. Roughlegs feed largely on small mammals and birds; they probably fill roughly the niche that snowy owls occupy in more mountainous upland country. They migrate south to warm temperate regions.

Red-tailed hawks are mostly confined to timbered country, where their niche seems more or less equivalent to that of roughlegs. They are more stocky birds, with a short, broad tail with conspicuous brick-red feathers on the upper surface. The overall color is variable, but generally darker than that of the roughleg.

The golden eagle is a huge, powerful, circumpolar eagle. Its great, broad wings may span nearly 2.5 meters. In the mature eagle the feathers are dark brown, with a golden wash on the head and neck. Younger birds show some white, particularly near the base of the tail. The legs are feathered all the way to the toes, unlike the bare feet of sea eagles.

Golden eagles are powerful predators. They feed on the larger rodents and hares. I have watched a pair of golden eagles carry out a serious and prolonged attack on a half-grown Dall sheep. Although it is unfashionable to say so, they can and do attack the young of some big-game animals successfully on at least some occasions. On the other hand, they are never common and they are generally confined to the more remote mountainous areas.

The sea eagles include the American bald eagle, the white-tailed eagle, which is its Eurasian counterpart, and the bizarre Steller's sea eagle of the North Pacific coast of Asia. With their tremendous hooked beaks, sea eagles are fearsome in appearance, but they tend to be fish and carrion eaters rather than aggressive predators, although they can and do attack mammals.

The bald eagle needs no introduction to U.S. readers. The other sea eagles have more or less white plumage, arranged in different locations over the body. Like the bald eagle, most are found along coasts and rivers northward to about the lower edge of the Arctic and in treeless coastal areas such as the Aleutian Islands. Coastal resources are rich enough to support quite large populations of these birds, and they often concentrate in dozens or hundreds in certain favored spots during the nonbreeding season. Because of their favored habitat and diet, sea eagles are vulnerable to both human predation and pollution. Bald eagles were nearly eliminated from the lower 48 states by DDT pollution, but remained common in Alaska and parts of northern Canada.

Other Raptors

Ospreys are somewhat similar to eagles, although smaller. Even more than sea eagles they depend on fish, and they are the only raptor that regularly dives like a tern to catch fish. Ospreys are circumpolar, reaching to the southern fringes of the Arctic. They also were devastated by DDT pollution, but are beginning to recover.

Harriers are slender, buteolike birds that hunt mainly by flying over open country at low elevation, sometimes hovering over some tempting object. They are very light and buoyant in appearance, with the wings usually held at a pronounced dihedral, like some vultures' wings. The common harrier of the far north, the marsh harrier, has a conspicuous white patch at the base of its long tail. It is often seen along the edges of lagoons and coastal wet tundra not far north of timberline.

Owls

Two species of owls are important in the tundra ecosystem throughout much of the circumpolar north. Several other species occur in the timberline forests. The short-eared owl is in many respects a counterpart of the marsh harrier, spending much of its time quartering coastal marshes and wet meadows looking for small mammals. It is usually a pale buff in color, and about the size of a gull or marsh harrier. Its body appears to be short, and the flight is often irregular, buoyant, and mothlike.

The snowy owl is one of the best known denizens of the tundra environment. A huge, often nearly pure white owl, it looks even larger than it is because it inhabits open tundra where the largest vegetation is about human ankle high. Snowy owls nest on the ground; each pair usually has a perch from which it maintains a lordly overview of its domain. The perch is generally a naturally occurring mound on the tundra, perhaps an exceptionally large tussock that has been fertilized by owl droppings and pellets for decades. In recent times the ubiquitous oil drum often serves as an owl perch.

Snowy owls are strongly dependent on lemmings and other microtines. As a result, their population and the success of their annual breeding are quite variable. In off years, the birds may not nest at all; they may also migrate southward into temperate regions in quantities, where they often sit on fenceposts in open pastures, a reasonable approximation of tundra conditions. Snowy owls are territorial, with a pair occupying an area averaging perhaps one square kilometer. After the snow has left the tundra, snowy owls are so conspicuous that they can easily be counted from a low-flying airplane. Snowy owls are particularly abundant in the vicinity of Point Barrow, Alaska. Since this area has long been a major study site for tundra biology, the overall role of the snowy owl in the arctic ecosystem has been well studied, and probably overemphasized.

The great horned owl is the boreal forest counterpart of the snowy owl, along with its close Eurasian relative, the eagle owl. Both are powerful predators that take animals up to the size of marmots and even porcupines. The great gray owl is a much shyer and rarer denizen of the deep boreal forest. Although it appears to be larger than the great horned owl, its soft, fluffy feathers enwrap a small body. The crow-sized hawk owl and the much smaller boreal owl are also forest dwellers found northward to the vicinity of timberline.

GROUSE AND PTARMIGAN

Grouse and ptarmigan are the boreal and arctic members of the *gallinaceous* (chickenlike) birds. Like other birds in this group, they are relatively weak flyers, particularly in terms of stamina. Hence, they are generally nonmigratory, or at most travel short distances. In winter, they may be the only member of the tundra avifauna over broad areas.

Ptarmigan are mottled brown or gray with white wings in summer, pure white or often appearing palest pink in winter. Their feet are feathered to the ends of the toes, justifying their Latin name, *Lagopus,* which means *rabbit foot.* Feet are often the only part of an animal left by a predator, and it is often difficult to decide whether the owner of a white foot found on the tundra was a rabbit or a ptarmigan, until a close look reveals either feathers or fur.

The rock ptarmigan, called simply the ptarmigan in Europe, is a circumpolar species that lives in the highest Arctic, inhabiting the barren fell fields and hardly withdrawing southward in winter except from the northernmost fringe of land. Farther to the south, the larger willow ptarmigan (see Figure 12–6) stays around brushland and likes to winter in riparian willow thickets. It is called willow grouse in Europe and is an important game species in Scotland. Both these ptarmigan have black feathers on the side of the tail even in white winter plumage. A third species, the white-tailed ptarmigan of the northern Rocky Mountains, is pure white.

Figure 12–6. Willow ptarmigan. These arctic grouse turn pure white in winter and have feathered feet. They spend the entire year on the tundra.

At the edge of the forest lives the spruce grouse, a somber, dark-feathered bird usually seen by itself. Spruce grouse are remarkably tame; they have earned for themselves the name *fool hen,* since they can be successfully hunted with nothing more than a stick. Several other species of grouse inhabit the boreal forests of America and Eurasia, but they seldom range to near timberline.

Ptarmigan and grouse show their chicken affiliation in a number of ways. Most species have a loud, raucous, crowing call. The willow ptarmigan's loud "tobacco, tobacco, tobacco" cry can be unnerving coming from a stretch of lonely and apparently un-inhabited tundra. The birds also take dust baths like barnyard fowl. The young are numerous, as many as 10 or 12 per clutch, and they are active as soon as they hatch (that is, they are precocial).

Ptarmigan feed mainly on vegetation. In winter they depend on the energy concentrated in buds, particularly willow buds. They often come to bulldozed areas and gravel pads of oil rigs in order to get the gravel to fill their gizzards that allows them to process the buds and seeds.

CRANES

Cranes are an ancient group of birds that seem to have largely outlived their time. Most species are in trouble, and several are in serious danger of extinction. Most cranes are highly migratory, and several breed in the far north. The sandhill crane of North American actually crosses the Bering Strait in some numbers and nests in Siberia, returning each fall to the American Midwest.

THE CHARADRIIFORMES

The Charadriiformes (sometimes called the Laro-Limocolae) are a large and extremely diverse group of birds. The order includes such distinct and seemingly unrelated birds as gulls, terns, and skuas, sandpipers and plovers, and the auks and puffins. The broad generalization one can make about this group is that most species are associated with the sea, coasts, and wetlands. No group of birds, not even waterfowl, is so broadly and uniformly distributed throughout the Arctic. It would be difficult to find a patch of tundra environment that had no species of this group breeding on it. On the other hand, most tundra-nesting Charadriiformes are highly migratory and vacate the Arctic after the close of breeding seasons that may last no more than a few weeks.

Plovers and Sandpipers

Plovers and sandpipers belong to separate families, the Charadriidae and Scolopacidae, respectively. The characteristics separating the groups are technical, and there is no obvious and sure way to separate a plover from a sandpiper. Plovers do tend to have shorter bills and a slightly greater preference for dry land over marshes and shores. Most plovers and sandpipers nest on the tundra, and they normally lay four eggs. The young are highly precocial, that is, they hatch with feathers, open eyes, and legs developed so that they can run about within minutes. They are able to fly within a few days, and they are often abandoned by the adults to find their way south in migration, often a distance of several thousand miles to the tropics, even the Southern Hemisphere. Most birds of this group feed on insect larvae and other invertebrates. They are generally known as the shorebirds, although many are found on uplands far from water, particularly during the breeding season.

Two common plovers of the tundra have elegant black faces and breasts in breeding plumage; these are the golden and black-bellied plovers. Both species are smaller than a pigeon. They often nest on upland fell fields and so are quite conspicuous. After the breeding season they become dull gray and are often seen on migration along temperate and tropical coasts.

Several smaller ringed plovers breed on the tundra. They have a dark ring around the neck (two in the case of the well-known killdeer, which sometimes is found on the tundra). Included here are the semipalmated plover, ringed plover, mongolian plover, and dotteral. The lapwing is a large plover with spectacular markings and a crest. It breeds north up to the tundra in Eurasia.

Another group of plovers are called turnstones. During migration they tend to remain around shingle and pebble beaches, but they nest on wet tundra. The ruddy turnstone is one of the most common nesting birds in high arctic areas.

There are many species of sandpipers, ranging in size from the near gull-sized curlews and godwits to several species of sparrow-sized birds often known collectively to bird-watchers as *peep*. Most of the larger species were nearly wiped out by market hunters a hundred years ago or so, and they have never recovered their former numbers. The existence of the eskimo curlew is about as precarious as that of any bird; a few individuals still may breed somewhere in the Arctic, perhaps in western Alaska. Curlews are easily distinguished from godwits by their down-curved rather than straight or upcurved bills.

The many other species of arctic-breeding sandpipers tend to divide up the habitat along interesting and subtle lines. The sanderling is seldom far from sandy beaches; the spotted sandpiper is usually around muddy river shores; the solitary sandpiper is found near marshy ponds; the buff-breasted sandpiper appears on grassy mesic tundra, and so forth. Many of the sandpipers are circumpolar, but others are local. For example, the wandering tattler breeds only along mountain streams and lakes in the uplands of interior Alaska.

Phalaropes

Phalaropes are like slender sandpipers in appearance, but have a number of unusual features. The two arctic species are the northern phalarope and the red phalarope (known as the gray phalarope in Europe, since it is seldom seen there in its brilliant breeding plumage). In phalaropes the usual gender roles of birds are reversed: the females have the more spectacular plumage and leave nurturing to the duller males after they have laid the eggs. Phalaropes spend most of their time in water, swimming like tiny ducks. The red phalarope is usually seen in salt water, the northern in fresh. Both species of phalaropes seem to disappear after the end of the breeding season. It is assumed that many of them winter on the open ocean, becoming true seabirds, but they are seldom seen in quantity at sea.

Skuas and Jaegers

Skuas and jaegers are dark, gull-like birds that have been aptly described as seagulls in the process of becoming hawks. The four species belong to the family Stercorariidae. The three smaller ones are all circumpolar arctic breeders; they are known in North America as jaegers (German for *hunter*). The name *skua* is reserved for a larger, heavier species in North America, but all four are called skua in Britain.

The skua (great skua, eagle guard, or bonxie in Britain) is the only bird breeding in both the Arctic and Antarctic. Skuas are dark, heavy set, fearless, and aggressive birds, about the size of one of the larger gulls but much more heavily built. They are identified by windows of white feathers near the wingtips and by the slightly projecting central tail feathers. Skuas are the dominant predatory bird, indeed the only major land predator, in the Antarctic. The northern race is quite rare and breeds only in the North Atlantic, although wanderers are sometimes seen in the Pacific and Bering Sea, perhaps straying in from the Antarctic.

The three jaegers (see Figure 12–7) are similar in appearance and closely related biologically and ecologically. The long-tailed jaeger is the smallest, not much bigger than an arctic tern. It is identified by its long, straight, pointed central tail feathers that project like a stinger and may be nearly as long as the rest of the bird. Like other jaegers, it is usually an elegant pale gray brown, with a darker cap, light-colored underparts, and a lemon yellow patch or collar on the throat. Long-tailed jaegers are found far inland, often in the high Arctic; they prey mainly on microtine rodents and may hover like a sparrow hawk.

The pomarine jaeger is a much larger bird with shorter, blunt, twisted central tail feathers. It is most common on coastal tundra and feeds largely on microtines. The parasitic jaeger (arctic skua in Britain) is intermediate in size, with short, pointed tail feathers. It often occurs in a dark-color phase, looking black and rapacious. This species is particularly adept at chasing other seabirds and forcing them to drop or even disgorge food.

Jaegers winter at sea and are seldom seen in temperate regions, so they are not well known. But they are of great importance to the tundra ecosystem; they are more widespread and generally much more abundant than hawks and owls, and they are important checks on rodent populations. They are also important to the aesthetic appearance of the Arctic, with their rakish lines and vivid, elegant plumage.

Figure 12–7. Jaeger. The long, pointed tail feathers identify this bird as a long-tailed jaeger, or skua, as it is called in Europe. The closely related parasitic jaeger (arctic skua) has shorter tail feathers, while the even larger pomarine jaeger has blunt, twisted tail feathers. Jaegers are among the most numerous predatory birds in the tundra environment.

GULLS AND TERNS

Gulls are abundant, varied, and ecologically important in virtually every arctic environment, both on land and at sea. The smaller terns are generally much more typical of tropical and temperate environments, and only one species, the arctic tern, is common north of timber.

The most imposing gull of the Arctic is the glaucous gull (see Figure 12–8), sometimes called the burgomeister. It is a large, heavily built, pure white gull with a wingspan not far short of two meters. Glaucous gulls live and breed on the cliff tops of seabird colonies and dominate the various smaller birds, feeding on eggs, young, and even on adults occasionally. In the North Atlantic, the same role is filled by the similar great black-backed gull.

Figure 12–8. Glaucous gull. The burgomeister, with its nearly two-meter wingspan, is an ever-present predator on seabird colonies throughout the Arctic.

The herring gull and its various close relatives (Iceland gull, lesser black-backed gull, and slaty-backed gull) also range into the Arctic. Not as aggressive as the largest gulls, it seems to be more of a scavenger.

The most abundant arctic gull, and quite possibly the most abundant seabird in the world, is the kittiwake. Kittiwakes have the familiar gray mantle, white underparts, and black wingtips of many gulls, but they are quite different in proportions and behavior. They are slender and graceful, with long wings and small bills. More strictly pelagic than the other gulls, they act more like petrels and seem to feed mainly on marine organisms instead of aggressively preying on other birds or fighting for carrion. Kittiwakes are cliff nesters and often occur in immense colonies; they are generally mixed with other cliff-nesting species, but seem to be comfortable on smaller ledges and niches than such birds as murres.

Several smaller gulls are found in the farthest north, often around the shores of the Arctic Ocean. The ivory gull has pure white plumage and black legs and bill. It seems to favor the vicinity of icebergs in the open ocean and is often seen perching on them. Sabine's gull extends a bit farther south, sometimes breeding on the Bering Sea coast; it has a gray head and triangular black wing patches. Bonaparte's gull is more common inland and breeds near timberline. Perhaps the most mysterious of the arctic gulls is Ross's gull, a small gull with a pointed tail and pinkish plumage. Seldom seen outside of the Arctic, it seems to breed mainly on the deltas of the larger Siberian rivers and then moves north into the Arctic Ocean basin in fall. In the 1980s, however, it began to breed, apparently for the first time, at several locations in the Canadian Arctic.

The arctic tern has the distinction of making the longest migration of any bird. It breeds in the Arctic and winters in the Southern Ocean in antarctic waters. Although usually seen near the coast in migration, arctic terns nest far inland throughout much of the tundra zone. They are very aggressive, feisty, and territorial. They will quite often actually attack a human interloper near their nest, even drawing blood with their sharp, red beak; this from a bird that weighs no more than a few ounces!

ALCIDAE: THE AUKS

At first or second glance, the group of birds known as the alcids has no obvious similarity or relationship to the other Charadriiformes. Alcids are chunky swimming and diving birds, generally with small wings and a bumblebeelike flight pattern. The best known alcid no longer exists; the great auk (see Figure 12–9) became extinct over 100 years ago. Originally common in the North Atlantic, it was the largest of the alcids and was flightless. It nested on islands and was easily harvested for food by sailors, who wiped it out. The great auk also has the distinction of being the original penguin. When sailors in the Antarctic found large, flightless, black and white birds, they applied the familiar name to them, about the time these last alcid so-called penguins were disappearing from the face of the earth.

Today, the *alcidae* are the dominant cliff-nesting, diving birds of the far north, with a few species reaching down into temperate regions. They reach their greatest diversity near the Bering Sea, but several species occur in the North Atlantic and a couple are endemic to that area.

Puffins

Puffins are stocky alcids, the size of small ducks. Their most distinctive feature is the deep, bright-colored, triangular bill, the brilliant outer covering of which is shed at the end of the breeding season. The bill gives puffins their other common name, sea parrot. The Latin name for the genus of the Atlantic puffin is *Fratercula,* which means *little brother.* Puffins have always had a special place, since little imagination is needed to give them human characteristics. This has not kept many people in coast-dwelling cultures from depending on puffins for food, however.

In the North Pacific, the niche occupied by the Atlantic puffin is filled by the closely related horned puffin. Also found there is the

Figure 12–9. Great auk. Drawn from an old museum specimen, this sketch probably does little justice to the now-extinct auk, the largest and only flightless alcid and the original penguin.

dark and bizarre-appearing tufted puffin, with its flowing blond topknot. The rhinoceros auklet might as well also be called a puffin. Puffins are abundant throughout cold northern waters. They generally breed in burrows or in crevices in cliffs and ledges, so their breeding colonies are not quite as spectacular as those of murres. But in overall numbers, they are probably the most common alcid. Puffins have tiny wings and normally have to work hard to stay in the air. On occasion, though, they find updrafts near their nesting cliffs and, given the opportunity, may soar for hours, like albatrosses.

Murres are the other prominent circumpolar alcid. Called guillemots in England, they are the quintessential cliff-nesting seabird, often occurring in colonies of tens or hundreds of thousands (see Figure 12–10). There are two species of murre, the common murre and the thick-billed, or Brunnich's, murre. The thick-billed murre is the more arctic of the two, but most colonies include both species nesting together apparently indiscriminately. How resources are partitioned among these closely related species to reduce or eliminate competition is not yet clearly understood.

Murres are black and white and look like penguins, but they are actually quite powerful flyers. They lay their eggs directly on bare rock ledges; the eggs are almost conical in shape, so that they roll in a tight circle, an obviously useful adaptation for a ledge nester.

A murre colony is one of the most spectacular biological features to be found in the Arctic, or, for that matter, anywhere. The colonies are usually found on towering sea cliffs, sometimes hundreds of meters high. The noise and odor are almost overpowering, particularly when one is precariously perched in a small boat in a high wind, heavy swell, and snow or rain squall. In addition to the murres there are usually kittiwakes, often puffins, perhaps smaller alcids, cormorants, and usually a few huge, predatory glaucous gulls perched on the cliff ramparts. The sheer quantity of concentrated life and activity is rarely matched even by a fur seal or sea lion colony.

The razorbill auk is confined to the North Atlantic. It is similar in size, appearance, and breeding behavior to the murres, but it is distinguished by its large, deep bill with a white stripe across it. It generally nests in colonies with murres.

The black guillemot of the North Atlantic and the closely related pigeon guillemot of the North Pacific are quite different alcids. They are dead black, with brilliant white wing patches, are rather slender and graceful, and are about the size of large

Figure 12–10. Murre colony. Murres are the major component of most of the greatest seabird colonies in northern seas. Two closely related species nest together seemingly indiscriminately, with no obvious competition for nesting sites or other resources.

pigeons. The feet and inside of the bill are brilliant coral red. Guillemots are much less gregarious than the other alcids and nest in small, loose colonies, usually in burrows or protected niches. Since these birds are much less concentrated in their nesting habitats, they are also much more widely distributed, and individuals and small flocks are seen in areas where no other alcids are found, such as stretches of coast where sea cliffs are few and low.

There are also several species of smaller alcids, some not much larger than small songbirds. They are generally called auklets and murrelets and occur in the North Pacific. An exception, the dovekie, or little auk, occurs in the Atlantic Arctic.

The smaller alcids are mainly burrow and talus slope nesters and are almost exclusively confined to islands, since they are susceptible to mainland predators. Although the birds are not often seen on the ground, the colonies may be immense; some have been estimated at a million individuals. But they are very much an either/or phenomenon: seemingly suitable islands may have no auklets nesting at all. This means that the smaller alcids, although abundant, are extremely sensitive to environmental change. A single major oil spill or the introduction of an exotic predator could wipe out a significant fraction of the world population of some smaller alcids in short order.

The small alcids include what may well be the most mysterious seabird in terms of its nesting location and behavior. The marbled murrelet and the more northern Kittlitz's murrelet are almost never discovered breeding, although both species are often quite abundant.

SONGBIRDS AND OTHER "LAND" BIRDS

What may seem to be a preponderance of marine and coastal birds in the Arctic makes sense in view of the general proximity of salt water, the length of coastline, and the dominance of ponds, marshes, and rivers even in inland areas. Overall, purely terrestrial species are lacking, in comparison to, say, a temperate woodland. This is a result not only of the abundance of coasts and wetlands but also of the absence of preferred habitat (trees and brush) for breeding of many land birds. A land bird breeding in any area north of the southern fringes of the Arctic is, by necessity, a ground nester. Nesting on the ground is satisfactory for precocial birds such as the shorebirds and grouse: they tend to have large clutches, and the young are able to escape and hide within hours of hatching. The typical songbird, though, is virtually helpless for a period of several weeks after hatching. Few would be able to survive to fledging stage on the tundra environment, where even small rodents such as lemmings are predatory when they have the chance.

In addition to the songbirds, which we will discuss, several other groups of terrestrial birds are represented in the arctic avifauna. In many cases, their presence is simply the result of their ability to fly, from which follows the likelihood that a few individuals will be lost or blown off course and arrive in some inhospitable environment like the tundra, where they may be observed or collected, but where they could never live, and from which they would probably never escape. This is the case for the occasional hummingbird or swift found shivering at some place like Barrow or Frobisher Bay.

The kingfisher is an interesting exception. It is in one sense a water bird, in that it feeds mainly on fish captured by diving in rivers and streams. It nests in holes or burrows excavated in riverbanks. A representative of a generally temperate and tropical family, kingfishers are common near timberline in North America and are also found in some numbers within the tundra zone. Wherever open water exists because of springs or swift current, kingfishers are likely to be found throughout the year and to be active at temperatures far below zero.

Woodpeckers, as might be expected, have the northward limit of their range near timberline. One group, the three-toed woodpeckers, is highly adapted to the boreal forest environment and is seldom seen south of the Subarctic. Three-toed woodpeckers are characterized not only by being one toe short of a typical woodpecker but also by the patch of yellow on the heads of the males. One species is circumpolar, another, the black-backed three-toed woodpecker, North American.

Three-toed woodpeckers are adapted for preying on the bark beetles that often attack northern conifers in explosive infestations. Since these insects are found at the surface of the wood, three-toed woodpeckers normally scale off the bark of dying trees rather than peck deeper holes. This work is quite visible and distinctive, so that the presence of the three-toed woodpeckers is usually obvious. Bark beetle infestations come and go something like lemming population cycles, so three-toed woodpeckers may also appear suddenly in numbers, then become rare as the infestation wanes.

The flicker is a somewhat aberrant woodpecker that is mainly a ground feeder of ants. Ants hardly make it into the Arctic, but isolated populations show up on dry, south-facing bluffs beyond timber. Ants are also a common denizen of the isolated cottonwood groves often found beyond timberline, so these copses usually support a flicker or two, giving them one more attribute of a patch of true forest lost in the tundra.

Flycatchers

Flycatchers are considered the most primitive of songbirds, and the majority of species are confined to the tropics of the New World. None are generally found in the tundra zone, but several species are common in subalpine brush land, riparian willow, and conifer forest. One species, the large, bull-necked, olive-sided flycatcher, is likely to be seen perched on the top of the tallest spruce in the last grove at timberline, calling "free beer" unmistakably, in a loud voice.

Larks

Larks are ground birds and include one of the few songbirds that is common over much of the tundra zone. The horned lark is a largish, somewhat sparrow- or longspur-like bird. It has a yellowish face with a dark mask and two small horns, or relatively inconspicuous tufts of feathers, on each side of the head. Like most ground-dwelling songbirds, larks have extremely elongated spurs, or hind toes, with long, sharp claws. These birds generally walk, rather than hop, across the short grass and barren habitats they prefer. Larks and the other tundra songbirds are highly migratory. They winter in temperate regions, generally occurring in flocks on habitats most nearly like the tundra. They are commonly seen on windy hillsides where the ground is swept bare of snow, and along seashores.

In Eurasia several additional species of larks may reach tundra or alpine regions or both. These include the sky lark and shore lark.

Swallows

Most species of swallows nest in holes in streambanks or in mud nests constructed on cliffs and under overhangs. Not dependent on trees, they do nest within the boundaries of the Arctic in some areas, although they are seldom seen far beyond timberline. They feed on flying insects that they capture on the wing and so would seem to be well designed to fill a niche in the tundra environment, but they don't seem to be tolerant of cold or midsummer snow squalls. The tree swallow and the cliff swallow are the species most likely to be seen in the North American Arctic.

The Corvids: Ravens, Jays, and Crows

The Corvids include the largest of all songbirds and one of the most important arctic birds, the raven (see Figure 12–11). Corvids are most easily characterized on the basis of their behavior, which is generally raucous, impudent, loud, and usually indicative of some sort of an intelligence at work.

The Canada jay, or gray jay, and its near relative, the Siberian

Figure 12–11. Raven. Ravens are omnipresent scavengers, predators, and observers in the arctic environment. The raven, considered the most intelligent of birds, figures prominently in the mythology of all northern peoples.

jay, are among the best known denizens of the northern forest and timberline zone. These are fluffy, gray-feathered birds, about the size of the more southern jays of North America and Eurasia. Compared to other jays, gray jays are rather quiet, but they are curious, unafraid, and often ravenous. No northern woodland camp is established for more than a day or two before a resident pair or group of gray jays begins to visit it as part of its daily rounds, checking particularly the garbage and cooking site. The birds act extremely tame as soon as they decide that they aren't endangered, and they will hang around for hours, often making a wide variety of surprising calls and what sound like bits of conversation. Gray jays are commonly known as camp robbers, but few travelers begrudge them a few scraps of food, particularly when they are the only sign of life near the end of a seemingly endless winter.

The raven is the most common and conspicuous bird in the tundra environment during much of the year. Ravens leave the more exposed parts of the higher Arctic during winter, but otherwise are pretty much ubiquitous year around. They have no special adaptations for the tundra environment; their jet-black plumage appears to be as unadaptive as anything could be in a snow-covered environment, but it doesn't seem to cause them any problem. In fact, it is surprising how easily a black bird disappears into a snow-covered environment, looking like a stump or a shadow.

Ravens are about the size of the largest hawks and are equally good at soaring. However, their flight is much more imaginative, and they are often seen doing acrobatics. This is most common when a pair or group are together. Such a performance can take place at any time of the year, and it appears to be much more related to fun and high spirits than courtship activities. Ravens also have a tremendous variety of calls that together are complicated enough to suggest a language. Furthermore, there seem to be raven dialects in parts of the circumpolar north.

Ravens generally nest on cliffs, laying their eggs in late winter. By spring the young are fledged and make their presence known by raucous cries and demands, often seeming to go on for 24 hours a day under the midnight sun. The adults feed the young and themselves on a wide variety of food. They specialize in carrion: wolf kills, washed-ashore marine mammal carcasses, salmon dying after spawning, and anything left by humans. They will also take small mammals and hatchling birds and have been seen attacking larger animals, mainly when these appeared to be sick or were young lost to their parents.

Other corvids include crows, rooks, magpies, and jays that may show up near the timberline or, particularly, along coastlines.

Chickadees and Tits

This group of birds is as familiar as any to people of the cooler temperate woodlands. Tits are among the smallest of nonmigratory birds, and physiological research has still not convincingly explained how they can maintain body temperatures sometimes nearly 100 degrees centigrade above that of the environment. Even their matchstick-thin legs seem to function perfectly well at 40° below. Tits are seldom seen much beyond timberline, but they can be seen in the northernmost timber and brushland at any time.

The most common northern tit has a brown cap, black bib, and buff-colored flanks. In North America it is called the brown-capped, boreal, or Hudsonian chicadee. The more familiar black-capped chickadee and its Eurasian counterpart, the willow tit, also range nearly as far north but fade out near timberline. The two species can be told from each other by voice: the brown-capped's song has a laconic, burry, slurred quality, different from the cheery "chick-a-dee" call of the black-capped. In northern and western Alaska is a rather rare and elusive chickadee called the gray-headed chickadee. Looking like a large, slightly frosted boreal chickadee, it is seldom seen and has not even been universally acknowledged to exist by ornithologists. It now appears to be a New World population of the Siberian tit, a Eurasian counterpart (or vicariant species), of the Hudsonian chickadee.

The Dipper, or Water Ouzel

The dipper, or water ouzel, is an odd bird that looks like a large, fat wren. There are species in western North America and Eurasia, both extending into the tundra zone in places like the Aleutian Islands and Iceland. Although the dipper is a true songbird, it feeds on aquatic invertebrates and actually dives under water, usually swift-flowing streams, to feed. It literally holds itself to the stream bottom with its strong feet! It can be seen around salmon spawning streams, even in winter.

Thrushes

Thrushes are slim, graceful, handsome birds, with a tremendous variety of plumage, behavior, and habitats. They are mostly insect eaters, are strongly migratory, and include several tundra-nesting species as well as several others common in brushland near timberline. There are more species in the Old World than the New, and several Eurasian species breed in the American Arctic but are seldom seen south of there. The thrush most familiar to North Americans is the robin. One of the most common breeding birds in much of the North American low Arctic, it is not found in Eurasia except as a straggler. It is replaced by the fieldfare and other thrushes in Old World tundra regions. Most of the larger thrushes have spotted breasts. The robin is only a partial exception, since the young are spotted. A few of these spotted thrushes reach timberline, as do the graycheeked thrush and fieldfare. But most of the true arctic species are smaller and without spots. The most common and widespread is the wheatear, a species that winters entirely in Eurasia but is essentially circumpolar as a breeder. It is a sparrow-sized thrush, slim, grayish, and elegant, with conspicuous white patches on each side of the tail. It is usually seen perching in low shrubbery or on rocks. The bluethroat is a similar bird with a brilliant blue throat and breast. In eastern Siberia is also found the rubythroat.

Old World Warblers, Including Kinglets

The word *warbler* refers to two distinct groups of birds. The wood warblers are strictly American and are known for their brilliant plumage. The Old World warblers are much duller and more nondescript. Several species do occur in North America; the two kinglets are the most familiar. These are generally birds of the timberline forest, similar in size and habits to chickadees, and with a brilliant patch of red feathers (ruby-crowned kinglet, or fire crest) or yellow and orange (golden-crowned kinglet, or goldcrest). Several other less conspicuous species are seen in brushland across the Siberian tundra and sometimes into Alaska.

Pipets and Wagtails

Pipets and wagtails belong to a family of largely ground-dwelling birds, much better represented in Eurasia than North America. Pipets are brown, streaky, sparrowlike birds most commonly seen walking (not hopping) in thin grassy areas, particularly near the shore. They are often seen with larks and longspurs. Wagtails are much more spectacular birds, generally slim, often with bright yellow, or contrasting black and white, plumage. They are common in coastal arctic brushland, where they usually are very active and conspicuous.

Waxwings

Waxwings are among the most unusual and elegant songbirds. They have gray plumage, black masks, conspicuous crests, and tiny but brilliant markings of red on the wings. The bohemian waxwing is a circumpolar species, often common in the timberline forest, where it often is seen in flocks and feeds on seeds and berries. The North American cedar waxwing is found farther to the south.

Shrikes

Shrikes, or butcher birds, are songbirds that have developed some of the behavior and physical attributes of small hawks. They prey on other birds, small mammals, and large insects. The one circumpolar, northern species is the northern, or great gray, shrike. It is reasonably common on the low arctic tundra, where it usually perches on shrubs. A handsome and conspicuous black, white, and pearly gray bird, it remains in the North throughout the year, wintering in the boreal forest.

New World, or Wood, Warblers, Including Vireos

New World, or wood, warblers are brilliant, little, insect-eating birds that migrate to the New World tropics in winter; some species reach the timberline and tundra in summer for breeding. None seem to have reversed the pattern of the wheatear to spread into the Old World as breeding species, possible exceptions being near the Bering Strait in Siberia. The most common species near timberline are the yellow, Wilson's, orange-crowned, and blackpoll warblers. The yellow-rumped, or myrtle, warbler is sometimes common as well. Several additional species are common within the boreal forest, as are a couple of species of the larger, duller related vireos.

Blackbirds and Starlings

Blackbirds are also mainly American birds, not related to the European blackbirds, which are actually thrushes. North American blackbirds include some nonblack species such as the meadowlark. Only a few blackbirds occur in the vicinity of timberline. The most important of these are the rusty blackbird, red-winged blackbird, and possibly the cowbird, or common grackle.

Starlings are Eurasian birds that look similar to blackbirds, but generally have longer bills. The common starling of Europe breeds northward to the tundra zone. It has become established in North America within the twentieth century and is now known to breed in and around villages on the fringes of the North American Arctic.

The Fringillidae: Grosbeaks, Sparrows, Finches, and Buntings

The Fringillidae are a large family of songbirds; the closest thing to a universal characteristic among them is the thick bill, which is generally adapted for eating seeds and other hard food. The fringillids include the two most common songbirds of the high arctic tundra, the Lapland longspur and snow bunting, but many more species occur in the brushland of the low Arctic, and members of another large group show up at timberline, where they are heavily dependent on conifer seeds. Food sources for fringillids are highly variable from year to year, and the birds are often sporadic in distribution. One year may see a huge flock in an area, the next year not a single bird. This is true both in summer and winter.

Redpolls are tiny birds, no larger than chickadees. Their nondescript brown plumage is in contrast with a brilliant red patch on the head. Redpolls are generally seen in small flocks, often in patches of grass and weeds. A tundra race that is often considered to be a separate species has a whiter, more frosty appearance.

The pine grosbeak is one of the largest finches, nearly the size of a robin. It has fluffy, soft plumage that in mature males is bright rose colored but in females and immature males is dull olive brown. Pine grosbeaks range north to timberline and are generally among the most common birds in the northernmost coniferous forest. They are quite tame.

Close relatives of the pine grosbeak are the crossbills. The tips of the bill are offset and cross each other, apparently as an adaptation for prying apart the scales of conifer cones. Two circumpolar species are known in North America as the red crossbill (raspberry colored, with plain black wings) and the white-winged crossbill (pale rose with conspicuous white bars on the wing).

The tiny pine siskin, no larger than a redpoll, with yellow markings, is often seen with pine grosbeaks and crossbills. Farther south in the boreal forest are a wide variety of finches; most are not circumpolar.

Sparrows seem to North Americans to be so ubiquitous that they are surprised to find that most species are confined to the

Western Hemisphere, even in the Arctic. Old World sparrows such as the familiar house sparrow are actually only distantly related to American sparrows. Although sparrows are the classic little brown bird, not too big and not too small, in the arctic timberline region the species are few enough and distinctive enough to be identified without much trouble. The savannah sparrow and song sparrow have streaked breasts, as does the much larger and darker fox sparrow. The white-crowned sparrow, which is one of the most conspicuous breeders in brush near timberline, has a brilliant black- and white-striped topknot. The tree sparrow and chipping sparrow have clear gray breasts and bright chestnut head patches; the tree sparrow is larger and has a large black spot in the middle of the breast. Juncos are sparrows with dull gray plumage and white stripes on the outer margins of the tail.

The only fringillids usually found deep into the Arctic are the Lapland longspur and the snow bunting. The longspur is a stocky, sparrowlike bird. In breeding plumage the male has a brilliant black face and head, with a chestnut-colored nape patch; it would be unmistakable even if there were other streaky brown birds in the same habitat. Females and immature males are duller brown, as is the male in winter.

In its summer plumage on the tundra, the snow bunting looks like a black and white sparrow. It is a common circumpolar nester well into the high Arctic. In general, longspurs are more common in sedge meadows, mesic tundra, and the richer, lower fell fields and shores. Snow buntings take over in uplands. The two species tend to come together in fall and migrate and winter together, often south to the temperate regions or along beaches near the edge of the Arctic. Snow buntings are actually darker, with more brown feathers, in winter than summer.

SUGGESTED FURTHER READING

For actual identification of birds, this chapter can best be utilized in conjunction with one of the well-known bird field guides to North America or Europe. Many more sources deal with specific groups of birds, and the voluminous periodical literature can be consulted as well.

Armstrong, R. *A Guide to the Birds of Alaska.* Anchorage: Alaska Northwest, 1981.

Bartonek, J. C. and D. N. Nettleship, eds. *Conservation of Marine*

Birds of Northern North America. Research Report No. 11. Washington, DC: U.S. Fish and Wildlife Service, 1979.

Fisher, J., and R. M. Lockley, *Seabirds*. Boston: Houghton Mifflin, 1954.

Gabrielson, I. N., and F. C. Lincoln. *The Birds of Alaska*. Harrisburg, PA: The Stackpole Co, 1959.

Godfrey, W. E. *The Birds of Canada*. Bulletin no. 203. Ottawa: National History Museum of Canada, 1966.

Haley, D., ed. *Seabirds of Eastern North Pacific and Arctic Waters*. Seattle: Pacific Search Press, 1984.

Harrison, P. *Seabirds: an Identification Guide*. Boston: Houghton Mifflin, 1983.

Kessel, B., and D. Gibson. *Status and Distribution of Alaska Birds*. Los Angeles: Studies in Avian Biology No. 1. Cooper Ornithological Society, 1978.

Salomonsen, F. *The Birds of Greenland*. Copenhagen: Munksgaard, 1950.

Sowls, A. L., S. A. Hatch, and C. J. Lensinck. *Catalogue of Alaskan Seabird Colonies*. Washington, DC: U.S. Fish and Wildlife Service, 1978.

Tuck, G. S. *A Field Guide to Seabirds of the Ocean Routes*. London: William Collins Sons, 1980.

Chapter 13

Ice Ages II

IN Chapter 7 we looked at the physical changes the Ice Ages made on the land and sea, and we discussed some of the theories on the causes of the Ice Ages. Now that we have an overview of the living world of the far north, we can develop a picture of how this assemblage of animals and plants was affected by the repeated tides of cold, and by the glacial ice that repeatedly swept down from the North as the climate continued to cool during the later part of the Quaternary.

THE PRE-QUATERNARY ARCTIC AND THE ORIGIN OF THE ARCTIC BIOTA

We saw in Chapter 7 that ice ages are an uncommon phenomenon over geologic time and that "our" Ice Ages only go back about half a million years. Therefore, we might well ask what the Arctic was like before the Ice Ages. Were there caribou a million years ago? If there were, did they live in an environment anything like modern tundra? And, of course, since the Quaternary is the Age of Man, we may well ask what the relationship was between humans and the deepening cold and advancing ice as the Arctic first spread southward.

There is ample evidence that many parts of the present Arctic were once temperate or subtropical. The widespread coal deposits in places such as Greenland, Spitzbergen, and Alaska contain fossils of plants, and occasionally animals, that could hardly have lived in a cold environment. Most of these deposits are so old, though, that they far predate the present locations of the continents. They tell us little or nothing about the origin of the arctic environment. Fossils from the later Tertiary, the period of time from perhaps 20 million to 2 million years ago, are much rarer, particularly in high latitudes. Part of the reason for this, of course, is that these relatively recent deposits were likely to be near the surface and unconsolidated; many were undoubtedly ground to dust by glaciers and exist now as particles of loess and boulder clay. Much of our evidence for the origin of arctic conditions is therefore indirect. If, for example, we find an increasing preponderance of animals that were adapted for cold temperate conditions in the western United States at a particular time, this suggests that the cold, and perhaps the tundra environment, were spreading in the far north.

Evidence suggests (see Chapter 7) that the world climate was becoming cooler and drier throughout the late Tertiary. As recently as 10 million or so years ago, though, temperate deciduous forests existed along the fringes of the Arctic Ocean in northern Canada. Five million years later, the boreal forest had taken over these northernmost areas, but there is still no evidence of widespread tundra conditions.

It is reasonable to suggest that what might be called the first tundra occurred in alpine regions, that many organisms became adapted to cold, snow, and otherwise bleak conditions, and then later colonized the expanding tundra as the climate cooled. This theory has drawn criticism because many of the major mountain ranges of the world are of recent origin, and it is possible that the cooling trend was associated with mountain building. Overall, though, it makes sense to assume at least limited alpine environments have existed for long periods of time.

We can easily imagine the newly expanding Arctic becoming a melting pot for cold-adapted plants and animals: some coming from central Asia, others from the high plains and mountains of North America, still others having been denizens of temperate woodlands with some natural talent for dealing with cold and seasonality. New forms of competition and symbiosis must have constantly sprung up, and selection pressure, or impetus to change and adapt, must have been intense. In fact, it has been suggested that the cold regions have long served as a staging area for highly competitive organisms, tested in the arctic crucible before colonizing the rest of the world. A weakness in this view, of course, is the assumption that arctic conditions are intrinsically more demanding than, say, those of tropical rain forests.

By the onset of the Quaternary period some two million years ago, there was a northern environment that would probably have been recognizable as such. It had forests of spruce, pine and larch, birch and willow. It had deer recognizable as the precursors of caribou and moose; it had archaic weasels, bears, and at least a selection of the birds, herbaceous plants, insects, and other organisms now typical of the far north. It also had a wide array of species that have since become extinct, or which no longer inhabit the polar regions. Huge, hairy elephants and near-elephants lived on the tundra, as did bison, rhinoceroses, and even great cats.

Let us consider the stage set, then, at about 500,000 years ago. We are at the time boundary between the lower Pleistocene and the middle Pleistocene. The first of the great Ice Ages has yet to occur, although there have been periodic major expansions of ice sheets in high northern latitudes, probably since before the beginning of the Quaternary, already almost a million and a half years earlier. The ancestors of most of our present large mammals are clearly recognizable (including *Homo erectus,* our own precursor). On the other hand, there are many unfamiliar animals in temperate and even cold regions, which have since become extinct. A few animals, such as the polar bear, have probably not yet come on the scene.

Cold, treeless, tundralike areas border the Arctic Ocean, although they probably do not cover quite as much area as present tundra. The vegetation is probably very different from modern tundra's, although we have little evidence to support this conclusion. It seems reasonable to suggest that many alpine species had not yet made their way to the Arctic and that the mass homogenization that must have happened with the repeated advancing and retreating migrations in front of the ice would have altered the vegetation dramatically.

We will look now at how the events of the following half-million years may have interacted with the land and organisms of the cold regions to produce the arctic environment we have described here. Much of what we can say on this is highly speculative. Tremendous mysteries still lie on all sides of the faint, winding trail we will try to follow up to the present.

LAND BRIDGES AND CONTINENTAL SHELF

We saw in Chapter 7 that the ice-free land area of higher latitudes was not greatly diminished during glacial maxima. What really happened was that the area of ice and the area of ocean water varied in relation to each other, while the land area stayed the same. This was a result of changes in sea level, mainly eustatic changes. Each time the ice sheets expanded, the sea level was lowered, exposing vast areas of continental shelf, creating of land bridges, and barriers to oceanic interchange, and diminishing the overall area of the surface of the ocean.

This stability of amount of ice-free land area suggests that the actual area of the earth's surface that was tundra, or some Ice Age counterpart of the present tundra environment, probably covered roughly the same area in higher latitudes as it does today, and that it probably occurred in at least a marginal strip along some of the southern borders of the continental ice sheets. The terrestrial arctic environment of the Ice Age was comparable in size to that of the present but was distributed very differently, and any organism occupying both the Ice Age tundra and the present tundra probably had to complete a major migration. In fact, it would have had to migrate repeatedly as the ice sheets waxed and waned. Furthermore, the differently shaped emergent land masses of the Ice Age tundra environment would have resulted in many physical differences in the environment. For example, the climate of an exposed continental shelf along the Arctic Ocean, bounded by a massive glacier to the south, would probably have been different from and far more rigorous than that of most tundra areas today. On the other hand, many areas that are now near the coast and have a maritime climate, with cool summers, might have been far inland during the height of glaciation. Even if the annual temperatures were colder than at present, summers might well have been comparatively warm and sunny. We know enough now about the critical nature of summer temperatures (see Chapters 8 and 9) to suggest that these inland areas could have supported a rich flora and fauna.

In any case, any organism that has continuously inhabited the Arctic since the onset of the Ice Ages has had to periodically and regularly pull up stakes. And the new homes available with the melting of the ice or the drying up of the shallow seas would have been very different from the land that was vacated, both in terms of features such as soil and in the climate itself. To survive the arctic Ice Ages, an organism had to be both mobile and adaptable. Many simply did not make it and became extinct. More importantly, though, those that did make it were undoubtedly changed by the experience. And, since organisms live in relationship to other organisms, the nature of these relationships changed as well. By now it should be clear that the emergence of the Arctic from the Ice Ages is a subject of considerable complexity.

TABULA RASA, THE NUNATAK HYPOTHESIS, AND CENTRIC DISTRIBUTIONS

By the late nineteenth century, biologists and geographers became convinced that ice ages had indeed occurred and began a search for data and concepts on how the glaciers had affected plants and animals. At first, it was assumed that ice had spread southward over the Northern Hemisphere from a single source near the North Pole. The glaciers presumably had simply obliterated everything living north of the terminal moraines, and the retreating glaciers had left a *tabula rasa,* an empty slate, that could only be recolonized by plants and animals that had retreated southward beyond the glacial margins. Very soon, however, more careful studies of the arctic and alpine floras of various areas, combined with the recognition that there had been numerous centers of glaciation around the circumpolar north, began to make inroads in this theory. Even before 1900, it was recognized that there were certain areas, in the mountains of Norway, for example, in which an unusually large number of species of plants, insects, and sometimes even mammals could be found. Not much later came the recognition that certain arctic areas never had been glaciated, as was the case in much of Alaska and eastern Siberia. The subsequent recognition of affinities between the arctic and alpine areas indicated that there might have once been closer geographical connections, and that the histories of mountain ranges and arctic tundra might be similar.

The American botanist M. L. Fernald suggested that the reformulation of the northern environment might have been much influenced by organisms that survived in unglaciated refugia far north of the glacial border, and which then reclaimed their earlier range. Since this idea rested on an earlier proposal that many of the refugia might have been mountaintops that protruded through the ice, the idea was often called the *nunatak hypothesis*. It was suggested that the refugia could be identified both by lack of physical evidence of glaciation and by the presence of rare organisms that had been genetically impoverished by the destruction of most of their populations and had thus somehow lost the ability to remigrate out into the newly ice-free environment.

The most celebrated refugia were supposedly located on the Gaspé peninsula of Quebec, in Newfoundland, in Labrador, and along the north shore of Lake Superior. As the concept was projected to other parts of the North, refugia were proposed in Iceland, Scandinavia, and the coast of British Columbia. By this time, it was clear that there were major unglaciated areas in Alaska, Siberia, and probably northern Canada, so no individual nunataks needed to be found there.

The nunatak hypothesis generated a surprising amount of controversy. The discovery of a glacial erratic where one wasn't supposed to be seems to have become a cause for celebration on more than one occasion. Over the years, extensive holes have been poked in most of the basic ideas of the nunatak hypothesis. Few scientists believe that the supposed loss of genetic variability of plants confined to isolated refugia accounts for their narrow distribution at present. (It is interesting to note, though, that the protection of genetic variability has become a major issue in conservation circles. It comes up repeatedly as the tropical forests are obliterated by human activities that approach glaciers in the magnitude of their overall destructive capacity.) Genetic concerns aside, it is hard to believe that a plant of temperate affinities could live out the millennia on a patch of bare rock with an ice cap climate.

The most important legacy of the nunatak hypothesis is simply the concept that many curious and difficult-to-explain things occurred in the lives of generations of plants and animals with the recurring advance and retreat of the ice. Of equal importance has been the vast amount of information gathered and the careful thought (and passionate argument) that went into trying to make some sense out of it all. The end result so far is an awareness that the situation is incredibly complex, full of local special cases, and probably not amenable to more than a few generalizations.

At the height of the interest in the nunatak hypothesis, the Swedish botanist Eric Hultén proposed a variation on the theme by suggesting that most of the arctic flora and fauna had retreated to the unglaciated region around the Bering Sea, now often called Beringia. From here, he suggested, many species reclaimed their earlier crcumpolar range, but others were slower to migrate, or, again, had lost the ability to recolonize the newly deglaciated land. Among the evidence used to support this idea was the existence of several centers of unusual floristic richness in Beringia. According to Hultén's theory, these represent the last strongholds of species that were virtually destroyed by glaciation and have never recovered. Hultén's theory is now pretty much in eclipse. A better explanation for the richness of the Beringian flora is the area's connection by mountain ranges to the highlands of both North America and Asia; the area may act as a staging area for new, preadapted alpine species to begin to colonize the Arctic.

These earlier controversies seem dated and simplistic to modern scientists who are trying to reconstruct the sequence of events and patterns of the Quaternary. Perhaps the most important single breakthrough to deepen our understanding of Ice Age events has been the development of carbon 14 (C^{14}) dating and other radiometric dating methods (see Chapter 7). It is true, though, that dating a piece of peat, bone, or mammoth meat, and placing that dated object in the context of the world in which it lived and died are two quite different things. Other new approaches to apprehending the nature of past environments, the patterns of change, and the directions of progress have come about since good dating methods have been available. The ability to reconstruct the past has more or less kept pace with the ability to date past events. The result has been an understanding of what has happened in the Arctic, and the rest of the world, over the past millennia that would have overwhelmed a scientist working in the early part of the twentieth century. The end result, though, has been the uncovering of a tremendous array of new mysteries, rather than providing a definitive answer to old questions such as those on the validity of the nunatak hypothesis. We have progressed to the point from which we can look at major questions of the nature of the earth 10,000 years ago with the subtlety and penetration of a historian rather than a fossil collector. But, just as increased knowledge and sophistication of research techniques do not reveal a more simple and straightforward version of the French Revolution or the Battle of Hastings, questions such as What killed off the woolly mammoth? have not received simple and straightforward answers.

POLLEN ANALYSIS

The most important techniques for reconstructing past events make use of fossils. The modern way of dealing with Quaternary-age fossils, though, places relatively little emphasis on bones and a great deal on fossils that are too small to be seen individually with the naked eye, and that collectively look like a smear of gritty mud. These microfossils preserve traces of many things: diatom shells, beetles' wings, fungal spores, and maybe an occasional rodent's tooth. By far the most important are the pollen grains of flowering plants and conifer trees, often with an admixture of the spores of more primitive plants.

Plants produce pollen grains in phenomenal quantities. They sift down through the branches of trees, are carried by the wind and water, and tend to end up in quantities on the floors of lakes and ponds. Here they may lie indefinitely. The living cell contents soon die, but the pollen walls consist of some of the hardest and most resistant organic substances known. Grains dropped in a proglacial lake at the end of the last Ice Age as the glaciers retreated look about the same as they did the day they fell from a pine tree or sedge plant. And it is perfectly possible to distinguish what sort of plant they did fall from: sedge pollen is totally different from pine pollen (see Figure 13–1). On the other hand, and this is often a serious problem, it is usually not possible to distinguish pollen of one sedge species, or one spruce species, from another.

Over time, a lake floor may build up a deep layer of pollen-containing sediment. This generally takes the form of thin, soft mud, including thousands of pollen grains per cubic centimeter. The bottom layers usually contain the first pollen laid down in

Figure 13–1. A sketch of several kinds of pollen grains typically found in boreal and arctic sediments. It is often possible to distinguish between closely related genera (for example, *Picea,* spruce, and *Pinus,* pine, or *Betula,* birch, and *Alnus,* alder). But it is seldom possible to determine which species the pollen came from. In some families such as the grasses and heaths, even genera are seldom distinguishable. The large grain with bladders at top left is spruce. Next to this are two birch grains, then two tetrads of four fused grains, typical of the *Ericaceae,* or heaths. Farthest right are the smooth, featureless grains of grass. The large grain on the upper right is a spore of a fern or some other lower plant, as shown by the characteristic trilete scar. Under a microscope, a wealth of detail would be visible, depending on such factors as focus, type of stain, and the quality of preservation in the natural environment. The largest grains are somewhat less than 100 microns, or one-tenth of a millimeter, in length.

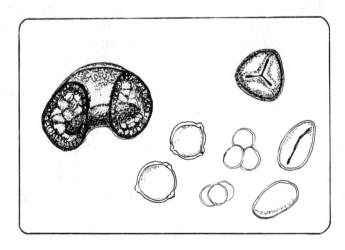

the lake, the top layers pollen from the last few years. With the use of a device something like an oversize apple corer, an undisturbed sample of sediment from the lake bottom can be removed. Since much of the mud is organic, it can be dated by its carbon 14 content. A series of dates from top to bottom will reveal the age of the lake, whether it has been disturbed, dried out for a time, or whatever else. An analysis of the pollen of the sample will then provide a handle on the vegetation that has surrounded the lake since the earliest days of its existence. The pollen data can then be correlated and interpolated in relation to the radiocarbon data, and a chronological history of the lake and its environs reconstructed.

In practice, of course, this is a much more difficult and complicated process. The processing of samples and gathering of data can be reasonably straightforward, but it is time-consuming and demands great experience and skill. A typical core might be sampled at 20 to 50 locations along its length. Each individual sample must be carefully carried through an array of chemical processes that get rid of extraneous material and bring out the features of the individual pollen grains. When the sample is mounted on a microscope slide, usually at least 250 to 500 individual grains are examined, and records are made of their type. Perhaps 50 or more pollen types, representing species, genera, or families of plants, might be found, and the scientist must be able to identify each quickly and accurately.

The end result is a diagram (see Figure 13–2) indicating the relative importance of pollen types at various levels of the core;

Figure 13–2. A simplified and generalized pollen diagram such as might be derived from a location in central or western Alaska. It represents some 16,000 years and thus extends back to the height of the last glacial advance. Three zones are easily distinguishable. Lowest and oldest is an herb zone, dominated by grass, sedge, and sagebrush *(Artemisia)*. The later birch zone seems to indicate greater moisture and possible warmth as the Ice Age ended and the Bering land bridge was submerged. The top zone, dominated by spruce, documents the spread of typical boreal forest into a previously treeless, or at least spruceless, environment. It should be noted that the changes from level to level are ones of proportion rather than total quantity, so introduction of a new type could lower the percentage of another type without changing the amount of that pollen falling. The few spruce grains at the lower level do not necessarily indicate the local presence of spruce trees. They may have blown long distances in the wind, or been redeposited from older sediments. In an actual diagram, there would be many additional minor pollen elements as well.

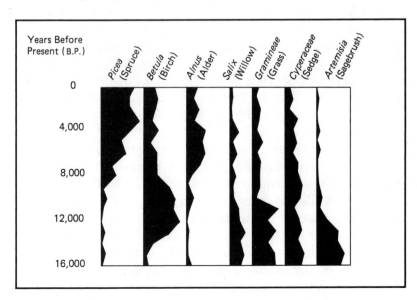

this is usually expressed in terms of percentages. At this point, the real work of analysis and interpretation begins.

A typical pollen diagram from a northern forest region of North America may show a high percentage of spruce pollen throughout much of its length. Does this mean that the area was dominated by spruce forest throughout the time the sediments were being deposited? More than likely not. Spruce tends to produce pollen in enormous quantities. Spruce pollen is distributed only by the wind, not insects, so pollination is a hit-or-miss proposition, dependent largely on the amount of pollen available. Spruce pollen, then, is generally overrepresented in the samples. A high percentage of spruce pollen suggests the presence of spruce trees in the immediate area; it doesn't prove that the pond was surrounded by boreal forest. On the other hand, if little or no spruce pollen is found at another level, it does suggest that the nearest spruce tree was far away. Perhaps the site was beyond timberline at the time. We might then look at birch pollen to see if we can answer the question. But remember that there are both tree birches of the boreal forest and scrub birches of the low arctic tundra. They usually can't be distinguished as pollen grains.

So the interpretation of pollen data is a far from exact science. It is most valuable when there are many samples from a given area that are well dated by radiocarbon. Then, trends usually appear. A spruce-free assemblage may be replaced by a spruce-rich one, and this may occur at about the same time over a broad area, or we may be able to see this trend move northward over time. What we are probably seeing in that case is the advance of timberline and the recovery of the boreal forest. Every so often, though, intelligent interpretation of a single pollen diagram can tell us about an event with surprising precision. For example, the sudden presence of pollen from a number of weeds may tell us almost exactly when the first farmer arrived in an area. Or a decline in spruce and a large quantity of fireweed may document some ancient forest fire.

The statistically less important elements in a pollen sample may have an important story to tell. For example, if two samples are dominated by spruce, but one includes a significant percentage of oak, while the other is rich in *Dryas,* it is a good bet that the first originated near the southern edge of the boreal forest at the time, while the second might have been at timberline.

Overall, though, the value of pollen data depends on the availability of quantities of carefully investigated samples. Intensive pollen work has been going on in the arctic and boreal regions for 20 to 30 or more years now, and the result is that clear pictures of overall trends are emerging. We can watch the spruce forest creeping northward in Canada during the period of time from 10,000 to 5,000 years ago. We can see oak and white pine colonizing northern New England and southern Canada several thousand years ago, then retreating under a new onslaught of spruce as the climatic optimum, or hypsithermal, waned. We can follow these trends around the world, and we can correlate them with other data that tell us about the changing climate and the correlation between a particular kind of vegetation and the prevailing climate. For example, as we follow the timberline northward after the retreat of the glaciers, we can at least hypothesize that we are also seeing a change in the location of the 10° isotherm for July, and the retreat of the tundra climate to the area of the present arctic tundra.

THE ARCTIC DURING THE ICE AGES

We know that huge areas in the far north were never covered by ice during the Ice Ages (see Chapter 7 for this discussion). Techniques of microfossil analysis provide at least a handle on the nature of the environment of these places, and we have radiocarbon and other dating techniques to tell what occurred when, and often what the sequence of events was. And we know now a good deal about the requirements and preferences of a sizable array of northern organisms, both plants and animals. So, we are in a position to make some serious suggestions about the history of the Arctic and how it came to be what it is now. This is a good time to throw a few additional concepts into the pot, so that we have some idea of the level of complexity (and mystery) we are dealing with.

The Pleistocene Megafauna

Paleontologists define the Quaternary period on the basis of the appearance of what might be thought of as modern fauna, known mainly on the basis of its large animals, which is often thought to have appeared about two million years ago. In fact, there have been many appearances, changes, and disappearances of animal species throughout the Quaternary. Of particular interest to us here is the fact that the Arctic has usually supported a much greater variety of large mammals than it does now. Our present large tundra herbivore is the caribou or reindeer. But at the height of the last Ice Age, many treeless northern environments almost certainly supported, in addition to reindeer, herds of bison, huge elephants called woolly mammoths, one or more species of horses, and quite likely a variety of less numerous herbivores including saiga antelope, one or more species of muskoxlike animals, perhaps one or more additional species of the deer/moose/elk family, and, quite possibly, various additional cattlelike, goatlike, and sheeplike animals. Although the evidence is less clear, there is some indication that small mammals, birds, and even insects lived on the treeless, Ice Age tundra that do not occur in the modern Arctic. Overall, though, the more spectacular and better-known animals of the ancient Arctic were large. So, we often talk about the Pleistocene megafauna, which simply means large animals of the Pleistocene. And while many of the megafauna species have become extinct, there is indeed a Holocene megafauna, perhaps best represented in Africa with its rhinos, elephants, and lions, but found in other parts of the world as well.

This ancient arctic environment also had a much broader array of predators. The grizzly had to share the environment with at least two other bears. Not only were there large, lionlike cats, but also the now-extinct saber-toothed tiger, which probably killed its victims by stabbing them with its huge canine teeth. The picture was completed not only by wolves, foxes, and wolverines, but by other, smaller predators such as badgers.

How do we know so much about this vanished fauna? Part of the answer, of course, is that we know less than we wish and that the picture we just pointed to reflects more than a little interpolation and possibly a fair amount of guesswork. The guesses and interpolations mostly concern the range of the animals in space and time, however. We know that they were all in northern areas at some time during the Würm/Wisconsinan glaciation. We do not necessarily know what the overall ranges of any given species were, or if two species were contemporaneous at any given location.

Most of our evidence for the presence of this tremendous array of animals is compelling. We have the frozen mammoths, we have them in quantity, and we have dates on many of them. Many placer mining operations in Alaska and Siberia yield almost endless quantities of bone and meat from the overburden of frozen muck. Research tasks are often more a matter of recording and analyzing an oversupply of material (much of it heavy, filthy, and vile smelling) than of looking for fossils. We have many other sources, too. An especially interesting one is fossil burrows of ground squirrels, which may preserve the plant material used to build the animal's hibernating nest and may include the mummified remains of the squirrel itself. Often of particular importance are the results of human activities: kill sites, butchered bones, or bone artifacts. Perhaps most interesting of all are the mammoth bone houses built on the Ice Age Eurasian steppe, discussed in the Chapter 14.

Much of the megafauna became extinct at about the time traditionally treated as the end of the last Ice Age and the beginning of the Holocene, about 10,000 years ago. The reasons for this rapid extinction (if indeed it was sudden) are far from clear. As might be expected, there is much discussion of this; we will return to the question again.

Ice Age Steppe-Tundra and Beringia

We are developing a picture of huge expanses of cold, treeless land, lying at high latitudes, often deep within the continents or on broad continental shelves, often at least partly surrounded by immense ice sheets and populated by an array of animals that are now extinct or occur only outside the modern tundra biome. What relationship, then, does this environment have to the tundra we described in Chapters 8, 9, and 10? There were almost certainly vast differences between the arctic environment of 20,000 years ago, in fact the northern ecosystems for most of the past 100,000 years or longer, and the present, Holocene, tundra biome. And yet this ancient and perhaps largely extinct environment was the immediate precursor of the Arctic as we know it. It was also, as we will see in Chapter 14, the environment in which many of our ancestors began their journey toward civilization. How, then, can we get a handle on it?

The answer lies in using the tools and techniques already mentioned: radiometric dating, microfossil analysis, more traditional archaeological and paleontological techniques, and a healthy but reasonably controlled dose of imagination. The most important single thing scientists studying the Ice Ages can do is to maintain close contact with people in distant but related fields. It is amazing how much an archaeologist, a botanist, and a specialist in modeling global weather patterns have to talk about if they simply put themselves in the same room to deal with the same question: What was it *like?*

The overall picture that has emerged is of a broad belt of cold, dry, continental steppe, stretching across Eurasia from central Europe, encompassing the mountains and uplands of central

Asia, replacing the forests of eastern Siberia and Chukotka, covering the emergent continental shelf of the Bering Sea, extending through central Alaska and into the present Yukon Territory of Canada, and then pinching out against the margins of the great North American ice sheets. Perhaps a similar environment occurred in a much smaller area south of the ice sheets in North America, although the evidence for this is scanty. Of particular interest is the possible existence of an ice-free corridor extending down the east side of the present Rocky Mountains during much of the last Ice Age and the further possibility that contact between Eurasia and the Americas was not always entirely blocked by ice throughout the Wisconsinan period. On the other hand, it is interesting to speculate on who or what would have traversed an icy-cold strip of desert, bounded on both sides by limitless ice fields, probably characterized by howling winds, frightful storms of blowing loess, and extending seemingly endlessly 2,000 or more kilometers into the heart of an unknown continent.

BERINGIA

The heart of the Ice Age North is often thought of as lying in the area we now usually call Beringia. During the Ice Age, the northern Bering Sea and Chukchi Sea floors were emergent in response to eustatic lowering of the sea level. A broad lowland plain stretched from what is now west central Alaska all the way to the Gulf of Anadyr. At the time, it must have been one of the great lowland plain systems of the world, an area of subcontinental proportions. It is sometimes referred to as the Bering land bridge but this implies a much narrower connection than the one that really existed. On the other hand, the Bering land bridge has been the main route of exchange for fauna between Eurasia and North America over the past many million years. There is little doubt that it was the route by which the first humans arrived in the Americas. In any case, a great deal of scientific work has been carried out in both North America and Siberia on the nature of Beringia throughout the Quaternary, and this provides the basis of much of what we have to say about the Ice Age North.

Pollen data has provided some of the best information on the nature of the environment, but it is much less than definitive and fuels more arguments than it settles. What we generally find in

pollen samples from the latter part of the Ice Age in the unglaciated North is this:

1. No evidence for spruce forest, although there is enough
   spruce pollen in many samples to suggest an occasional
   isolated spruce tree
2. A good deal of pollen from grasses, indicating perhaps
   more grassland but telling nothing about the species of
   grass
3. Also a good deal of pollen from sedges, but no answer to
   the question of whether they were the familiar denizens of
   sedge meadows or some upland species—or both, in varying quantities at different times
4. Exceptional quantities of pollen from *Artemisia,* a large
   genus of plants that includes sagebrush and is generally
   found in dry areas, but some species of which occur in the
   present tundra
5. Small but regular quantities of pollen from plants that now
   normally do not live in a typical tundra environment; examples are members of the spinach family *(Chenopo-
   diaceae)*

Overall, this is not a compelling assemblage of evidence. It
isn't even proof that the Ice Age North was unforested, since
poplar and aspen *(Populus)* pollen is one of the rare pollen types
that does not preserve well. We've seen (see Chapter 8) that
poplar often occurs far out on the present tundra, and we've seen
that it can live and reproduce as vegetative groves probably more
or less indefinitely. On the other hand, this evidence does not
create a clear picture of a rich grassland and woodland environment in the Ice Age North, as has sometimes been suggested. A
conservative interpretation of the evidence is that it suggests a
cold, dry, steppelike environment, possibly related to the deserts
of high Asia, as in Mongolia or Sinkiang, or possibly like some of
the foothills of the northern Rocky Mountains. This putative
environment has been called by a number of names; *steppe-
tundra* is probably as good as any other.

If this interpretation is correct, what did the mammoths,
horses, and bison eat? We can't imagine them except as herd
animals, or at least as living in good-sized family groups. Could
they have survived on forage that was little different from the
upland fell fields of the modern Arctic? If they could survive on
such forage, why did they become extinct or at least no longer

inhabitants of the modern tundra? Alternatively, were these animals really in the unglaciated North throughout the last Ice Age, or are the fossils mainly those of a few miserable stragglers, or from earlier times when conditions were less rigorous?

We are going to leave this discussion in a very unsatisfactory state. Arguments on what the Ice Age North was really like continue hot and impassioned. A middle-of-the-road reconstruction of this great ancient environment, probably guaranteed to please no one, runs roughly as follows:

1. Large mammals, now extinct or no longer found at high latitudes, probably lived in the unglaciated northern areas throughout even the coldest times of the last Ice Age.
2. The climate of a typical example of this environment was dry and continental. It was extremely cold in winter, with low snowfall, and was cold in terms of mean annual temperature. Summers, however, were probably dry, sunny, and comparatively warm. The growing season began early because of the low snow cover, and depth of thaw allowed deep-rooted plants to grow.
3. The overall vegetation of the ice-free areas was sparse and steppelike. But woodlands, marshes, and meadows occurred locally. There were probably also huge expanses of vegetation similar to modern riparian willow thickets. These supplied winter browse and shelter for animals such as horses and mammoths, as they do for moose today.
4. Just as in the modern Arctic, the environment was complex and provided a mosaic of greatly varying conditions and resources. Animal migrations occurred then, as they do now. Changes in vegetation and climate over time were important.
5. Every aspect of the Ice Age arctic environment was profoundly different from the modern tundra biome. Many denizens of the ancient Arctic don't exist any more, and reconstruction of the past by analogy with modern situations is risky.

We leave this section, then, with the idea that the events and inhabitants of the North during the last Ice Age were profoundly important in shaping the present day arctic tundra environment, but that those who lived in that time and place—the mammoths, horses, and, unquestionably, humans—looked out on a world that no longer exists anywhere, nor ever will again. The Arctic as we know it is new, having come into existence as a biome only within the past few thousand years. Unraveling the secrets of its ancestry will continue to be a challenging field for a long time to come.

THE END OF THE ICE AGE

As we saw in Chapter 7, it is conventional to place the Pleistocene-Holocene boundary at 10,000 years B.P. Changes occurred rapidly at about this time. The continental ice sheets had been in a state of retreat for over 5,000 years, but ice was still present in the vicinity of the north shores of the Great Lakes and large ice sheets covered northern Scandinavia. Several minor readvances had taken place within the past couple of thousand years, but the ice was now definitely on the wane. It would still persist in central Quebec and the area near the west shore of Hudson Bay for several thousand years more.

Sea levels were rising rapidly. Ten thousand years ago, the Bering land bridge was already severed, but broad areas of the Bering-Chukchi plain were still emergent. Parts of the North Sea, Grand Banks, and other fringes of continental shelf near the earlier ice margins must have been disappearing rapidly. By this time, there must have been human beings on many northern coastlines who could probably see clearly over their lifetime the encroachment of the seas.

CLIMATIC CHANGE

The global climate was becoming warmer from the time of the onset of glacial retreat, about 16,000 to 17,000 years ago until a few thousand years ago. The postglacial high point in global temperatures occurred roughly between 3,000 and 6,000 years ago. It is known as the *climatic optimum,* or *hypsithermal,* and it has been followed by a cooling trend that may well be still going on, taking us into the next ice age. Various estimates have been made of the difference in mean temperatures between a full-glacial climate and that of the present or of a climatic optimum. The differences are generally agreed to be on the order of perhaps 3° to 5°C on an annual basis, but they vary from place to place and are probably more intense at higher latitudes. A difference this size between an unusually cold year and a warm one is common; it is common for a given month to vary this much from year to year in temperate and cold regions. This difference seems surprisingly small to control the waxing and waning of continental ice sheets, but apparently it is enough.

Superimposed on this global climatic change are local or regional changes. An extreme example would be the climate of, say, northern New England, which was covered by the Laurentide ice sheet and presumably had an ice cap climate 18,000 years ago, but now is temperate. Here the presence or absence of glacial ice was the dominant controlling factor. More subtle, but comparably important differences in regional climates would have reflected the differences between continental and maritime climatic regimes.

We have seen several times that the present day distribution of tundra climates, and tundra itself, is related to the presence of nearby large bodies of water and their cooling action on summer temperature regimes. Whatever the similarities between the steppe-tundra environment of the Ice Ages and the modern tundra, one clear difference is that many areas dominated by steppe-tundra were far from the sea and must have had highly continental climates. And, because of changes in land-water relationships, many of these earlier steppe-tundra areas are now near water and covered by modern arctic tundra. The shores of the Bering and Chukchi seas are excellent examples of this situation. Nome, Alaska, is a coastal city, but its location was 600 or 700 kilometers inland at the height of the Wisconsin glaciation. Eighteen thousand years ago, summer temperatures at this site may have been comparable to those of the present, or even warmer. But the environment must have been radically different. The present environment, then, has come into existence as a result of the flooding of Beringia, and the most significant change has quite possibly been a local climatic one, from a continental to a maritime climate. Similar trends must have taken place in most parts of the present Arctic.

VEGETATION CHANGES

Throughout the Ice Age North, the first sign of the winds of change in vegetation with the waning of the ice is a tremendous rise in birch pollen. This is more or less simultaneous over broad areas at about 14,000 to 12,000 years B.P. This pollen rise is probably correlated with a dramatic shift from steppe-tundra to a brushland dominated by dwarf birch scrub over huge areas of the present low Arctic.

Other changes in the pollen record are generally less marked, or less closely synchronous over wide areas, than the birch rise. Willow sometimes reaches peaks at about the time of the birch high. Spruce often becomes suddenly conspicuous, but the time of its arrival is quite variable. In some areas it becomes a major part of the pollen rain soon after the birch rise, but in other areas it is hardly important until 5,000 or so years ago. *Artemisia* pollen generally drops down to low levels at the onset of the birch rise and seldom shows up in any quantity again. Percentages of sedges and grasses change, but it is hard to tell if this is related to any real change in the importance of these plants rather than a sort of general swamping by pollen of birch and, later, spruce.

It has been suggested that both dwarf birch scrub and another major component of the low arctic tundra, tussock fields, may have been rare and have occurred only locally during the height of the Ice Age. With the changing climate, particularly the increased moisture resulting from a change to maritime climates, this type of vegetation might have spread rapidly at the end of the Ice Age. The steppe-tundra, which had persisted in one form or another for many thousands of years, might have been overwhelmed simultaneously from two directions. While much of its habitat was becoming sea floor, it was elsewhere being invaded by birch scrub and tussocks.

Of course, many other factors could be at least potentially involved. For example, some forms of steppe-tundra might have depended on loess deposition for stability, and such deposits would have decreased with the waning of the ice. Or fire could have become an important element in the tundra environment with the rise of tussocks, and, along timberline, spruce forest. A moister climate might have encouraged increased growth of mosses such as *Sphagnum,* effectively insulating the ground and diminishing the depth of thaw during summer. The lack of evidence of peatlands in unglaciated northern areas during the Ice Ages, for example, stands high on the list of arctic paleoecological phenomena that we need to know more about.

EXTINCTION OF THE PLEISTOCENE MEGAFAUNA

The greatest Ice Age question of all concerns the loss of the major portion of the large animals of the Ice Age tundra. This is not a purely arctic phenomenon. Over huge areas of the earth, faunas containing all sorts of exotic animals—elephants, mastodons, giant ground sloths, saber-toothed "tigers," and others—were replaced by the more prosaic Holocene faunas during the period of perhaps 12,000 to 9,000 years ago. Some evidence shows that these extinctions were not confined to large animals. Birds, rodents, and other small mammals seem to have suffered comparably, although the fossil record is much less complete for these than for large-boned creatures.

There are many questions to be answered regarding the timing of these events or extinctions. Mammoths seem to be widespread in both North America and Eurasia at 15,000 years ago. They are found in numbers, often at human kill sites, as recently as 11,000 B.P. But this appears to be the end, everywhere. No one has ever dated mammoth remains at less than 10,000 years old. Whether the same dates hold true for arctic horses or bison, though, is by no means clear. Some evidence suggests that bison hung on in Alaska for thousands of years into the Holocene. The American elk (or wapiti) appears to have been present in Alaska for some time in the earlier Holocene, followed by a much later extinction there. In other parts of the world, Africa for example, there were few if any extinctions.

The end of the last Ice Age, then, was evidently a time of catastrophic events, and these were felt particularly strongly in the higher latitudes of the circumpolar north. The locations and relative importance of ice, water, uplands, and lowlands changed dramatically. Probably equally dramatic were changes in the significance and distribution of major vegetation types. Some combination of all these events was too much for many of the species of animals, probably both large and small, that had inhabited the Ice Age North for perhaps the preceding 100,000 years. We need to remember, too, that the mammals, particularly the large grazers, probably had their own direct effect on the vegetation. Just as thheee American bison affected and helped maintain the prairie environment, the grazing, galloping, defecation, and death of large mammals may well have been important in stabilizing the steppe-tundra environment. The end of the Ice Age was not just a series of major but somewhat isolated catastrophes; it was the extinction, or at least the radical alteration, of one of the earth's major ecological systems.

A final major phenomenon, perhaps the most important of all, was occurring in the arctic environment during the last Ice Age and into the Holocene. This was the coming of human beings.

SUGGESTED FURTHER READING

Much information in this area can be found in technical papers and scientific journals. Perhaps the closest to a standard journal in the field is *Quaternary Research,* published quarterly by Academic Press, New York.

Birks, H. J. B., and R. G. West. *Quaternary Plant Ecology.* Oxford: Blackwell Scientific Publications, 1973.

Bradley, R. S. *Quaternary Paleoclimatology.* Boston: Allen and Unwin, 1985.

Hopkins, D. M., J. V. Matthews, Jr., C. Schweger, and S. Young, eds. *The Paleoecology of Beringia.* New York: Academic Press, 1982.

Kurtén, B. *Pleistocene Mammals of Europe.* Chicago: Aldine, 1968.

Kurtén, B., and E. Anderson. *Pleistocene Mammals of North America.* New York: Columbia University Press, 1980.

West, R. G. *Pleistocene Geology and Biology.* London: Longman, 1977.

Chapter 14

The Human Presence in the Arctic

IT is fashionable to think of human beings as interlopers, an unnatural force causing artificial alterations and despoliations of the otherwise pristine natural environment. Whether this is true at the present time is a moot philosophical question. Certainly the human impact on the world has grown exponentially and changed qualitatively during the past couple of hundred years. But people have been around for quite a while; during most of our tenure on the planet our role in the environment has been exceptional and reasonably enduring but has hardly resulted in profound alterations.

Obviously, the human potential to do incredible damage to the arctic environment is not to be underestimated. A reader who has read this far in this book cannot help being aware that serious potential for destruction exists in such areas as artificial thermokarst, chemical or heat pollution of the Arctic Ocean, oil spills and seabird or sea mammal colonies, overhunting of marine mammals, overfishing, and so forth. What is probably less obvious is the complex nature of these environmental problems in terms of social and economic issues as well as straight biology or chemistry. The nature of these individual problems is beyond the scope of this book, but the hard science aspects of the questions may have been clarified by the information here.

Rather than concentrate on humans as destroyers or usurpers in the Arctic, this final chapter will look at humanity as a natural part of the arctic environment, a role it has played for a period of probably at least 100,000 years. People may have been around as long as polar bears, and while we outlived the woolly mammoth and may even have had a hand in its demise, our role in the arctic environment may well until recently have only been of roughly comparable significance.

THE FIRST NORTHERNERS

As we've seen in the past several chapters, polar regions have expanded and contracted repeatedly during the Quaternary, and have generally encompassed lower latitudes than they currently reach. This means that if the first human incursions into polar environments took place during any of the glacial ages, they may have occurred in areas that are now temperate rather than arctic. It also means that if humans ranged far to the north during interglacial periods, the succeeding glacial advances would probably have wiped out all traces of their culture.

These factors obviously complicate our search for the earliest colonists of the North. The only way we can tell for certain whether prehistoric people lived under true polar conditions would be to reconstruct their culture—what they hunted or gathered, whether they used fire, whether they could manufacture clothing. If we assume, for example, that the woolly mammoth was an animal strictly confined to cold climates, and if we find evidence that these animals were hunted by humans, then it is a reasonable inference that the hunters were also inhabitants of cold climates.

Of course, if we find datable remains of human cultures, such as hearths with radiocarbon datable charcoal, and if we have a general picture of climatic conditions at the time at which the cultural remains are dated, then we can make obvious climatic inferences. However, it appears that the critical time for the early colonization of polar regions is in that maddening period before radiocarbon datability (earlier than 35,000 to 50,000 years ago) and later than the time when other isotope methods such as potassium/argon (K/A) dating are useful.

We do not now have, and may never have, satisfactory evidence of who the first inhabitants of the cold regions were and when they began their first trek north. But from the 1950s on, we have obtained a provocative array of new archaeological sites and other pieces of fragmentary evidence that allow us to trace the peopling of the cold regions with some confidence back to near the beginning of the last Ice Age in Europe, perhaps 80,000 years ago. We have some basis for speculating that any earlier incursions into boreal forest or cold steppe environments were probably marginal, brief, and seasonal, if they occurred at all.

Humans, presumably still in the *Homo erectus* stage, were hunting elephants and other animals of the temperate forest, mountains, and cool steppe in Europe as early as 300,000 years ago. This is well documented by excavations at the famous sites of Terra Amata in southern France, and Torralba and Ambrona, in the uplands of eastern Spain. However, it is at least 150,000 years later that the first evidence for human culture shows up in northern Europe, in areas such as the North German Plain. A number of sites in the area have been tentatively dated as coeval with the warming trends at the end of the next to last Ice Age (Riss or Saale glaciation, as it is known locally). Finally, in the early Würm-Weichsel period, we begin to find clear evidence of the hunting of reindeer, woolly mammoths, and a variety of cold-adapted animals; which makes it clear that hunters were using the cold, Ice Age steppes of northern Europe at least seasonally at that time. The dates are still not precise, and it is possible that we are dealing with temporary migration or colonization during one or more interstadials, but it seems clear that culture had progressed to the point that the resources of cold regions were available and useful to humans early in the last glacial period. In Europe, at least, evidence of habitation is continuous enough after some 60,000 to 80,000 years ago to justify the conclusion that humans inhabited cold, periglacial regions more or less continuously throughout the rest of the Pleistocene. This period of time is often called the upper Pleistocene. All human cultures of this time are referred to as the Paleolithic, or Old Stone Age. The upper Pleistocene contains both the middle and upper Paleolithic; the upper Paleolithic supplants the middle Paleolithic with the beginning of the Aurignacoid traditions (see below). In the Arctic, the Old Stone Age extends, in one sense, into historical times.

NEANDERTALERS AND THE MOUSTEROID TRADITIONS

Who were these earliest inhabitants of the polar regions? A human skull fragment found in Germany indicates clearly that we are dealing with the much maligned Neanderthals or Neandertalers. (Newer works commonly use the spelling *Neandertal,* since the *h* is silent.)

The question of who (or what) Neandertalers were has probably occupied as much discussion on early humans as any other, and it is worth spending some time on here. Most physical anthropologists today classify Neandertalers as full members of the human species *(Homo sapiens),* but as a distinct subspecies. Thus, the formal classification is *H. sapiens neanderthalensis.* These people are generally considered to have been an intermediate stage between the earlier *Homo erectus* and the modern subspecies, *H. sapiens sapiens.* Nonetheless, the classic Neandertaler of Europe exhibits a number of specialized, and extremely interesting, physical characteristics. Among these are a broad, low-crowned skull with immense brow ridges and a brain capacity at least as large, on the average, as that of modern humans, and a small, receding chin. Postcranially, Neandertalers seem to have been rather short by modern standards but with very heavy bone structure and remarkably large joints, indicating tremendous musculature and physical strength. The hands and feet were exceptionally large, and there is evidence that the fingers were more mobile than our own.

Many artists' reconstructions of Neandertalers show them as squat, shambling individuals with flat faces, beetling brows, surly stares, much body hair, and skin of an indeterminate brownish color. They are usually shown carrying rude wooden bludgeons or ragged masses of bloody meat. In fact, we have little information on which to base a fully-fleshed picture of Neandertalers. One eminent paleontologist has pointed out that they may, like some more modern northern peoples, have been pale skinned and flaxen haired. There is certainly a basis for suggesting that a Neandertaler in a business suit might present a somewhat odd and perhaps impressive sight, but not necessarily any indication that he or she was any really exceptional sort of human being.

With respect to Neandertaler culture, we are on firmer, and especially interesting, ground. Perhaps the most basic cultural phenomenon we have records of is the production of tools. Advances over the long-lasting and generally conservative hand-ax, or Acheulian, tradition seem to have evolved at roughly the time of the first onset of the last Ice Age. The new advances involve a variety of forms of stone tools, usually made from flakes of flint, chert, or obsidian, and carefully fashioned for specific functions. There are also a variety of bone and antler tools, although these are preserved only under certain conditions. Presumably, wood was widely used also. Stone tools found in Neandertaler sites have been assigned to what is called a *Mousterian industry,* named after a site at which some of such tools were found. Generally comparable tools, although with many local and temporal variations, are widespread throughout much of the Old World, often outside the area (and sometimes the time) of the Neandertalers. This group of flake tool industries is now sometimes called *Mousteroid,* to point out the overall similarity of the tools without implying a close connection to the physical or cultural group of Europe and the Near East that we regard as typically Neandertaler.

Presumably, Neandertalers could not have inhabited the cold regions without some form of clothing. Many of the stone tools found at their sites seem to be skin scrapers, but there is no evidence of needles. What sort of clothing could be functional in an Ice Age winter, but would not require sewing? Could Neandertalers, for example, have invented felt?

Neandertalers are commonly thought of as the quintessential cave man, and early Neandertaler discoveries were often made at the mouths of shallow overhangs called *abris,* or rock shelters. These would have offered little protection from the Ice Age climate of interior Europe. Until fairly recently, it was only assumed that some sort of huts must have been built. Now Soviet scientists have excavated a site in the Ukraine (Molodova 1) that seems beyond a doubt to represent a house, to date from perhaps 50,000 years ago, and to contain large quantities of Mousteroid tools and several hearths. The walls of the house were supported by mammoth bones, and it presumably was covered with skins and perhaps brush and sod. At 5 by 8 meters, it was considerably larger than the typical houses of many modern polar peoples and could comfortably have housed one or more good-sized families. Assuming that it is indeed a dwelling place, and there is no reason to doubt this, it is the oldest-known house in the world. Its invention was certainly one of the keys to the opening up of the polar world to human habitation. Fire, of course, had long been tamed in some fashion. Clearly, Neandertalers could produce fire and maintain it at will, but we have no direct evidence of how they did this.

One reason that we know as much about Neandertalers as we do is that they disposed of their dead by burial and, in some cases, accompanied these dead with what can only be interpreted as ritual objects. The earliest human burials known are Neandertaler. They tell us a number of interesting things. First, simply making the effort to dispose of a corpse by burial indicates some form of respect for the dead and can be interpreted as at least an incipient phase of ceremonialism or spirtuality or both. This view gains credence from the fact that some burials include red ochre, a substance that at later times was widely used as a ritual means of restoring lifelike color to a corpse before interment. Of further interest is the apparent inclusion of flowers in at least one Neandertaler grave.

Remains from Neandertaler graves also indicate something of the nature of the society and its ethical nature. One skeleton is of a crippled man of relatively advanced age who would clearly have been unable to participate in many activities and would have had to have been cared for throughout his life. Another skeleton is of an elderly man who had been ravaged by arthritis for many years. On the other side of the coin, the evidence for cannibalism among Neandertalers is compelling and may have involved systematic butchering for food, rather than the ritual cannibalism that has been described in a few more modern societies.

To summarize, we find evidence of the human occupation of cold regions extending back 80,000 or more years in western Eurasia, and these cold-adapted cultures presumably developed over a period extending to considerably earlier times. The people of these cultures appear to have been those we think of as Neandertalers; they had fire, a sophisticated tool kit, skills to hunt large mammals and build shelters, and at least the beginnings of a spiritual life. It is widely believed that these were the only people in the cooler regions of the Northern Hemisphere until about 40,000 years ago. Then they disappeared rapidly, perhaps suddenly, and were replaced by modern humans *(homo sapiens sapiens)*, who spread rapidly around the circumpolar North and throughout the habitable world.

MODERN HUMANS AND THE AURIGNACOID TRADITION

The disappearance of the Neandertalers has been the subject of a great deal of speculation, some of it imaginative in the extreme. All that can be said with certainty is that no skeletons of the distinctively Neandertaloid type are found anywhere after roughly 40,000 years ago, and that by that time or a few thousand years later, modern humans had inhabited essentially all the terrain previously occupied by their predecessors. It has often been suggested that the modern race (often called Cro-Magnon people, after a classic site in France) overwhelmed the Neandertalers, while other scientists suggest that Neandertalers simply disappeared by interbreeding with the newcomers. In any case it is clear that the transition took place within a few thousand years and that it was associated with a series of major advances in toolmaking and in other cultural phenomena. It is also important to point out that the change was contemporaneous with the general warming of the climate and with a series of climatic oscillations often called the mid-Würm/Wisconsinan interstadial. It appears that when Cro-Magnon people migrated into northern Eurasia and set the stage for the development of probably most of the classic arctic and boreal cultures as we know them, they migrated into a newly temperate environment not altogether different from that of the present. Perhaps the Neandertalers had already left, following the retreating Ice Age game animals northward toward the polar sea.

Blades and Burins

The characteristic feature of the lithic (stone) material associated with the Aurignacoid (or upper Paleolithic toolmaking) tradition is known as blade-and-core technology. A blade in this context is a long, narrow flake of stone that is struck from a larger core (see Figure 14–1). Blades could be the result of any flint-chipping technique. The significance of blade-and-core technology lies in the fact that a large number of blades, each with a perfect, ready-made cutting edge on each side, can be struck from a

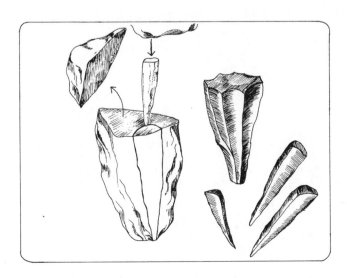

Figure 14–1. Blade-and-core technology. When a properly prepared core of flint, chert, or similar stone is struck a blow directed and transmitted by a piece of antler, a long, sharp blade is produced. The process can be repeated, producing many linear feet of razor-sharp edge. The remaining core can then often be utilized for some other purpose.

single core of material if the core is carefully prepared in advance and the proper force and direction are employed in striking the blows that dislodge the individual blades. This technique has several important implications. First, the amount of usable edge per volume of material is multiplied many times over earlier chipping techniques. Given the right materials and techniques, it has been shown that perhaps 5 to 25 meters of razor-sharp edge can be produced from a single kilogram of stone. Second, the edge can be produced rapidly, and the resulting blade can often be used for its intended purpose with little or no additional work. So if the blade became dull or chipped, it was often better to discard it and replace it with another easily made tool. Thus, while certain blade-and-core tools are exceptionally beautiful and well fashioned (see Figure 14–2), many actually are rather crude in appearance and may be mistaken for waste, or be considered to indicate primitive techniques. Another implication is that the quality of the raw material is of paramount importance to the number, size, and quality of blades that can be produced. This situation can provide impetus for long journeys to sources of stone, to the development of mining techniques, and the establishment of trade. Finally, the smaller the blades, the more edge that can be produced from a core. So, if several small blades are fixed on a matrix of wood or bone, stone may be economized—stone that may have arrived by some circuitous trade route and have, in Paleolithic terms, "cost" a great deal. The general tendency through the roughly 30,000-year history of blade-and-core technology is toward smaller and smaller blades, culminating in the microblades of the Arctic Small Tool tradition, which we will discuss shortly.

Although many blades were used as tools with little further

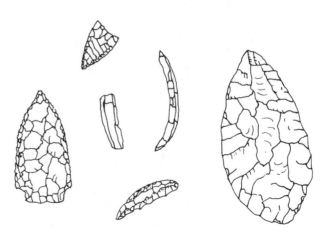

Figure 14–2. Several chipped stone implements, created by a variety of methods. The two thinner central ones are made from small blades.

alteration, a wide variety of specialized tools were also made. Further manufacture often involved the dulling of one edge to make a backed blade that could be used as a knife or scraper, or the removal of a large chip so that the tool could be used as a spokeshave on a round wooden shaft. One of the most common and characteristic tools of the Aurignacoid traditions is called a *burin*. Modern burins are steel engraving tools consisting of a shaft, square or diamond shaped in cross section and sharpened on a diagonal to provide a sharp but strong and thick point. While differing in proportions, a stone burin (see Figure 14–3) also has a sharp, thick point that is useful for engraving lines and, particularly, for cutting deep grooves in wood, bone, or other comparatively soft material. Under this heavy usage, stone burins would obviously be rapidly dulled. However, they can be easily resharpened by removing a small chip. These chips have a characteristic shape and are called *burin spalls*. They were produced in quantity, and are a characteristic feature of many upper Paleolithic sites. Burins are well adapted to producing long, narrow splinters of bone, and it is probably no coincidence that burins and bone needles, evidence of the first skin sewing, seem to arrive more or less simultaneously. Fishhooks and gorges are another evident product of this technology. In any case, some scientists posit a train of connections between artifacts that goes like this: burin spalls = burins = bone splinters = needles = tailored clothing = cold weather adaptations = ability to live in a cold, northern, Ice Age environment.

Without going into great detail on the comparative dating of innovations, we can suggest that by about 30,000 years ago human beings who were physically modern were widespread throughout the range occupied by Neandertalers some 10,000 years earlier. In many cases, they had also occupied new territory. They had a newly complex and sophisticated tool technology based on blades and cores, but evidence of the survival of Mousteroid features exists, more in some areas than others. These new people were thus well established at roughly the time of the mid-Würm interstadial. And the northern populations of these people were soon to be plunged into the intense cold and advancing ice sheets of the last glacial maximum. During the period of about 30,000 to 10,000 years ago, we see the flowering of a culture that thrived on the margins of the great ice sheets and the cold periglacial steppes. These northerners in a sense originated art or pictorial representation, invented more technological innovations than had occurred in all previous human history, populated the New World, and very likely made the first

Figure 14–3. A stone burin. Burins vary widely in shape and general appearance, but all typically have a strong, sharp point useful for tasks such as grooving bone or antler; they can be resharpened by the removal of a burin spall.

attempts to domesticate plants and animals that led to the so-called Neolithic Revolution starting at about the end of the Ice Age. This is not to say that northerners were the only people on the forefront of human development. For only a single example from another area, deep water crossings to Australia were made at about the beginning of the time we are discussing. But enough evidence exists to support the idea that the people who hunted reindeer and mammoths on the cold plains of northern Europe and the interior of Asia were as seminally involved in the origin of human civilization as were the Sumerians, Egyptians, and Hellenes in their own later time.

ICE AGE HUNTERS IN EURASIA

To recapitulate briefly the climatic and glacial events of the later Würm period: a general cooling and drying trend began shortly after 30,000 years ago and culminated in the last glacial maximum at about 20,000 to 18,000 years ago. This was followed by an overall warming trend that seems to have gathered speed after about 15,000 years ago and to have culminated in conditions similar to those of the present in most cool temperate regions of Eurasia and North America by about 10,000 years ago, the time that is considered to be the boundary between the late Glacial and the Holocene periods. However, the retreat of the major continental glaciers was by no means complete at the beginning of the Holocene, and Ice Age conditions persisted for several thousand additional years in areas such as northern Scandinavia, the Quebec-Labrador peninsula, and Greenland.

In Europe and northeastern Asia, these climatic events resulted first in the advance of the Scandinavian ice sheet and the local ice caps on the Alps, Pyrenees, Caucasus, and other mountains to the eastward. Forest retreated from the ice-free portions of northern Europe so that by about 18,000 years ago a cold periglacial steppe extended from the unglaciated portion of southern England eastward across to Poland, the Ukraine, and, probably in a more extreme continental form, deep into Siberia and even to unglaciated Beringia. In southern Europe, the forests remained, but temperate species such as oak were increasingly replaced by pine and fir. Shortly after 18,000 years ago, the forests reversed their retreat and again spread northward into northern Europe as the ice retreated. Thus, the history of the Northern Hemisphere during the last glacial age was a history of changing emphasis or importance in terms of area of forest versus steppe vegetation and fauna. The boundaries between the two areas were probably seldom sharp, and they probably changed rapidly enough to be evident at some times to a single long-lived human. The situation is particularly complex in Europe, since glaciers advanced both from the north and from mountain ranges such as the Alps and Pyrenees. Forests in, say, France or Germany would have been caught in a pincers of steppe and tundra moving in from several directions.

In the last chapter, we discussed the concept of steppe-tundra in Beringia and suggested that it was related in climate, flora, and fauna to the steppe of Eurasia. Whatever the similarities and differences between the two areas are, they clearly share one major faunal feature: the presence of mammoths. European prehistorians now commonly refer to the steppe in their area as *mammoth steppe*. The game hunted by the people with whom we are concerned in this section consisted essentially of large animals, and they were, for the most part, denizens of this mammoth steppe.

We know far more about the upper Paleolithic peoples of Europe than we do about any earlier or contemporaneous culture, or for that matter, many later cultures. The most obvious reason for this knowledge is the fact that Europe is the heartland of Paleolithic archaeology. The search in Europe for clues as to who these people were and what they did has been long and intense, and the area comparatively small and accessible. There are undoubtedly sites of tremendous importance yet to be discovered in Asia and North America, and there is no question that some of the yet-to-be-made findings will alter our understanding of humans of the last Ice Age, probably in fundamental ways. Nonetheless, real grounds exist for suggesting that Ice Age northern Europe was as important in the early development of civilization as it has been in the study of the beginning of the rise of modern humans.

Cave Art

The well-known Quaternary scientist C.V. Haynes has suggested that European rock art depicting large mammals may have been an appeal to the gods to save the prey from extinction. The painted caves of later Ice Age times in Europe are renowned for showing the first major flowering of art, as well as for providing evidence of many aspects of the culture, ranging from hunting and other forms of subsistence to spiritual development. These paintings, and other art forms such as sculpture, were the work of the people who created the Aurignacoid tradition. Much of the cave art depicts an Ice Age fauna, including reindeer, mammoths, and bison. Classic cave art extends well back into the classic Aurignacoid phase, before the height of the last ice advance. It reaches its peak during the last few thousand years of the Pleistocene, during a late offshoot of the Aurignacoid called the Magdalenian. At this time we are probably coming to the final decline of the Ice Age megafauna; Haynes' suggestion is thus an appealing one.

MAMMOTH HUNTERS

The Ice Age hunters of western Europe probably had a reasonably broad potential larder to choose from, since their environment was complex and variable. Hundreds of kilometers to the north and east, in what is now Poland, the Ukraine, and the steppes of interior Asia, life must have been much harsher, particularly as the grip of the last glacial advance reached deeply into the continent some 25,000 years or so ago. Even in these cold, arid wastes, though, there were people. These people seem to be closely associated with one animal: the mammoth.

The most compelling evidence for this relationship is in architecture. The inhabitants of the bleak, cold plains made buildings of the bones of mammoths. Nor were these structures mere tents with mammoth bones for poles and pegs; rather, they were solidly constructed on a masonry of carefully laid bones. The remains of scores of mammoths went into a single house, often with the herringbone-shaped jawbones arranged to form a pattern.

There is some question as to whether the mammoth bone structures (they could as well have been temples as houses) were the result of wide-scale, intensive mammoth hunting. It has been suggested that the bones may have been scavanged over wide areas. But there can be no question that the mammoth was an important element in the lives of these people, and it is interesting to see mammoth hunting occurring a few thousand years later and nearly half a world away, in North America, at the final closing of the Ice Age and near the time when the last mammoth died.

So-called mammoth people were established on the steppes as the last cold closed in. There is little evidence of their presence during the most intense cold period, about 20,000 to 18,000 years ago. As the ice waned, though, and as Magdalenian culture flourished to the west, mammoth-bone builders were living on the steppes. There are even indications that the social structure of the communities had undergone subtle changes during the cold time.

We don't know for certain how widespread inland peoples of the Ice Ages were in Asia. Some scientists believe that people reached the shores of the North Pacific and Beringia as early as 50,000 years or more ago. If this is true, these earlier arrivals may have been unrelated to the mammoth people. All things considered, it is probably not overly conservative to suggest that the colonization of the northern interior of Asia took place before and during the mid-Würm/Wisconsinan interstadial. Humans were probably in central Beringia, the Bering land bridge region, as the sea level fell some 25,000 years ago, and they probably inhabited all of unglaciated Beringia, and hunted large mammals, during and after the last glacial maximum some 18,000 to 20,000 years ago.

PEOPLING THE NEW WORLD

Virtually all prehistorians who are concerned with the origin of human populations in North and South America assume that the first Americans arrived from Asia, and that they arrived by way of the Bering land bridge or, just possibly, crossed Bering Strait at some time when the land bridge was at least partially submerged. Since there is evidence that at least one deep water crossing was made to Australia as long as 25,000 to 30,000 years ago, a sea (or sea ice) crossing in Beringia is certainly plausible. This human arrival across Beringia is about the last piece of the puzzle on which there is any agreement. The questions that remain unanswered concern the timing of the crossing or crossings, and the identity and culture of the people who may have crossed into North America, as well as their subsequent history.

Old Crow Basin

Some distance before it crosses the Yukon border into Alaska, the Porcupine River is already a large river flowing through a series of flats, called the Old Crow Flats, which are the beds of ancient, shallow proglacial lakes. Currently, the river actively downcuts through the clay of the lake beds, and the erosive action constantly exposes a wide variety of organic materials, including fossil bones of a variety of animals. These bones and other objects can be picked up in some quantity along the shores of the river and on the sides of bluffs as they wash out. They are seldom found in any stratigraphic context, so that any dating must be done by radiometric rather than stratigraphic methods.

The Old Crow Flats became a household phrase, at least in northern archaeological households, shortly after 1966. In that year a piece of caribou tibia, or shin, bone was recovered from the riverbank; it had clearly been altered by human activity. In fact, it was obviously a skin scraper, remarkably similar to scrapers in use by the local Athabascan Indians within living memory. Part of the original artifact was sacrificed for radiocarbon dating, and a date on the apatite fraction showed it to be about 27,000 years old. Although there have been a number of roughly comparable dates suggested for other sites in North America, the Old Crow scraper was, at the time of its discovery and dating, the closest thing known to hard evidence of humans in North America before about 12,000 years ago.

The flurry of activity touched off by the initial Old Crow discoveries is probably unmatched in northern archaeology. Nonetheless, the overall results of subsequent activities were rather disappointing. No stone tools or other artifacts were found. In fact, the area is devoid of any stone because of its lake bed origin. Most of the artifacts recovered are pieces of bone from mammoths and other animals. While they appear to have been worked on by a flake technology and, in some cases, seem to show signs of wear that would only result from use as tools, the overall picture is not impressive when compared to even the most rudimentary European contemporary Aurignacoid sites. Critics of the Old Crow material question its significance on the following grounds:

1. Radiocarbon dates on bone apatite fractions are not fully accepted as being reliable. Several examples of anomalously "old" dates have been cited, as will be discussed further here.
2. The few undoubted artifacts could have been made much later of old bone that had washed out of the frozen ground and been picked up by later people as raw materials.
3. Many of what seem to be artifacts have been shaped by natural events such as tumbling in streams or gnawing and cracking by carnivores.

In 1986 a staggering blow landed on the Old Crow Basin proponents. Advances in radiocarbon techniques made it advisable to redate the original caribou bone scraper. The new date indicated that it was of modern origin!

The most ambitious Old Crow partisans had suggested that a 25,000- to 30,000-year-old date for human habitation at the site was the upper end, and that dates of 50,000 to 60,000 years ago were plausible. In fact, there are some sites in Alberta where artifacts and even human remains have supposedly been dated back this far, but these dates have been generally rejected, for a variety of reasons. With the rejection of the main piece of evidence for a mid-Wisconsinan presence of man in Beringia, rethinking has taken place. While Old Crow is being at least partially deflated, though, new evidence continues to be found south of the ice sheets in both North and South America that at least suggests the presence of humans in the 13,000 to 17,000 years B.P. range. Assuming that the dating *is* solid, we have evidence of humans in Beringia during land bridge times. This is in keeping with some documented colonization of northeastern Asia (Yakutia and possibly Chukotka) at probably roughly the same time or a bit earlier.

Unless we can be sure humans were in Beringia well before the height of the last glaciation—18,000 B.P.—we are faced with the problem of figuring out how they got south of the North American ice sheets before the Late Wisconsinan was well on the wane, say 12,000 years ago. The most plausible solution to this problem depends on the fact that present day Canada was covered by ice from two major ice sheets, the Laurentide and the Cordilleran. The Laurentide ice sheet stretched from the Atlantic coast to the foot of the Rocky Mountains, while the Cordilleran extended from the eastern slope of the Rockies westward to the Pacific shores. While little or no land at the area of contact between these two great glaciers was *never* ice covered, there is reason to believe that the time of maximum expansion of the two ice sheets was somewhat different for each one, with the Cordilleran reaching its greatest extent eastward after the Laurentide was well on the wane. This *could* mean that further colonization to the south could have taken place through an open corridor that presumably existed between the shrunken Laurentide and Cordilleran ice sheets. As we discussed in Chapter 13, there is some evidence that an ice-free corridor existed between these two ice sheets throughout most or even all of the late Wisconsinan.

However, accepting a 20,000 B.P. or earlier date for early humans in Beringia provides only a new data point, rather than a breakthrough to the real nature of the colonization of the Americas and, for our interest, the New World north. At this time, we know essentially nothing about these people, if we accept that they were there at all. We have no dependable evidence that people occupied Beringia or any other portion of the American north before about 15,000 years ago. We know nothing of the ways of life of the earlier people, or even whether they survived to be the ancestors of any later inhabitants.

It is only at the close of the Ice Age, about 12,000 to 10,000 years ago, that we begin to find evidence of inhabitants in the cold regions of North America. Powerful evidence points to a major change in the human role in the American ecosystem perhaps 12,000 years ago. This suggests that any earlier people were few in number, sparsely distributed, and had an impoverished culture that left little evidence of their passing. Considering the immense amount of investigation that has taken place, the story of early humans in North America remains fragmentary and unsatisfactory until about 12,000 years ago. The critical date in northern regions is more in the neighborhood of 8,000 to 10,000 years ago.

LATE GLACIAL HUMAN ACTIVITIES IN NORTHERN AMERICA

We know that early humans inhabited much of North America (and parts of South America) before the end of the Late Glacial, which we somewhat arbitrarily placed at 10,000 B.P. (in radiocarbon years) in the last chapter. About 12,000 years ago, the Clovis culture emerged in the American Southwest, the first American people about whom we know enough to reconstruct some features of their way of life. Clovis people were apparently consummate hunters of large mammals, particularly mammoths. Their characteristic projectile points, with fluted bases, have been found actually embedded in the bones of butchered mammoths. These Clovis points are *not* made of blades, and they bear only the most minimal resemblance to any Eurasian tradition. Within probably less than 1,000 years of their emergence, these points have been found all the way across North America, and south into Mexico. They also evolve rapidly into a variety of other forms, the most famous of which is probably the Folsom point. This was used by a bison-hunting culture in the southwestern Great Plains, probably immediately after the demise of the last mammoths in the area.

Derivatives of the Clovis culture or its near relatives, or both, spread into northern regions in Canada by the end of the Late

Glacial, where they form the baseline of a group of traditions known as Northern Archaic and Maritime Archaic. These, in turn, are quite possibly the precursors of at least some of the recent Indian cultures of the Subarctic.

Not only does no line of descent reach back from Clovis to an earlier Asian or Beringian culture, but Clovis-type material also begins to occur in Beringia considerably later than it emerges in the American southwest. So, we continue to assume that Clovis is a derivative of an Asian culture that colonized Beringia, but the only part of the Clovis/Beringia picture we can document is a spread into Beringia of Clovislike material dated some thousands of years after the emergence of true Clovis in the southwest. Although we are pretty sure that humans were indeed in Beringia during the time from 20,000 years ago to the end of the Ice Age, and thus present for several thousand years before the "return" of Clovis, this human presence is documented by only a few sites, and they tell us little about the actual inhabitants and their ways of life.

As a final comment on these people and times, we note that the story of the mammoth, and of many other animals such as the mastodont and giant ground sloth, ends here. We can easily imagine the remnant herds, trapped by rising seas and by the disappearance of grazing lands under a sea of brush, being sent to their final extinction by skilled and determined bands of Clovis-type hunters. There is little doubt that humans were in on the kill of the last of the Pleistocene megafauna. The real questions to be answered concern their role in the events that led up to this last stand.

EARLY HOLOCENE

We find ourselves now at a time when the ice has retreated to a few centers in central Canada and Scandinavia. The seas have risen to about their present level, the climate has taken on a modern configuration, and the northern forest has migrated back to a timberline position not too dissimilar to that of the present. And the first human inhabitants of the modern North are dealing with the environment as it now stands, mammothless, bisonless, but with a newly created seacoast rich in fish and marine mammals, and with herds of reindeer and caribou flourishing in the coastal tundra.

The newly constituted, true tundra environment stretches far to the northward in Canada, Alaska, and Greenland. People have not yet figured out how to deal with it, and it will remain uninhabited for several thousand years yet. In Eurasia, tundra has become a narrow coastal strip bounded by forests, and extending to a few islands that will remain mostly uninhabited. Eurasians may learn to utilize the tundra environment, but they can always retreat to the forest. A truly arctic culture comparable to that of the Eskimos of North America will never develop there.

We have early Holocene sites in many places. In Europe and the Near East this seems generally to have been a time of poor conditions and thinly spread cultures that were shortly to give rise to the so-called Neolithic Revolution, involving agriculture, animal husbandry, pottery, polished stone implements, and so forth. We find advanced cultures around the Pacific basin, including northern areas. Various related cultures appear in northern North America from Alaska to Labrador. These people and their various so-called archaic cultures can be seen as representing a way of life roughly comparable to today's subarctic Indian cultures, such as the Cree and Athabaskan. Since these people were only marginally inhabitants of the tundra, we will not discuss them or the similar cultures in Eurasia, but rather, will move on to the middle of the Holocene and take a brief look at the origin of the one true arctic culture, that of the Eskimo.

The word *Eskimo* is actually a Cree Indian word and means eaters of raw flesh. While this may not be particularly complimentary, the story has it that the Eskimo name for the Indians translates as *lice*. In any case, many Eskimo groups now prefer to be called by their own name for themselves, *Inuit,* meaning simply *the people,* or, more precisely *The people*. The problem is that the majority of the Eskimo people currently alive speak a language that doesn't include the word *Inuit.* We'll use the word *Eskimo* here, while recognizing that it isn't much better than calling all the inhabitants of the British Isles, past and present, British.

ORIGINS OF ESKIMO CULTURE

At about 5,000 years ago, we first begin to find archaeological material that can be definitely linked to a modern northern culture. The first site discovered, at Cape Denbigh, near the Bering Strait in Alaska, contained mainly large quantities of well-made flint tools fashioned from exceptionally small blades (microblades). So small were the artifacts that they suggest that only miniature people could have made or used them. Actually, of course, they were hafted on stone or bone implements, which long since mouldered away in the acid soil. This first site gave its name to the Denbigh Flint culture. Soon, though, similar implements were being found all over arctic Alaska and in much of northern Canada. The name Arctic Small Tool tradition (ASTt) is now in general use for the whole complex of material.

There is no real question that the ASTt people were the ancestors, both culturally and physically, of the modern arctic Eskimos. The situation is less clear in the case of the people of southern and southwestern Alaska and the Aleutian Islands, where the environment and relations with other people were more complex. In any case, Arctic Small Tool tradition people exhibited one of the typical features of later Eskimo groups: they spread rapidly across the North American Arctic. By 2000 B.C. they had reached Greenland and the eastern Canadian Arctic. Here, their descendants can be traced for long periods of time, most particularly as the well-known Dorset culture, which was the dominant Eskimo culture in the eastern Arctic for many centuries.

At least in the early stages, there is reason to believe that the ASTt people were much less coastal than modern Eskimos. It has been suggested that they may have been strongly dependent on muskox, and that their apparent disappearance in much of Alaska by about 3,000 years or so ago was related to the decline in muskox. In any case, ASTt in most of Alaska and in easternmost Siberia was replaced by, or became, a more maritime-related group of cultures that are generally called Norton or Norton-Ipiutak. This seems to have been the dominant culture of much of arctic Alaska at about the time of the beginning of the Christian era, and its development can be traced with some confidence 1,000 years or so further back. The art and culture of Norton-Ipiutak people is a fascinating subject that has never been studied as a whole, though it certainly deserves definitive treatment. Some of their burial customs seem to have been exceptionally bizarre and in need of interpretation.

The final major story of the Eskimo culture opens about 2,000 years ago along the shores of the Bering Strait, and, particularly, on St. Lawrence Island. Here we see evolving a people who are truly adapted to, and dependent on, the seacoast. These are boat-building and boat-using people, closely attuned to marine mammals, dependent on them for things such as oil for lamps as well as food. We first see these people in somewhat sedentary communities, living off the rich resources of the Bering Strait, able to take time to develop art forms comparable to those of the

Magdalenean cave painters. This art shows up in what is known as Okvik and Old Bering Sea material: carved ivory implements, objects of unknown use and with fantastic faces, forms, and figures, and somber statuettes sometimes called Okvik Madonnas. A serious international trade in these beautiful objects has developed in the late twentieth century. This tells us something about the quality of the artwork, but it also results in the destruction of archaeological sites that might hold some of the main keys to the origins of present Eskimo culture.

A more streamlined phase of this culture spreads out from the center in the millennium after the beginning of the Christian era. This is generally known as Thule culture, and it rapidly made its way across Canada, even as the climate declined toward the Little Ice Age. Where Thule met Dorset, Dorset disappeared. (It has been suggested that this phenomenon is similar to the replacement of Neandertalers some 40,000 years earlier in Europe.) Thule, in fact, spread all the way to East Greenland, the very backyard of Europe. An occasional lost kayaker must have landed on Iceland at about the time it was first colonized by Europeans. The first confrontations between Europeans and native American peoples of the Arctic took place probably some time around the year 1,000. Northerners from Europe were making incursions into the true Arctic, perhaps for the first times. Aided by the comparatively warm climate of the period, Norse farmers landed on Greenland and even Newfoundland, trying to adapt their culture to the southern fringes of the Arctic. But, at various points they met with the Inuit of the Thule culture.

The two cultures, although vastly different, were probably about evenly matched in terms of survival. The Thule people were better nomads, probably better subsistence hunters, more at home in the true arctic environment. The Norse, with their agriculture, were better at creating stable communities, and they could build up much larger populations. Ultimately the Norse culture disappeared; the Thule culture, perhaps enriched by contact with the Norse, survived. So, we reach modern times with the one truly successful arctic culture derived from an ancient Beringian tradition and probably extending its roots back even to the time of the Bering land bridge. Even further back, there may be dim but vibrant connections to the Ice Age hunters of the European steppe and the painted caves. Like reindeer, or bears, the circumpolar peoples may share a single heritage extending around the globe and back into the cold recesses of the Ice Age. When the Norse and the Inuit met on some fiord in west Greenland a thousand years ago, it may have been more of a meeting of cousins separated by ten millennia than a confrontation of East and West.

SUGGESTED FURTHER READING

Many important recent discoveries in this area have yet to come to press in the form of overviews or general popular literature. Among the many journals dealing with concerns of this chapter, *Arctic Anthropology,* published quarterly by the University of Wisconsin Press, is a good starting point for further reading.

Bailey, G., ed. *Hunter-Gatherer Economy in Prehistory: A European Perspective.* Cambridge: Cambridge University Press, 1983.

Bandi, H. G. *Eskimo Prehistory.* College, AK: University of Alaska Press, 1969.

Bibby, G. *The Testimony of the Spade.* New York: Alfred A. Knopf, (Though dated, a classic synthesis of northern European prehistory), 1956.

Dumond, D. E. *The Eskimos and Aleuts.* London: Thames and Hudson, 1977.

Giddings, J. L. *Ancient Men of the Arctic.* New York: Alfred A. Knopf, 1967.

Hadingham, E. *Secrets of the Ice Ace.* New York: Walker, 1979.

Klein, R. G. *Ice Age Hunters of the Ukraine.* Chicago: University of Chicago Press, 1973.

Maxwell, M. S. *Prehistory of the Eastern Arctic.* Orlando, FL: Academic Press, 1985.

McGhee, R. *Canadian Arctic Prehistory.* Toronto: Van Nostrand Reinhold, 1978.

Philips, P. *The Prehistory of Europe.* Bloomington, IN: University of Indiana Press, 1980.

Soffer, O. *The Upper Paleolithic of the Central Russian Plain.* San Diego: Academic Press, 1985.

Thorson, R., ed. *Interior Alaska.* Anchorage: The Alaska Geographic Society, 1986.

Tuck, J. A. *Newfoundland and Labrador Prehistory.* Toronto: Van Nostrand Reinhold, 1976.

West, F. H. *The Archaeology of Beringia.* New York: Columbia University Press, 1981.

SUBJECT INDEX

INDEX TO COMMON AND LATIN NAMES OF PLANTS AND ANIMALS